KnowThis?®:
Marketing Basics

Second Edition

Paul Christ, Ph.D.

KnowThis?
Media

KnowThis: Marketing Basics, Second Edition
Paul Christ

Published By:
KnowThis Media, A Division of KnowThis LLC
615 Juniper Drive
Blue Bell, PA 19422

Publisher Website: KnowThisMedia.com
Book Website: KnowThis.com/books/marketing-basics.htm

Trademark: KnowThis is a registered trademark of KnowThis LLC

ISBN: 978-0-9820722-1-9

Printed and bound in United States of America

10 9 8 7 6 5 4 3 2 1

Contents

Preface

Why This Book?

In 1998, *KnowThis.com* was launched as one of the first Internet websites to address the specific needs of those involved in marketing and related fields. In short order, *KnowThis.com* became a leading authority website as evidenced by high rankings on search engine queries, the large number of links on university websites, and strong website traffic. A key part of *KnowThis.com* is the <u>Principles of Marketing</u> series, which offers a detailed look at marketing concepts. This series brought a great deal of positive comments and many requests for a printed version. This led to the first edition of ***KnowThis: Marketing Basics,*** which was well received by both the academic and business communities. The success and satisfaction received from publishing the first edition has led to this update.

Overall, we feel the second edition continues our practice of offering comprehensive coverage of marketing concepts. In fact, this new edition expands on the coverage offered in the first edition. Compared to the first edition, the second edition of ***KnowThis: Marketing Basics*** presents a number of enhancements including:

- This edition contains nearly <u>20% new material</u>.
- This edition inlcudes over <u>150 newly presented real-world marketing examples</u> connecting marketing concepts with issues facing organizations around the world.
- This edition presents <u>new Marketing Story boxes</u> that take an in-depth look at over 40 selected marketing stories found in major media publications.
- This edition features <u>significantly expanded coverage</u> of global marketing and emerging technologies.
- This edition offers an <u>enhanced design</u> including a larger book size and improved graphics.

As with the first edition, the second edition **IS NOT SIMPLY A REPRODUCTION OF CONTENT FOUND ON THE WEBSITE**. This book offers significantly broader coverage of marketing issues.

Who is the Book For?

KnowThis: Marketing Basics was written with several audiences in mind including:

- ◆ *The Marketing Novice* – This book is ideal for anyone who is new to marketing, as it covers all essential marketing areas. By spending time with this book, the *Marketing Novice* will quickly gain the foundation needed to appreciate what marketers do and understand the full scope of marketing decision making. For some, reading this book may also offer insight into career options in the marketing field.

◆ *The Marketing Professional* - Experienced marketers will also find this book useful. Often, seasoned marketers tend to focus on just a few areas of marketing as part of their day-to-day activities. This book may serve as a good refresher for areas of marketing for which they have not recently spent much time.

◆ *The Marketing Educator* – Teachers of marketing now have an alternative to high-priced marketing textbooks. This book offers nearly all of the same coverage found in expensive textbooks at a fraction of the price (educators see more information below).

Additionally, most of what is covered applies to all types of businesses including those whose objective is to make money (i.e., for-profit businesses) as well as those not driven by a profit-making motive (i.e., not-for-profit organizations).

Quality at an Affordable Cost?

Yes! *Know This: Marketing Basics* is written by a marketing professor and covers much of the same ground as found in much more expensive books. But it also provides insight not found in other publications and, therefore, holds its own as a unique offering and not simply a remaking of other books.

We are able to maintain affordable pricing by using printing strategies and methods that reduce overall printing costs and inventory carrying costs. However, be assured this book does not sacrifice quality. Whether this book is used in the classroom to help students learn basic concepts or used outside the classroom to assist in professional marketing activities, readers will find the material to be comprehensive and relevant. Additionally, it is written in a way that is intended to bridge the gap that often exists between business practice and academic textbooks.

Looking For More?

As you might guess, the support website for *Know This: Marketing Basics* is *Know This. com*. Along with the usual resources found on the general site, there is also a special section for this book. The location of this section is:

KnowThis.com/books/marketing-basics.htm

Included in this section are links to many of the references cited in the book along with other resources.

For Educators

As noted, *KnowThis: Marketing Basics* is ideal as a textbook for an entry-level marketing course or as a supplemental reference for a more advanced class. This book covers the same ground as far more expense textbooks, while also offering new information not covered in other books. Additionally:

♦ This book takes a contemporary view of marketing including covering numerous new developments and how these affect marketing. For instance, coverage includes such topics as social networks, mobile device applications ("apps"), neuro-research, group couponing, smartphone payments, quick response codes, and much, much more.

♦ Extensive material is presented focusing on real-world examples selected from leading media outlets. Students will find that most of these examples are still current and directly accessible via links on the book's support website.

♦ There is new material that takes an in-depth look at select marketing stories found in popular media. These unique feature boxes also contain questions that are useful for class discussion or outside assignments.

♦ With *KnowThis.com* as the book's support website, educators are directing their students to a high-quality resource that has served the marketing community since 1998.

♦ While the book contains over 150 real-world examples and over 40 in-depth stories, educators will find even more support on *KnowThis.com* including:

 • The *KnowThis Blog* offers detailed insight into selectively chosen marketing stories. These posting tie stories to marketing concepts and include discussion questions. Additionally, stories are tagged by topic area and notices of new postings are available via RSS feed.

 • In addition to current marketing stories, *KnowThis.com* has a database of over 4,000 more stories dating back to 2004. The stories are categorized by topic area. While we cannot guarantee that all are accessible, many, in fact, can be located with a simple click. This database could prove quite valuable as a research resource for students and instructors.

♦ Slide presentations, end-of-chapter discussion questions and test bank are available for qualified instructors who adopt the book.

For information on obtaining exam or desk copies see KnowThis Media website at: **KnowThisMedia.com**

About the Author

Paul Christ (pronounced with soft "i") holds a Ph.D. (marketing concentration) from Drexel University. He is a Professor of Marketing at West Chester University (AACSB accredited), the second largest university in the Pennsylvania State System of Higher Education and one of the largest universities in the Philadelphia region. Paul teaches MBA-level courses titled *Marketing Management, Marketing and Technology*, and *Business Research and Data Analysis*.

In addition to teaching, Paul has held several administrative positions including currently serving as the university's MBA Program Director. Also, in 1999 he was responsible for developing one of the first E-Commerce focused MBA programs in the world.

Paul has written and presented on marketing and technology topics in numerous academic publications, conferences and other public forums and has spoken throughout the world on the topic of marketing and Internet business. Paul is editor of *KnowThis. com*, one of the Internet's leading marketing references sites. In addition to academic experience, Paul has extensive experience in various marketing and sales positions with Fortune 500 companies and served in a management position for a successful startup in the consumer electronics industry. Additionally, he has been a consultant to many marketing and technology companies, including startup Internet-based firms.

Acknowledgements

I would like to thank my friends and colleagues at West Chester University for their support. I am especially grateful to the members of the Marketing Department, who provided excellent feedback, and also to Dean Chris Fiorentino and Associate Dean Michelle Patrick, for providing access to resources needed to finish this project. Also, a special thanks goes to my MBA Program staff, Chris Odorisio and Betsy Heckman, for understanding the importance of this project and for picking up the slack when needed.

P.C.

This book is lovingly dedicated to my parents, Anne and Ed, who taught me the importance of hard work and dedication to the task at hand. It is also dedicated to my wife Carol and children – Katie, Kelly, Mark and Tom –who continue to support and inspire.

Chapter 1: What is Marketing?

Welcome to the world of marketing! The main intention of *KnowThis: Marketing Basics* is to offer a straightforward examination of one of the most important, exciting, and challenging business activities crucial to nearly all organizations.

In this first chapter, we lay the groundwork for our study of the field of marketing with a look at marketing's key concepts and the important tasks marketers perform. Coverage includes a close examination of the definition of marketing. A dissection of the key terms in the definition shows that marketing's primary focus is to identify and satisfy customers in a way that helps build a solid and, hopefully, sustained relationship that encourages customers to continue doing business with the marketer. We also show how marketing has evolved from a process centered on simply getting as many people as possible to purchase a product to today's highly complex efforts designed to build long-term customer relationships. Additionally, we'll see marketing is not only necessary for individual organizations it also carries both positive and negative influences at a broader societal level. Finally, we look at the key characteristics that define successful marketers.

||||||||||||||||||||||||||||||||||||||||||||||||||||||||||||||||||||||||||||||||||||||||||||||||||||||||||||||||||

MARKETING DEFINED

Marketing is defined in many different ways. Some definitions focus on marketing in terms of what it means to an organization, such as being the main functional area for generating revenue. Other definitions lean more toward defining marketing in terms of its most visible tasks, such as advertising and creating new products.

There probably is no one best way to define marketing, however, whatever definition is used should have an orientation that focuses on the key to marketing success – customers.

We define marketing as follows:

Marketing consists of the strategies and tactics used to identify, create, and maintain satisfying relationships with customers resulting in value for both the customer and the marketer.

Dissecting Marketing

Let's examine our definition of marketing in detail by looking at the key terms.

Strategies and Tactics

Strategies are the direction the marketing effort takes over some period of time while tactics are actionable steps or decisions made in order to follow the strategies established. For instance, if a company's strategy is to begin selling its products in a new country, the tactics may involve the marketing decisions made to carry this out. Performing strategic and tactical planning activities in advance of taking action is considered critical for long-term marketing success.

Identify

Arguably the most important marketing function involves efforts needed to gain knowledge of customers, competitors, and markets (i.e., where marketers do business). To gain knowledge marketers will continually undertake marketing research.

> *American food companies, including McDonalds, Pizza Hut and General Mills, have frequently encountered problems when trying to market in the fast growing Asian market. These firms have learned the food needs in Asian markets are quite different compared to the needs of U.S. consumers. After many years of conducting customer research, American companies have learned they cannot simply sell their U.S. products in Asia but must adjust their offerings to local tastes. (1)*

Create

Competition forces marketers to be creative. When marketers begin new ventures, such as building a new company, it is often based around something that is new (e.g., a new product, a new way of getting products to customers, a new advertising approach, etc.). However, once something new is launched innovation does not end. Competitive pressure is continually felt by the marketer, who must respond by again devising new strategies and tactics that help the organization remain successful. For marketers, the cycle of creating something new never ends.

Maintain

Today's marketers work hard to ensure their customers return to purchase from them again and again. Long gone are the days when success for a marketer was measured simply by how many sales are made each day. Now, in most marketing situations, marketing success is evaluated not only in terms of sales but also by how long a marketer retains their customers. Consequently, marketers' efforts to attract customers do not end when a customer completes a purchase. It continues in various ways for, hopefully, a long time after the initial purchase.

Satisfying Relationships

A key objective of marketing is to provide goods and services that customers really want AND to make customers feel their contact with the marketer is helping build a strong relationship between the two. In this way, the customer becomes a partner in the transaction, not just a source of revenue for the marketer. While this concept may seem intuitive and a natural part of what all businesses should do, as Box 1-1 points out, this has not always been the case.

Value for Customer and Marketer

Value refers to the perception of benefits received for what someone must give up. For customers, value is most often measured by how much benefit they feel they are getting for their money, though the value one customer feels may differ from what another customer feels even though they purchase the same product. On the other side of the transaction, the marketer for a for-profit organization may measure value in terms of how much profit they make for the marketing efforts and resources expended. For a successful marketing effort to take place, both the customer and the marketer must feel they are receiving something worthwhile in return for their efforts. Without a strong perception of value, it is unlikely a strong relationship can be built.

Box 1-1

MARKETING CONCEPT

In the old days of marketing (before the 1950s) sellers of products were keen on identifying strategies and tactics that focused solely on selling more goods and services with little regard for what customers really wanted. Often this meant companies embraced a "sell-as-much-as-we-can" philosophy with little concern for building relationships for the long term.

But starting in the 1950s, companies began to see that old ways of selling were wearing thin with customers. As competition grew stiffer across most industries, organizations looked to the buyers' side of the transaction for ways to improve. What they found was an emerging philosophy suggesting that the key factor in successful marketing is understandings the needs of customers.

This now famous "Marketing Concept" suggests marketing decisions should flow from FIRST knowing the customer and what they want. Only then should an organization initiate the process of developing and marketing goods and services.

The Marketing Concept continues as the root of most marketing efforts. Marketers know they can no longer limit their marketing efforts to just getting customers to purchase more, they must have an in-depth understanding of who their customers are and what they want.

Marketing Story

New Retail Strategies: Offering a Better Fit for Today's Careful Consumers
Knowledge @ Wharton

Many marketers assume that during slow economic times customers will adjust their buying habits and seek out less expensive products. The assumption is based on the notion that during down times customers are forced to reevaluate their needs. This leads them to focus on just the basic or core benefits of products and forego products offering enhanced options. For instance, vacationers may change where they stay when traveling by booking economy hotels, where the core benefits are available (e.g., simple room furniture), instead of more luxurious hotels, where many more benefits are offered (e.g., high-end furniture). For customers, lower priced products offering fewer bells-and-whistles are now more appealing since, in the customers' mind, they offer more value compared to higher priced product.

But marketers need to remember that customers' perception of "best value" does not always mean they will choose the lowest priced product. What "best value" means is that customers have compared the benefits offered by different products and have decided they are getting their money's worth from the one they have chosen. (As we will see in Chapter 4, the benefits sought by customers can vary from one consumer to another.) For marketers, knowing the key benefits sought by customers will often require extensive marketing research. However, when done right the research may also show that products offering more benefits at a higher price are perceived as providing greater value than products offering fewer benefits at a lower price, even when the economy is not strong.

In this story, we see a clear example of how this works. Coca-Cola has introduced a new vending machine, called Freestyle, that enables customers to choose from over 100 flavor options. Better yet customers can mix and match to make their own flavor. While some may think this extreme (who needs to decide among over 100 beverage choices?), it clearly is empowering customers by giving them choices. Even in a slow economy, Coke expects that many customers will see the Freestyle as offering significant benefits and customers will be willing to spend more to obtain it.

What it does mean is that the price has to be right. To the value-conscious consumer, for example, a classic suit made of cheap fabric would be no more appealing than a trendy outfit made of the finest silk: Neither would last long -- the first because of the material, the second because of style. A better fit for today's careful consumer: a classic suit made well, or a fashionable outfit made affordably. (2)

Is the Freestyle vending machine a fad or will consumers continue to seek out and pay more for customizable products that can be purchased through vending?

||||||||||||||||||||||||||||||||||||||||||||||||||||||||||||||||||||||||||||||||||||||||||||||||||||||||||||||||||

THE MARKETER'S TOOLKIT

In order to reach the goal of creating a relationship that holds value for customers and the organization, marketers use a diverse Toolkit (see Figure 1-1). The Toolkit represents the key tasks performed by the marketer. These tasks include:

1. Selecting Target Markets

This task involves the selection of customers identified as possessing needs the marketer believes can be addressed by its marketing efforts. In almost all cases, marketers identify target markets prior to making other decisions since satisfying the needs of the target market drives all other marketing decisions. This task is discussed in detail in Chapter 5.

2. Creating Products

Marketers use tangible (e.g., goods) and intangible (e.g., services) solutions to address the needs of their target market. For many customers, the product is the main reason why the customer will or will not do business with the marketer. Product decisions have several dimensions and are discussed in detail in Chapters 6 and 7.

3. Establishing Distribution

Products are only of value to the target market if they can be obtained. Selecting distribution methods that enable customers to acquire products requires extremely careful consideration of different distribution options. As we will discuss in Chapters 8 and 9, gaining distribution almost always requires marketers seek assistance from others.

4. Developing Promotions

Most organizations must communicate information about their products to their target market. While advertising is the most notable form of promotion, there are others including sales promotion, personal selling, and public relations. In depth coverage of promotion is discussed in Chapters 10 through15.

5. Setting Price

Marketing often results in a transaction taking place between customers and the marketing organization. While product decisions determine what the marketer will exchange with the customer, it is pricing decisions that determine what the customer will give up in order to obtain the product. Pricing decisions can be quite complex and is addressed in detail in Chapters 16 and 17.

Figure 1-1: The Marketer's Toolkit

Characteristics of the Marketer's Toolkit

In addition to containing the five key marketing decisions, other key characteristics of the Toolkit include:

INTEGRATION OF TASKS

Each task within the Marketer's Toolkit is tightly integrated with all other tasks so that a decision in one area could, and often does, impact decisions in other areas. For instance, a change in the price of a product, such as lowering the price, could impact the distribution area by requiring increased product shipments to retail stores.

SEQUENCE OF TASKS

While the five key marketing tasks are shown with a number, the order of decision making does not necessarily follow this sequence. However, as we will discuss, marketers will generally first identify target markets (#1) prior to making decisions #2 through #5 (also called the **marketing mix**) since these decisions are going to be directed toward satisfying the desired target markets.

ADDITIONAL SKILLS

To use the Toolkit properly, marketers must possess additional skills including the ability to:

- <u>Conduct Marketing Research</u> – As we will see in Chapter 2, marketing decisions should not be made without first committing time and resources for gathering and analyzing information through marketing research. For this reason marketing research can be viewed as the foundation of marketing and, as shown in Figure 1-1, supports all marketing decisions.

- <u>Understand Customers</u> – While the Marketer's Toolkit centers on making decisions that satisfy customers, marketers must take extra steps to know as much as they can about their customers. In Chapters 3 and 4, we will see what marketers do to understand and manage their customers.

- <u>Monitor the External Environment</u> – As shown in Figure 1-1, options within the Marketer's Toolkit are affected by factors that are not controlled by the marketer. These factors include economic conditions, legal issues, technological developments, social/cultural changes, and many more. While not managed in the way marketers control their Toolkit, these external factors must be monitored and dealt with since these have the potential to cause considerable harm to the organization. Also, ignoring outside elements also can lead to missed opportunities in the market especially if competitors are the first to take advantage of the opportunities.

- <u>Create a Marketing Plan</u> – While some marketers may find success making decisions on the spur of the moment, most marketers must put much more thought into their decision making. As discussed in Chapter 20, developing a formal plan is a critical part of marketing.

‖‖

MARKETING'S ROLE

The key objective of an organization's marketing efforts is to develop satisfying relationships with customers that benefit both the customer and the organization. These efforts lead marketing to serve a pivotal role within most organizations and within society.

At the organizational level, marketing is a vital business function that is necessary in nearly all industries whether the organization operates as a for-profit or a not-for-profit. For the for-profit organization, marketing is responsible for most tasks that generate revenue and profits. For the not-for-profit organization, marketing is responsible for attracting customers needed to support the not-for-profit's mission, such as raising donations or supporting a cause.

> *Marketing is considered to be essential to the growth of almost all organizations with large sums being spent on the effort. In fact, it is estimated that globally spending for just one area of promotion, advertising, is more than $470 billion per year (3). This amount is greater than the GDP of such industrial areas as Sweden, Argentina and Malaysia. (4)*

Marketing is also the organizational business area that interacts most frequently with the public and, consequently, what the public knows about an organization is determined by their interactions with marketers. For example, customers may believe a company is dynamic and creative based on its advertising message.

At a broader level, marketing offers significant benefits to society. These include:

♦ Developing products that satisfy needs, including products that enhance society's quality of life

♦ Creating a competitive environment that helps lower product prices

♦ Developing product distribution systems that offer access to products to a large number of customers and many geographic regions

♦ Building demand for products that require organizations to expand their labor force

♦ Offering techniques having the ability to convey messages that change societal behavior in a positive way (e.g., anti-smoking advertising)

CRITICISMS OF MARKETING

While marketing is viewed as offering significant benefits to organizations and to society, the fact that marketing is a business function operating in close contact with the public opens this functional area to extensive criticism.

Among the issues cited by those who criticize marketing are:

Marketing Makes People Purchase What They Don't Need

Possibly the criticism most frequently made about marketing is that marketers are only concerned with getting customers to buy whether they need the product or not. The root of this argument stems from the belief that marketers are only out to satisfy their own needs and really do not care about the needs of their customers.

While many marketers are guilty of manipulating customers into making unwanted purchases, the vast majority understand such tactics will not lead to loyal customers and, consequently, is unlikely to lead to long-term success.

Marketers Embellish Product Claims

Marketers are often criticized for exaggerating the benefits offered by their products. This is especially the case with methods used for customer communication, such as advertising. The most serious problems arise when product claims are seen as misleading customers into believing a product can offer a certain level of value that, in fact, it cannot.

But sometimes there is a fine line between what a rational person should accept as a "reasonable exaggeration" and what is considered downright misleading. Fortunately, many countries offer customers some level of protection from misleading claims since such business practices may subject the marketer to legal action. Of course, using such tactics is also likely to lead to marketing failure as customers will not be satisfied with their experience and will not return.

> *The Center for Science in the Public Interest (CSPI), a U.S- based health advocacy group, participated in a class action lawsuit against Coca-Cola for the marketing of its Vitaminwater sports drink. The group claims the name, Vitaminwater, is misleading customers to believe the product is a healthy drink since it contains high levels of sugar in addition to vitamins. Coke disagrees claiming the sugar information is clearly marked on the product's label. (5)*

Marketing Discriminates in Customer Selection

A key to marketing success is to engage in a deliberate process that identifies customers who offer marketers the best chance for satisfying organizational objectives. This method, called **target marketing** (see Chapter 4), often drives most marketing decisions including product development and price setting. But some argue target marketing leads marketers to focus their efforts primarily on customers who have the financial means to make more expensive purchases. They contend this intentionally discriminates against others, especially lower income customers, who cannot afford to purchase higher priced products. Additionally, critics say lower income customers are targeted with lower quality products.

While this criticism is often valid, it is worth noting that while many "lower quality" products are inferior to current high-end products, comparison of their quality to similar products from just a few years ago shows there has been significant improvement. For instance, low cost electronic equipment, such as digital cameras, offer more features compared to low cost cameras of just a few years ago. Thus, while certain customer groups may not be the primary target market for some new product offerings, within a short period of time they may benefit from the development of higher-end products.

Marketing Contributes to Environmental Waste

One of the loudest complaints against marketing concerns its impact on the environment through:

- the use of excessive, non-biodegradable packaging (e.g., use of plastics, placing small products in large packages, etc.)

- the continual development of resource consuming products (e.g., construction of new buildings, golf courses, shopping malls, etc.)

- the proliferation of unsightly and wasteful methods of promotions (e.g., outdoor billboards, direct mail, etc.)

Marketers have begun to respond to these concerns by introducing **green marketing** campaigns that are not only intended to appease critics but also take advantage of potential business opportunities. For example, auto makers see opportunity by creating new fuel efficient electric and hybrid vehicles, the demand for which has accelerated due to increasing fuel prices and the heightened awareness of the environmental impact of gasoline-powered vehicles. Also, awareness of environmental issues has affected product design. For example, Paper Mate has introduced biodegradable pens with outer shells that when placed into a composter will break down to organic material in about a year. (6) It is expected that, as environmental activism gains political clout and more consumer support, marketers will see even more opportunity to market environmentally friendly products.

Marketing Encroaches on Customers' Right to Privacy

Gathering and analyzing information on the market in which marketers conduct business is a vital step in making smart marketing decisions. Often the most valuable information deals with customers' buying behavior and especially determining which factors influence how customers make purchase decisions.

But to some, digging deep into customer behavior crosses the line of what is considered private information. Of most concern to privacy advocates is marketers' use of methods that track user activity. In particular, they are critical of the growing use of advanced technologies allowing marketers to gain access to customer shopping and information gathering habits (see Box 1-2).

Privacy issues are not restricted to marketing research. Other areas of marketing have also experienced problems. For instance, there have been many incidents affecting consumer purchasing, most notably those involving mishandled credit card payment information, where a breach in privacy has placed customers at risk. This has affected many well-known companies including Sony, who saw hackers access the credit card data of members of its highly popular online Playstation Network. (7)

The issue of customer privacy is likely to become one of the most contentious issues marketers face in the coming years and could lead to greater legal limits on how marketers gather customer information and perform other activities.

Wal-Mart's decision to place radio frequency identification tags (RFID) on certain products, including men's jeans, has drawn criticism from privacy proponents. These "smart tags" allow Wal-Mart employees to know what products are being removed from the store for inventory purposes. However, privacy advocates say such systems may be capable of reading other RFID tags, including those found on some state drivers' license. They claim such methods could allow Wal-Mart and other retailers to better identify and track shoppers. (8)

Box 1-2

TRACKING CUSTOMERS ONLINE AND OFFLINE

Marketers have at their disposal numerous highly advanced techniques for tracking user activity both online and offline.

Online Tracking

At the most rudimentary level, marketers operating websites and mobile device applications ("apps") can track user activity that may include determining: how many are using a services (e.g., visit a website); what areas of the service are used (e.g., page within app); how they arrived at the service (e.g., via a search engine); where in the world users are located (e.g., geographic location); and many other types of information. This information is left by visitors each time they access a website or app and does not require the marketer to do much extra work to obtain the data. In fact, Google through its Analytics service enables marketers to have access to website and app tracking information for free. (9)

While tracking is widely used and generally considered an acceptable marketing tool, some marketers do engage in questionable practices, such as loading tracking software onto computers, without the knowledge or permission of the user. (10) For instance, one type of tracking software, called **adware,** allows marketers to monitor the website browsing activity of unsuspecting users and use this information to deliver advertisements based on users' Internet habits. To address online tracking concerns, several U.S. consumer advocacy groups and politicians have raised the prospect of legislation to limit the extent to which these techniques are used.

Offline Tracking

Privacy issues are not limited to concerns with online tracking; marketers also use techniques to track customers' offline purchase activities. One example of offline tracking occurs when retail stores match sales transactions to individual shoppers. This is easy to do when customers use purchase cards (a.k.a. loyalty cards, discount cards, club cards, etc.) as part of the buying process. This information can then be used to create individualized promotions, such as printing coupons that are based on the customer's previous buying activity.

||||||||||||||||||||||||||||||||||||||||||||||||||||||||||||||||||||||||||||||||||||||||||||||||||||||||||

ETHICAL AND SOCIAL CONCERNS

In addition to problems cited above, some critics also argue that the money-making motive of some marketers has encouraged many to cross the line in terms of ethical and social business behavior.

Ethical Issues

Ethics is concerned with what is right and wrong. Many people assume that only actions that violate laws are considered unethical. While it is true that illegal activity is also unethical, a business activity can be unethical even though no laws are violated. For instance, some consider it unethical for companies to aggressively promote unhealthy foods to children, though such promotional practices are generally not viewed as illegal.

Sometimes the line between what is ethical and unethical is difficult to distinguish since what is right and wrong differs depending on such factors as nationality, culture, and even industry. For example, many websites offer users free access to their content (e.g., articles, videos, audio clips, etc.), but do so only if users register and provide contact information including an email address. Some of these sites then automatically add registrants to promotional email mailing lists. Some view the practice of automatic "**opt-in**" to a mailing list as being unethical since customers do not request it and are forced to take additional action to be removed from the list ("**opt-out**"). However, many marketers see no ethical issue with this practice and simply view adding registered users to an email list as part of the "cost" to customers for accessing material.

MARKETING CODE OF ETHICS

The call for marketers to become more responsible for their actions has led to the development of a code of ethics by many companies and professional organizations.

Company Code

A company code of ethics includes extensive coverage of how business is conducted by members of an organization. For instance, Google's Code of Conduct lays out an extensive list of what is expected of their employees (11). Among the issues covered are:

- Offering Gifts - "We want to avoid the possibility that the gift, entertainment or other business courtesy could be perceived as a bribe, so it's always best to provide such business courtesies infrequently and, when we do, to keep their value moderate."

- Receiving Gifts - "Google policy prohibits Googlers accepting significant gifts, entertainment or any other business courtesy (including discounts or benefits that are not made available to all Googlers) from any of our customers, suppliers, partners or competitors."

- Competitor Information - "If an opportunity arises to take advantage of a competitor's or former employer's confidential information, don't do it."

- Friends and Relatives - "Don't tell your significant other or family members anything confidential, and don't solicit confidential information from them about their company."

> *The code of ethics for international retailer Ikea includes a policy against accepting or handing out bribes, even though such payments are understood to be how business is done in some parts of the word. To support this policy, when Ikea entered Russia with their first store, they refused pay a kickback to local businesspeople who threatened to withhold access to electrical power. Instead of paying, Ikea leased its own power generators. (12)*

Organization Code

Marketers often join professional organizations for the purpose of associating with others who share similar interests. These organizations include industry associations, whose membership is mostly limited to those working within a particular industry, and professional services associations, whose membership consists of those sharing similar job responsibilities. Marketers joining these organizations often find that a code of ethics has been developed that is intended to be followed by all organization members. For example, the Canadian Marketing Association lays out rules for its membership, which includes marketers from many for-profits and not-for-profit organizations, in its *Code of Ethics and Standards and Practices*. (13) The Code discusses such issues as:

- Accuracy of Representation of Products - "must accurately and fairly describe the product or service offered"

- Support of Claims Made About Products - "must be able to substantiate the basis for any performance claim or comparison"

- Acceptability for Using the Word Free - "products or services offered without cost or obligation"

- Guidelines for Advertising Which Compares One Product to Another - "must be factual, verifiable and not misleading"

The concern over ethical behavior in marketing continues to draw attention from customers, the news media, and other external groups. The issue is so important many companies now mandate their employees engage in ethics training and commit to performing their work with an understanding of what falls inside and outside of ethical boundaries. As more questionable marketing practices are publicized for potential ethical violations, marketers may expect to hear an increasing call for more emphasis in this area.

Marketing Story

How to Write a Code of Ethics for Business
Inc. Magazine

Business ethics is much discussed in the business press and within the academic arena, but few firms outside of the largest companies bother to write a formal Code of Ethics statement for their employees. Considering the potential loss of trust from customers, not to mention possible legal ramifications that may result from a perceived violation of expected ethical standards, it is probably wise for companies of all sizes to produce a business ethics statement. While a Code of Ethics applies to all within an organization, it is particularly useful for marketing personnel as they are the ones most connected to customers, suppliers, channel partners, the media, and other influential stakeholders.

In this story, the author provides good ideas for developing a stated ethics policy. The story also provides links to samples of ethics statements.

A code of ethics is a collection of principles and practices that a business believes in and aims to live by. A code of business ethics usually doesn't stand alone, it works in conjunction with a company's mission statement and more specific policies about conduct to give employees, partners, vendors, and outsiders an idea of what the company stands for and how it's members should conduct themselves. (14)

What are the key issues that should be addressed within a Code of Ethics statement that are most specific to the marketing side of an organization?

Social Responsibility in Marketing

Most marketing organizations do not intentionally work in isolation from the rest of society. Instead, they find greater opportunity exists if the organization is visibly accessible and involved with the public. As we've seen, because marketing often operates as the "public face" of an organization, when issues arise between the public and the organization marketing is often at the center. In recent years, the number and variety of issues raised by the public has increased. One reason for the increase is the growing perception that marketing organizations are not just sellers of products but also have an inherent responsibility to be more socially responsible, including being more responsible for its actions and more responsive to addressing social concerns.

Being socially responsible means an organization shows concern for the people and environment in which it transacts business. It also means these values are communicated and enforced by everyone in the organization and, in some cases, with outside business partners, such as those who sell products to the company (e.g., supplier of raw material for product production) and those who help the company distribute and sell to other customers (e.g., retail stores).

In addition to ensuring these values exist within the organization and its business partners, companies often pursue social responsibility through methods that fall under the heading of **cause marketing**. As the name suggests, these techniques involve activities intended to align a company or a product with a specific cause. For instance, marketers may sponsor charity events or produce cause-related advertising.

> *Another example of approaches taken by companies engaged in cause marketing is to create new products that are specifically intended to serve as fundraisers. For instance, Ben & Jerry's Ice Cream has a philosophy of being involved in social causes (15) and that includes developing unique products, such as the AmeriCone Dream ice cream developed for television personality Stephen Colbert's charity. (16)*

Marketers who are pursuing a socially responsible agenda should bear in mind such efforts do not automatically translate into increased revenue or even an improved public image. Additionally, if not handled correctly, socially responsible activities could negatively affect a company. However, organizations that consistently exhibit socially responsible tendencies may eventually gain a strong reputation that could pay dividends in the form of increased customer loyalty.

||||||||||||||||||||||||||||||||||||||||||||||||||||||||||||||||||||||||||||||||||||||||||||||||||

CHARACTERISTICS OF THE MODERN MARKETER

As we've seen, marketing is a critical business function operating in an environment that is highly scrutinized and continually changing. Today's marketers undertake a variety of tasks as they attempt to build customer relationships while meeting organizational objectives. The "know-how" needed to perform these tasks successfully is also varied. Possessing basic marketing knowledge is just the beginning. Successful marketers must also be comfortable with a wide-range of knowledge and skill sets including:

Basic Business Skills

Marketers are first and foremost business people who must perform necessary tasks required of all successful business people. Many of these tasks depend on marketers possessing an assortment of basic skills including problem analysis and decision making, oral and written communication, quantitative skills, and the ability to work well with others.

Understanding Marketing's Impact

Marketers must know how their decisions will impact other areas of the company and their business partners. They must realize that marketing decisions are not made in isolation and that decisions made by the marketing team could lead to problems for others in the organization. For example, a decision to run a special sale that significantly lowers the price of a product could present supply problems if the production area is not informed well in advance of the sale.

Technology Savvy

Today's marketers must have a strong understanding of technology on two fronts. First, marketers must be skilled in using technology as part of their everyday activities. Not only must they understand how basic computer software is used to build spreadsheets or create slide presentations, marketers must also investigate additional technologies that can improve their effectiveness and efficiency, such as multifunction smartphones, GPS navigation services, and web-based productivity applications.

Second, as we will see throughout this book, the evolution of the Internet and mobile technology is transforming many marketing functions. Marketers must understand emerging technology and applications in order to spot potential business opportunities as well as potential threats. For instance, the rapid growth of **social media** requires marketers firmly understand how these fit within an overall marketing strategy.

The Need for a Global Perspective

Thanks in large part to the Internet, nearly any company can conduct business on a global scale. In fact, the World Trade Organization estimates that over $15 trillion is transacted as part of international commerce. (17) Yet, just having a website that is accessible to hundreds of millions of people worldwide does not guarantee success. Marketers selling internationally must understand the nuances of international trade and cultural differences that exist between markets. One key issue facing marketers selling globally is choosing the appropriate strategy for reaching international customers. As discussed in Box 1-3, two distinctly different methods are often pursued.

Information Seeker

The field of marketing is dynamic. Changes occur continually and often quickly. Marketers must maintain close contact with these changes through a steady diet of information. As we will see, information can be obtained through formal marketing research methods involving extensive planning that includes the use of a variety of information gather techniques. However, marketers also must be in tune with day-to-day developments by paying close attention to news that occurs in their industry, in the markets they serve, and among their potential customers.

Box 1-3

APPROACHES TO GLOBAL MARKETING

Marketers seeking to expand beyond their home market face many decisions that are often new to them. However, for most companies the most important decision they face is deciding whether they should follow a marketing approach policy that is the same world-wide (i.e., standardization) or one that is customized for the markets served (i.e., adaptation). It should be understood, this topic is a broad one encompassing not only issues regarding decisions to produce the same or different products but all marketing mix decisions.

Standardization

Under a standardization strategy, a marketing organization follows a "one-for-all" approach where all global markets are targeted with the same combination of marketing mix elements. The main advantage to the standardization approach is the cost savings realized from common production, research and development, and marketing decisions across multiple countries. On the negative side, standardization may only be effective if there are enough customers in each market whose needs are very similar.

Adaptation

Under an adaptation strategy, firms operating globally allow both conception and execution of the marketing plan to originate in the foreign market. This provides local managers the opportunity to custom-design the marketing mix for local conditions. The main advantage of this approach is that it fits the marketing concept by allowing local management to satisfy the target market's needs while taking into consideration issues that may exist within the local environment. However, the cost of implementation of this approach can be higher compared to standardization as costs cannot be spread over all markets the way they can with standardization.

||||||||||||||||||||||||||||||||||||||||||||||||||||||||||||||||||||||||||||||||||||||||||||||||||||||||||||||||||||

REFERENCES

1. Chu, K., "Fast-Food Chains in Asia Cater Menus to Customers," *USA Today*, September 7, 2010.

2. "New Retail Strategies: Offering a Better Fit for Today's Careful Consumers," *Knowledge@Wharton*, August 31, 2011.

3. *ZenithOptimedia*, Press Release, July 13, 2011.

4. *The World Bank* website.

5. Gregory, S., "Is Vitaminwater Really a Healthy Drink?" *Time*, July 30, 2010.

6. Hunt, W. and A. Reid, "2011 Trends in Packaging," *Brand Packaging*, December 27, 2010.

7. Snider, M., "Sony: Credit Card Data at Risk in PlayStation Hack," *USA Today*, April 27, 2011.

8. D'Innocenzio, A., "Wal-Mart Plan to Use Smart Tags Raises Privacy Concerns," *USA Today*, July 25, 2010.

9. *Google Analytics* website.

10. Angwin, J., "The Web's New Gold Mine: Your Secrets," *Wall Street Journal*, July 30, 2010.

11. *Google Investor Relations* website.

12. Spiro, J., "How to Write a Code of Ethics for Business," *Inc. Magazine*, February 24, 2010.

13. *Canadian Marketing Association* website.

14. Spiro, J., "How to Write a Code of Ethics for Business," *Inc. Magazine*, February 24, 2010.

15. *Ben & Jerry's Ice Cream* website.

16. Elliott, S., "A Brand That Takes a Stand," *New York Times*, October 17, 2011.

17. *World Trade Organization*, Press Release, April 7, 2011.

Full text of many of the references can be accessed via links on the support website.

Chapter 2: Marketing Research

Many organizations find the markets they serve are dynamic with customers, competitors, and market conditions continually changing. They also recognize that marketing efforts that work today cannot be relied upon to be successful in the future. Meeting changing conditions requires marketers have sufficient market knowledge in order to make the proper adjustments to their marketing strategy. For marketers, gaining knowledge is accomplished through marketing research.

In this chapter, we look at the importance of research in marketing. We explore what marketing research is and see why it is considered the foundation of marketing. Our examination includes a detailed look at the key methods marketers use to gather relevant information. Finally, we look at the trends shaping marketing research.

‖‖

THE FOUNDATION OF MARKETING

Research, in general, is the process of gathering information to learn about something that is not fully known. Nearly everyone engages in some form of research. From the highly trained geologist investigating newly discovered earthquake faults to the author of best-selling spy novels seeking insight into new surveillance techniques, to the model train hobbyist spending hours hunting down the manufacturer of an old electric engine, each is driven by the quest for information.

For marketers, research is not only used for the purpose of learning, it is also a critical component needed to make good decisions. Marketing research does this by giving marketers a picture of what is occurring (or likely to occur) and, when done well, offers alternative choices that can be made. For instance, research may suggest multiple options for introducing new products or entering new markets. In most cases, marketing decisions prove less risky (though these are never risk free) when the marketer can select from more than one option.

Using an analogy of a house foundation, marketing research can be viewed as the foundation of marketing. Just as a well-built house requires a strong foundation to remain sturdy, marketing decisions need the support of research in order to be viewed favorably by customers and to stand up to competition and other external pressures.

Consequently, all areas of marketing and all marketing decisions should be supported with some level of research.

While research is key to marketing decision making, it does not always need to be elaborate to be effective. Sometimes small efforts, such as doing a quick search on the Internet, will provide the needed information. However, for most marketers there are times when more elaborate research work is needed and understanding the right way to conduct research, whether performing the work themselves or hiring someone else to handle it, can increase the effectiveness of these projects.

> *Marketing research is essential for all types of businesses including not-for-profit organizations. For instance, the Guggenheim Museum in New York uses research to understand the needs and interests of its members. The museum utilizes several different research techniques to learn the reasons why members join, what benefits they value, and their overall level of satisfaction. (1)*

Research in Marketing

As noted, marketing research is undertaken to support a wide variety of marketing decisions. Table 2-1 presents a small sampling of the research undertaken by marketing decision area. Many of the issues listed under Types of Research are discussed in greater detail in other parts of this book.

Options for Gathering Research Information

Marketers engage in a wide range of research from simple methods done spur of the moment to extensive, highly developed research projects taking months or even years to complete. To gather research marketers have three choices:

♦ Acquire pre-existing research conducted by others

♦ Undertake new research themselves

♦ Out-source the task of new research to a third-party, such as a marketing research company

The first option is associated with **secondary research**, which involves accessing information that was previously collected. The last two options are associated with **primary research**, which involves the collection of original data generally for one's own use. In many instances, the researcher uses both secondary and primary data collection as part of the same research project. While both secondary and primary research have advantages and disadvantages, as discussed in Box 2-1, the value in using these is dependent on how the information is collected.

Table 2-1: Examples of Research in Marketing

Marketing Decision	Types of Research
Target Markets	sales, market size, demand for product, customer characteristics, purchase behavior, customer satisfaction, website traffic
Product	product development, package protection, packaging awareness, brand name selection, brand recognition, brand preference, product positioning
Distribution	distributor interest, assessing shipping options, online shopping, retail store site selection
Promotion	advertising recall, advertising copy testing, sales promotion response rates, sales force compensation, traffic studies (outdoor advertising), public relations media placement
Pricing	price elasticity analysis, optimal price setting, discount options
External Factors	competitive analysis, legal environment, social and cultural trends
Other	company image, test marketing

‖‖

SECONDARY RESEARCH

By far the most widely used method for collecting data is through secondary data collection, commonly called secondary research. This process involves collecting data from either the originator or a distributor of primary research (see *Primary Research* discussion below). In other words, accessing information already gathered.

In most cases, this means finding information from third-party sources, such as industry research reports, company websites, magazine articles, and other sources. But in actuality any information previously gathered, whether from sources external to the marketer's organization or from internal sources, such as previously undertaken marketing research, old sales reports, accounting records, and many others, falls under the heading of secondary research.

Box 2-1

RISK AND DOING RESEARCH RIGHT

Marketing research is a process that investigates both organizations and people. Of course, organizations are made up of people so when it comes down to it, marketing research is a branch of the social sciences. Social science studies people and their relationships and includes such areas as economics, sociology, and psychology. To gain understanding into their fields, researchers in the social sciences use scientific methods that have been tested and refined over hundreds of years. Many of these methods require the institution of tight controls on research projects. For instance, many companies conduct surveys (i.e., by asking questions) of a small percentage of their customers (called a **sample**) to see how satisfied they are with the company's efforts. For the information obtained from a small group of customers to be useful when evaluating how all customers feel, certain controls must be in place including controls on who should be included in the sample. Also, for results to be truly relevant, research must stand up to scrutiny using **statistical analysis**.

Thus, doing research right means the necessary controls are in place. Relying on results of research conducted incorrectly to make decisions could prove problematic if not disastrous. Thousands of examples exist of firms using faulty research to make decisions, including many dot-com companies that failed when the Internet bubble burst between 1999 and 2002 as well as financial firms that failed between 2008 and 2009.

But marketers must be aware following the right procedures to produce a relevant study does not ensure the results of research will be 100 percent correct as there is always the potential that results are wrong. Because of the risks associated with research, marketers are cautioned not to use the results of marketing research as the only input in making marketing decisions. Rather, smart marketing decisions require considering many factors, including management's own judgment. But being cautious with how research is used should not diminish the need to conduct research. While making decisions without research input may work sometimes, long-term success is not likely to happen without regular efforts to collect information.

ADVANTAGES

Secondary research offers several advantages for research gathering including:

- Ease of Access – Before the Internet era, accessing reliable secondary data required marketers visit libraries or wait until a report was shipped by mail. When online access initially became an option through dial-up services, marketers needed training to learn different rules and procedures for accessing each data source. However, the Internet has changed how secondary research is accessed by offering convenience (e.g., easy, nearly anywhere access) and generally standardized usage methods for accessing data sources.

- Low Cost to Acquire – Researchers are often attracted to secondary data because getting this information is much less expensive than if the researchers had to carry out the research themselves.

- May Help Clarify Research Question – Secondary research is often used prior to larger scale primary research to help clarify what is to be learned. For instance, a researcher doing competitor analysis, but who is not familiar with competitors in a market, could access secondary sources to locate a list of potential competitors and use this information as part of his/her own primary research study.

- May Answer Research Question – As noted, secondary data collection is often used to help set the stage for primary research. In the course of doing so, researchers may find the exact information they are looking for is available via secondary sources, which eliminates the need and expense of carrying out primary research.

- May Show Difficulties in Conducting Primary Research – The originators of secondary research often provide details on how the information was collected. This may include discussion of difficulties encountered. For instance, a research report written by a large marketing research company reveals a high percentage of people declined to take part in the research. After obtaining this study, a marketer contemplating doing similar research may decide it is not worth the effort given the potential difficulties in conducting the study.

DISADVANTAGES

While secondary research is often valuable, it also has drawbacks that include:

- Quality of Researcher – As we will discuss, research conducted using primary methods is largely controlled by the marketer. However, this is not the case when it comes to data collected by others. The quality of secondary research should be scrutinized closely since the origins of the information may be questionable. Organizations relying on secondary data as an important component in their decision making must take care to evaluate how the information was gathered, analyzed, and presented to ensure the research was done correctly and is relevant (see Box 2-1).

- Not Specific to Researcher's Needs – Secondary data is often not presented in a form that exactly meets the marketer's needs. For example, a marketer obtains an expensive research report examining how different age groups feel about certain products within the marketer's industry. Unfortunately, the marketer may be disappointed to discover the way the research divides age groups (e.g., under 13, 14-18, 19-25, etc.) does not match how the marketer's company designates its age groups (e.g., under 16, 17-21, 22-30, etc). Because of this difference the results may not be useful.

- Not Available in All Markets – In some cases, marketers will find much of their research needs are satisfied with secondary research available in their current market. However, marketers relying on specific data may find such information is not available in all markets. This is especially the case for marketers seeking to expand to foreign markets. They may discover that secondary research that is readily available in their home markets is either not available or the quality is poor. Additionally, there may be differences in how the data is collected and presented; thus, making comparisons between markets somewhat difficult.

- Inefficient Spending for Information – If the research received is not specific to the marketer's needs, an argument can be made that research spending is inefficient. That is, the marketer may not receive a satisfactory amount of information for what is spent.

- Incomplete Information – Many times a researcher finds research that appears to be promising is, in fact, a "teaser" released by the research supplier. This may occur when a small portion of a study is disclosed, often for free, but the full report, which is often expensive, is needed to gain the full value of the study.

- Not Timely – Caution must be exercised in relying on secondary data collected well in the past. Out-of-date information generally offers little value especially for companies competing in fast changing markets.

- Not Proprietary Information – In most cases, secondary research is not undertaken specifically for one company. Instead, it is made available to many either for free or for a fee. Consequently, there is rarely an information advantage gained by those who obtain the research.

Types of Low-Cost Secondary Research

Many marketers mistakenly believe marketing research is something that is far too expensive to do on their own. While this is true for some marketing decisions, not all marketing research must be expensive to be useful. There are secondary research sources that are easily obtainable and relatively low cost and often free. (2) These include:

TRADE ASSOCIATIONS

Trade associations are generally membership-supported organizations whose mission is to offer assistance and represent the interests of those operating in a specific industry. One of the many tasks performed by trade associations is to provide research information and industry metrics through efforts, such as conducting member surveys. Accessing this information may be as simple as visiting a trade association's website, although some associations limit access to the best research to members only, in which case joining the association (if they permit) may include paying dues.

An example of a trade association undertaking research can be found with the Color Marketing Group which produces research forecasting color trends, often years in advance. Members of the association then have time to plan for adjusting the colors used in their products, packaging, and promotional material. (3)

GOVERNMENT SOURCES

Many national, regional, and local governments offer a full range of helpful materials including information on consumers, domestic businesses, and international markets. For those operating in the United States, information available through the U.S. Government is staggering. The U.S. Government is a behemoth with agencies and offices found in more nooks and crannies than one could ever imagine and the uninitiated can spend hours on end trying to find relevant information. But once found and digested, the reports are often very useful for many marketing purposes.

COMMUNITY GROUPS AND ORGANIZATIONS

When searching for information related to regional business areas, marketers can often tap into groups and organizations connected to these areas. Some examples of groups offering access to low cost secondary data include regional chambers of commerce, economic development agencies, and local colleges and universities.

COMPANY PROVIDED INFORMATION

If the need is for information on a specific company and if research seekers are willing to believe what a company reports in its own literature, then value may be found in company provided information. While many materials published by organizations are promotional pieces (see *Research as Promotional Tool* discussion below), there may be beneficial information found amongst the hype. Options for finding information include company websites, annual reports, press releases, white papers, and presentations.

NEWS AND MEDIA SOURCES

Possibly the most widely used method for acquiring secondary research is through articles and other reports found through commercial news sources. Options include magazines, newspapers, television news, and other video/audio programming. Nearly all of these sources are available online.

ACADEMIC RESEARCH

College professors often cite industry research as part of their own scholarly efforts when they conduct their own research studies. Many of these academic works can be found in academic journals and within research centers established by many universities. The websites of these centers frequently post articles and working papers containing market data, most of which are freely accessible. An Internet search using the keywords "research center" along with industry or product keywords may yield a list.

CAUSE-RELATED GROUPS

Many non-profit groups have an organizational mission directed at supporting causes they feel are not well-supported in society. Examples include groups focusing on the environment, education, and health care. As would be expected, a considerable portion of their focus looks at how business impacts these issues. Research seekers will find the best funded of these groups carry out an active marketing research agenda with many of their studies freely available on their websites.

Types of High-Cost Secondary Research

While research seekers can get lucky finding information through inexpensive means, the realty is that, in many situations, locating in-depth market information is difficult and expensive. Companies in the business of producing market studies are mostly doing so to make money and do not give the information away for free. Consequently, in many research situations, especially those in which reliable market numbers and estimates are critical, acquiring the best researched market information requires a fee.

Expensive sources of information generally include accessing reports from the originators of the research, such as marketing research firms. However, since gaining access to quality research can be costly, on the surface it may not seem practical for small companies or individuals to take advantage of these sources. Yet, research seekers also know that the level of detail available in a single report may be enough to provide answers to most of their questions in which case these reports can be real time savers (though marketers are cautioned against relying on a single source of information when making marketing decisions).

Also, while the cost of reports can appear prohibitive, today's reports are much more accessible than in the past when research suppliers required clients to sign up for high-priced subscription services. Purchasing a subscription would then give the client access to a large number of reports. Today, many information sources permit the purchase of a single research report without the requirement to commit to a subscription.

It should be noted that some of these sources may make a limited amount of material available for free, so it is worth a look no matter how much money the research seeker has to spend.

High-cost marketing research sources include (4):

MARKETING RESEARCH COMPANIES

Many companies engaged in marketing research services offer both customized research activities (i.e., produce work only for a specific client) and commercial research (i.e., produce work that nearly anyone can buy). Commercial reports produced by reputable firms are often well researched and contain extensive product/industry metrics and statistics, including forecasts and trend analysis. Often these reports are generated by a specific researcher, who has been following the market/industry for many years. An industry-focused researcher will produce regular updates, which include offering comments and insight that go beyond the numbers. But these reports come with a high price tag. It is not uncommon to pay a large sum for a report that is less than 100 pages long. However, many research reports are updates of existing reports and the older reports may be available for lower cost.

FINANCIAL SERVICES COMPANIES

Financial institutions, such as brokerage firms and other financial consulting firms, are also in the business of producing original research. Financial firms assist investors by offering research reports presenting the financial firm's analysis of an industry or company including providing market metrics. While such reports may be free to a broker's clients, many reports can also be purchased by non-clients through financial portal websites.

CONSULTING FIRMS

Consulting firms consist of individuals specializing in particular business areas, such as by job function (e.g., sales training), business need (e.g., strategy development) or industry (e.g., transportation). In addition to working for individual clients, consulting firms also produce reports covering their specialties that are made available to the general public. By and large the bigger the consulting firm the more valid and reliable are the reports they produce. One group of companies to consider as a starting point is large accounting firms. Nearly all major accounting firms have divisions focused on management consulting. These divisions regularly make available industry reports.

MARKET INFORMATION DEALERS

The marketing research business consists of a large number of suppliers who provide many products (i.e., research studies and other documents) targeted to a wide-range of buyers. To get research into the hands of buyers, the creators of the research can attempt to sell the reports themselves or they can enlist the services of companies serving an intermediary role (i.e., bring buyers and sellers together). For their services, these dealers receive a percentage of the sale price.

For research seekers, these dealers offer several advantages. First, they carry reports from many different suppliers increasing the likelihood of finding a report that meets the researcher's needs. Second, they allow for the purchase of individual reports and, in some cases, pieces of reports offered at lower cost, whereas marketing research creators often require clients to purchase a complete report at full price. Third, they offer excellent search functionality making it easy to locate reports.

COMPREHENSIVE INFORMATION SOURCES

Marketers, who frequently need to locate market information, may consider establishing an account with one of the major comprehensive information sources. These are the heavyweight sources of business research used by university libraries and leading corporations.

Comprehensive sources offer one-stop shopping for research reports, industry news, and even government information. In fact, much of the information available from sources already mentioned is also available through comprehensive information sources. However, gaining access to these services can be prohibitively expensive. Fortunately, several comprehensive information sources are now offering pay-per-item access.

PRIMARY RESEARCH

When marketers conduct research to collect original data for their own needs it is called primary research. This process has the marketer or someone working for the marketer designing and then carrying out a research plan. Primary research is often undertaken after the researcher has gained some insight into the issue by collecting secondary data.

While not as frequently used as secondary research, primary research still represents a significant part of overall marketing research. For many organizations, especially large firms, spending on primary research far exceeds spending on secondary research.

The primary research market consists of marketers carrying out their own research as well as an extensive group of companies offering their services to marketers. These companies include:

♦ <u>Full-Service Marketing Research Firms</u> – These companies develop and carryout the full research plan for their clients.

♦ <u>Partial-Service Research Firms</u> – These companies offer expertise addressing a specific part of the research plan, such as developing methods to collect data (e.g., design surveys), locating research participants or undertaking data analysis.

♦ <u>Research Tools Suppliers</u> – These firms provide tools used by researchers and include data collection tools (e.g., survey websites), data analysis software, and report presentation products.

ADVANTAGES

Marketers often turn to primary data collection because of the benefits it offers including:

- Addresses Specific Research Issues – Carrying out its own research allows the marketing organization to address issues specific to its own situation. Primary research is designed to collect the information the marketer wants to know and report it in ways benefiting the marketer. For example, while information reported with secondary research may not fit the marketer's needs, no such problem exists with primary research since the marketer controls the research design.

- Greater Control – Primary research enables the marketer to focus on specific issues and have a higher level of control over how the information is collected. In this way the marketer can decide such issues as size of project (e.g., how many responses), location of research (e.g., geographic area), and time frame for completing the project.

- Efficient Spending for Information – Unlike secondary research where the marketer may spend for information that is not needed, primary data collection focuses on issues specific to the researcher. This helps improve the chances research funds will be spent efficiently.

- Proprietary Information – Information collected by the marketer using primary research is its own and is generally not shared with others. Thus, information can be hidden from competitors and potentially offer an **information advantage** to the company that undertook the primary research.

DISADVANTAGES

While primary data collection is a powerful method for acquiring information, it does pose several significant problems including:

- Cost – Compared to secondary research, primary data may be very expensive since it requires a high-degree of marketer involvement and the cost of carrying out the research can be high.

- Time Consuming – To be done correctly, primary data collection requires the development and execution of a research plan. Going from the starting point of deciding to undertake a research project to the end point of having results is often much longer than the time it takes to acquire secondary data.

- Not Always Feasible – Some research projects, while potentially offering information that could prove quite valuable, are not within the reach of a marketer. Many are just too large to be carried out by all but the largest companies while some research projects are not feasible at all. For instance, it would not be practical for McDonalds to attempt to interview every customer visiting its stores on a certain day since doing so would require hiring an enormous number of researchers, an unrealistic expense. Fortunately, there are ways for McDonalds to use other methods (e.g., sampling) to meet its needs without talking to all customers.

> *For some forms of primary research, disadvantages are enhanced due to the time and money needed to find participants willing to take part in a study. To improve participation in surveys conducted at shopping malls, market research firm Olinger Group used newly introduced Apple iPads as a tool in the research collection process. The resulting high response rate was attributed to customer curiosity with the new iPad and enabled Olinger to complete the research in less time than was planned. (5)*

Types of Primary Research

In general, there are two basic types of primary research – quantitative data collection and qualitative data collection.

Quantitative Data Collection

Quantitative data collection involves the use of numbers to assess information. This information can then be evaluated using statistical analysis, which offers researchers the opportunity to dig deeper into the data and look for greater meaning (see Box 2-2). Quantitative data collection comes in many forms, but the most popular forms are:

- Surveys – This method captures information through the input of responses to a research instrument, such as a questionnaire. Information can be input either by respondents themselves (e.g., complete an online survey) or the researcher can input the data (e.g. phone survey, shopping mall intercept). The main methods for distributing surveys are via postal and electronic mail, phone, website, and in-person. However, newer technologies are creating additional delivery options including through wireless devices, such as smartphones.

- Tracking – With tracking research marketers monitor the behavior of customers as they engage in regular purchase or information gathering activities. Possibly the most well-known example of tracking research is used by websites and mobile device applications as they track customer visits and usage. Yet, tracking research also has offline applications (see Box 1-2 in Chapter 1) including using point-of-purchase scanners to track product purchases at retail stores. This method of research is expected to grow significantly as more devices are introduced with tracking capability.

- Experiments – Marketers often undertake experiments to gauge how the manipulation of one marketing variable affects another (i.e., **causal research**). The use of experiments has applications for many marketing decision areas including product testing, advertising design, setting price points, and creating packaging. Unfortunately, performing highly controlled experiments can be quite costly. Some researchers have found the use of computer simulations can work nearly as well as experiments and may be less expensive, though the number of simulation applications for marketing decisions is still fairly limited.

For many years, newspapers relied on customer feedback through reader surveys distributed either by mail or through phone calls. Such methods for finding out what customers are interested in were not always timely and, when they did learn customers' interests, it would take newspapers some time to make adjustments. Today, many newspapers use tracking of their website editions to determine what is of interest to it readers. For instance, in the newsroom of the Washington Post, a television screen displays current website traffic data for all to see. This provides a way for editors and journalist to see in real time what issues are of interest to site visitors. (6)

Box 2-2

RESEARCH BY THE NUMBERS

Primary research is collected using a **research instrument** designed to record information for later analysis. Marketing researchers use many types of instruments from basic methods that record participant responses to a survey on a piece of paper to highly advanced electronic measurement that has those participating in research hooked up to sophisticated equipment. Depending on the type of research instrument used, the researcher may be able to evaluate the results by turning responses into numbers which then allows for analysis using statistical methods (see Box 2-1).

Of course, certain information is by nature numerical. For example, asking a person their actual age or weight will result in a number. But under the right circumstances, numbers can also be used to represent certain characteristics, which are not on the surface considered numerical. This most often occurs with data collected within a structured and well-controlled scientific **research design**. For instance, a company researching its customers' attitudes toward products they purchased may ask a large number of customers to complete a survey. Contained in the survey is the following:

Place an "X" on the line that best indicates your impression of the overall quality of our company's products:

Poor __ __ __ __ __ __ __ Excellent

In this example each line, which represents a potential customer response, could be assigned a number. For example, checking the left-most line could result in the researcher entering a "1", the next line a "2", the next line a "3", and so on.

Once research is gathered for all customers completing the survey, information for this item can then undergo statistical analysis and interesting comparisons can be made. For example, different types of customers (e.g., female vs. male) can be compared on their mean or average score for this item. Statistical analysis can then be used to determine if a difference exists in how they responded.

Qualitative Data Collection

Often called "touchy-feely" research, qualitative data collection requires researchers to interpret the information gathered, most often without the benefit of statistical support. If the researcher is well trained in interpreting respondents' comments and activities, this form of research can offer valuable insight. However, this data collection method may not hold the same level of relevancy as quantitative research due to the lack of scientific controls. An additional drawback of qualitative research is that it can be time consuming, expensive, and only a very small portion of the marketer's desired market can participate. Due to the lack of strong controls in the research design, using results to estimate characteristics of a larger group is more difficult.

Qualitative data collection options include:

- Individual Interviews – Talking to someone one-on-one allows a researcher to cover more ground than may be covered if a respondent was completing a survey. The researcher can dig deeper into a respondent's comments to find out additional details that might not emerge from initial responses. Unfortunately, individual interviewing can be quite expensive and may be intimidating to some who are not comfortable sharing details with a researcher.

- Focus Groups – To overcome the drawbacks associated with individual interviews, marketers can turn to focus groups. Under this research format, a group of respondents (generally numbering 8-12) is guided through a discussion by a moderator. The power of focus groups as a research tool rests with the environment created by the interaction of the participants. In well run sessions, members of the group are stimulated to respond by the comments and the support of others in the group. In this way, the depth of information offered by a respondent may be much greater than that obtained through individual interviews. However, focus groups can be costly to conduct especially if participants must be paid. To help reduce costs, online options for focus groups have emerged. While there are many positive aspects to online focus groups, the fact that respondents are not physically present diminishes the benefits gained by group dynamics. However, as technology improves, in particular Internet video conferencing, the online focus group could become a key research option.

- Observational Research – Marketers can gain valuable insight by watching customers as they perform activities, especially when observed in a natural setting (e.g., using products at home). In fact, an emerging research technique called **ethnographic research** has researchers following customers as they shop, work, and relax at home in order to see how they make decisions, use products, and more.

Marketing researchers are continually experimenting with new methods for acquiring information. As an example, Spark, a New York-based research firm, developed an interactive technique where research participants create collages intended to represent how consumers feel about products or advertisements. The marketing director for Unilever, which used the technique to evaluate its Suave hair-care brand, feels the concept give valuable insight into the emotional side of consumer decision-making. (7)

Marketing Story

Going Where CPGs Do Research
Shopper Marketing

Just how valuable an organization views marketing research can often be determined by looking at the resources directed toward this important function. However, for competitive reasons, most companies prefer to keep such details secret and do not often share their research techniques in a public way. Though, occasionally information does leak out, mostly through articles in the trade press.

For example, this story explains methods used by several leading companies for measuring customers' response to marketing decisions. Most methods are employed within an internal research laboratory where qualitative research is collected. These labs include mock-ups of retail store aisles, product demonstration and usage areas (including one company's research facility that contains a house), and advanced focus groups facilities.

Hewlett-Packard's lab is designed to mock the aisles of many major big box stores selling its products. The company tests many of its campaigns as it receives the first prototypes, approximately three to six months before launch. "It's the ideal store for shoppers based on their insights and what they want," Stermitz says. (8)

What are the key advantages and disadvantages with operating an in-house marketing research laboratory?

||||||||||||||||||||||||||||||||||||||||||||||||||||||||||||||||||||||||||||||||||||||||||||||||||||||||||||||||||||

TRENDS IN MARKETING RESEARCH

In recent years, the evolution of marketing research has been dramatic with marketers getting access to a wide variety of tools and techniques to improve their hunt for information. Below we discuss a few notable trends shaping the marketing research field:

GAINING AN INFORMATION ADVANTAGE

In its role as the foundation of marketing, marketing research is arguably the key ingredient in making marketing decisions and a critical factor in gaining advantage over competitors. Because organizations recognize the power information has in helping create and maintain customer relationships, there is an insatiable appetite to gain even more insight into customers and markets. Marketers in nearly all industries are expected to direct more resources to gathering and analyzing information especially in highly competitive markets. Many of the trends discussed below are directly related to marketers' quest to acquire large amounts of customer, competitor, and market information.

INTERNET AND MOBILE DEVICE TECHNOLOGIES

To address the need for more information, marketing companies are developing new methods for collecting data. This has led to the introduction of several technologies to assist in the information gathering process. Many of these developments are associated with measuring the activities of website visitors or with users of mobile device applications ("apps") and include:

- Enhanced Tracking – As noted earlier, the Internet and mobile technology offer an unparalleled ability to track and monitor customers. Each time a visitor accesses a website or uses a mobile application they provide marketers with extensive information (see Box 1-2 in Chapter 1). With tracking software becoming more sophisticated, many marketers now view it as an indispensable research tool.

- Improved Communication – Internet and mobile technologies offer a significant improvement in customer-to-company communication, which is vital for marketing research. For instance, the ability to encourage customers to offer feedback on the company's goods and services is easy using website popup notices, email reminders and smartphone apps.

- Research Tools – A large number of Internet websites offer services to assist with the collection of market information. These include online survey tools, virtual focus groups, and access to large databases containing previous research studies (i.e., secondary research).

The influence of social media in marketing has led to a number of new research tools. New research companies are focused on research methods that measure the influence companies, brands, and people have in social media. For example, by plugging in a name, research firm Klout, provides a detailed report covering 35 different variable that then produces a score suggesting how influential the company, product, or person may be. (9) Also, research company, Communispace, specializes in creating, monitoring, and reporting of online communities set up for certain customer groups. Clients include Best Buy, Verizon and Mattel. (10)

OTHER TECHNOLOGIES

In addition to the Internet, marketing research has benefited from other technological improvements including:

- Global Positioning Systems (GPS) – GPS enables marketers to track inventory and even track sales and service personnel. GPS is also becoming a common feature of customers' communication devices, such as smartphones, offering marketers the potential to locate and track customers.

- Virtual Reality and Simulations – Marketers can use computer-developed virtual worlds to simulate real-world customer activity, such as in-store shopping. While this research is mostly performed in a controlled laboratory setting, there are emerging virtual worlds on the Internet (e.g., Second Life) where marketers can test concepts and communicate with customers.

- Tablet Computers – The rapid advance of small, highly portable computers has significantly enhanced researcher's ability to capture user information during one-on-one research gathering. Developments, including Apple's iPad and other low-profile computers, allow researchers to capture and transmit consumer response to surveys without the need to request consumers move to special survey facilities. The tablets also enable the consumer to provide feedback on visual issues, such as offering evaluations on advertisements presented on the tablet.

- Data Analysis Software – The research process not only includes gathering information, it also involves a full analysis of what is collected. A number of software and statistical programs have been refined to give marketers greater insight into what the data really means. In fact, everyday spreadsheet programs, such as Microsoft Excel, now offer advanced statistical tools that previously were only available with more expensive computer programs.

- Neuro-Research – Companies have begun to explore the use of brain-imaging technology for marketing research. Using such technologies as Magnetic Resonance Imaging (MRI) and Electroencephalogram (EEG) sensors, researchers scan the brains of research subjects as they are exposed to neuro-stimuli, such as imagery and sound, in order to detect the effect the stimuli.

AFFORDABLE RESEARCH

For many years, formal research projects were considered something only the largest marketers could afford due to the expense in carrying out such projects. However, the technologies discussed above make it affordable for companies of all sizes to engage in research. For instance, surveying customers is quick and easy using one of the many online survey services which charge low fees to create, distribute, and analyze results.

MERGING OF DATA SOURCES

The wide range of technologies used to gather data has led to the creation of data centers where information is stored. Today many of these data centers are sharing information with other centers in a manner that offers the marketer a fuller picture of its customers. As we will discuss in Chapter 3, many companies have multiple contact points where customers can interact with the company (e.g., in-person, on the web, via phone call). In the past, the information gathered at these points was often stored separately. Companies now see the value in knowing what customers do across all contact points and, consequently, they now work to integrate customer information from many sources.

Additionally, some marketers go outside their own data collection and seek information on their customers from other sources, such as information provided by credit card companies. This information is then merged with the company owned information to get a fuller picture of customer activity.

PRIVACY CONCERNS

As we discussed in Chapter 1, the continual demand for customer information, along with advances in technology and the merging of information sources, has led marketing organizations to gather information in ways that raise concerns among privacy advocates and government regulators. Many customers are unaware of the amount and nature of the data marketers collect. As new information gathering techniques and technologies emerge, customer response to issues of privacy may determine whether these methods are feasible or forbidden.

USER COOPERATION AT ISSUE

The growing concern with privacy is leading many customers to limit their participation in research activities. This includes customers choosing not to respond to company requests to take part in research studies. Customers are also becoming more aware of how their Internet activities are tracked and are responding by using techniques to restrict marketers tracking efforts. For example, marketers can place small data files called **cookies** on customers' computers and then use this to track user activity. Many customers are learning to set the privacy setting on their web browser to reject cookies and, in doing so limit the marketer's ability to track customer activity. Additionally, in the United States there is growing support for the Federal Trade Commission to institute new requirements that could significantly restrict online tracking.

The issues surrounding how users are tracked on the Internet is leading to calls for government regulation to limit such activity. However, marketers have expressed concern regarding the institution of tracking limitations saying that such a move could dramatically affect a large number of websites that derive a major portion of their revenue from advertising. These sites use tracking research for many reasons including using the information for "targeting" relevant ads to website visitors. (11)

Marketing Story

Neuroscience: A New Perspective
Millward Brown

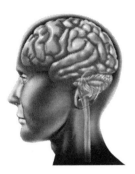

When most marketers think of marketing research techniques, they often focus on traditional methods, such as surveys, experiments, and focus groups. While these methods continue to be at the top of the list of how marketers gather customer information, new technology-driven methods are increasingly gaining favor among a growing number of marketers. Some of these methods, including website analytics, are already well established and necessary for managing many marketing decisions. But there are a number of others that have evolved over the last few years which marketers should watch closely.

In this story, market research firm Millward Brown explores three unconventional methods for measuring consumer behavior – implicit association measurement, eye-tracking, and brainwave measurement. These are grouped as neuroscience techniques, which we will define as methods for measuring brain activity when customers are exposed to certain neuro-stimuli (e.g., advertisement).

While each method uses a different approach for gathering customer information, each shares the goal of enabling marketers to learn something about customers that customers may not be willing to share or may not be able to express. For instance, they may not be able to tell the marketer what part of a magazine advertisement first caught their attention, while eye-tracking methods can.

While the story offers nice coverage of these high-tech research methods, it does caution marketers to be careful in how the data is interpreted.

...marketers should use neuroscience-based research in conjunction with established techniques when (and only when) it adds value. If used in isolation, such methods can be hard to interpret, but when combined with qualitative or survey-based research, they can add a powerful new dimension of insight. (12)

Besides using these techniques to test advertising, what other marketing decisions could be supported using these methods?

RESEARCH AS A PROMOTIONAL TOOL

While most people do not equate marketing research with promotion, many companies are discovering research can also function as an influential promotional tool. The practice of distributing company-produced research reports to potential customers and the news media has been used for a number of years in scientific and technology industries. In recent years, the practice has expanded into many other fields, particularly among firms involved in consulting, healthcare, and financial industries. Such reports often provide readers with information related to product features and benefits, comparisons with competitor's offerings, and target market perceptions. These reports are produced using high quality graphs and charts backed up by carefully created narratives that proudly emphasize the company's strengths.

Unfortunately, many research reports produced for promotional reasons are not scientific; therefore, these may not carry much value. While companies may claim the research supports their products, many of these claims may, in fact, be more fluff than substance since they are not grounded in sound research methods.

||||||||||||||||||||||||||||||||||||||||||||||||||||||||||||||||||||||||||||||||||||||||||||||||||||||||

REFERENCES

1. "Guggenheim Foundation and Museum," *Audience Research & Analysis*, April 17, 2011.
2. For an extensive list of links to low-cost secondary research websites see the Weblinks Collection section of *KnowThis.com*.
3. *Color Marketing Group* website.
4. For an extensive list of links to high-cost secondary research websites see the Weblinks Collection section of *KnowThis.com*.
5. Horovitz, B., "Market Researchers Get New Tool in iPad," *USA Today*, July 28, 2010.
6. Peters, J. W., "Some Newspapers, Tracking Readers Online, Shift Coverage," *New York Times*, September 5, 2010.
7. Vega, T., "Focus Groups That Look Like Play Groups," *New York Times*, May 29, 2011.
8. Altman, R., "Going Where CPGs Do Research," *Shopper Marketing*, October 1, 2010.
9. Smith, D., "How to Measure Your Brand's Online Influence," *Inc. Magazine*, February 12, 2011.
10. Bruno, K., "Secrets of Engaging Customers in Online Communities," *Forbes*, August 7, 2010.
11. Vega, T. and V. Kopytoff, "In Online Privacy Plan, the Opt-Out Question Looms," *New York Times*, December 5, 2010.
12. Page, G., "Neuroscience: A New Perspective," *Millward Brown*, June 2010.

Full text of many of the references can be accessed via links on the support website.

Chapter 3: Managing Customers

In Chapter 1, we noted marketers make decisions which result in value to both the marketer and its customers. Throughout this book, we emphasize the importance customers play in helping marketers meet their business objectives.

To drive home this point, in Chapter 3 we concentrate our discussion on understanding customers and examining their role in the marketing process. We show that for most organizations understanding customers is necessary not only because of its effect on marketing decisions but because customers' activities influence the entire organization.

In this chapter, we explore the techniques marketers use to manage customers. We begin by defining what a customer is and why they are important to an organization. We then look at what tools and strategies must be in place to manage customers skillfully, including the crucial requirement that marketers work hard to build relationships with their customers. Finally, we conclude with a discussion of how servicing customers after the sale is often just as critical as pre-sale marketing efforts.

||||||||||||||||||||||||||||||||||||||||||||||||||||||||||||||||||||||||||||||||||||||||||||||||||||||||||||||

WHAT IS A CUSTOMER?

In general terms, a customer is a person or organization that a marketer believes will benefit from the goods and services offered by the marketer's organization. As this definition suggests, a customer is not necessarily someone who is currently purchasing from the marketer. In fact, customers may fall into one of three customer groups:

EXISTING CUSTOMERS

The first group consists of customers who have purchased or otherwise used an organization's goods or services, typically within a designated period of time. For some organizations, the timeframe may be short. For instance, a coffee shop may only consider someone to be an existing customer if they have purchased within the last three months. Other organizations may view someone as an existing customer even though they have not purchased in the last few years (e.g., automobile manufacturer).

Existing customers are by far the most important of the three customer groups since they have a current relationship with a company and, consequently, they give a company a reason to remain in contact with them. Additionally, existing customers also represent the best market for future sales, especially if they are satisfied with the relationship they presently have with the marketer. Getting existing customers to purchase more products is significantly less expensive and time consuming than finding new customers. This is because existing customers know and hopefully trust the marketer and, if managed correctly, are easy to reach with promotional appeals (e.g., emailing a special discount offer for a new product). Yet, as discussed in Box 3-1, not all existing customers should be treated the same as some offer more value to the marketer than others.

FORMER CUSTOMERS

This group consists of those who have formerly had relations with the marketing organization typically through a previous purchase. However, the marketer no longer feels the customer is an existing customer because they have not purchased from the marketer within a certain timeframe or due to other indications (e.g., a former customer just purchased a similar product from the marketer's competitor). The value of this group to a marketer will depend on whether the customer's previous relationship was considered satisfactory to the customer or the marketer. For instance, a former customer who felt she was not treated well by the marketer will be more difficult to persuade to buy again compared to a former customer who liked the marketer but decided to buy from another company offering a similar product but at a lower price.

POTENTIAL CUSTOMERS

The third category of customers includes those who have yet to purchase but possess what the marketer believes are the requirements to become customers. As we will see in Chapter 5, the requirements to become a potential customer include such issues as having a need for a product, possessing the financial means to buy, and having the authority to make a buying decision.

Locating potential customers is an ongoing process for two reasons. First, existing customers may become former customers (e.g., decide to buy from a competitor) and must be replaced by new customers. Second, while we noted above that existing customers are the best source for future sales, it is new customers that are needed for a business to expand. For example, a company selling only in its own country may see less room for sales growth if a high percentage of people in the country are already existing customers. In order to realize stronger growth, the company may seek to sell their products in other countries where the percentage of potential customers may be quite high.

Motorcycle manufacture Harley-Davidson is discovering their existing customer base, which consists mostly of white, middle-aged males, is aging and are not prone to continue purchasing. The company now faces challenges in reaching new customers. However, potential customers, such as younger males, women and growing ethnic populations, have yet to show strong interest in Harley's products. (1)

Box 3-1

THE "GOOD" CUSTOMER

For marketers simply finding customers who are willing to purchase their goods or services is not enough to build a successful marketing strategy. Instead, as we note in our definition of marketing in Chapter 1, marketers should look to manage customers in a way that will "identify, create, and maintain satisfying relationships with customers." By using marketing efforts that are designed to "maintain satisfying relationships" rather than simply pursuing a quick sale, the likelihood increases that customers will be more trusting of the marketer and exhibit a higher level of satisfaction with the organization. In turn, satisfied customers are more likely to become "good" customers.

For our purposes, we define a "good" customer as one who holds the potential to undertake activities offering long-term value to an organization. The activities performed by "good" customers not only include purchasing products, these also include such things as:

- offering a higher level of profitability since they buy more while costing proportionally less to satisfy

- making prompt payment for their purchases

- offering insight and feedback that help create new products and improve services

- voluntarily promoting the company's products to others

These activities, along with many others, represent the value (i.e., benefits for costs spent) an organization receives from its customers. In the case of "good" customers, their potential for providing value should be a signal for marketers to direct additional marketing efforts in building, strengthening, and sustaining a relationship with these customers.

The fact that we place the descriptive term "good" in front of customers should not be taken lightly. Not all existing customers who currently have relationships with an organization should be treated on an equal level. Some consistently spend large sums to purchase products from an organization; others do not spend large sums but hold the potential to do so; and still others use a large amount of an organization's resources but contribute little revenue. Clearly there are lines of demarcation between those in the existing customer category. For marketers, identifying the line that separates "good" customers from others is critical for marketing success. And in some cases, that line may result in the marketer "letting go" a customer who is not considered to be offering the value sought by the marketer.

Marketing Story

Capturing Hearts, One Upgrade at a Time
New York Times

Marketers face a difficult task when introducing products that are considered upgrades of existing products. The key decision confronting these marketers is what to do about a potentially large percentage of customers who already own an older version of the product. To drive higher sales, many marketers maintain the mindset that existing customers must purchase the new product if they want the latest features. They take the position that new is new and if customers want the new stuff they need to pay to upgrade to the new product.

But, other companies have learned it is not a good idea to upset existing customers by forcing them to pay the full purchase price for a product upgrade. These companies know continued customer service is important for existing customers since these customers may someday want to purchase new products. To keep existing customers happy, marketers need to look for ways to let existing customers know they are not being forgotten once an upgraded product is marketed.

The high-tech industry provides an excellent example of how companies can strengthen their relationships with existing customers when the company rolls out product upgrades. One way this is done is to offer purchasers protection in case a product upgrade occurs within a certain period of time. For instance, the marketer can offer existing customers heavy discounts (and possibly free product) if a product upgrade happens within one year from the date of purchase. Such methods are a way of reassuring the customer that their original purchase decision was not a mistake in timing.

As discussed in this story, companies whose products run on software, such as smartphones, video games, and computers, are finding they can build more loyalty among their existing customers by offering free upgrades to the latest software even though the software is primarily intended to create interest in the latest hardware product. In this way, existing customers continue to feel attached to the brand even though they do not have the latest hardware.

Suddenly, that old phone could run an application in the background while another app was being used, apps could be organized into folders, and users gained access to Apple's new electronic bookstore. Without having to spend a dime, people got what was essentially a brand new phone, one that could do nearly everything the newer model could do. (2)

How can companies outside the high-tech industry keep their existing customers happy once an upgraded product is introduced?

||||||||||||||||||||||||||||||||||||||||||||||||||||||||||||||||||||||||||||||||||||||||||||||||||||||||||||||||||||||

CUSTOMERS AND THE ORGANIZATION

For most organizations, understanding customers is the key to success, while not understanding them is likely to result in failure. It is so important that the constant drive to satisfy customers is not only a concern for those responsible for carrying out marketing tasks, it is a concern of everyone in the entire organization.

Whether someone's job involves direct contact with customers (e.g., salespeople, delivery drivers, telephone customer service representatives) or indirect contact (e.g., production, accounting), all members of an organization must appreciate the role customers play in helping the organization meets its goals. To ensure everyone understands the customer's role, many organizations continually preach a "customer is most important" message in department meetings, organizational communication (e.g., internal emails), and corporate training programs. To drive home the importance of customers, the message often contains examples of how customers impact the company. These examples include:

SOURCE OF INFORMATION AND IDEAS

Satisfying the needs of customers requires organizations maintain close contact with them. Marketers can get close to customers by conducting research, such as surveys and other feedback methods (e.g., website comment forms), that encourages customers to share their thoughts and feelings. With this information, marketers are able to learn what people think of their present marketing efforts and receive suggestions for making improvements. For instance, research and feedback methods can offer marketers insight into new goods and services sought by their customers.

When Twiddy & Company, a North Carolina vacation rental firm, deployed an online customer commenting tool they quickly learned of serious shortcoming with their website. Customers were complaining that a limited search feature resulted in few properties being displaying when, in fact, many were available. The company quickly adjusted their search tool resulting in an immediate increase in vacation bookings. (3)

AFFECTS ACTIVITIES THROUGHOUT THE ORGANIZATION

For most organizations, customers not only affect decisions made by the marketing team, they are also the key driver for decisions made throughout the organization. For example, customers' reaction to the design of a product may influence the type of raw materials used in the product manufacturing process. With customers impacting such a significant portion of a company, creating an environment geared to locating, understanding, and satisfying customers is imperative.

Needed to Sustain the Organization

Finally, customers are the reason an organization is in business. Without customers or the potential to attract customers, a company is not viable. Consequently, customers are not only key to revenue and profits they are also crucial to creating and maintaining jobs within the organization.

||||||||||||||||||||||||||||||||||||||||||||||||||||||||||||||||||||||||||||||||||||||||||||||||||||||||||

CHALLENGE OF MANAGING CUSTOMERS

While, on the surface, the process for managing customers may seem to be intuitive and straightforward, in reality organizations struggle to accomplish this. The challenges marketers face when it comes to managing customers include:

Customers Are Different

One reason managing customers can be difficult is because no two customers are the same. What is appealing to one customer may not necessarily work for another. For instance, a marketer may change how it issues coupons to customers by reducing the frequency of issuing coupons by regular mail and instead direct customers to electronic coupons found on its website. The marketer makes this move with the hope it will: lead to cost savings (e.g., sending out traditional coupons by mail requires postage expense); allow the marketer to acquire more customer information (e.g., monitor their activities when they visit the website); and give the marketer the opportunity to sell more products to the customer (e.g., special promotional messages on the website). However, while many customers will like visiting the website to acquire coupons, some long-time customers may feel they will now need to do more work to acquire coupons compared to having these delivered through regular mail. In this example, the introduction of a new feature may satisfy some customers while irritating others.

Customers Interact at Different Contact Points

Another problem is that customers may interact with organizations at different contact points. A contact point is the method a customer uses to communicate with a company. For instance, consider the different ways customers interact with an organization:

- In-Person – Customers seek in-person assistance for their needs by visiting retail stores and other outlets, and through discussion with company salespeople who visit customers at their place of business or in their homes.

- Telephone – Customers seeking to make purchases or to have a problem solved may find it more convenient to do so through phone contact. In many companies a dedicated department, called a **call center**, handles all incoming customer inquiries.

Marketing Story
Gap Scraps New Logo After Taking Flak Online
MSNBC

A classic marketing mistake taught in nearly all basic marketing courses is Coca-Cola's 1985 decision to change the formula of their flagship Coke product. In a nutshell, during the mid-1980s Coke was being hammered by their main competitor, Pepsi. At the time, Pepsi was running highly effective taste test advertisements showing their brand being favored over Coke. As hard as Coke tried to counter this with its own ads and other promotions, Pepsi continued to gain market share. With changes to promotion, pricing and even distribution not working, Coke felt the need to respond with the only marketing mix decision it had not changed, the product. In particular, they altered the Coke formula, a drastic decision as the formula had not changed for almost 100 years.

While the "New" Coke got off to a favorable start, long-time customers quickly turned on the company and demanded the return of the old formula. In these pre-Internet, pre-social network days, the angry customer response involved public demonstrations and letter writing campaigns that caught the media's attention. Things grew so intense that Coke had no choice but to reinstate the old product, renamed Coke Classic, while retaining the new formula product under the New Coke name.

The key lesson to be learned in Coke's mistake is not to underestimate customers' relationship with a brand, especially when the marketer is considering changing a key component. Marketers, who are considering substantial changes to their product, need to engage in marketing research to address the key issues of concern to their customers. In the Coke case, the company was highly skilled at conducting marketing research. However, they made the mistake of not asking customers critical questions about their feelings toward the original product.

Of course, Coke is not alone in reversing a poor marketing decision. Many companies face this including the one featured in this story. As discussed, the clothing retailer, Gap, decided to change the design of their logo, which their marketing team felt is dated. And, just as in the Coke case, the decision had to be reversed when customers voiced their complaints on social media sites.

The new design was meant to show how the Gap chain has evolved from its long-standing, even preppy image. It was meant to complement Gap's sleeker new designs, new fits for black pants and khakis and more modern feel, company officials said. But instead the logo flap served as a lesson in the power of the Internet to influence a company's brand message. (4)

Can it be argued that Gap's response to online criticism will benefit them in the long-run? If so, how?

- Internet and Mobile Networks – The fastest growing contact points are through electronic communication over the Internet and through mobile networks. The use of these networks for purchasing (called **electronic commerce**) has exploded and is now the leading method for purchasing certain types of products including music. These communication networks have also become the primary area many customers look to first for help with their purchases such as seeking online help, product usage information, and recommendations for additional products.

- Kiosks – A kiosk is a standalone, interactive computer, often equipped with a touch-screen, offering customers several service options including product information, ability to make a purchase, and review of a customer's account. Kiosks are now widely used for airline check-in, banking, and, most recently, within grocery stores.

Kiosks are evolving to the point where there is virtually no limitation on where these are placed. While most kiosks require placement near electrical and/or telecommunication access points, this is not always the case. In Europe, Eco Tech Computers is offering kiosks operating on a combination of solar power and user power. The unit features a solar panel that will operate the kiosk on sunny days. But, on overcast days and at night users can turn a crank that will provide two minutes of power for each turn. (5)

- In-Person Product Support – Some in-person assistance is not principally intended to assist with selling but is designed to offer support once a purchase is made. Such services are handled by delivery people and service/repair technicians.

- Financial Assistance – Customer contact may also occur through company personnel who assist customers with financial issues. For instance, employees in a company's credit department help customers arrange the necessary funds to make a purchase while personnel in accounts receivable work with customers who are experiencing payment problems.

The challenge of ensuring customers are handled properly no matter the contact point they use is daunting for many companies. For some organizations, the customer contact points cited above operate independently of others. For instance, retail stores may not be directly connected to telephone customer service. The result is that, for different contact points, many companies have developed different procedures and techniques for handling customers. And, for some firms, there exists little integration between contact points so customers communicating through one point one day and another point the next day may receive conflicting information. In such cases, customers are likely to become frustrated and question the company's ability to provide adequate service.

Customer Relationship Management

In order to overcome the challenges faced as they attempt to cultivate and manage customers, many marketers must continually conduct marketing research to evaluate customers to determine what they want. And, uncovering what customers want is made significantly easier if a company establishes methods designed to manage its customers. The most widely adopted method for managing customers is a business concept known as Customer Relationship Management (CRM).

CRM AND MARKETING STRATEGY

CRM is a strategic approach whose goal is to get everyone in an organization, not just the marketer, to recognize the importance of customers. Under CRM, the key driver for marketing success is to treat "good" customers in a way that will increase the probability they will stay "good" customers. This is accomplished, in part, by ensuring a customer receives accurate information and has a consistent and satisfying experience every time he/she interacts with a company.

While CRM is primarily used to manage existing customers, it also has application for other customer groups. For instance, CRM is used to help identify former customers that may hold potential to buy again. This is often possible due to the amount of information obtained and subsequently retained within a CRM system when former customers were considered existing customers. Additionally, CRM can serve an integral role in helping locate potential customers. As we will explore in Chapter 5, one method for locating potential customers is to use information contained in CRM to determine key characteristics exhibited by existing customers This information can then be used to pursue new customers in untapped markets who possess similar characteristics.

CRM AND TECHNOLOGY

Computer technology plays a key part in carrying out CRM. A proper technology-based system is needed so that nearly anyone in an organization that comes into contact with a customer (e.g., sales force, service force, customer service representatives, accounts receivable, etc.) has access to information and is well prepared to deal with the customer. For large firms with many employees, this requires the purchase of expensive CRM software along with the necessary hardware to implement CRM throughout the company. For smaller firms with only a few employees, a more cost-effective and potentially less complicated way to implement CRM is to use Internet-based services that charge monthly fees to access the technology. (6)

While the benefits of CRM are easy to appreciate, the actual execution presents many challenges. As discussed in Box 3-2, the combination of adapting to a new customer management philosophy as well as learning new technologies has presented significant obstacles for organizations implementing CRM.

Box 3-2

CRM IS NOT ALWAYS EASY

While maintaining close and consistent relationships with customers through all contact points via CRM makes good business sense, accomplishing this has often been a challenge. Numerous problems, from technology failures and lack of communication between contact points, as well as lack of adequate employee training or outright employee resistance, have derailed many CRM efforts.

For example, as we will see in Chapter 16, salespeople have been extremely reluctant to accept CRM since a key requirement of CRM is for members of the organization to share what they know about their customers. But for those involved in selling, what they know about their customers is often a critical component of what makes them successful.

And, in organizations where salespeople compete against each other for clients, withholding valuable client information could offer an advantage to the salesperson possessing it. Of course, this type of situation places the company at a disadvantage if others in the organization, who also deal with the customer, do not have access to the information.

Though CRM is now widely adopted and is becoming an essential tool for a large number of business organizations, it still has a long way to go before it is ingrained as an essential business function within most organizations. In fact, many experts feel that a large majority of companies are still a long way from fully integrating CRM throughout their organizations. This suggests the full benefits of CRM are not likely to be realized for some time.

CUSTOMER SERVICE AND MARKETING

As we have noted, to manage customers effectively, marketers must be concerned with the entire experience a customer has with a company. While much of the value sought by customers is obtained directly from the consumption or use of goods or services they purchase (i.e., benefits from using the product), customers' satisfaction is not limited only to benefits from the actual product. Instead, customers are affected by the entire purchasing experience, which is a mix of product and **non-product benefits**.

When it comes to managing customers, a pivotal non-product benefit affecting customers' feelings about a company is customer service, which is defined as activities used by the marketer to support the purchaser's experience with a product. Customer service includes several activities including:

♦ Training – services needed to assist customers in learning how to use a product

♦ Repair – services needed to handle damaged or malfunctioning products

♦ Financial Assistance – services needed to help customers with the financial commitment required to purchase or use the product

♦ Complaint Resolution – services needed to address other problems that have arisen with customers' use of a product

In many industries, customers' experience with a company's customer service can significantly affect their overall opinion of the product. Companies producing superior products may negatively impact their products if they back these up with shoddy service.

On the other hand, many companies compete not because their products are superior to their competitors' products but because they offer a higher level of customer service. In fact, many believe customer service will eventually become the most significant benefit offered by a company because global competition (i.e., increase in similar products) makes it more difficult for a company's product to offer unique advantages.

Customer service manifests itself in several ways, with the most common being a dedicated department to handle customer issues. Whether a company establishes a separate department or spreads the function among many departments, being responsive and offering reliable service is critical and likely to be demanded by customers.

What companies are tops in customer service? According to a survey, the leading firms are all retailers. When market research firm, Temkin Group, surveyed 6,000 U.S. consumers the results show that 15 of the top 20 rankings were for retailers with Amazon, Kohl's and Costco leading the way. Possibly more revealing is that only 24 of the 143 companies rated received a customer service score of "good" or "excellent." (7)

Trends in Customer Service

Marketers have seen the customer service process evolve from an area receiving only marginal attention into a primary functional area. In response to customers' demands for responsive and reliable service, companies are investing heavily in innovative methods and processes to strengthen their service level. These innovations include:

INCREASED CUSTOMER SELF SERVICE

A major trend in customer service is the move by companies to encourage customers to be involved in helping solve their own service issues. This can be seen in the retail industry where self-service ranges from customers placing their own grocery products in shopping bags all the way to having customers do their own checkout, including scanning products and making payment.

Also, as we will soon discuss, customers needing information are being encouraged by companies to undertake the effort themselves, often by visiting special company-provided information areas (see *Website and Phone Accessible Knowledge Base* discussion below). Only after they have explored these options are customers advised to contact customer service personnel.

REVENUE GENERATORS

Companies maintaining a customer service staff have found these employees not only help solve customer problems, but they also may be in a position to convince customers to purchase more. Many companies now require sales training for their customer service personnel. At a basic level, customer service representatives may be trained to ask if customers are interested in hearing about other goods or services. If a customer shows interest, then the representative will transfer the customer to a sales associate. At a more advanced level, the representative will shift to a selling role and attempt to get the customer to commit to additional product purchases.

OUT-SOURCING

One of the most controversial developments impacting customer service is the move by many companies around the world to establish customer service functions outside of either their home country or the country in which their customers reside. Called out-sourcing, companies pursue this strategy to both reduce cost and to increase service coverage. For instance, having multiple customer service facilities around the world allows customers to talk via phone with a service person no matter what time of day.

The ability to move service to another country is only viable in large part due to technological developments (see *Internet Telephone* discussion below). But such moves have raised concerns on two fronts. First, many see this trend as leading to a reduction of customer service jobs within a home country. Second, customer service personnel located off-shore may not be sufficiently trained and often lack an understanding of the conditions within the customer's local market both of which can affect service levels. At the extreme, a poorly managed move to outsource customer service can lead to a decrease in customer satisfaction, which in the long-run could affect sales.

CUSTOMER SERVICE TECHNOLOGIES

As we will see throughout this book, technological innovation has significantly impacted all areas of marketing. Within customer service improvements in computer hardware and software, as well as expansion of electronic communication networks such as the Internet and mobile networks, has led to numerous innovative methods for addressing customer needs. These methods include:

- Online Chat – Companies are finding value in using Internet chat as a way to address customer questions. Typically the chat feature is presented via a pop-up browser window that appears when a customer clicks on a website link. However, newer technology using computer programming, dubbed AJAX, allows for chat to take place right on a webpage and not through pop-up windows. Whether presented as a separate window or contained within a regular webpage, online chat sessions are undertaken in real-time with customers and company service people exchanging text messages. More advanced chat technology, called **collaborative browsing** or co-browsing, allows customer service representatives to manipulate a customer's web browser by sending webpages containing relevant information.

> *Newer technology is now allowing chat sessions to offer a video option. For instance, retailer Lands End offers Live Video Chat that enables customers to see the customer service representative who is assisting them. Customers communicate with the Lands End service representative either by verbal communication using a microphone or through standard keyboard messaging. (8)*

- Website and Phone Accessible Knowledge Base – As part of customers' desire to be more involved in solving their own problems, companies have moved to offering technological solutions in ways that appeal to customers' desire for self service. The predominant method for doing this is by maintaining a collection of answers to commonly asked questions. The collection may be part of a Knowledge Base accessible either online, through such methods as **frequently asked questions (FAQ)**, or through a call system where an automated helper or a **virtual attendant** guides customers to an answer.

- <u>Social Media</u> – More and more companies are embracing Internet and mobile technology options in their efforts to improve customer satisfaction. The use of social media, such as Twitter and Facebook, give marketers the opportunity to reach out to customers that actively use these sites. It also enables marketers to watch what is being said about their company and take appropriate action if needed.

Electronics retailer Best Buy has a staff of 15 employees dedicated to monitoring and responding to comments made on social media sites and to company run discussion forums. The team monitors the web 24/7 and responds quickly to quell rumors or in situations where someone's posting places the company in a bad light. (9)

- <u>Really Simple Syndication (RSS)</u> – Made popular by its use on Internet blogs and now widely used on most popular websites, Really Simple Syndication (RSS) allows a company to send out information quickly, and to a large number, with little manual effort compared to traditional methods. Subscribers who have installed the proper software or have access to an online RSS reader will see the information appear automatically. Customer service has found RSS to be useful for: communicating product updates; technical matters, such as product defects or recalls; and general company communication, such as notification of special promotions.

- <u>Wireless Data Access</u> – Providing a high-level of customer service does not only occur when the customer initiates contact with an organization. Customer service takes place during any potential interaction including those that may be initiated by a company representative who is meeting face-to-face with a customer. For instance, an organization may send salespeople and other support personnel to a customer's location and their ability to address customer concerns is vital to maintaining strong customer service. To ensure field people have the most up-to-date information, many companies now equip their field teams with portable devices, including smartphones and touch pads computers. These devices are capable of accessing the Internet from virtually any location, thus, enabling the field person to tap into customer data found on company computers.

- <u>Text Messaging</u> – Once considered a play-toy for teenagers, text messaging has found a useful place customer service tool. Many companies and organizations, including colleges and universities, now use text messaging as a means to communicate with their customers. For instance, colleges and universities have set up instant alert security systems where students can receive a text message in the case of an on-campus emergency or weather-related problem.

- Internet Telephone – No matter the organization's size, the cost of maintaining telephone support services can be quite high. One major expense lies with the cost of using traditional telecommunication lines. Commonly referred to as plain old telephone service (POTS), this system is more expensive because telephone lines are generally dedicated to individual users. That is, a single line can only handle one phone call, fax transmission, or computer data connection at a time. While a discussion of technical issues behind this is beyond the scope of this book, suffice to say the POTS system is inefficient since a single telephone line has the capacity to handle a far larger volume of phone and data transmission. For this reason, companies have moved to a technology called **Voice over Internet Protocol (VoIP)**. With VoIP, telephone calls are delivered over the Internet with multiple phones sharing the same connection. With more people using the same line, the cost per call is reduced. While the audio quality of the call may not be as reliable as POTS technology, improvements over the last few years have narrowed the quality gap to the point where most customers cannot distinguish the difference.

- Intelligent Call Routing – Another innovation associated with telephone support deals with technologies for identifying and filtering incoming customer calls. One method is the use of software that attempts to identify the caller (usually based on the incoming phone number) and then automatically directs the call for proper servicing. For instance, an appliance manufacturer may be able to distinguish between those who purchased refrigerators and those who purchased microwave ovens. But some marketers go a step further and can program their call routing system to distinguish "good" customers from others. This may result in these customers receiving preferential placement in the calling order or queue, so they will be serviced before lower rated customers who sequentially called before the "good" customer.

Customer service technology is not only focused on helping companies communicate with their customers, it also includes methods that help improve customers' overall experience with the company. For instance, Disney employs highly advanced technologies to help customers move more rapidly through their amusement parks. From an underground control center, employees use crowd monitoring tools alerting them to problem areas. The employees can then make adjustments, such as adding more cars to rides or instructing a meet-and-greet character to go to less crowded areas where it may attract customers away from more populated attractions. (10)

||||||||||||||||||||||||||||||||||||||||||||||||||||||||||||||||||||||||||||||||||||||||||||||||||||||||||||

REFERENCES

1. Taylor, A., "Harley-Davidson's Aging Biker Problem," *Fortune*, September 17, 2010.

2. Darlin, D., "Capturing Hearts, One Upgrade at a Time," *New York Times*, November 13, 2010.

3. Waxer, C., "Find Out What Your Buyers Are Thinking," *CNN Money*, March 31, 2010.

4. "Gap Scraps New Logo After Taking Flak Online," *MSNBC*, October 12, 2011.

5. Butler, C., "Inside the Kiosk: European Company Cranks Out Earth-friendly Kiosks," *Self Service World*, March 4, 2011.

6. "How to Buy Small Business CRM Software," *Small Business Computing.com*, May 17, 2011.

7. Swartz, J., "Amazon.com Tops Customer-Service Rankings," *USA Today*, April 4, 2011.

8. Briggs, B., "Lands' End Launches Live Video Chat," *Internet Retailer*, October 6, 2010.

9. Enright, A., "Listen Up," *Internet Retailer*, May 31, 2011.

10. Barnes, B., "Disney Tackles Major Theme Park Problem: Lines," *New York Times*, December 27, 2010.

Full text of many of the references can be accessed via links on the support website.

Chapter 4: Understanding Customers

Possibly the most challenging concept in marketing deals with understanding why buyers do what they do. Such knowledge is critical for marketers since having a strong understanding of buyer behavior helps shed light on what is important to the customer, including what influences their purchasing.

However, factors affecting how customers make decisions are extremely complex. Buyer behavior is deeply rooted in psychology with dashes of sociology thrown in just to make things more interesting. Since every person in the world is different, it is impossible to have simple rules explaining how buying decisions are made. But those who have spent many years analyzing customer activity have presented us with useful "guidelines" in how someone decides whether or not to make a purchase.

In this chapter, we look at how customers make purchase decisions. We begin with a discussion of customer needs and why understanding this is fundamental to understanding why customers make purchases. The perspective we take in this chapter is to touch on just the basic concepts that appear to be commonly accepted as influencing customer behavior. We look at the buying behavior of consumers (i.e., when people buy for personal reasons) and examine factors that influence buyers' decisions in the business market.

||||||||||||||||||||||||||||||||||||||||||||||||||||||||||||||||||||||||||||||||||||||||||||||||||||||||||||||||||

WHY CUSTOMERS BUY

Customers make purchases in order to satisfy **needs**. Some of these needs are basic and must be filled by everyone on the planet (e.g., food, shelter), while others are not required for basic survival and vary depending on the person or organization making a purchase. It probably makes more sense to classify needs that are not a necessity as **wants** or **desires**. In fact, in many countries where the standard of living is high, a large portion of the population's income is spent on wants and desires rather than on basic needs.

Whether the buyer is buying for personal use (i.e., consumer purchase) or the purchase is for use by a business, it is critical for marketers to understand how their customers make decisions including the dynamics that influence the decision-making process.

We use the term customer to refer to the actual buyer, the person spending the money. But it should be pointed out the one who does the buying is not necessarily the user and others may be involved in the buying decision. For example, in planning for a family trip the mother may make the hotel reservations but others in the family may have input on the hotel choice. Similarly, a father may purchase snacks at the grocery store, but his young child may be the one who selects them from the store shelf. Consequently, analysis of factors affecting why a customer buys should not be limited to only the person doing the buying transaction; others who are not performing the purchasing activity may also be involved.

> *The influence children have on household purchase decisions is most evident during the U.S. back-to-school shopping season. In a survey conducted for the National Retail Federation, nearly two-thirds of parents of children in grades K-12 report their children influence 50 percent or more of back-to-school purchases. The total value of this influence is quite high considering sales of the back-to-school items, which include clothing, supplies and electronics, is estimated to exceed $22 billion. (1)*

Influences on Customer Purchasing

The decision-making process used by customers to make purchases is anything but straight forward. There are many factors affecting this process. The number of potential influences on customer buying behavior is limitless. However, marketers are well served to understand the key influences. By doing so, they may be in a position to tailor their marketing efforts to take advantage of these influences in a way that will satisfy the customer.

The influences of purchasing break down into two main categories: Internal and External (see Figure 4-1). For the most part, the influences are not mutually exclusive. Instead, they are all interconnected and work together to form who we are and how we behave. Additionally, not all influences affect all buying decisions. For example, a business buyer mulling over a purchase decision for high-priced electronics equipment that his company has never purchased before may be influenced by different factors compared to a consumer seeking to make a low-priced purchase she makes several times a week. Finally, while purchase situations facing consumers may be different from those facing business buyers, in many ways the influences on both types of decisions are similar. For this reason, we present the influences as covering both consumer and business purchasing.

Figure 4-1: Influences on Customer Purchasing

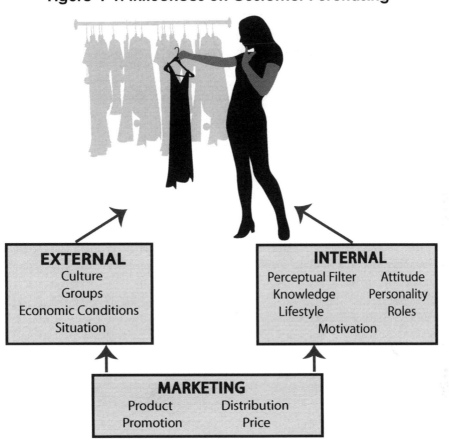

IIIIIIIIIIIIIIIIIIIIIIIIIIIIIIIIIIIIIIIIIIIIIIIIIIIIIIIIIIIIIIIIIIIIIIIIIIIIIIIIIIIIIIIIIIIIIIIIIIIIIIIIIIIIIII

INTERNAL INFLUENCES

We start our examination of the influences on customer purchase decisions by first looking inside ourselves to see which are the most important internal factors affecting how we make choices.

Perceptual Filter

Perception is how we see ourselves and the world we live in. However, what ends up being stored inside us does not always get there in a direct manner. Often our mental makeup results from information consciously or subconsciously filtered as we experience it, a process we refer to as a perceptual filter. To us this is our reality, though it does not mean it is an accurate reflection of what is real. Thus, perception is the way we filter stimuli (e.g., someone talking to us, reading a newspaper story) and then make sense from it.

Perception has several steps:

◆ <u>Exposure</u> – sensing a stimuli (e.g. seeing an advertisement)

◆ <u>Attention</u> – an effort to recognize the nature of a stimuli (e.g. recognizing it is an advertisement)

◆ <u>Awareness</u> – assigning meaning to a stimuli (e.g., it is a humorous advertisement for a particular product)

◆ <u>Retention</u> – adding the meaning to one's internal makeup (i.e., this product has fun advertisements)

How these steps are eventually carried out depends on a person's approach to **learning**. By learning we mean how a person changes what they know, which in turn may affect how they act. There are many theories of learning, a discussion of which is beyond the scope of this book, however, suffice to say people are likely to learn in different ways. For instance, one person may be able to focus intensely on a certain advertisement and retain the information after being exposed only one time while another person may need frequent exposure to the same advertisement before he/she even recognizes what it is. Customers are also more likely to retain information if a person has a strong interest in the stimuli. For example, if a person is in need of a new car they are more likely to pay attention to a new advertisement for a car while someone who does not need a car may need to see the advertisement many times before they recognize the brand of automobile.

For marketers, getting through customers' perceptual filters takes careful planning as outlined in Box 4-1.

Knowledge

Knowledge is the sum of all information known by a person. It is the facts of the world as he/she knows it and depth of knowledge is a function of the breadth of worldly experiences and the strength of an individual's long-term memory. Obviously what exists as knowledge to an individual depends on how their perceptual filter makes sense and retains the information it is exposed to.

As we will see, when it comes to making product decisions many factors influence customer purchase behavior. In most cases, these other factors are, in large part, shaped by what is known. Thus, developing methods (e.g., incentives) to encourage customers to accept more information (or correct information) may affect other influencing factors.

Box 4-1

GETTING THROUGH THE PERCEPTUAL FILTER

Marketers spend large sums of money to get customers to have positive impressions of their products. But clearly the existence of a perceptual filter suggests getting to this stage is not easy. Each stage in the perceptual filter presents challenges and opportunities:

Exposure

Exposing customers to a product can be extremely difficult especially when competing products are attempting to accomplish the same objective. To stand out from others requires marketers be creative and use a variety of different methods (e.g., different types of promotion) to deliver their messages. Additionally, marketers often find that a large number of attempts (e.g., frequently running advertisements) must be made before customers are exposed to their product.

Attention

Once the message reaches the customer, it must be viewed as interesting in order to capture his/her attention. This often means the marketer's message must not only be engaging but must also highlight a product's benefits and how these can satisfy customers' needs. It is important to understand that being exposed to a product does not mean a customer will pay attention to it. Of course, most people experience this every day as they are bombarded with products in stores or ads on television, but they attend to only a very small percentage.

Awareness

Simply attending to the marketer's message is not enough to get a customer to retain the message. For marketers, the most critical step in getting through the perceptual filter is the one that occurs with awareness where customers give meaning to what they experience. To ensure the message is getting through as intended (i.e., customers accurately interpret the message), marketers must continually monitor and respond if their message becomes distorted in ways that negatively shape its meaning. This can happen due in part to competitive activity, such as a competitor creating advertisements that position their product in a stronger light than the marketer's product, or through published comments, such as news media reports or website postings, containing negative and possibly inaccurate statements related to the marketer's product.

Retention

Finally, making sure customers are retaining positive product information requires continual customer research. If they discover the wrong information is being retained (e.g., wrong idea of how product works) then new strategies must be employed (e.g., new message delivered). Marketers can reinforce the retention process by establishing ongoing communication with the customer. This can be accomplished through such techniques as email newsletters, social media updates, and follow-up service calls.

Attitude

In simple terms, attitude refers to what a person feels or believes about something. Additionally, attitude may be reflected in how an individual acts based on his or her beliefs (i.e., knowledge). Once formed, attitudes can be difficult to change. If a customer has a negative attitude toward a particular product or company, it may take considerable effort to change what she/he believes to be true.

Marketers facing customers with negative attitudes toward their product must work to identify the key issues shaping a customer's attitude then adjust marketing decisions (e.g., advertising) in an effort to change the attitude. For companies competing against strong rivals to whom loyal customers exhibit a positive attitude, a key strategy is to work to see why customers feel positive toward the competitor and then try to meet or beat the competitor on these issues. Alternatively, a company can try to locate customers who have negative feelings toward the competitor and then target its efforts to this group.

Personality

An individual's personality relates to perceived personal characteristics they consistently exhibit, especially when interacting with others. In most, but not all, cases the behaviors projected in one situation are similar to the behaviors exhibited in another situation. In this way personality is the sum of sensory experiences others get from experiencing a person (i.e., how one talks, reacts, etc.).

While one's personality is often interpreted by those we interact with, a person has his/her own vision of their personality, called **self concept**, which may or may not be the same as how others view them. For marketers, it is necessary to know customers, and especially consumers, make purchase decisions to support their self concept. Using research techniques to identify how customers view themselves may give marketers insight into products and promotion options that are not readily apparent. For example, when targeting consumers a marketer may initially build its marketing strategy around more obvious clues to consumption behavior including consumers' demographic indicators, such as age, occupation and income (for more on targeting see Chapter 5).

However, in-depth research may yield information showing consumers are purchasing products to fulfill self concept objectives that have little to do with the demographic category they fall into. For instance, research by a clothing manufacturer may show senior citizens, who are not currently targets for a company's product, are making purchases because it makes them feel younger. In this example, appealing to consumer's self concept needs could expand a product's customer base by including customers not initially envisioned to be in the target market.

Many companies appeal to consumers' personality traits by offering them the opportunity to customize products in ways that appeal to their personality. One example is candy maker Mars whose MY M&Ms website (2) offers customers the option to create their own snack including customizing colors and creating a personalized message. (3)

Marketing Story

Men's Jewelry: A Recession-Proof Luxury
Time

Vanity purchases occur when a customer buys a product with the intention of using it to enhance or support their perceived personality (i.e., self concept). The most well known example of this is the personalized license plate, though many other products also fall into this category such as designer clothing, sports cars, housing and jewelry. From this short list, it is pretty clear vanity purchases skew toward high-end, expensive offerings, and are most frequently bought by high-income buyers.

What is additionally intriguing about some vanity purchases is that these are often viewed as being recession proof. A case in point is men's high-end jewelry. As discussed in this story, this product category experienced a 10% sales increase between 2007 and 2009, the height of U.S. recession. For some, this may not seem all that surprising as the target market for high-end jewelry are those earning over $100,000. However, the recession was widely viewed as impacting a large cross-section of the population including high-income consumers. It would seem logical that the high-end jewelry business would suffer. Yet, the opposite seemed to happen.

The motivation for continuing strong purchases in this category, despite a tough economy, is the key characteristic of vanity goods. Purchasers are motivated to acquire these products with the express intention of enhancing their image, which includes how they are perceived by others. As noted in the story, buyers have stated they purchase expensive jewelry so that others will think they are doing well. From a consumer behavior perspective, these buyers believe perception may be more important than reality.

Unity's study found that rings accounted for 51% of men's jewelry purchases made last year, excluding wedding bands. The fastest-growing accessories, however, are bracelets and necklaces — up 23% and 21% respectively, from 2008. (4)

How would a marketer of vanity goods, such as jewelry, use the information contained in this study to aid their marketing efforts?

Lifestyle

This internal influencing factor relates to the way we live through the activities we engage in and interests we express. In simple terms, it is what we value out of life. Lifestyle is often determined by how we spend our time and money. Additionally, customers often associate with others who share similar lifestyles.

In the consumer market, goods and services are purchased to support consumers' lifestyles. Marketers have worked hard researching how consumers in their target markets live their lives since this information is key to developing products, suggesting promotional strategies, and even determining how best to distribute products (e.g., consumer lifestyle shows preference for shopping online).

Motivation

Motivation relates to our desire to achieve a certain outcome. Many internal factors we've already discussed can affect a customer's desire to achieve a certain outcome, but there are others. For instance, when it comes to making purchase decisions customers' motivation could be affected by such issues as financial position (e.g., *Can I afford the purchase?*), time constraints (e.g., *Do I need to make the purchase quickly?*), overall value (e.g., *Am I getting my money's worth?*), emotional attachment (e.g., *Will this product remind me of something that is special to me?*), and perceived risk (e.g., *What happens if I make a bad decision?*).

Motivation is closely tied to the concept of **involvement**, which relates to how much effort the customer exerts in making a decision. Highly motivated customers will want to get mentally and physically involved in the purchase process. Not all products have a high percentage of highly involved customers (e.g., purchasing milk), but marketers who market goods and services with a high level of customer involvement should prepare options to attract this group. For instance, marketers should make it easy for customers to learn about their product (e.g., information on website, free video preview) and, for some products, allow customers to experience the product (e.g., free trial) before committing to the purchase.

The practice of offering customers the opportunity to experience a product prior to purchasing appears to be growing. Dubbed **experiential marketing***, the idea is to have customers immerse themselves in the product prior to making a commitment. In most cases, customers experience the product at locations that are away from the marketer's location. For instance, House Party Inc, (5) offers marketers the ability to have their products be the centerpiece of hundreds of parties, often held on the same day. This method was used by Singer Sewing Company when 800 locations in 37 states hosted parties at which a new sewing machine was tested by nearly 12,000 participants. (6)*

Box 4-2

ROLES IN THE BUYING CENTER

In the business market, those associated with the purchase decision are known to be part of a Buying Center, which consists of individuals within an organization performing one or more of the following roles:

- <u>Buyer</u> – responsible for dealing with suppliers and placing orders (e.g., purchasing agent)

- <u>Decider</u> – has the power to make the final purchase decision (e.g., CEO)

- <u>Influencer</u> – has the ability to affect what is ordered, such as setting order specifications (e.g., engineers, researchers, product managers)

- <u>User</u> – those who will actually use the product when it is received (e.g., office staff)

- <u>Initiator</u> – any Buying Center member who is the first to determine that a need exists

- <u>Gatekeeper</u> – anyone who controls access to other Buying Center members (e.g., administrative assistant)

For marketers confronting a Buying Center, it is crucial that first they identify who plays what role. Once identified the marketer must address the needs of each member, which may differ significantly. For instance, the Decider, who may be the company president, wants to make sure the purchase will not negatively affect the company financially while the Buyer wants to be assured the product is delivered on time. The way each Buying Center member is approached and marketed to requires careful planning in order to address their unique needs.

Roles

Roles represent the position we feel we hold or others feel we should hold in a group environment whether in a personal or business situation (see Box 4-2). These positions carry certain responsibilities, yet it is essential to understand that some of these responsibilities may be perceived and not spelled out or even accepted by others. In support of their roles, customers make product choices that vary depending on which role they are assuming. As an illustration, a person, who is responsible for selecting snack food for an office party his boss will attend, may choose higher quality products than he would when purchasing snacks for his family.

Advertisers often show how the benefits of their products aid customers as they perform certain roles. Typically, the underlying message of this promotional approach is to suggest using the advertiser's product will raise one's status in the eyes of others while using a competitor's product may have a negative effect on status.

‖‖‖

EXTERNAL INFLUENCES

Customer purchase decisions are often affected by factors outside of their control but have direct or indirect impact on how they live and what they consume.

Culture

Culture represents the behavior, beliefs and, in many cases, the way we act which is learned by interacting with and observing other members of society. In this way, much of what we do is shared behavior passed along from one member of society to another. Culture is learned from those with whom we directly interact (e.g., family, co-workers) and from those that we observe from a distance (e.g., movie stars).

Culture can be analyzed from many levels. At a broad level, culture is shaped by the general behaviors, belief and the way people act shared by a large portion of society, such as citizens of a country sharing patriotic beliefs. However, marketers are much more concerned with culture as it pertains to smaller groups or **sub-cultures**. Customers simultaneously belong to multiple sub-cultures whose cultural attributes may be different. For instance, people may simultaneously belong to different groups based on ethnicity, religious beliefs, geographic location, musical tastes, sports team allegiance, and many others. In a business situation there exist sub-cultures within an organization. For example, the organization's formal policies and procedures may be pivotal in developing an overall corporate culture, while other sub-cultures are developed in less formal ways (e.g., members of the company bowling team).

As part of their efforts to convince customers to purchase their products, marketers often use cultural representations, especially in promotional appeals. The objective is to connect to customers using cultural references that are easily understood and often embraced by the customer. By doing so, the marketer hopes customers feel comfortable with or can relate better to the product since it corresponds with their cultural values. Additionally, smart marketers use strong research efforts to identify differences in how sub-cultures behave. These efforts help pave the way for spotting trends within a sub-culture, which the marketer can capitalize on through new marketing tactics, such as developing new products. Finally, when selling globally marketers must understand cultural differences are pervasive. Many marketers make the mistake of assuming that what works in their home market will also work in foreign markets. Unfortunately, when success does not come the marketer may discover that cultural differences are at the root of the problem and until these differences are addressed marketing efforts will continue to struggle.

Marketing Story

Fast-Food Chains in Asia Cater Menus to Customers
USA Today

Marketing on a global scale is almost never easy. The efforts and costs required in establishing a marketing base in foreign countries can be significant. This often means only the largest firms become full-fledged global marketers. While the Internet is helping make all companies visible throughout the world, to be truly a global player requires much more than a website and a FedEx or UPS shipping account.

Instead, companies looking to go global must invest significant capital, manpower and time if they want to compete in foreign markets. For marketers, this includes gaining a deep understanding of the markets they are entering. And, this is no simple task as each country is different and the marketing decisions needed to reach customers in each country may be different.

While expanding beyond a home market is risky, for marketers seeking to become global players the rewards are often well worth the effort as foreign markets offer new opportunities for growing a business. Additionally, for other marketers, becoming a global player is a necessity if the marketer wants to stay in business especially if the marketer's home market is showing signs of slow growth.

This story looks at how marketers are embracing globalization in the Asian market by painting a nice picture of what companies, such as McDonalds, General Mills and Pizza Hut, are doing from a customer research side to make sure sales continue to grow. While the story looks only at examples in the Asian market, the overall ideas presented here are fundamental to virtually all global markets.

In the past, most of what Western companies sold in Asia were the same products offered in the U.S., with "very superficial ... cosmetic changes," says David Tse, an international marketing professor at the University of Hong Kong. But as China's economic might has grown, so has American companies' willingness to fundamentally revamp their menus in Asia. "China has become too big to ignore," says Tse. (7)

Should marketers expect the need for product adaption to exist across all types of consumer markets or is this primarily limited to certain markets, such as consumer food products?

Other Group Membership

In addition to cultural influences, customers belong to many other groups with which they share certain characteristics and which may influence purchase decisions. Some of the basic groups include:

- ♦ <u>Social Class</u> – represents the social standing one has within a society based on such factors as income level, education, and occupation

- ♦ <u>Family</u> – a person's family situation can have a strong effect on how purchase decisions are made

- ♦ <u>Reference Groups</u> – most consumers simultaneously belong to many other groups with which they associate or, in some cases, feel the need to disassociate

- ♦ <u>Industry Groups</u> – a company and many of its employees may belong to a large number of trade and community groups

Identifying and understanding groups, which customers belong to, is a key strategy for marketers. And, as discussed in Box 4-3, marketers can gain further insight through those who are perceived to be group leaders.

Box 4-3

MARKETING TO OPINION LEADERS

When appealing to groups, a key marketing strategy is to seek out group leaders and others to whom group members look to for advice or direction. Termed opinion leaders, these individuals may have influence over what others purchase if they are perceived as well-respected by the group.

Marketers may find value in researching opinion leaders to learn more about how they behave and the means by which they influence a group. For instance, research may show that an Internet blogger is viewed as an opinion leader within the marketer's industry and regularly reading the blogger's posts could yield insight on the group.

Additionally, marketers may find promotional opportunities with opinion leaders. For instance, marketers may target influential bloggers with free products and other material hoping this effort will encourage bloggers to write about a product. (8) Also, opinion leaders can be approached to represent the company in a promotional way, such as serving as a spokesperson for the marketer's products.

Marketing Story

How to Measure Your Brand's Online Influence
Inc. Magazine

Marketers are creatures that feast on numbers. Metrics are used for such important marketing functions as uncovering opportunities, creating marketing plans, and determining if decisions actually yield positive results. While research has been an integral part of marketing for a long time, the explosion of data available from customers' interaction on the Internet has vaulted analysis of metrics to a new level. Unfortunately, not all of this information is easily understood.

For instance, one area that has been difficult to measure is the impact social media has on marketing. Everyone believes Facebook, Twitter and the like are essential for marketing, but placing an actual monetary value on this has been problematic. One reason is that it has been hard to connect a social media posting to customers making an actual purchase. Yes, the referral measures are there (e.g., Facebook's Like, Twitter's Retweet), but many marketers want the answer to a simple question: "If I spend the money to use social media what money am I getting back?"

As this story discusses, several companies are trying to provide some answers to the social media measurement question. All companies discussed are small, start-up firms. Each offers analytic tools to help measure the "influence" a person, brand or company has within the social media space.

So how exactly is the information used? While the services discussed cannot convert a specific posting, tweet or other social media communication into real dollars, they may be able to direct marketers to sites on the Internet that exert influence over the marketer's target market. In other words, these metrics tools could help identify Opinion Leaders.

Of course, this still does not address marketers' concern of how social media translates into real money, but it may be a start.

Chief marketing officers surveyed by BazaarVoice and the CMO Club were likely to say their business engaged in at least three forms of social media. But nearly 35 percent of all CMOs didn't know if their Facebook presence yielded any return on investment. (9)

Once the marketer identifies social media influencers, what can they do to take advantage of this?

Economic Conditions

The current state of economic conditions has a direct impact on buyers. While, in certain cases, a customer's financial status is controllable (i.e., control wasteful spending), in other instances what the customer has available for spending is affected by economic factors that are beyond their control. Clearly, if someone has suddenly lost their job the impact on purchasing may be immediate and force major adjustments in what is purchased.

Additionally, expectation of future economic conditions could impact purchasing. For instance, if the sentiment exists that the economy is posed to grow than buyers may feel that engaging in purchasing of expensive items holds less risk than if the same decision were made during times when the forecast is for an economic slowdown.

> *The extended economic slowdown, that started in 2008 and gripped countries throughout the world, continues to have lingering effects on consumer purchasing. One effect is seen on shopping behavior, where the downturn forced consumers to become more educated shoppers. Even though the personal economic situation of many consumers has now improved, the shopping tips and lessons they learned continue to be used. These changes are also forcing marketers to adapt as they see many of the changes in consumer behavior as being permanent. (10)*

Situation

A purchase decision can be strongly affected by the situation in which people find themselves. This external factor can be influenced by many elements including: features of the buyer's current physical environment (e.g., presence of an in-store display); the circumstances in which the buyer is currently in or will be in some time in the future (e.g., hosting a party that unexpectedly runs out of food); market conditions in which the buyer is buying (e.g., a product that is in short supply); and time constraints (e.g., limited amount of time to make a purchase).

On many occasions, a situation is not controllable, in which case a customer may not follow her/his normal purchase decision process. For instance, if a person needs a product quickly and a store does not carry her/his normal brand, the customer may choose a competitor's product.

Marketers can take advantage of decisions made in uncontrollable situations in at least two ways. First, marketers can use promotional methods to reinforce a specific selection of products when the customer is confronted with a particular situation. For example, automotive services can be purchased promising to service vehicles if the user runs into problems anywhere and at anytime. Second, marketers can use marketing methods to convince customers a situation is less likely to occur if the marketer's product is used. This can be seen with financial services firms targeting business customers, where marketers explain that their clients' assets are protected in the case of unexpected economic problems.

An example of a situation in which market conditions can impact customer purchasing can be seen with the McDonald's McRib sandwich. In the U.S., McDonald's views the McRib as a promotional item and makes it available for only a short time at irregular intervals. Yet the product has built a loyal following with customers clamoring for it when it is available. These customers often purchase large numbers of the sandwich realizing it will only be around for a short time. (11)

HOW CUSTOMERS BUY

So now that we have discussed the factors influencing a customer's decision to purchase, our next task is to examine the process customers follow when making purchase decisions. Our focus is on the types of decisions two different customer groups – consumers and businesses - face and the steps they may take in getting to their final decision. We define consumers as those making purchases for their own or others personal consumption while businesses make purchases for organizational use.

However, before we describe how each group makes buying decisions, we first examine how the purchasing characteristics of consumers differs from those associated with business purchasing.

How Consumer and Business Purchasing Differs

It is necessary for marketers to understand that while the influences on purchasing are similar, the circumstances surrounding purchase decisions are quite different for consumers and businesses. The differences between these customers require marketers take a different approach when selling to business customers than they do when selling to consumers. Among the differences between consumer and business customers are:

- How Decisions Are Made - In the consumer market, a large percentage of purchase decisions are made by a single person. In the business market, while single person purchasing is not unusual, a large percentage of buying, especially within larger organizations, requires the input of many (i.e., Buying Center).

- Purchasing Experience - Organizations often employ purchasing agents or professional buyers whose job is to negotiate the best deals for their company. Unlike consumers, who often lack information when making purchase decisions, professional buyers are generally as knowledgeable about the product and the industry as the marketer who is selling to them.

- Decision Making Time - Depending on the product, business purchase decisions can drag on for an extensive period. Unlike consumer markets, where **impulse purchasing** (i.e., purchase decisions that are not planned) is rampant, the number of people involved in business purchase decisions results in decisions taking weeks, months, or even years.

- Size of Purchases - For products regularly used and frequently purchased, businesses will often buy a larger volume at one time compared to consumer purchases. Because of this, business purchasers often demand price breaks (e.g., discounts) for higher order levels.

- Importance of Price - In certain business markets, purchase decisions hinge on the outcome of a bidding process between competitors offering similar goods and services. In these cases, the decision to buy is often simply who has the lowest price. Unlike consumer, markets where customers will often purchase a brand with little consideration for its price, in the business market this is generally not the case.

- Number of Buyers - While there are several million companies worldwide operating in the overall business market, within a particular market the number is much smaller. Within some industries, buyers are highly concentrated in certain geographic areas. Consequently, compared to consumer products, where millions of customers make up a market, marketing efforts for the business market may be confined to a smaller targeted group.

- Promotional Focus - Companies who primarily target consumers likely use mass advertising methods to reach an often widely dispersed market. For business-to-business marketers the size of individual orders, along with a smaller number of buyers, makes person-to-person contact by sales representatives a more effective means of promotion.

Types of Consumer Purchase Decisions

Consumers are faced with purchase decisions nearly every day. But not all decisions are treated the same. Some decisions are more complex than others requiring more effort by the consumer. Other decisions are fairly routine and require little effort. In general, consumers face four types of purchase decisions:

◆ Minor New Purchase – These purchases represent something new to a consumer. However, in the consumer's mind, it is not a critical purchase in terms of need, money, or other reason (e.g., does not affect status within a group).

♦ Minor Re-Purchase – These are the most routine of all purchases and often the consumer returns to purchase the same product without giving much thought to other product options (i.e., consumer is loyal to a product).

♦ Major New Purchase – These purchases are the most difficult of all purchases because the product being purchased is important to the consumer. However, the consumer has little or no previous experience making these decisions. The consumer's lack of confidence in making this type of decision often (but not always) requires the consumer to engage in an extensive decision-making process.

♦ Major Re-Purchase – These purchase decisions are also important to the consumer, though, the consumer feels more confident in making the decision since they have previous experience purchasing the product.

For marketers, it is essential to understand how consumers treat the purchase decisions they face. If a company is targeting customers who feel a purchase decision is difficult (i.e., Major New Purchase), its marketing strategy may vary considerably compared to a company targeting customers who view the purchase decision as routine. In fact, the same company may face both situations at the same time; for some consumers the product is new, while others see the purchase as routine. The implication for marketers is that different purchase situations require different marketing efforts.

Steps in Consumer Purchasing Process

The consumer purchasing process can be viewed as a sequence of five steps (Figure 4-2). However, whether a consumer will actually carryout each step depends on the type of purchase decision that is faced. For instance, for Minor Re-Purchases the consumer may be quite loyal to the same brand and the decision is a routine one (i.e., buy the same product) with little effort needed to make a purchase decision.

In cases of routine brand loyal purchases, consumers may skip several steps in the purchasing process since they know exactly what they want. This allows the consumer to move quickly to the actual purchase. But for more complex decisions, such as Major New Purchases, the purchasing process can extend for days, weeks, or months. While evaluating these steps, marketers should realize that, depending on the circumstances surrounding the purchase, the importance of each step may vary.

Step 1: Need Recognized

In the first step, the consumer determines that, for some need, he/she is not happy with his/her perceived actual level of satisfaction. Consequently, he/she seeks to improve to a desired level of satisfaction. For instance, internal triggers, such as hunger or thirst, may tell the consumer that food or drink is needed. External factors can also trigger consumers' needs. Marketers are particularly effective doing this through advertising, in-store displays, and even the intentional use of scent (e.g., perfume counters in retail stores). At this stage, the decision-making process may stall if the consumer is not motivated to continue (see *Motivation* discussion above). However, if the consumer does have the internal drive to satisfy the need he/she will continue to the next step.

Online marketers have developed several methods designed to trigger customers' recognition of a need. One widespread approach, employed by such companies as Amazon, eBay and Netflix, is the use of sophisticated computer-based **product recommendation systems**, *which offer suggestions of products a customer may find of interest. Using a technique called* **collaborative filtering**, *the recommendation system suggests products to online shoppers based, in part, on purchases made by other customers who show similar behavioral patterns. (12)*

Figure 4-2: Decision Making Process

Step 2: Search for Information

Assuming a consumer is motivated to satisfy her or his need, she/he will next undertake a search for information on possible solutions. The sources used to acquire this information may be as simple as remembering information from past experience (i.e., memory) or the consumer may expend considerable effort to locate information from outside sources (e.g., Internet searching, talking with others, etc.). How much effort the consumer directs toward searching depends on such factors as the importance of satisfying the need, familiarity with available solutions, and the amount of time available to search. To appeal to consumers who are at the search stage, marketers should make efforts to ensure consumers can locate information related to their product. For example, for marketers whose customers rely on the Internet for information gathering, attaining high rankings in search engines for likely keyword searches done by consumers has become a critical marketing objective.

Step 3: Evaluate Options

Consumers' search efforts may result in a set of options from which a choice can be made. It should be noted there may be two levels to this stage. At level one, the consumer may create a set of possible solutions to her/his needs (i.e., different product types), while at level two the consumer may be evaluating particular products (i.e., different individual brands) within each solution. For example, a consumer who needs to replace a television has multiple solutions to choose from such as plasma, LCD, rear projection, and even old-style CRT screens. Within each type of solution will be multiple brands from which to choose. Marketers need to understand how consumers evaluate product options and why some products are included while others are not. Most importantly, marketers must determine which criteria consumers are using in their selection of possible options and how each criterion is evaluated. Returning to the television example, marketing tactics will be most effective when the marketer can tailor their efforts by knowing: 1) what benefits are most relevant to consumers (e.g., picture quality, brand name, screen size, price, etc.), and 2) determining the order of importance of each benefit.

Store-based retailers are finding their customers purchasing behavior is changing in terms of what customers expect from a retailer when evaluating products. Because of the many interactive services online retailers offer, such as visual access to large amounts of product, detailed product information, and product usage tips, retail stores have had to respond with more technology options including touch screens offering expanded product details. Additionally, research is being undertaken that someday may result in allowing a shopper to project clothing on their body without having to try it on. (13)

Step 4: Purchase

In many cases, the solution chosen by the consumer is the same as the product whose evaluation is the highest. However, this may change when it is actually time to make the purchase. The "intended" purchase may be altered at the time of purchase for many reasons such as: the product is out-of-stock; a competitor offers an incentive at the point-of-purchase (e.g., store salesperson mentions a competitor's offer); the customer lacks the necessary funds (e.g., credit card not working); or members of the consumer's reference group take a negative view of the purchase (e.g., friend is critical of purchase).

Marketers whose product is most desirable to the consumer must make sure the transaction goes smoothly. For example, Internet retailers have worked hard to prevent consumers from abandoning an online purchase (i.e., **online shopping carts**) by streamlining the checkout process. For marketers whose product is not the consumer's selected product, last chance marketing efforts may be worth exploring, such as offering incentives to store personnel to "talk up" their product at the checkout line.

> *Research suggests that over half of online customers who begin the purchasing process never complete the transaction. To overcome abandoned online shopping carts, marketers at SmileyCookie.com employ a retargeting campaign in hopes of getting customers to return to their website to complete the purchase. Using customer login information and web browser cookies, SmileyCookie.com identifies those who did not complete the transaction and within a few minutes sends out emails with a reminder message and other incentives. (14)*

Step 5: Post-Purchase Evaluation

Once the consumer has made the purchase they are faced with an evaluation of the decision. If the product performs below the consumer's expectation then he/she will question their decision. At the extreme, this may result in the consumer returning the product and seeking a replacement or a refund, while in less extreme situations the consumer will retain the purchased item but may take a negative view of the product. Such evaluations are more likely to occur in cases of expensive or highly important purchases. To help ease the concerns consumers have with their purchase evaluation, marketers need to be receptive and even encourage consumer contact. Customer service centers and follow-up marketing research are useful tools in helping to address purchasers' concerns.

Types of Business Purchase Decisions

While it would appear business customers face the same four purchase situations faced by consumers (Minor New Purchase, Minor Re-Purchase, Major New Purchase, Major Re-Purchase), the nature of the business market has led to categories that are somewhat different from those seen with consumer purchasing. This is primarily due to the differences that exist between these two markets. In particular, marketers targeting business buyers often see little value in pursuing business customers undertaking minor purchases (e.g., small orders) compared to consumer marketers who may actively pursue such customers. Consequently, while minor purchases certainly do occur, especially within small businesses, few business suppliers choose to direct their selling efforts to this type of purchase.

For buyers in business markets the types of decisions they face include:

♦ Straight Re-Purchases – These purchase situations involve routine ordering. In most cases buyers simply reorder the same products previously purchased. Many larger companies have programmed re-purchases into an automated ordering system that initiates electronic orders when inventory falls below a certain pre-determined level. For the supplier, benefiting from the re-purchase situation is ideal since the purchaser is not looking to evaluate other products. For competitors, it may require extensive marketing efforts to persuade the buyer to consider other product options.

♦ Modified Re-Purchases – These purchases occur when products previously considered a Straight Re-Purchase are now under a re-evaluation process. There are many reasons why a product is moved to the status of a Modified Re-Purchase including: end of the purchase contract period; change in who is involved in making the purchase; supplier is removed from an approved suppliers list; mandate from top level of the organization to re-evaluate all purchasing; or strong marketing efforts by competitors. In this circumstance, the incumbent supplier faces the same challenges they faced when they initially convinced the buyer to make the purchase. For competitors, the door is now open and they must work hard to make sure their message is heard by the decision makers.

♦ New Task Purchases – These purchases are ones the buyer has never or rarely made before. While not all New Task purchases are considered to have equal importance, in general, the buyer will spend considerably more time evaluating alternatives than would be considered for re-purchase situations. For marketers, the goal when selling to a buyer facing a New Task Purchase is to make sure to be included in the set of evaluated products as discussed in Step 2 of the business purchasing process.

Steps in Business Purchasing Process

Business purchasing follows the same five-step buying process (Figure 4-2) faced by consumers – Need Recognition, Search, Evaluate Options, Purchase, and After-Purchase Evaluation. While the steps are the same, the activities occurring within each step are quite different.

As we examine the business purchasing process, it is necessary to keep in mind the Buying Center concept discussed in Box 4-2. In particular, marketers must be aware that members of the Buying Center can affect the process at different stages.

Step 1: Need Recognized

In a business environment needs arise from just about anywhere within the organization. The Buying Center concept shows Initiators are the first organizational members to recognize a need. In most situations, the Initiator is also the User or Buyer. Users are inclined to identify the need for new solutions (i.e., new products), while Buyers are more likely to identify the need to re-purchase products. But marketers should also understand more companies are replacing human involvement in re-purchase decisions with automated methods, which makes it more challenging for competitors to convince buyers to replace currently purchased products. In Straight Re-Purchase situations, the purchasing process often jumps from Step 1 to Step 4 and little search activity is performed.

As part of this step, a specifications document may be generated laying out the requirements of the good or service to be purchased. Several members of the Buying Center may be involved in the creation of the specifications. For the marketer, establishing close contact with those who draw up the specifications may help position the marketer's product for inclusion in the search phase.

Step 2: Search for Information

The search for alternatives to consider for satisfying recognized needs is one of the most significant differences between consumer and business purchasing. Much of this has to do with an organization's motive to reduce costs. While a consumer will not search hard to save two cents on gas, a company with a large fleet of cars will. In fact, this step in the purchase process is where professional buyers make their mark. The primary intention of their search efforts is to identify multiple suppliers who meet product specifications and then, through a screening process, offer a selected group the opportunity to present their products to members of the Buying Center. Although, in some industries, online marketplaces and auction websites offer buyers access to supplier information without the need for suppliers to present to the Buying Center.

For suppliers, the key for success at this step is to make sure they are included within the search activities of the Buyer or others in the Buying Center. In some instances, this may require a supplier work to be included within an approved suppliers list. In the case of online marketplaces and auction websites, suppliers should work to be included within relevant sites.

Step 3: Evaluate Options

Once the search has produced options, members of the Buying Center then choose among the alternatives. In more advanced purchase situations, members of the Buying Center evaluate each option using a checklist of features and benefits sought by the buying organization. Each feature/benefit is assigned a weight that corresponds to its importance to the purchase decision. In many cases, especially when dealing with Government and Not-For-Profit markets, suppliers must submit bids with the lowest bidder often being awarded the order, assuming goods or services meet specifications.

Step 4: Purchase

To actually place the order may require the completion of paperwork (or electronic documents), such as a purchase order. Acquiring the necessary approvals can delay the order for an extended period of time. And for extremely large purchases, such as buildings or large equipment, financing options may need to be explored.

Step 5: Post-Purchase Evaluation

After the order is received, the purchasing company may spend time reviewing the results of the purchase. This may involve the Buyer discussing product performance issues with Users. If the product is well received it may end up moving to a Straight Re-Purchase status, which eliminates much of the evaluation process on future purchases.

‖‖

REFERENCES

1. "Back-to-School Sales Expected to be Flat as Parents Practice Restraint," *National Retail Federation*, July 21, 2011.

2. *MyMMS.com* website.

3. Conare, C., "Shopping: Not About Product or Place, but Interaction," *Millward Brown*, June 2010.

4. Tulshyan, R., "Men's Jewelry: A Recession-Proof Luxury," *Time*, July 27, 2010.

5. *HouseParty.com* website.

6. Lillis, M., "Two Local Women Weave Themselves Into Sewing History," *Las Vegas Review Journal*, May 24, 2011.

7. Chu, K., "Fast-Food Chains in Asia Cater Menus to Customers," *USA Today*, September 7, 2010.

8. Byron, E., "In-Store Sales Begin at Home," *Wall Street Journal*, April 25, 2011.

9. Smith, D., "How to Measure Your Brand's Online Influence," *Inc. Magazine*, February 17, 2011.

10. Horovitz, B., "Retailers Respond as Value Mania Hits Even the Well-to-Do," *USA Today*, June 9, 2011.

11. Rayworth, M., "Does McRib's Limited Availability Make It So Popular?" *USA Today*, November 11, 2010.

12. Woyke, E., "EBay Tests Serendipitous Shopping," *Forbes*, August 3, 2011.

13. Steel, E., "Luring Shoppers to Stores," *Wall Street Journal*, August 26, 2010.

14. Siwicki, B., "Target Practice," *Internet Retailer*, September 1, 2010.

Full text of many of the references can be accessed via links on the support website.

Chapter 5: Targeting Markets

In the first four chapters, we saw that the essential building blocks for creating a strong marketing program rests with marketing research and a deep understanding of customers. With this groundwork in place, it is now time to turn our attention to strategic decisions undertaken by the marketer to address customers' needs and help the organization meet its objectives.

In this chapter, we examine decisions affecting the selection of target markets. This is a critical point in marketing planning since all additional marketing decisions are going to be directed toward satisfying customers in the markets selected. We explore what constitutes a market and look at basic characteristics of consumer and business markets. We see not all markets are worth pursuing, and marketers are often better served developing a plan identifying specific markets to target. In particular, we look at the process of market segmentation where larger markets are carved into smaller segments offering more potential. Our discussion includes methods used to identify markets holding the best potential. Finally, we discuss the concept of product positioning and see how this fits into target marketing strategy.

IIIIIIIIIIIIIIIIIIIIIIIIIIIIIIIIIIIIIIIIIIIIIIIIIIIIIIIIIIIIIIIIIIIIIIIIIIIIIIIIIIIIIIIIIIIIIIIIIIIIIIIIIIIIIIIIIIIIIIIIIIIIIIIIIII

WHAT IS A MARKET?

The simple definition of a market is that it consists of all the people or organizations that may have an interest in purchasing a company's goods or services. In other words, a market comprises all customers who have needs that may be fulfilled by an organization's offerings. Yet just having a need is not enough to define a market. Several other factors also come into play.

The first factor is that markets consist of customers who are *qualified* to make a purchase. As spelled below, customers must meet several criteria to be qualified. A second factor for defining a market is that a market can only exist if the solutions sought by customers can be satisfied with the company's offerings. Thus, if a company identifies a group qualified to make purchases, it only becomes a market when the company is in a position to execute marketing activities designed to service these customers.

Therefore, a market is defined as all people or organizations that are qualified to make purchases of goods or services that a marketer is able to offer.

Criteria for Qualifying Customers

Many people may say they have a need for a California mansion overlooking the Pacific Ocean. Yet, just because someone says they have a need for this type of property does not mean a real estate agent will automatically consider them to be a potential customer. Instead, marketers are interested in customers who are qualified; they meet certain criteria which suggest they are good candidates to be the target of a company's marketing efforts.

In general, there are five basic criteria customers must meet to be considered qualified:

Must Seek a Solution to a Need

The customer must either consider the marketer's product to be a potential solution to a need or the marketer must believe the customer is likely to do so. In some cases, the customer may not realize or accept they have a need (e.g., *I don't need insurance*). These so-called **latent needs** may be unknown to the customer until something triggers them. For instance, latent needs may be triggered by exposure to certain marketing actions, such as product demonstrations, testimonials and other promotional methods, leading the customer to decide a previously unknown need does exist.

Must be Eligible to Make a Purchase

Some marketers limit who is eligible to purchase their products. The best example is legal restrictions on who can purchase alcohol, firearms, and tobacco products. Other examples of limitations include manufacturers only selling to certain retailers (see Chapter 9) and legal firms only handling certain types of clients.

Must Possess the Financial Ability to Make a Purchase

In our example of the California mansion, financial ability is most likely the criterion that will disqualify most people. Marketers are not likely to consider someone to be a customer if they do not have the funds to make a purchase. This is a major evaluative measure in the business market where purchasing companies lacking a strong financial position may be viewed as a risk to a supplying firm.

Must Have the Authority to Make the Purchase Decision

In some buying situations, the person responsible for the decision may not be the one with the need for a product. For example, in our Buying Center discussion in Chapter 4 (see Box 4-2), the Decider may be the one with the power to make the decision but Users are the ones with the need for the product. In these situations, while Users may fit the criteria of need, eligibility, and financial ability, they ultimately may not have the authority to make the purchase.

Must be Reachable

What good are potential customers if the marketer is not able to communicate with them? When the marketer is unable to reach a customer it is not reasonable to consider them as a qualified customer even though they meet all other criteria. For example, a newly created small business marketing custom, high-end footwear may feel presidents of leading companies are potential customers, yet establishing personal communication with these executives may prove all but impossible. Thus, it would be a stretch for these executives to be reasonably considered qualified customers.

It is crucial to note a customer must meet ALL criteria listed above to be considered qualified. However, in some markets the customer may have a **surrogate** who handles some of these qualifications. For instance, a market may consist of pre-teen customers who have a need for certain clothing items but the actual purchase may rest with the pre-teen's parents. So the parents could possibly assume one or more surrogate roles (e.g., financial ability, authority) that will result in the pre-teen being a qualified customer.

> *By one estimate, children under the age of 16 influence over $1 trillion dollars in purchases each year. Knowing the importance children play in household purchasing, many leading marketers, including McDonalds and American Eagle, aggressively target this market with a number of high-tech approaches, such as having kids click on ads that offer credits to be used in virtual worlds. These marketing techniques have caught the attention of parents and consumer groups, who feel the emphasis on promoting directly to children has gone too far, and that more controls are needed. (1)*

‖‖

CONSUMER AND BUSINESS MARKETS

As we discussed in Chapter 4, a marketer's customers may be consumers, businesses or both. A brief profile of each of these broad markets is presented below.

Consumer Market

The consumer market is comprised of anyone who purchases goods and services for their own personal consumption or for the personal consumption of others (e.g., household members, gift for friend, etc.). Most consumer purchasing takes place at retail outlets of which there are many types (see Chapter 9), though consumers also spend in other ways, such as through auctions, flee markets, and yard sales.

For 2009, it was estimated that worldwide consumer spending (measured as household final consumption expenditure) was nearly (US) $35 trillion. (2) Yet, this number is most likely much higher as it does not account for many unreported purchases, such as those that occur with private exchanges (e.g., neighbor selling to another neighbor). In the United States, according to the *United States Bureau of Labor*, the average consumer expenditure for a household (measured as Average Annual Expenditures per Consumer Unit) was over (US) $49,000 in 2009. (3)

When marketers look at the overall consumer market for a specific geographic area, they will see overall spending tends to change at slow rates from one year to the next. For instance, total consumer spending, adjusted for inflation (i.e., price increases) in developed countries may rise or fall by less than a few percentage points from one year to the next.

Who Makes Up the Consumer Market

The consumer market is made up of nearly everyone in the world! This means well over 6.5 billion people exist in the consumer market. Within this population, companies create markets by locating customers that share similar needs. For instance, the consumer market can be sub-divided into a large number of categories based on needs such as food, clothing, electronics, entertainment, leisure, etc. Furthermore, each of these can be sub-divided. For example, clothing has hundreds of sub-markets such as women, men, children, athletic, formal, and many, many more.

Business Market

The business market is comprised of organizations involved in the manufacture, distribution, or support of products sold or otherwise provided to other organizations. The business market easily dwarfs total spending in the consumer market even though there are far fewer buyers than in the consumer market. (4) This is because the business market not only includes businesses making purchases for their own needs (e.g., equipment, office supplies), it also includes purchases of items that are contained in products businesses produce (e.g., raw materials) and purchases of items that one business resells to another business (see *Resellers* discussion below). Additionally, as we noted in Chapter 4, businesses tend to place large orders compared to consumers.

The demand by businesses for goods and services is affected by consumer purchases (called **derived demand**) and because so many organizations play a part in creating consumer items, a small swing in consumer demand can create significant changes in overall business purchasing. Automobile purchases are a good example. If consumer demand for cars increases companies connected with the automobile industry also see demand for their goods and services increase (we will later refer to these companies as supply chain members). Under these conditions, companies ratchet up their operations to ensure demand is met, which leads to new purchases by a large number of companies. An increase of just one or two percent for consumer demand can increase business demand for products and services by five or more percent. Unfortunately, the opposite is true if consumer demand declines. Trying to predict these swings requires businesses use marketing research to know the conditions facing their direct customers (e.g., retail stores, other businesses) as well as customers to whom they do not sell directly (e.g., final consumer).

Who Makes Up the Business Market

There are millions of organizations worldwide selling their goods and services to other businesses. They operate in many industries and range in size from huge multinational companies with thousands of employees to one-person small businesses. For our purposes, we will categorize the business market based on the general business function an organization performs rather than by industry (of which there are thousands). We break the business market down into two broad categories - Supply Chain Members and Business User Markets.

Supply Chain Members

The supply chain consists of companies engaged in activities involving product creation and delivery. Essentially the chain represents major steps needed to manufacture a product that is eventually sold as a final product.

The supply chain includes:

- Raw Material Suppliers – These companies are generally considered the first stage in the supply chain and provide basic products (e.g., mining, harvesting, fishing, etc.), that are key ingredients in the production of higher-order products. *Example: Copper mine that extracts and refines copper from copper ore.*

- Processed Materials or Basic Component Manufacturers – Firms at this level use raw materials to produce more advanced materials or products contained within more advanced components. *Example: Electrical wire manufacturer that purchases copper.*

- Advanced Component Manufacturers – These companies use basic components to produce products offering a significant function needed within a larger product. *Example: Manufacturer of electrical power supplies purchases electrical wire.*

- Product Manufacturers – This market consists of companies purchasing both basic and advanced components and then assembling these components into a final product designated for a user. These products may or may not be sold as stand-alone products. Some may be included within larger products. *Example: Computer manufacturer purchases electrical power supplies.*

- Supporting Firms – These companies offer services at almost any point in the supply chain and to buyers in the business user market (see *Business User Markets* discussion below). Some services are directly related to the product while others focus on areas of the business not directly related to production. *Example: A trucking company moves products from one supply chain member to another.*

Business User Markets

Several additional user markets also make purchases for their own consumption or with the intention of redistributing to others. In these purchase situations, the buyer generally does not radically change the product from its purchased form. While technically these markets are also part of the supply chain, members of the business user market do not, in most cases, engage or directly assist in production activities.

The business user market consists of:

- Governments – They use purchases to assist with the functioning of the government which may include redistributing to others, such as medical supplies. *Examples: Federal, State, Local, and International governments.*

- Not-For-Profits – This category includes organizations whose tax structure precludes earning profits from operations and whose mission tends to be oriented to assisting others. *Examples: Educational institutions, charities, hospitals, and industry associations.*

- Resellers – Also called distributors, these companies operate in both the consumer and the business markets. Their function involves purchasing large volumes of products from manufacturers (and sometimes from other resellers) and selling these products in smaller quantities. *Examples: Wholesalers, retailers and industrial distributors.* (Resellers are discussed in detail in Chapters 9 and 10.)

||||||||||||||||||||||||||||||||||||||||||||||||||||||||||||||||||||||||||||||||||||||||||||||||||||||||||||||||||||||||

THE NEED FOR TARGET MARKETS

Earlier we defined a market as consisting of customers who are qualified to purchase goods or services offered by an organization. Yet, as we saw in our discussion of consumer and business markets, depending on how a market is categorized, qualified customers can exist in multiple markets. With potential customers in many markets, marketers face the challenge of deciding on the best approach for reaching these customers.

For many inexperienced marketers, the strategy for reaching these customers is simple: "*We will just sell to whoever wants to buy.*" Yet, for most marketing organizations, the notion of marketing to ALL qualified customers is unrealistic because:

REACHING CUSTOMERS REQUIRES RESOURCES

The fact customers are qualified by no means ensures they will actually do business with the marketer. No matter where customers are located, marketers must invariably spend money reaching them. In situations where qualified customers are spread throughout many markets, the idea of reaching all is both ineffective and inefficient as the marketer is likely to drain resources in its quest to locate those willing to buy.

SATISFYING BASIC CUSTOMER NEEDS MAY NOT BE ENOUGH

How customers' needs are defined (see *Criteria for Qualifying Customers* discussion above) is critical to determining a market. One approach to defining needs is to identify markets as consisting of qualified customers who have a basic need that must be satisfied. For example, one could consider the beverage market as consisting of all customers that want to purchase liquid refreshment products to solve a thirst need. While this may be the largest possible market a company could hope for (it would seem to contain just about everyone in the world!), in reality, there are no manufactured products that would appeal to everyone in the world since individual nutritional needs, tastes, purchase situations, economic conditions, and many other issues lead to differences in what people seek to satisfy their thirst needs.

Instead of directing resources to every conceivable customer, marketers are better off being selective in the markets they will target with their marketing efforts. **Target markets** are the markets that offer the best fit for an organization's goals and objectives. Using a target market approach, an organization attempts to get the most from its resources by following a planned procedure to identify customers that appear to be the best candidates to respond to the marketer's message.

With this in mind, we now turn our attention to examining the process marketers follow to choose which markets are best to target with their marketing effort.

||||||||||||||||||||||||||||||||||||||||||||||||||||||||||||||||||||||||||||||||||||||||||||||||||||

TARGETING MARKETS THROUGH SEGMENTATION

The market selected by a company as the target for its marketing efforts is critical since all subsequent marketing decisions will be directed toward satisfying the needs of these customers. But what approach should be taken to select markets the company will target?

As we saw in Chapter 4, marketers strive to understand as much as possible about their customers including identifying the main benefits they seek. Because people are different and seek different ways to satisfy their needs, nearly all organizations, whether for-profits or not-for-profits, must select their target markets using a **market**

segmentation approach. Market segmentation divides broad markets, consisting of customers possessing different characteristics, including different needs, into smaller market segments in which customers are grouped by characteristics shared by others in the segment.

To successfully target markets using a segmentation approach, organizations should engage in the following three-step process:

1. Identify segments within the overall market.

2. Choose the segment(s) that fits best with the organization's objectives and goals.

3. Develop a marketing strategy that appeals to the selected target market(s).

Below we examine these steps in detail.

Step 1: Identify Market Segments

The first step in targeting markets through market segmentation is to separate customers who make up large general markets (i.e., basic needs) into smaller groupings based on selected characteristics (called **bases of segmentation**) shared by those in the group. General markets are most often associated with basic product groups, such as automobile, beverage, footwear, home entertainment, etc.

The purpose of segmentation is to look deeper within the general market in order to locate customers who: 1) possess specific needs (e.g., seek hybrid automobiles), and 2) who share similar characteristics (e.g., college educated, support environmental issues, etc.). When grouped together these customers may form a smaller segment of the general market (e.g., segment of the automobile market). By focusing marketing research on these smaller segments, the marketer can learn a great deal about these customers and, with this information, craft highly targeted marketing campaigns.

In the last few years Comic-Con International, the annual convention for comic book and science fiction fans, has experience a significant increase in the number of pre-teen girls attending the event with their parents. Corporate exhibitors have taken notice of this new market segment by introducing new products. Mattel, for example, has introduced a new product line called Monster High featuring dolls, books and clothing targeted to this young group. (5)

The variables used to segment markets can be classified into a three-stage hierarchy (see Figure 5-1) with higher stages building on information obtained from lower stages in order to reach greater precision in identifying shared characteristics. More precise segmentation efforts require sufficient funding, strong research skills, and other capabilities. For instance, a marketer entering a new market may not have the ability to segment beyond the first two stages since the precision needed in Stage 3 segmentation may demand an established relationship with customers in the market.

The three-stage segmentation process presented below works for both consumer and business markets, though the variables used to segment these markets may be different. Each segmentation stage includes an explanation along with suggestions for variables the marketer should consider. This is not meant to be an exhaustive list, as other variables are potentially available. However, for marketers new to segmentation, these offer a good starting point for segmenting markets.

Figure 5-1: Stages of Segmentation

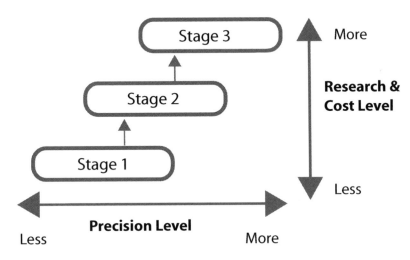

STAGE 1 SEGMENTATION VARIABLES

Stage 1 segmentation consists of variables (see Table 5-1) that can be easily identified through **demographics** (i.e., statistics describing a population), geographics (i.e., location), and financial information. For both consumer and business segmentation (see Box 5-1) this information focuses mostly on easy to obtain data from such sources as government data (e.g., census information), examining secondary data sources (e.g., news media), trade associations, and financial reporting services. While Stage 1 segmentation does not offer the segmentation benefits available with higher-level stages, the marketer benefits from accomplishing the segmentation task in a short time frame and at lower cost.

> *When it comes to targeting markets, marketers may use a number of segmentation approaches to attract different customer groups to the same product. This can be seen at Universal Studios Hollywood where they segment on many variables including ethnicity. For instance, Universal updated it Halloween Horror Nights program to include a mythological character from Latin America called La Llorona. A key reason for this addition was to appeal to the large Hispanic market that resides in Southern California. (6)*

Table 5-1: Stage 1 Segmentation Variables

Segmentation Variables Consumer Markets	Segmentation Variables Business Markets
Demographics age group (e.g., teens, retirees, young adults), gender, education level, ethnicity, income, occupation, social class, marital status **Geographics** location (e.g., national, regional, urban/suburban/rural, international), climate	**Demographics** type (e.g., manufacturer, retailer, wholesaler), industry, size (e.g., sales volume, number of retail outlets), age (e.g., new, young growth, established growth, mature) **Geographics** location (e.g., national, regional, urban/suburban/rural, international), climate **Business Arrangement** ownership (e.g., private versus public, independent versus chain), financial condition (e.g., credit rating, income growth, stock price, cash flow)

STAGE 2 SEGMENTATION VARIABLES

Some firms, especially companies with limited funds or those who feel they need to move quickly to get their product to market, stop the search for segmentation variables at the Stage 1 level. However, moving beyond Stage 1 segmentation offers a rich amount of customer information allowing marketers to more effectively target customers' needs.

To segment using Stage 2 variables (see Table 5-2) marketers must use research techniques to gain insight into customers' current purchase situations and the environment in which customers operate. Information at this stage includes learning what options customers have chosen to satisfy their needs, what circumstances within customers' environment affect how purchases are made, and understanding local conditions impacting purchase decisions. Marketers

---

Box 5-1

FINDING BUSINESS TARGET MARKETS

On the surface, segmentation of business markets may not always seem as clear as segmenting consumer markets. This can especially be a problem for marketers who are not familiar with a particular business market. For these marketers, a convenient starting point for segmentation efforts is to utilize business classification systems set up by international governments, such as the North American Industrial Classification System (NAICS), which covers Canada, Mexico and the United States, and the International Standard Industrial Classification (ISIC), which is widely used in Europe.

These systems provide descriptions of hundreds of industry classifications. For instance, the table below shows how U.S. operators of "Golf Pro Shops" are listed in the NAICS coding system. Note the numeric sequence that occurs as one "drills down" in order to locate individual industry groups.

Level	Code	Description
Sector	45	Retail Trade
Subsector	451	Sporting Goods, Hobby, Book, and Music Stores
Industry Group	4511	Sporting Goods, Hobby, and Musical Instrument Stores
Industry	45111	Sporting Goods Stores
US Industry	451110	Golf Pro Shops

Once industry codes are known, these can be used within various government and industry research reports to locate industry information, such as the number of firms operating in the industry, total industry sales, number of employees, and more. Additionally, these codes can be used to locate individual businesses. This can be done through business directory services specializing in listing company information. (7)

might locate some of this information through the same sources used in Stage 1, but most variables require the marketer to engage in at least casual contact with customers in the market. This can be done through primary research methods, such as surveying the market, having sales personnel contact customers, purchasing research reports from commercial marketing research firms, or hiring consultants to undertake research projects. The cost and time needed to acquire this information may be significantly greater than that of Stage 1 segmentation.

STAGE 3 SEGMENTATION VARIABLES

Marketers choosing to segment at the Stage 3 level face an enormous challenge in gathering useful segmentation information but, for those committed to segmenting at this level, the rewards may include gaining competitive advantage

Table 5-2: Stage 2 Segmentation Variables

Segmentation Variables Consumer Markets	Segmentation Variables Business Markets
Current Purchasing Situation brands used, purchase frequency, current suppliers	**Current Purchasing Situation** brands used, purchase frequency, current suppliers
Purchase Ready possess necessary equipment, property, knowledge, skill sets	**Purchase Ready** possess necessary equipment, property, knowledge, skill sets
Local Environment cultural, political, legal	**Local Environment** cultural, political, legal
	Customers Served by the Business identify the business' market
	Business' Perceived Image identify how targeted businesses are perceived by their customers

over rivals whose segmentation efforts have not dug this deep. However, the marketer must invest significant time and money to amass the detailed market intelligence needed to achieve Stage 3 segmentation. Additionally, much of what is needed at Stage 3 is information that is often well protected and not easily shared by customers. In fact, many customers are unwilling to share certain personal information (e.g., psychological) with marketers with whom they are not familiar.

Consequently, segmenting on Stage 3 variables (see Table 5-3) is often not an option for marketers new to a market unless they acquire this via other means (e.g., hire a consultant who knows the market). To get access to this information marketers, who already serve the market with other products, may be able to use primary research, such as focus groups, in-depth interviews, observational research, and other high level marketing research techniques. Additionally, companies with existing customer relationship management (CRM) technologies may be in position to tap into their customer information in order to identify customer characteristics that may potentially lead to new segments.

Kraft Foods learned from focus group research that Latino shoppers, who purchased single serving cheese products, were primarily purchasing lower priced competitors' products and not Kraft Cheese Singles. However, in the course of research they discovered that these consumers were willing to pay more for cheese that was made from real milk. Kraft took this information and segmented their market based on this specific feature and realized a 12% growth in sales. (8)

Table 5-3: Stage 3 Segmentation Variables

Segmentation Variables Consumer Markets	Segmentation Variables Business Markets
Benefits Sought price, overall value, specific feature, ease-of-use, convenience, support services, etc.	**Benefits Sought** price, overall value, specific feature, services, profit margins, promotional assistance, etc.
Product Usage how used, why used, situation when used, used in combination with other goods or services, etc.	**Product Usage** how used (e.g., raw material, component product, major selling item at retail level), situation when used, etc.
Purchase Conditions time of day/month/year when purchased, require product usage assistance, credit terms, trade-in option, etc.	**Purchase Conditions** length of sales cycle, set product specifications, bid pricing, credit terms, trade-in option, product handling, etc.
Characteristics of Individual Buyer purchase experience, how purchase is made, influencers on purchase decision, importance of purchase	**Characteristics of Buying Center** purchase experience, number of members, make-up of key influencers, willingness to assume risk
Psychographics personality, attitudes, and lifestyle combined with demographics	

Step 2: Choosing Market Segments

The second step in selecting target markets requires the marketer to evaluate critically the segments identified in Step 1 in order to select those which are most attractive. For small firms, this step may not be very involved since they may lack the resources to do it effectively. Consequently, these firms are often left with using their own intuition or judgment to determine which segments are the most promising. For companies with the time and money to commit to this step, the results may offer greater insight as to which segments are primary candidates for current marketing efforts. Additionally, it may present segments that could serve as future targets for the company's offerings.

In determining whether a segment is a worthwhile target market, the marketer needs to address the following:

♦ *Is the segment large enough to support the marketer's objectives?* This is an especially critical question if the marketer is entering a market served by many competitors.

♦ *Is the segment showing signs of growth?* One of the worst situations for a marketer is to enter a market whose growth is flat or declining, especially if competitors already exist.

♦ *Does the segment meet the mission of the company?* The segment should not extend too far beyond the direction the company has chosen to take.

Marketing Story

How to Disrupt an Overlooked Market
BusinessWeek

One marketing advantage small companies can have over large firms is to target market segments that are underappreciated by their larger competitors. This may be especially true for smaller privately held firms that do not face the same level of financial scrutiny that confronts bigger public companies. Facing less external pressure, small companies can gradually build presence in an underappreciated market segment even if profits are not initially very high. They can also often do this without bigger companies taking much notice.

For relatively small or niche segments that do not show much growth potential, large firms are perfectly happy letting smaller companies handle these customers. Yet, sometimes large firms just do not understand these markets and cannot see the opportunity that lies there. They often unable see what smaller marketers see for the market segment. In particular, smaller marketers see that if underappreciated segments are targeted in the right way with the right marketing mix, these segments may actually have the potential to grow substantially and become highly profitable.

When these underappreciated segments do take off, firms that were first to address these customers are often well placed to ride the wave to higher profits. Large firms are often forced to play catch-up, principally by paying a premium to buyout smaller early entrants that were deeply entrenched in these markets.

As this story points out, TracFone Wireless is an example of a company targeting an underappreciated market segment that bigger companies have overlooked. TracFone offers basic, no-frills cellphone service primarily aimed at lower income and restricted income consumers. While it is owned by a large Latin American telecommunication firm, TracFone is viewed by some as being a relatively small player in the U.S. mobile device market. However, this perception is quickly changing as the company is growing rapidly and has established a sizeable customer base. With a foothold in the U.S. market, TracFone is now beginning to expand its offerings and could one day be a threat in larger, more lucrative mobile device markets served by the major U.S. carriers.

While wars between Androids and iPhones have dominated the headlines, TracFone has quietly built a U.S. subscriber base of 18 million customers. In one recent quarter, TracFone signed up more customers than Verizon Wireless. Quarterly revenue clocked in at nearly $800 million, growing at a vibrant 62 percent rate. (9)

What will TracFone need to do if it wants to appeal to the higher-end customer currently serviced by the leading mobile device carriers?

♦ *Does the company have the necessary skills, knowledge, and expertise to service the segment?* The company should understand and be able to communicate with customers in the segment, otherwise they may face a significant learning curve in understanding how to market effectively to a segment.

> *Consumer products companies are finding valuable, growing markets among Muslim consumers. However, many leading marketers have not serviced these markets well because they failed to appreciate how the needs of these consumers may differ from consumers in other markets. With over 1.5 billion Muslims worldwide, marketers, such as Nike, Unilever and Colgate-Palmolive, have realized they must learn more. These firms are undertaking extensive marketing research projects in an attempt to gain a stronger understanding of Muslim consumers. (10)*

Once one or more segments have been identified the marketer must choose the most attractive option(s) for its marketing efforts. At this point, the choice becomes the firm's target market(s).

Step 3: Develop Strategy to Appeal to Target Market(s)

In the final step of the segmentation process, the marketer must decide a strategy for reaching the segments identified in Step 2. The options include the following target marketing strategies:

♦ Undifferentiated or Mass Marketing – Under this strategy, the marketer attempts to appeal to one large market with a single marketing strategy. While this approach offers advantages in terms of lowering development and production costs, since only one product is marketed, there are few markets in which all customers seek the same benefits. This approach was extremely popular in the early days of marketing (e.g., Ford Model-T), but today few companies view this as a feasible strategy.

♦ Differentiated or Segmentation Marketing – Marketers choosing this strategy try to appeal to multiple smaller markets with a unique marketing strategy for each market. The underlying concept is that bigger markets can be divided into many sub-markets and an organization chooses different marketing strategies to reach each sub-market it targets. Most large consumer products firms follow this strategy as they offer multiple products (e.g., running shoes, basketball shoes) within a larger product category (e.g., footwear).

♦ Concentrated or Niche Marketing – This strategy combines mass and segmentation marketing by using a single marketing strategy to appeal to one or more small markets. It is primarily used by smaller marketers, who have identified small **sub-segments** of a larger segment that are not served well by larger firms. In these situations, a smaller company can do quite well marketing a single product to a narrowly defined target market.

♦ <u>Customized or Micro Marketing</u> - This target marketing strategy attempts to appeal to targeted customers with individualized marketing programs. For micro marketing segmentation to be effective, the marketer must, to some degree, allow customers to "build-their-own" products. This approach requires extensive technical capability for marketers to reach individual customers and allow customers to interact with the marketer. The Internet and mobile networks have been catalysts for target marketing strategy. As more companies become comfortable utilizing these technologies, micro marketing is expected to flourish.

> *Through its NIKEiD site, Nike offers customers the opportunity to customize their own apparel. Customers can choose from a large selection of footwear, clothing, and equipment and then customize their purchase to their own needs. For instance, for some footwear products customers can adjust several different color elements including the look of the general base material, the heel, the Nike Swoosh logo, and the laces. Customization also includes the imprinting of text on the tongue of the shoe. (11)*

||||||||||||||||||||||||||||||||||||||||||||||||||||||||||||||||||||||||||||||||||||||||||||||||||||||||||||

POSITIONING PRODUCTS

No matter which target marketing strategy is selected, the overall marketing strategy should involve the process of positioning the firm's offerings in ways that will appeal to targeted customers. Positioning is concerned with the perception customers hold regarding a product or company. In particular, it relates to marketing decisions an organization undertakes to get customers to think about a product or company in a certain way compared to its competitors.

The goal of positioning is for marketers to convince customers their product offers key benefits not found with competitor's offerings. For instance, if a customer has discovered she has a need for an affordable laptop computer, a company, such as Dell, may come to mind since its marketing efforts position its products as offering good value at a reasonable cost.

To position successfully, the marketer must have thorough knowledge of the key benefits sought by the market. Obviously the more effort the marketer expends on segmentation (i.e., reached Stage 3 segmentation) the more likely it will know the benefits sought by the market. Once known, the marketer must: 1) tailor marketing efforts to ensure its offerings satisfy the most sought after benefits, and 2) communicate to the market in a way that differentiates the marketer's offerings from competitors.

For firms seeking to appeal to multiple target markets (i.e., segmentation marketing), positioning strategies may differ for each market. For example, a marketer may sell the same product to two different target markets, but in one market the emphasis is on styling while in another market the emphasis is on ease-of-use benefits. The key point is that the overall marketing strategy must be evaluated separately for each target market since what works well in one market may not work as well in another market.

> *Television informercials are well known for selling products that are positioned against existing products. For instance, Snuggie, is one of the most successful products to be sold through informercials. Allstar Products Group has been selling Snuggie by positioning it as a blanket without the problems of a blanket, such as it sliding off when watching television. The company has sold over 25 million Snuggies by convincing customers that such benefits are important. (12)*

Marketing Story

U.S. Food Giants Tailor Products, Marketing to International Palates
Los Angeles Times

When it comes to marketing globally, all companies should clearly understand this truism: just because a marketing strategy works in your home country does not mean it will work in other countries. This story offers support for this truism as it presents several examples of companies who experienced problems marketing their products in different areas of the world.

In particular, companies are finding the target marketing methods designed to meet customers' needs in emerging markets (i.e., countries with small but growing economies) are often significantly different compared to methods used to reach customers in more advanced markets. Unfortunately, many companies recognize this only after suffering significant losses. Yet much of the pain experienced in their initial marketing efforts may have been avoided if companies had first engaged in extensive marketing research.

Catering to local tastes is vital, as New Jersey-based Campbell Soup found out in its first foray into China in the early 1990s. The company essentially slapped a Chinese label on its classic U.S. condensed soups, said Larry McWilliams, president of Campbell's international operations. "They sold well for a while, but they were a novelty. They had no staying power," he said. Campbell returned to China in 2007, but only after two years of research revealed that in China, as well as Russia, there's a cultural disposition to cooking soup from scratch. (13)

In addition to what is mentioned in this story, what other factors do marketers face in emerging markets that may not be present in more advanced markets?

‖‖

REFERENCES

1. Horovitz, B., "Marketing to Kids Gets More Savvy With New Technologies," *USA Today*, August 15, 2011.

2. "Household Final Consumption Expenditure – 2009," *The World Bank*.

3. "Consumer Expenditures in 2009," *Bureau of Labor Statistics - United States Department of Labor*, October 5, 2010.

4. Hutt, M.D. and T.W. Speh, <u>Business Marketing Management: B2B</u>, South-Western College Publishing, 2009.

5. Schmidt, G., "Girls at Comic-Con Find Marketers Ready for Them," *New York Times*, August 10, 2010.

6. Martin, H., "Universal Studios Turns to Folklore to Woo Latinos for Halloween," *Los Angeles Times*, September 29, 2010.

7. For a list of links to business directory services see the **Market Research** section of *KnowThis.com*.

8. Elliott, S. and T. Vega, "TV Steps Up Pitch to Hispanic Market," *New York Times*, May 17, 2011.

9. Johnson, M.W., "How to Disrupt an Overlooked Market," *BusinessWeek*, June 2, 2011.

10. Gooch, L., "Advertisers Seek to Speak to Muslim Consumers," *New York Times*, August 11, 2010.

11. *NIKEiD* website.

12. Newman, A.A., "Lots of Laughs, and Even More Sales," *New York Times*, December 21, 2010.

13. Hughlett, M., "U.S. Food Giants Tailor Products, Marketing to International Palates," *Los Angeles Times*, March 25, 2010.

Full text of many of the references can be accessed via links on the support website.

Chapter 6: Product Decisions

As we stress throughout this book, organizations attempt to provide value to a target market by offering solutions to customers' needs. These solutions include tangible or intangible (or both) product offerings marketed by an organization. In addition to satisfying the target market's needs, the product is crucial because it is how organizations generate revenue. It is what a for-profit company sells in order

to realize profits and satisfy financial stakeholders (e.g., stockholders). Products are also important for many nonprofit organizations where they are used to generate revenue needed to support operations (e.g., fund raising). Without a well-developed product strategy that includes input from the target market, a marketing organization will not have long-term success.

In this chapter, we define what a product is and look at how products are categorized. We also take a close look at the key decisions marketers face as they formulate their product offerings including what features to include in a product, how a product's identity is established through branding, important issues in packaging design, and what to consider when labeling products. We discuss each in detail and see how these impact product strategy.

||||||||||||||||||||||||||||||||||||||||||||||||||||||||||||||||||||||||||||||||||||||||||||||||||||||||||||||||||||||||||||||||||||

WHAT IS A PRODUCT?

In marketing, the term **product** is used as a catch-all word to identify solutions a marketer provides to its target market. We will use the term "product" to cover offerings that fall into one of the following categories:

GOODS

Something is considered a **good** if it is a tangible item. That is, it is something that is felt, tasted, heard, smelled or seen. For example, bicycles, cellphones, and donuts are all examples of tangible goods. In some cases, there is a fine line between items that affect the senses and whether these are considered tangible or intangible. We often see this with digital goods accessed via the Internet or mobile devices, such as listening to music online. For these products, there does not appear to be anything that is tangible or real since it is essentially computer code proving the solution. However, for our purposes, we distinguish these as goods since these products are built (albeit using computer code), are stored (e.g., on a computer), and generally offer the same benefits each time (e.g., quality of a digital song is always the same).

SERVICES

Something is considered a **service** if it is an offering a customer obtains through the work or labor of someone else. Services can result in the creation of tangible goods (e.g., a publisher of business magazines hires a freelance writer to write an article) but the main solution purchased is the service. Unlike goods, services are not stored and are only available at the time of use (e.g., hair salon) and the consistency of the benefit offered can vary from one purchaser to another (e.g., not exactly the same hair styling each time).

IDEAS

Something falls into the category of an **idea** if the marketer attempts to convince the customer to alter his/her behavior or perception in some way. Marketing an idea is often an approach used by nonprofit groups or governments in order to get targeted groups to avoid or change certain behavior. This is seen with public service announcements directed toward such activity as youth smoking, automobile safety, and illegal drug use.

While some marketers offer solutions providing both tangible and intangible attributes, for most organizations their primary offering is concentrated in one area. So, while a manufacturer may offer intangible services or a service firm provides certain tangible equipment, these are often add-ons that support the organization's main product.

Categories of Consumer Products

Most products intended for consumer use can be further categorized as:

♦ Convenience Products – These products appeal to an extremely large market segment. Products in this category tend to be consumed regularly and purchased frequently. Examples include most household items, such as food, cleaning products, and personal care products. Because of the high purchase volume, pricing per item tends to be relatively low and consumers often see little value in shopping around since additional effort yields minimal savings. From the marketer's perspective, the low price of convenience products means that profit per unit sold is low. In order to make high profits marketers must sell in large volume. Consequently, marketers attempt to distribute these products in mass through as many retail outlets as possible (see *Mass Coverage* discussion in Chapter 8).

♦ <u>Shopping Products</u> – These are products consumers purchase and consume on a less frequent schedule compared to convenience products. Consumers spend more time locating these products since they are relatively more expensive than convenience products and because these may possess additional psychological benefits for purchasers, such as raising their perceived status level within their social group. Examples include many clothing products, personal services, electronic products, and household furnishings. Because consumers are purchasing less frequently and are willing to shop to locate these products, the target market for shopping products is much smaller than for convenience goods. Consequently, marketers often are more selective when choosing distribution outlets to sell these products (see *Selective Coverage* discussion in Chapter 8).

♦ <u>Specialty Products</u> – These are products that carry a high price tag relative to convenience and shopping products. Consumption may occur at the same rate as shopping products, but consumers are much more selective. In fact, in many cases consumers know in advance which product they prefer and will not shop to compare products. But they may shop at retailers that provide the best value. Examples include high-end luxury automobiles, expensive champagne, and celebrity hair care experts. The target markets are generally very small and outlets selling the products are highly limited to the point of being exclusive (see *Exclusive Coverage* discussion in Chapter 8).

> *While most consumer convenience and shopping products can easily be purchased over the Internet, the same is not true for many high-end specialty products. For the most part, it is the specialty product marketer who is not allowing their products to be sold online. They are concerned that a product, which built a reputation for being unique and exclusive, will lose this perception given the openness of the Internet. Additionally, they believe luxury products require the marketer to build close, personal relationships with customers, something that is much easier to do in-person than over the Internet. (1)*

In addition to the three main categories above, consumer products are classified in at least two additional ways:

♦ <u>Emergency Products</u> – These are products sought due to sudden events and for which pre-purchase planning is not considered. Often the decision is one of convenience (e.g., whatever works to fix a problem) or personal fulfillment (e.g., perceived to improve purchaser's image).

♦ Unsought Products – These are products whose purchase is unplanned but occur as a result of marketers' actions. Such purchase decisions are made when the customer is exposed to promotional activity, such as a salesperson's persuasive presentation, or purchase incentives, including appealing pricing discounts. These promotional activities often lead customers to engage in impulse purchasing.

> *Retailers have long used in-store promotion techniques, including coupon dispensers and product displays, to get customers to make unplanned purchases. But marketers are finding that demand for unsought products can be stimulated well before customers enter a store. Retailer are now expanding promotions, called shopper marketing, to social media with the goal of getting shoppers to add products to the shopping list that they may not have previously considered. (2)*

Categories of Business Products

Products sold within the business market fall into the following categories:

♦ Raw Materials – These are products obtained through mining, harvesting, fishing, etc., that are key ingredients in the production of higher-order products.

♦ Processed Materials – These are products created through the processing of basic raw materials. In some cases, original raw materials are refined while in other cases the process combines different raw materials to create something new. For instance crops, including corn and sugar cane, can be processed to create ethanol used as fuel to power car and truck engines.

♦ Equipment – These are products used to help with production or operations activities. Examples range from conveyor belts to large buildings housing the headquarters staff of a multinational company.

♦ Basic Components – These are products used within more advanced components and are often built with raw or processed material. Electrical wire is an example.

♦ Advanced Components – These use basic components to produce products offering a significant function needed within a larger product. By itself, an advanced component is not a final product. In computers, the motherboard is an example since it contains many basic components but without the inclusion of other products (e.g., memory chips, microprocessor, etc.) would have little value.

♦ Product Components – These are products used in the assembly of a final product though these could also function as stand alone products. Dice included as part of a children's board game is an example.

♦ MRO (Maintenance, Repair and Operating) Products – These are products used to assist with the operation of the organization but are not directly used in pro- ducing goods or services. Office supplies, parts for a truck fleet, and natural gas to heat a factory would fall into this category.

Components of a Product

On the surface, it seems a product is simply a marketing offering, whether tangible or intangible, that someone wants to purchase and consume. One might believe product decisions are focused exclusively on designing and building the consumable elements of goods, services or ideas. In actuality, while decisions related to the consumable parts of the product are extremely important, the TOTAL product consists of more than what is consumed. The total product offering, and the decisions facing the marketer for the product, can be broken down into three main parts:

Core Benefits

As we discussed in Chapter 1, customers seek to obtain something of value from marketers in exchange for their willingness to give up something they value, generally money. What customers obtain are solutions to their needs or, stated another way, they receive **benefits**. For customers, benefits drive their purchase decisions (see Box 6-1). Consequently, at the very heart of all product decisions is determining the core benefits a product provides. These benefits, hopefully, address those sought by the marketer's target market. From this decision, the rest of the product offering can be developed. In most cases, the core benefits are offered by features of the actual product, though, for some customers, benefits offered by other aspects or augmented features (see *Augmented Product* discussion below) of the product are also important (e.g., access to customer service).

Actual Product

For most customers, the core benefits are offered through the components that make up the actual product. When a consumer returns home from shopping and takes an item out of her shopping bag, the actual product is the item she holds in her hand. Within the actual product is the **consumable product**, which is the main good, service or idea the customer is buying. For example, while toothpaste comes in a package that makes dispensing it easy, the consumable product is the paste that is placed on a toothbrush. But marketers must understand that while the consumable product is the most critical of all product decisions, as we will soon see the actual product includes many separate product decisions, including product features, branding, packaging, labeling, and more.

Augmented Product

Marketers often surround their actual product with goods and services that provide additional value to the customer's purchase. While these factors may not be key reasons leading customers to purchase (i.e., do not offer core benefits), for some the inclusion of these items strengthens the purchase decision while for others failure to include these may cause the customer not to buy. Items considered part of the augmented product include:

- Guarantee – This provides a level of assurance that the product will perform up to expectations and if not the company marketing the product will support the customer's decision to replace, repair or return for a refund.

- Warranty – This offers customers a level of protection often extending past the guarantee period to cover repair or replacement of certain product components.

- Customer Service – As discussed in detail in Chapter 3, these services support customers through such methods as training, repair, and other types of assistance.

- Complementary Products – The value of some product purchases is enhanced with add-on products or complementary products. Such items make the main product easier to use (e.g., laptop carrybag), improve styling (e.g., cellphone face plates) or extend functionality (e.g., portable keyboard for table computers).

||||||||||||||||||||||||||||||||||||||||||||||||||||||||||||||||||||||||||||||||||||||||||||||||||||||||||||||||||||||||

KEY PRODUCT DECISIONS

The actual product is designed to provide the core benefits sought by the target market. The marketer offers these benefits through a combination of factors making up the actual product. Below we discuss four key factors that together help shape the actual product.

Consumable Product Features

Features are characteristics of a product that offer benefits to the customer. When it comes to developing a consumable product, marketers face several decisions related to product features, including:

♦ Features Set vs. Cost – For marketers, a key decision focuses on the quantity and quality of features (i.e., features set) to include in a product. In most cases, the more features included or the higher the quality level for a particular feature, the more expensive the product is to produce and market.

♦ Is More Better? – Even if added cost is not a major concern, the marketer must determine if more features help or hurt the target market's perception of the product. A product with too many features could be viewed as too difficult to use.

> *According to a survey conducted by Consumer Reports, the technology that most frustrates consumers is the computer which contains hundreds of features. Over 95% of respondents indicated they had computer problems that they needed help solving. Other products also rated among the most frustrating include cellphones, cameras and televisions. (3)*

Box 6-1

MARKETERS SELL BENEFITS

The benefits a customer obtains from a product are contained within the actual and augmented product through product features. Features are the separate attributes of a product. For example, for the purchase of a flat panel television, features include screen size, screen resolution, surround sound, and remote control.

The benefits a customer receives from the purchase and use of the product fall into two main categories:

Functional Benefits
These are benefits derived from features that are part the consumable product. For instance, in our flat panel television example, features and benefits may include:

Feature	Functional Benefit
• screen size	offers greater detail and allows for more distant viewing
• screen resolution	provides clear, more realistic picture
• surround sound	immerses all senses in the viewing experience
• Internet connectivity	allows access to online content, such as movies
• remote control	allows for greater comfort while viewing

The benefits offered by these features are called functional because they result in a benefit the user directly associates with the product. Functional benefits are often the result of materials, design, and production decisions. How the product is built can lead to benefits, such as speed, ease-of-use, durability, and cost savings.

Psychological Benefits
These are benefits the customer perceives she/he receives when using the product. These benefits address psychological needs, such as status within a group, risk reduction, sense of independence, and happiness. Such benefits are developed through promotional efforts that are aimed at customers' internal influences on purchase behavior (see Chapter 4).

In communicating with customers, marketers should always associate a benefit with a product feature. Benefits are what customers seek; the feature is simply how the benefit is delivered. Thus, in our flat panel television example, a magazine advertisement promoting the television is more effective if it speaks directly to benefits it offers such as:

Our new high-definition televisions offer screen resolutions (feature) *that provide the clearest, most realistic picture* (functional benefit) *that will make your house the place to be* (psychological benefit) *for the big game!*

♦ <u>Who Should Choose the Features?</u> – Historically marketers determined what features to include in a product. However, the Customized or Micro Marketing targeting strategy we discussed in the Chapter 4 offers customers the opportunity to choose their own features to custom build a product. For instance, companies offering website hosting services allow website owners to choose from a list of service options (e.g., data storage options, overall website speed, customer help services) that best suit their needs. Also, for traditional products, such as clothing, companies allow customers to stylize their purchases with logos and other personalized options.

Branding

Branding involves decisions establishing an identity for a product with the goal of distinguishing it from competitors' offerings. In markets where competition is fierce and where customers may select from among many competitive products, creating an identity through branding is essential. It is particularly important in helping position the product (see Chapter 5) in the minds of the product's target market.

While consumer products companies have long recognized the value of branding, it has only been within the last 15-20 years that organizations selling in the business market have begun to focus on brand building strategies. One well-known business marketer to develop a brand is Intel, maker of component products, such as computer chips, which created a brand through its now famous "Intel Inside" slogan. Intel's success has led many other business-to-business marketers to incorporate branding within their overall marketing strategy.

BRAND NAMES AND BRAND MARKS

At a basic level, branding is achieved through the use of unique brand names and brand marks. Developing a brand name, which may be the individual product name or a name applied to a group or family of products, offers several advantages. First, brand names may suggest to customers what the product is or does (e.g., Mop & Glo). This can catch the attention of customers needing a product for a certain usage or who are seeking a specific benefit, but do not know what products to choose. Second, the name is what we utter when we discuss a product with others. This is helpful in creating and spreading product awareness.

The creation of brand names must be done carefully if a marketer looks to expand outside its home country. This can especially be a problem if a company looks to follow a standardization approach to marketing (see Chapter 1), where a single product name is used throughout the world. Whether using a single name or developing a new name for each market that is entered, marketers must fully understand the local language to ensure there are no issues in the translation of a brand name.

Starbucks found that their logo, which was essentially unchanged since it was introduced in 1992, was proving too limiting as the company looks to expand. The primary concern was with the words "Starbucks" and "Coffee" which appeared on the logo. While the company is retaining the widely recognized twin-tailed mermaid figure and the green logo, the company dropped the words. By dropping the company name, Starbucks avoids potential translation problems that may arise as it seek to grow in global markets while dropping "Coffee" enables the company to move away for being recognized as a coffee company. (4)

BRANDING STRATEGY

With competition growing more intense in almost all industries, establishing a strong brand allows an organization's products to stand out and avoid potential pitfalls, such as price wars. A clear understanding of branding is essential in order to build a solid product strategy. Marketers should be aware of various branding approaches that can be pursued and deployed to establish a product within the market. The purpose of these approaches is to build a brand that will exist for the long term. Making smart branding decisions in the early stages of a new product is crucial since a company may have to live with the decision for a long time.

Branding approaches include:

- Individual Product Branding – With this branding approach, new products are assigned new names with no obvious connection to a company's existing brands. Under individual product branding, the marketing organization must work hard to establish the brand in the market since it cannot ride the coattails of previously introduced brands. The chief advantage of this approach is it allows brands to stand on their own. This lessens threats that may occur to other brands marketed by the company. For instance, if a company receives negative publicity for one brand this news is less likely to influence the company's other brands since these carry their own unique names. Under an individual branding approach, each brand builds its own separate equity (see *Brand Equity* discussion below), which allows the company to potentially sell off individual brands without impacting other brands owned by the company. The most famous marketing organization to follow this strategy is Procter & Gamble, which has historically introduced new brands without any link to other brands or even to the company name. (5)

- Family Branding – Under this branding approach, new products are placed under the umbrella of an existing brand. The principle advantage of family branding is it enables rapid building of market awareness and acceptance, since the brand is already established and known to the market. The potential disadvantage is that the market already has established perceptions of the brand. For instance, a company selling low-end, lower priced products may have a brand viewed as an economy brand. If the company attempts to introduce higher-end, higher priced products using the same brand name this may create customer confusion and hinder sales. Additionally, any negative publicity for one product within a brand family could spread to all other products that share the same brand name.

- Co-Branding – This approach takes the idea of individual and family branding a step further. With co-branding, a marketer seeks to partner with another firm, which has an established brand, in hopes the synergy of two brands on a product is more powerful than a single brand. The partnership often has both firms sharing costs but also sharing the gains. For instance, major credit card companies, such as Visa and MasterCard, offer co-branding options to companies and organizations. The cards carry the name of a co-branded organization (e.g., university name) along with the name of the issuing bank (e.g., Citibank) and the name of the credit card company. Besides tapping into awareness for multiple brands, the co-branding strategy is designed to appeal to a larger target market, especially if each brand, when viewed separately, does not have extensive overlapping target markets with their co-brand partner. Therefore, co-branding allows both firms to tap into market segments where they previously did not have a strong position.

- Private Label or Store Branding – Some suppliers are in the business of producing products for other companies, including placing another company's brand name on the product. This is most often seen in the retail industry where stores or online sellers contract with suppliers to manufacture the retailer's own branded products. In some cases, the supplier not only produces products for the retailer's brand but also markets its own brand so that store shelves will contain both brands. In recent years, the rapid growth of private label products has resulted in more shelf space being dedicated to these products and less to branded products. (6)

- No-Name or Generic Branding – Certain suppliers provide products that are intentionally "**brandless**." These products are mostly basic commodity-type products consumer or business customers purchase as low price alternatives to branded products. Basic household products, such as paper goods, over-the-counter medicines, and even dog food are available in a generic form.

- Brand Licensing – Under brand licensing, a contractual arrangement is created in which a company owning a brand name allows others to produce and supply products carrying the brand name. This is often seen when a brand is not directly connected with a product category. For instance, several famous children's characters, such as Sesame Street's Elmo, have been licensed to toy and food manufacturers who market products using the branded character's name and image.

ADVANTAGES OF BRANDS

A strong brand offers many advantages for marketers including:

- Enhances Product Recognition – Brands provide multiple sensory stimuli to enhance customer recognition. A brand can be visually recognizable from its packaging, logo, shape, etc. It can be recognizable via sound, such as hearing the name on a radio advertisement or verbally when someone mentions the product.

- Builds Brand Equity – Strong brands can lead to financial advantages through the concept of brand equity in which the brand itself becomes valuable. Such gains can be realized through the out-right sale of a brand or through licensing arrangements.

- <u>Helps Build Brand Loyalty</u> – **Brand loyal** customers are frequent and enthusiastic purchasers of a particular brand. Cultivating brand loyalty among customers is the ultimate reward for successful marketers since these customers are far less likely to switch to other brands compared to non-loyal customers.

- <u>Helps with Product Positioning</u> – Well-developed and promoted brands make product positioning efforts more effective. The result is that upon exposure to a brand (e.g., hearing it, seeing it) customers conjure up mental images or feelings of the benefits of that brand. The reverse is even better. When customers associate benefits with a particular brand, the brand may have attained a significant competitive advantage. In these situations the customer who recognizes he needs a solution to a problem (e.g., needs to bleach clothes) may automatically think of one brand that offers the solution to the problem (e.g., Clorox). This "benefit = brand" association provides a significant advantage for the brand.

- <u>Aids in Introduction of New Products</u> – A successful brand can be extended by adding new products under the earlier discussed Family Branding strategy. Such branding may allow companies to introduce new products more easily since the brand is already recognized within the market.

BRAND EQUITY

For marketers, intellectual property (see Box 6-2), particularly trademarks, is important in building brand identity. As we discussed, a uniquely identified brand, that is well known to a target market, may occupy a position in the minds of customers that sets it apart from other brands (e.g., Apple computers vs. PC computers) or associates it with a specific benefit (e.g., digital music player = Apple iPod). By doing this, the marketer is creating a company asset from a recognizable name, symbol or other unique feature. Called brand equity, the marketer's work can lead to an asset that can grow in value and eventually offer the company a financial reward.

For example, Company A may have a well-recognized brand (Brand X) within a market, yet they have decided to concentrate efforts in other markets. Company B is looking to enter the same market as Brand X. If circumstances are right, Company A could sell to Company B the rights to use the Brand X name without selling any other part of the company. That is, Company A simply sells the legal rights to the Brand X name while retaining all other parts of Brand X, such as the production facilities and employees. In cases of well developed brands, this kind of transaction may carry a large price tag. Thus, through strong branding efforts Company A achieves a large financial gain by simply signing over the rights to the brand name.

But why would Company B seek to purchase a brand for such a high price tag? Because, by buying the brand Company B has already achieved a significant marketing goal – building awareness within the target market. The fact the market is already familiar with the brand allows Company B to concentrate on other marketing decisions.

Brand equity almost always requires the establishment of a trademarked brand name or other identifiable image, such as a logo. In Wisconsin, Al Johnson's Swedish Restaurant has registered a unique aspect of their business – goats on the roof. The restaurant uses the concept of goats in its promotion and as part of the overall ambiance of their building. They actively protect the trademark including filing a cease-and-desist lawsuit against a restaurant in Georgia that also had goats grazing on its roof. (7)

Box 6-2

BRANDS AND INTELLECTUAL PROPERTY

When most people think of a business asset they generally think of machinery, computers, buildings, and other physical items purchased and used by a business. But companies can also create and grow their own assets that are, in essence, intangible. These assets principally exist as legally protected "rights" that often prevent others from doing the same thing. If managed well, such rights can become enormously valuable.

In marketing, the most likely source for acquiring protected rights is through government-controlled registration systems collectively referred to as intellectual property. Intellectual property provides protection in four ways (8):

Patent
Offers legal protection for inventions, such as new products, preventing others from offering the same product for a specified period of time. For example, a company may develop certain features in a product that others can not include in their product for the period of the patent which may be as long as 20 years.

Trademark
Offers legal protection on unique words, names, symbols, and other identifiable features that distinguish one item from another. For example, a product's name, the design of a logo, special symbols, and even characters associated with a brand can be trademarked.

Copyright
Offers legal protection for original authored work, such as writings and recordings. For example, in addition to protecting authors of books and music, copyright can also be used to protect website materials, music tied to product advertising, and print advertising copy.

Trade Secret
Offers legal protection for information, tightly protected by a company, which is used within the regular course of doing business and intended to give a company an advantage over competitors. For example, the formula used to produce Coca-Cola is protected as a trade secret.

Marketing Story

From Retired Brands, Dollars and Memories
New York Times

A well-marketed, recognizable brand can often obtain financial benefits in which the name of the brand becomes a valuable commodity. That is, the name, exclusive of the actual product, has value. When this happens the marketer is said to possess a product with significant brand equity. For instance, just think how much value there is in the brand name, iPod. Because this name is so well known, anyone using this name to sell digital music devices would realize tremendous consumer awareness.

Obviously, Apple is not about to let others use their iPod brand name. Apple, like most marketers, is highly protective of its brand names and the equity these have created. They control these legally by obtaining trademarks and enforce their names by threatening lawsuits against potential violators.

Brand equity is greatest when a product is a current market leader, yet it is possible for equity to extend well beyond a product's life. This can be seen when a product is no longer being sold either because it is a retired brand, or because the brand suffered financially and eventually went out of business. So even though a product may be off the market for several years, as long as customers recognize the brand a marketer may still reap value from the name.

A case in point can be found in this story which reports on just how valuable some old brand names may be. The story discusses an auction in which bidders are bidding on previously established and trademarked brand names. However, the owners of the original trademarks have let these names lapse, and now a speculator has filed for use of the names. At the auction, the speculator sold the rights to the application for the trademark. In other words, the trademarks have not actually been awarded, only an intention to use the name has been filed. But, this did not prevent many from seeing future value in the old brand names.

It featured names in categories like beverages (Meister Brau beer, Snow Crop frozen orange juice) financial services (the Kuhn Loeb and Shearson brokerage firms), packaged foods (Allsweet margarine, Lucky Whip dessert topping), personal care (Mum and Stopette deodorants), publishing (Collier's, Saturday Review) and retail (Computer City, Phar-Mor). (9)

For those who were successful in their bid, what risks are associated with their purchase?

Packaging

Nearly all tangible products (i.e., goods) are sold to customers in a container or package that serves many purposes, including protecting the product during shipment. In a few cases, such as with certain produce items, the final customer may purchase the product without a package, but the produce marketer still faces packaging decisions when it comes to shipping its produce to others, such as resellers. Consequently, for many products there are two packaging decisions – final customer package and distribution package.

Final Customer Package

This relates to the package the final customer receives in exchange for his/her payment. When the final customer makes a purchase he or she is initially exposed to the outermost container holding the product. This exterior package generally contains product information (see *Labeling* discussion below), graphic design (e.g., logo, colors scheme), special handling features (e.g., a carrying handle), and other characteristics.

Depending on the type of product being purchased, there may be several components to the package holding the product. These components can be divided into the following:

- First-Level Package – This is packaging that holds the consumable product (e.g., Tylenol bottle holding tablets). In some cases, this packaging is minimal since it only serves to protect the product. For instance, certain frozen food products are sold to consumers in a cardboard box with the product itself contained in a plastic bag found inside the box. This plastic bag represents the first-level package. In other cases, frozen food products are sold to final customers only in plastic bags. In these cases, the plastic bag is the only packaging obtained by the customer.

- Second-Level Package – For some products, the first-level package is surrounded by one or more outer packages (e.g., box holding the Tylenol Bottle). This second-level package would then serve as the exterior package for the product.

- Package Inserts – Marketers use a variety of other methods to communicate with customers after they open the product package. These methods are often inserted within, or sometimes on, the product's package. Insertions include information, including instruction manuals and warranty cards; promotional incentives, including coupons; and items that add value, including recipes and software.

Distribution Package

This packaging is used to transport the final customer package through the supply chain. It generally holds multiple final customer packages and offers a higher level of damage protection than that of customer packaging. The most obvious examples are card board boxes and wooden crates.

FACTORS TO CONSIDER WHEN MAKING PACKAGING DECISIONS

Packaging decisions are crucial for several reasons, including:

- Protection – Packaging is used to protect the product from damage during shipping and handling, and to lessen spoilage if the product is exposed to air or other elements. Products being shipped long distances, such as overseas, are more likely to require more durable packaging in order to protect the product from damaged that can occur due to potential temperature fluctuations and repeated handling.

- Visibility – Packaging design is used to capture customers' attention as they are shopping or glancing through a catalog or website. This is particularly useful for customers who are not familiar with the product and in situations where a product must stand out among thousands of other products, such as those found in grocery stores. Packaging designs that standout are more likely to be remembered on future shopping trips.

A key decision in package is design is choosing the right colors. Research shows color has a significant emotional influence and some believe it represents the first point of interaction customers have with a product. Because of this, researchers suggest color decisions should not be left up to designers, but must be viewed as more of a business decision involving customer research in order to determine the right colors to use in packaging design. (10)

- Added Value – Packaging design and structure can add value to a product. For instance, benefits can be obtained from package structures that make the product easier to use while stylistic designs can make the product more attractive to display in the customer's home.

- Distributor Acceptance – A packaging decision must not only be accepted by the final customer, it may also have to be accepted by distributors who sell the product for the marketer. For instance, a retailer may not accept a product unless the packaging conforms to requirements the retailers has for storing products on its shelves.

- Cost – Packaging can represent a significant portion of a product's selling price. For example, in the cosmetics industry, it is estimated that packaging cost of some products may be as high as 40 percent of a product's selling price. Smart packaging decisions can help reduce costs and possibly lead to higher profits.

- Expensive to Create – Developing new packaging can be extremely expensive. The costs involved in creating new packaging include: graphic and structural design, production, customer testing, possible destruction of leftover old packaging, and possible advertising to inform customers of the new packaging.

- Long-Term Decision – When companies create a new package it is most often with the intention of having the design on the market for an extended period of time. In fact, changing a product's packaging too frequently can have negative effects since customers become conditioned to locating the product based on its package and may be confused if the design is altered.

- Environmental or Legal Issues – Packaging decisions must also include an assessment of its environmental impact especially for products with packages that are frequently discarded. Packages that are not easily biodegradable could draw customer and governmental reaction. Also, caution must be exercised in order to create packages that do not infringe on another firm's intellectual property, such as copyrights, trademarks or patents.

Marketing Story

Brands Without Borders
Brand Packaging

When it comes to product decisions, many consumer products marketers do not devote enough attention to elements of the package that will contain the main product. In particular, they fail to consider the importance of the outer or second-level package that may be the first experience a customer has with the product.

The lack of attention to packaging decisions is particularly an issue with products sold on a global scale. For some marketers, there is not much thought placed in whether a product should be packaged differently for each market. Instead, apart from using the local language on the package, product design is pretty much the same for all global markets in which the product is sold.

However, marketers selling internationally need to do much more with their packaging than simply change the language. Packaging decisions must be in tune with such issues as how the target market purchases, transports, uses, and stores the product. For instance, depending on the country, consumer products may be sold in different types of outlets.

For example, in one country the marketer's product may be sold in high-end retail outlets where products are spaced apart and customers spend considerable time browsing store aisles. In these countries, because of extended customer shopping time and product spacing, packaging can be rich in the information it provides as customers have longer eye-contact with the product.

Yet, in other countries the product may predominately be available in much smaller, congested outlets where it is difficult for the product to stand out. In these markets, it may be best if packaging contains much less information and, instead, focuses on the package colors, product image, and simple attention-grabbing information.

As this story notes, there are many different packaging issues marketers face when selling globally. And, rarely is a one-for-all packaging approach a good idea.

The net is that any global design system must be tailored to work across a wide range of retail formats. Mandating a "template" (without appropriate adaptation) is very likely to result in packaging that doesn't work on shelf or, for that matter, in the home. (11)

Of all the elements that make up a package, which one is likely to be the easiest to adapt to global markets? Which is likely to be the most difficult?

Frito-Lays' intention to provide its SunChips snacks in biodegradable packaging proved more difficult than expected. What is most interesting is the problem is not due to one of the main factors marketers general consider when it comes to package design (e.g., product protection, visibility, cost, etc.). Instead, the problem is with customers' response to their experience with the package. Namely, customers did not like the perceived loud noise that resulted from handling the snack's bag. (12)

Labeling

Most packages, whether final customer packaging or distribution packaging, are imprinted with information intended to assist customers and distributors. For consumer products, careful focus on labeling decisions is needed for the following reasons:

♦ Captures Attention - Labels serve to capture the attention of shoppers. The use of catchy words and graphics may cause strolling customers to stop and evaluate the product.

♦ Offers First Impression - The label is likely to be the first thing a new customer sees leading to his/her first impression of the product.

♦ Provides Information - The label provides customers with product information to aid their purchase decision or help improve customers' experience when using the product (e.g., recipes).

♦ Aids Purchasing - Labels generally include a universal product codes (UPC) and, in some cases, radio frequency identification (RFID) tags, making it easy for resellers, such as retailers, to process customers' purchases and manage inventory.

♦ Addresses Needs in Global Markets - For companies serving international markets or diverse cultures within a single country, bilingual or multilingual labels may be needed.

♦ Meets Legal Requirements - In some countries, certain products, including food and pharmaceuticals, are required by law to contain certain labels, such as listing ingredients, providing nutritional information, or including usage warning information.

Warning labels are common on a large cross-section of products. For many companies, these labels are included as a protection against legal action that may occur by someone sustaining an injury when using their product. However, some see warning labels as going too far by covering usage situations that border on the absurd. For instance, sleep aid Nytol warns the product may cause drowsiness; Vidal Sassoon warns not to use their hair dryer while sleeping; and the maker of Vanishing Fabric Markers warns consumers not to use its marker for signing checks or legal document. (13)

II

REFERENCES

1. Enright, A., "Classy Examples*,*" *Internet Retailer*, May 31, 2011.

2. Elliott, S., "The Impulse to Buy Can Start Anywhere," *New York Times*, December 19, 2010.

3. "This Does Not Compute: More technology = More Complaints," *Consumer Reports*, May 2010.

4. "Logo Overhaul: Will Customers Still Answer the Siren Call of Starbucks?" *Knowledge@ Wharton*, February 2, 2011.

5. *Procter & Gamble* website.

6. "Global Private Label Report: The Rise of the Value-Conscious Shopper," *Nielsen*, March 4, 2011.

7. Scheck, J. and S. Woo, "Lars Johnson Has Goats on His Roof and a Stable of Lawyers to Prove It," *Wall Street Journal*, September 17, 2010.

8. "What is Intellectual Property?" *United States Patent and Trademark Office* website.

9. Elliott, S., "From Retired Brands, Dollars and Memories," *New York Times*, December 8, 2010.

10. Markowitz, E., "How to Choose the Right Colors for Your Brand," *Inc. Magazine*, October 14, 2010.

11. Young, S., "Brands Without Borders," *Brand Packaging*, November 5, 2010.

12. Horovitz, B., "Frito-Lay Sends Noisy, 'Green' SunChips Bag to the Dump," *USA Today*, October 5, 2010.

13. Nelson, B. and K. Finneran, "Dumbest Warning Labels," *Forbes*, February 23, 2011.

Full text of many of the references can be accessed via links on the support website.

Chapter 7: Managing Products

In Chapter 6, we saw how marketers are confronted with many issues when building the product component of their marketing strategy. While product decisions represent just one aspect of marketers' overall activities, these decisions are often the most critical because they lead directly to the reasons (i.e., benefits offered, solutions to problems) why the customer decides to choose the organization's goods, services, or ideas.

In this chapter, we extend the coverage of product decisions by exploring additional product issues facing the marketer. First, we look at how companies structure their product offerings and identify the scope of a manager's responsibilities within this structure. Second, we spend a large part of this chapter covering the importance of new product development, including an analysis of the steps firms may follow to bring new products to market. Finally, we show once new products have been established in the market numerous factors force the marketer to adjust its product decisions. As part of this, we examine the concept of the Product Life Cycle and see how it offers valuable insight and guidance for new product decisions.

||||||||||||||||||||||||||||||||||||||||||||||||||||||||||||||||||||||||||||||||||||||||||||||||||||||||||||||||||

STRUCTURE OF PRODUCT MANAGEMENT

Marketers are often responsible for a wide array of decisions required to manage a company's product offerings. As we will discuss shortly, these decisions include both creation of new products and management of existing products. But what a marketer does on a day-to-day basis will depend on how a company structures the management of its products. Possible structures include:

PRODUCT ITEM MANAGEMENT

At this level, responsibilities are associated with marketing a single product or brand. By "single" we are limiting the marketer's responsibility to one item. For instance, a startup software development company may initially market just one product. In some organizations, the person in charge has the title Product Manager, though in smaller companies this person may simply be the Marketing Manager.

BRAND PRODUCT LINE MANAGEMENT

At this level, responsibilities are associated with managing two or more similar product items. By "similar" we are referring to products carrying the same brand name that fit within the same product category and offer similar solutions to customers' needs. Procter & Gamble, one of the largest consumer products companies in the world, markets Tide laundry detergent in many different packaging sizes (e.g., 50oz., 100oz., 150oz.), in different forms (e.g., regular powder, powder packs, high efficiency liquid), and with different added features (e.g., softener, bleach, freshener) resulting in a product line consisting of over 100 different versions of the product. (1) Differences in the product offerings indicate these are targeted to different segments within the larger market (e.g., those preferring liquid vs. those preferring powder), however, it may also represent a choice for the same target market who may seek variety. A product line is measured by its depth, relative to competitors, with deep product lines offering extensive product options. Brand product lines are often managed by a Brand or Product Line Manager.

CATEGORY PRODUCT LINE MANAGEMENT

At this level, responsibilities are associated with managing two or more brand product lines within the same product category. In this situation the marketer may manage products offering similar basic benefits (e.g., detergent to clean clothes) but target its offerings to slightly different needs (e.g., product for tough to clean clothing vs. product to clean delicate clothing). Multiple brand product lines allow the marketer to cover the needs of more segments and, consequently, increase its chance to generate sales. Often in larger companies, category product lines are the responsibility of the Product Category or Divisional Marketing Manager who may have several Brand Product Managers reporting to him/her.

PRODUCT MIX MANAGEMENT

At this level, responsibilities include two or more category product lines directed to different product categories. In some cases the category product lines may yield similar general solutions (e.g., cleaning) but are aimed at entirely different target markets (e.g., cleaning dishes vs. cleaning automobiles). In large companies, the product lines are often diverse and offer different solutions. For example, BIC sells writing instruments, shaving products, and butane lighters. (2) This diversification strategy cushions against an "all-eggs-in-one-basket" risk that may come if a company directs all resources to one product category. A product mix can be classified based on its **width** (how many different category product lines) and its **depth** (how many different brand product lines within a category product line). In most situations, responsibility for this level belongs to a company's Vice President for Marketing.

For those seeking information on marketing careers in the U.S., several websites offer information on different career options. These websites include: 1) Salary.com, which offers salary information by job title (3), and 2) the Occupational Employment Statistics section of the U.S. Department of Labor, which offers employment totals and salary information. (4)

MANAGING NEW PRODUCTS

By its nature marketing requires new ideas and successful marketers are constantly making adjustments to their marketing efforts. New ideas are essential for responding to changing market demand and competitive pressure. The reasons for developing new products will vary by company and industry. Yet, for most organizations, the motivation to develop new products is a direct result of the need to respond to one or more of the following situations:

♦ Customers Change - Over time customers' needs may evolve. What attracted customer interest in the past is not guaranteed to do the same in the future. This is especially the case for products targeted to narrow age groups where not only are customers' needs changing but customers themselves change. For example, Nickelodeon, a cable television network targeted to young children and teenagers, faces a situation where customers are only in their target market for 10 to 12 years (from young child to early teen). The constant influx of new customers, along with continually losing existing customers, requires frequent evaluation of programming to ensure the network is meeting the needs of an ever changing target market.

♦ Attract Different Customers - Almost all companies face a point at which appealing to the current target market is not enough to grow the business. Instead, the company must attract different customers who are not yet major purchasers of the company's products. To appeal to new customers often requires a different set of products.

Mercedes-Benz discovered the average age of its car buyers in the U.S. was older than buyers of cars sold by key competitors BMW and Audi. To attract younger buyers, Mercedes completely redesigned its C-Class automobile with elements intended to appeal to much younger buyers. (5)

♦ Profit in Newer Products - Many new products earn higher profits than older products. This is often the case for products considered innovative or unique which may enjoy success and initially face little or no competition.

♦ Keep Ahead of Competition - Fierce global competition and technological developments make it much easier for competitors to learn about products and replicate them. In other instances, marketers may find their own brands are being duplicated by unapproved manufacturers, especially in foreign markets. These "**knockoff**" products are then sold to unwitting customers. To stay ahead of true competitors and product duplicators, requires marketers to innovate with new offerings.

♦ Helps with Repositioning - New products can help reposition the company in customers' minds. For instance, a company with a reputation for selling low-priced products with few features may shift customers' perceptions by introducing products with more features and slightly higher pricing.

♦ Fill Out Product Line - Companies with limited product line depth may miss out on more sales unless they add new products to fill out the line. For example, companies may have a strong high-end and high priced product but lack a good quality, mid-price offering.

♦ Expand Product Mix - Some firms market seasonal products that garner their highest sales during a certain time of the year or sell cyclical products whose sales fluctuate depending on economic or market factors. Expanding the firm's product mix into new areas may help offset these fluctuations. For manufacturing firms, an additional benefit is realized as new products utilize existing production capacity that is under-used when seasonal or cyclical products are not being produced.

Categories of New Products

New products fall into several categories defined by: 1) the type of market the product is entering, which includes newly created, existing but not previously targeted, or existing and previously targeted, and 2) the level of product innovation, which includes radically new, new, or upgrade.

Creates New Market with Radically New Product

This category is represented by new breakthrough products that are so revolutionary they create an entirely new market. A relatively recent example is the Segway Personal Transporter. (6) Highly innovative products are rare so very few new products fall into this category.

Enters Existing but Not Previously Targeted Market with New Product

In this category, a marketer introduces a new product or product line to an existing market which they did not previously target. Often these products are similar to competitors' products already available in the market but with some level of difference (e.g., different features, lower price, etc.). Under Armour's introduction of athletic apparel aimed at the women's market is an example. (7)

Stays in Existing and Previously Targeted Market with New or Improved Product

Under this category, the marketer attempts to improve its current market position by improving or upgrading existing products or by extending a product line by adding new products. This type of new product is seen in our earlier example of Procter & Gamble's Tide product line, which contains many product variations.

Marketing Story

From Four Wheels to Two: Has Mini Gone Too Far?

Time

One of the most difficult decisions facing marketers is figuring out how to grow their business beyond what originally made them successful. For most marketers, there comes a time when the products that led to initial success have hit their peak and a decision has to be made on how to grow the company further.

Many marketers, who see product sales stagnate, will often look to make changes to the product (e.g., new features, target new market, introduce lower-price models) in order to keep sales going.

But, sometimes the company can no longer expect its key products to grow, no matter what changes are made. At this point, they often consider whether growth can be achieved by introducing entirely new products. If so, they must decide whether to leverage the existing brand name for the new product or develop a new name.

This is what seems to be occurring with the Mini Cooper car brand owned by BMW. As discussed in this story, Mini is launching what would appear to be an entirely new product in the form of an electric scooter. However, even though they are perceived as a car company, Mini is applying its brand to the scooters. Considering that, for over 50 years, the brand has been associated with automobiles, attaching the name to scooters has caught many by surprise, thus raising questions.

Critics charge that BMW, which acquired Mini, is pushing the brand too far; appreciators are singing the scooter's praises for its eco-credentials. But all are asking: When is a Mini not a Mini? (8)

Consumers have long associated the Mini brand name with automobiles. What will the company need to do in order to change this?

How New Products Are Obtained

Marketers have several options for obtaining new products. First, products can be developed within an organization's own research operations. For some companies, such as service firms, this may simply mean the marketer designs new service options to sell to target markets. For instance, a marketer for a mortgage company may design new mortgage packages offering borrowers different rates or payment options. At the other extreme companies may support an extensive research and development effort, where engineers, scientists, or others are engaged in new product discovery.

A second way to obtain products is to acquire them from external sources. This can occur in several ways, including:

♦ Purchase the Product – With this option, a marketer purchases the product out-right from another firm that currently owns the product. The advantage is the product is already developed, which reduces the purchasing company's time and potential costs related to developing it themselves. The disadvantage is the purchase cost may be high and, under some conditions, the purchase may not include valuable assets (e.g., equipment, facilities, people) associated with the product.

♦ License the Product – Under this option, the marketer negotiates with the owner of the product for the rights to market the product. This may be a particularly attractive option for companies who have to fill a new product need quickly (e.g., give a product line more depth) or it may be used as a temporary source of products while the marketer's company is developing its own product. On the negative side, the arrangement may have a limited timeframe at which point the licensor may decide to end the relationship leaving the marketer without a source for the product.

♦ Purchase Another Firm – Instead of purchasing another company's products marketers may find it easier just to purchase the whole company owning the products. One key advantage to this is that the acquisition often includes the people and resources that developed the products, which may be a key consideration if the acquiring company wants to continue to develop the acquired products.

A number of companies are experimenting with product development methods that combine both internal and external development. One method for doing this is by using promotional contests to get customers to offer their own product design ideas. When Baskin-Robbins did this, over 40,000 customers offered recipes for a new ice cream flavor. The winner was a 62-year old grandmother whose product was added to the ice-cream chain's stores around the U.S. (9).

New Product Development Process

Because introducing new products is necessary to the future success of many organizations, marketers in charge of product decisions often follow set procedures for bringing products to market. In the scientific area this may mean the establishment of ongoing laboratory research programs for discovering new products (e.g., medicines), while other industries may pull together resources for product development on a less structured basis.

In this section, we present a 7-step process comprising the key elements of new product development. While some companies may not follow a deliberate step-by-step approach, the steps are useful in showing the information input and the decisions required to develop new products successfully. The process also shows the importance marketing research plays in developing products.

However, while the new product development process offers insight into how products come to market, marketers should also understand potential limitations with this approach that include:

♦ Developing Radically New Products - While the 7-step process works for most industries, it is less effective in developing radically new products (see *Categories of New Products* discussion above). This is due to the target market's inability to provide sufficient feedback on advanced product concepts, as they often find it difficult to understand radically different ideas. So, while many of these steps are used to research breakthrough ideas, the marketer of radically new products should exercise caution when interpreting the results.

♦ New Product Development in Less Developed Markets - Marketers should recognize that it may be more difficult to obtain significant marketing research information in less developed countries compared to what can be obtained in more developed markets. Often this is due to the lack of a reliable communication infrastructure. Though it may not be possible to gain the same level of market analysis in less developed markets, some level of marketing research should still be considered as even a small amount of research may prove to be effective.

STEP 1: IDEA GENERATION

The first step of new product development requires gathering ideas to be evaluated as potential product options. For many companies, idea generation is an ongoing process with contributions from inside and outside the organization.

Many marketing research techniques are used to encourage ideas including:

- running focus groups with consumers, channel members, and the company's sales force

- encouraging customer comments and suggestions via toll-free telephone numbers, email, social media postings or online discussion forums

- gaining insight on competitive product developments through secondary data sources

One effective research technique used to generate ideas is **brainstorming,** where open-minded, creative thinkers from inside and outside the company gather and share ideas. The dynamic nature of group members floating ideas, where one idea often sparks another idea, can yield a wide range of possible products that can be further explored.

> *Design firm Ideo, whose clients have included such firms as Apple and Fisher-Price, has embraced brainstorming as its principle technique for developing new product ideas. The ideas associated with this research technique are so ingrained in the corporate culture that they include their rules for brainstorming on company business cards. (10)*

STEP 2: SCREENING

In Step 2, the ideas generated in Step 1 are critically evaluated by company personnel to isolate the most attractive options. Depending on the number of ideas, screening may be done in rounds with the first round involving company executives judging the feasibility of ideas while successive rounds may utilize more advanced research techniques. As the ideas are whittled down to a few attractive options, rough estimates are made of an idea's potential in terms of sales, production costs, profit potential, and competitors' response if the product is introduced. Acceptable ideas move on to the next step.

STEP 3: CONCEPT DEVELOPMENT AND TESTING

With a few ideas in hand, the marketer now seeks initial feedback from customers, distributors, and its own employees. Generally, focus groups are convened where the ideas are presented to a group, often in the form of **concept board** or **storyboard** presentations. For instance, customers may be shown a concept board displaying drawings of a product idea or even an advertisement featuring the product. In some cases, focus groups are exposed to a **mock-up** of the idea, which is a physical but, in most cases, a nonfunctional version of the product concept. During focus groups with customers, the marketer seeks information including: likes and dislikes of the concept, level of interest in purchasing the product, frequency of purchase (used to help forecast demand), and price points to determine how much customers are willing to spend to acquire the product.

STEP 4: BUSINESS ANALYSIS

At this point in the new product development process, the marketer has reduced a large number of ideas down to one or two options. Now in Step 4 the process becomes highly dependent on marketing research as efforts are made to analyze the viability of the product ideas. The key objective at this stage is to obtain useful forecasts of market size (e.g., overall demand), operational costs (e.g., production costs), and financial projections (e.g., sales and profits). Additionally, the organization must determine if the product fits within the company's overall mission and strategy. Much effort is directed at both internal research, such as discussions with production and purchasing personnel, and external marketing research, such as customer and distributor surveys, secondary research, and competitor analysis.

STEP 5: PRODUCT AND MARKETING MIX DEVELOPMENT

Ideas passing through business analysis are given serious consideration for development. Companies direct their research and development teams to construct an initial design or **prototype** of the idea. Marketers begin to construct a Marketing Plan for the product (see *The Marketing Plan* discussion in Chapter 20). Once the prototype is ready, the marketer seeks customer input. However, unlike the concept testing stage, where customers were only exposed to the idea, in this step the customer gets to experience the real product as well as other aspects of the marketing effort, such as advertising, pricing, and distribution options (e.g., retail store, direct from company, etc.). Favorable customer reaction helps solidify the marketer's decision to introduce the product and provides other valuable information, such as estimated purchase rates and understanding how the customer will use the product. Less favorable reaction may suggest the need for adjustments to elements of the Marketing Plan. Once these are made the marketer may have the customer test the product again. In addition to gaining customer feedback, this step is used to gauge the feasibility of large-scale, cost-effective production for manufactured products.

STEP 6: MARKET TESTING

Products surviving to Step 6 are ready to be tested. While, in some cases, the marketer accepts what was learned from concept testing (see Step 3) and skips over market testing to launch the idea as a fully marketed product, many companies will seek more input from a larger group before moving to commercialization (see Step 7). The most common type of market testing, used especially for consumer products sold at retail stores, uses methods that make the product available to a selective, small segment of the target market (e.g., one city). This market is then exposed to a full marketing effort, just as they would be to most other products they could purchase. In **conventional test markets**, the marketer must work hard to get the product into the market by convincing distributors to purchase and place the product on their store shelves. In more **controlled test markets** distributors may be paid a fee if they agree to place the product on their shelves for testing. Another form of market testing for consumer products is even more controlled with customers recruited to a "laboratory" store where they are given shopping instructions. Product interest is then measured based on customers' shopping responses. Finally, there are several high-tech approaches to market testing including virtual reality and computer simulations. With **virtual reality testing** customers are exposed to a computer-projected environment and asked to locate and select products. With **computer simulation testing** customers may not be directly involved at all. Instead, certain variables are entered into a sophisticated computer program and estimates of a target market's response are calculated.

> *Would anyone really be interested in a 12 inch burger? Apparently the company that operates fast food restaurants Hardees and Carl's Jr. thinks there is a market for such a massive sandwich. To find out whether their main target market of 18-24 year old, young men would be interested, they test marketed the 850 calorie sandwich in 50 stores in California and another 50 stores in Indiana. (11)*

STEP 7: COMMERCIALIZATION

If market testing displays promising results, the product is ready for market introduction. Some firms introduce or roll-out the product in waves with different parts of the market receiving the product on different schedules. This allows the company to ramp up production in a more controlled way and to fine-tune marketing decisions as the product is distributed to new areas.

MANAGING EXISTING PRODUCTS

Marketing strategies developed for initial product introduction almost certainly need to be revised as the product settles into the market. While commercialization may be the last step in the new product development process, it is just the beginning of managing the product. Adjusting the product's marketing strategy is required for many reasons including:

♦ changing customer tastes

♦ domestic and foreign competitors

♦ economic conditions

♦ technological advances

Marketing Story

Inventions That Were Accidents
Forbes

In order to sustain growth in the face of stiff competition, most companies find they have little choice but to continually find new products. For some companies, this means looking for products outside the organization, such as by purchasing or licensing products created by other companies. However, for the vast majority of firms, the search for new products is an ongoing internal process requiring a collaborative effort involving potentially hundreds of employees from different functional areas, such as research and development, business operations, finance, and, of course, marketing.

Yet, even with a dedicated development plan in place, most companies will discover in-house efforts for creating new products are risky. The success rate for new product development is often quite low, with few ideas actually reaching the testing stage. But, some companies find failure is sometimes a good thing. How can this be?

Well, sometimes failure of one idea leads to success for another idea. This can occur when the marketer is looking for one type of product only to find another product has evolved. Some examples of products that were not part of the original product development idea phase are found in this story. Among the products discussed are Kleenex, Kotex, Ivory Soap, Popsicle and Zout.

Overall, this story provides clear examples of why companies need to have an open mind with what they develop. Sometimes marketers have products showing little promise in one area but possessing potential if marketed for solving a different need.

The story also provides insight into the accidental development of several other products including chewing gum, potato chips and chocolate chip cookies.

Kimberly-Clark's famous facial tissue brand started life as a cold cream remover. But Ernest Mahler, a hay fever sufferer who ran K-C's research, technical and engineering departments, started using it as a disposable handkerchief, and then he realized he could sell it for that new use. (12)

Besides the products discussed in this story, what other products were developed by accident or found success when marketed for different uses?

> *Car rental company Rent-a-Wreck has found that it needs to update its product offering in order to expand its market and attract more customers. While the company's roots are in renting older used cars at low prices, the company is now offering higher-end cars in an effort to compete against industry leaders, such as Avis and Hertz. However, unlike leading rental companies, which purchase new cars, Rent-a-Wreck only purchase used luxury cars which they then can rent at lower rates. (13)*

To stay on top of all possible threats, the marketer must monitor all aspects of the marketing strategy and make changes as needed. Such efforts require the development and refinement of the product's Marketing Plan on a regular basis. In fact, marketing strategies change as a product moves through time leading to the concept called the Product Life Cycle.

The Product Life Cycle

The basic premise of the Product Life Cycle (PLC) is that products go through several stages of "life" with each stage presenting the marketer with different challenges that must be met with different marketing approaches. For example, marketers may find what works when appealing to customers early in the life of a product may be different than marketing methods used to attract customers in later stages.

There have been several attempts over the years to define the stages that make up the PLC. Unfortunately, the PLC may be different for different products, different markets, and different market conditions (e.g., economic forces). Consequently, there is not a one-model-fits-all PLC. Yet there is enough evidence to suggest most products and product groups (see Box 7-1) experience patterns of activity that divide the evolution of the product into five distinct stages. As shown in Figure 7-1 these stages are:

♦ Development – Occurs before the product is released to the market and is principally a time for honing the product offering and preparing the market for product introduction.

♦ Introduction – Product is released to the market and sales begin though often gradually as the market becomes aware of the product.

♦ Growth – If the product is accepted it may reach a stage of rapid growth in sales and profits.

♦ Maturity – At some point sales of a product may stabilize. For some products, the maturity phase can be the longest stage as the product is repeatedly purchased by loyal customers. However, while overall sales may grow year-over-year, sales in terms of percentage increase may be small compared to previous years.

♦ Decline – All products eventually see demand decline as customers no longer see value in purchasing the product.

Figure 7-1: Stages of the Product Life Cycle

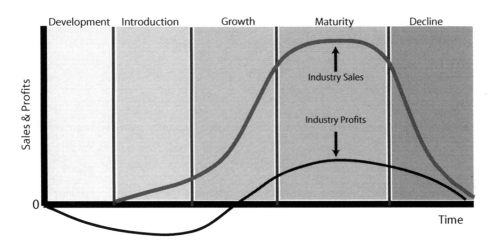

Adoption of New Products

The PLC is tied closely to the concept of the **Diffusion of Innovation**, which explains how information and acceptance of new products spreads through a market. Innovation is anything new that solves needs by offering a significant advantage over existing methods (e.g., other products) customers use (see Chapter 19 for a detailed discussion). Innovation can encompass both highly advanced technology products, such as new computer chips, and non-technological products, such as a new soft drink. In fact, the seminal work of the Diffusion of Innovation concept occurred in the 1950s when researchers in the agricultural industry observed how new corn seeds were adopted by farmers in the U.S. Midwest. (14)

For marketers, a key concept to emerge from research on new product diffusion is the identification of adopter categories into which members of a market are likely to fall. These categories include:

Innovators

These adopters represent a small percentage of the market that is at the forefront of trying new products. These people are often viewed as enthusiasts and are eager to try new things, often without regard to price. While a useful test ground for new products, marketers find Innovators often do not remain loyal as they continually seek new products.

Early Adopters

This group contains more members than the Innovator category. They share Innovators' enthusiasm for new products, though they tend to be more practical about their decisions. They also are eager to communicate their experiences with

Box 7-1

LEVELS OF ANALYSIS OF THE PLC

The Product Life Cycle is commonly referenced in many business publications as a way of describing the current conditions facing a market or product. The fact it is used to describe either markets or individual products points out the need to understand the different levels of analysis for which the PLC can be used. These levels include:

Product Category

This level considers the macro market view for the general category of products that meet a general need. For instance, automobiles would be a general category that meets the need for personal motorized transportation (obviously there are others, such as motorcycles, scooters, and trucks but we will focus only on automobiles) and includes hundreds of products. Since the PLC for a product category includes sales for all products, the timeframe for the automotive PLC is quite long with the Introduction stage beginning around 1900.

Product Form

This level looks at product groupings that fall within a product category. The product form contains many different groupings that, taken together, make up the product category. These groupings include products that not only satisfy the general need of the product category, but do so by also offering additional benefits. In our example, hybrid cars would be a product form, since it satisfies the general need for personal motorized transportation and offers additional benefits in the form of fuel efficiency and environmental friendliness. Other product forms in the product category include sports cars, minivans, luxury sedans, etc. Clearly there can be a unique PLC for each form of a product. Marketers are very concerned with analysis at this level since it provides evidence for what is occurring in specific markets, and for this reason is considered the most important level of analysis.

Individual Brand

This level concerns the life cycle of a specific brand within a product form. In our example, this would include the Toyota Prius. While it may seem marketers would be most concerned with this level, they actually gain more value from analyzing what is happening in the overall market (i.e., product form). For instance, a marketer may make a serious mistake if she assumes the entire market has entered the Decline stage just because her company's brand has seen a sales drop. Doing so may mean a total misread of what is happening in the market and lead to the marketer missing out on additional opportunities if the market for the product form is still growing.

We should note in most cases the PLC considers what is happening for the total market (i.e., worldwide sales). However, more information could be obtained by applying the concepts of the PLC to more narrowly defined market segments, such as geographic regions or segments based on customer characteristics (e.g., by age, education level, etc.).

the Early Majority (next group) and, because of their influence, they are vital to the future success of the product (i.e., act as opinion leaders).

Early Majority

This represents the beginning of entry into the mass market (i.e., large number of potential customers). The Early Majority account for up to one-third of the overall market. The Early Majority like new things but tend to wait until they have received positive opinions from others (i.e., Early Adopters) before purchasing. Adoption by the Early Majority is key if a new product is to be profitable. On the other hand, many new products die quickly because they are not accepted beyond early trials by Innovators and Early Adopters and never reach mass market status.

Late Majority

Possibly as large as the Early Majority, this group takes a wait-and-see approach before trying something new. Marketers are likely to see their highest profits once this group starts to purchase.

Laggards

This is the last group to adopt something new and, in fact, may only do so if they have no other choice. Depending on the market this group can be large, though because of their reluctance to accept new products marketers are not inclined to direct much attention to them.

ADOPTER CATEGORIES AND THE PLC

The adopter categories help explain the shape of the life cycle for many products. For instance, consider how a new household cleaning product may become successful. At first Innovators may experience the product during the Development stage and then become the key targeted customers at the beginning of the Introduction stage. Early Adopters will also be targeted during the Introduction stage and their adoption will determine whether the product makes it to the Growth stage. If the product survives the Innovator and Early Adopter stages, it moves to the Growth stage where acceptance by the Early Majority means the product is entering the mass market. The product can continue to be successful as it is adopted by the Late Majority and, to a much lesser extent, by Laggards. Eventually product sales decline as Innovators and Early Adopter move to something new and the cycle starts over.

It should be noted, an assumption of a person's placement in a certain adopter category for one product does not imply that person will also occupy the same category for other products. For example, someone who is an Innovator for one product may be a Laggard for another. However, with research, marketers may find an individual's adopter classification for one product applies across a similar set of products. For instance, those classified as Innovators for computer hardware may have a high probability of being categorized the same for computer software. This assumption may be necessary as a software company develops its target marketing strategies in advance of the launch of a new product.

Additionally, marketers should not view an adopter category as being a single market segment. Instead, each adopter classification consists of multiple market segments that together make up the category. For example, the Early Majority may be made up of many markets that can be segmented on different variables, such as geographic location, age, income, etc. Consequently, aiming to satisfy all customers in an adopter category using a single marketing plan is likely not an effective strategy.

Criticisms of the PLC

The PLC has the ability to offer marketers guidance on strategies and tactics as they manage products through changing market conditions. Unfortunately, the PLC does not offer a perfect model of markets as it contains drawbacks preventing it from being applicable to all products. Among the problems cited are:

◆ Shape of Curve – Some product forms do not follow the traditional PLC curve. For instance, clothing may go through regular up and down cycles as styles are in fashion then out then in again. **Fad products**, such as certain toys, may be popular for a period of time only to see sales drop dramatically until a future generation renews interest in the toy.

◆ Length of Stages – The PLC offers little help in determining how long each stage will last. For example, some products can exist in the Maturity stage for decades while others may be there for only a few months. Consequently, it may be difficult to determine when adjustments to the Marketing Plan are needed to meet the needs of different PLC stages.

◆ Competitor Reaction not Predictable – As we discuss in greater detail in Chapter 20, the PLC suggests competitor response occurs in a somewhat consistent pattern. For example, for a new product form, the PLC says competitors will not engage in strong brand-to-brand competition until the product form has gained a foothold in the market. The logic is that, until the market is established, it is in the best interest of all competitors to focus on building interest in the general product form and refrain from claiming one brand is better than another. However, competitors do not always conform to theoretical models. Some will always compete on brand first and leave it to others to build market interest for the product form. Arguments can also be made that competitors will respond differently than what the PLC suggests on such issues as pricing, number of product options, and spending on declining products, to name a few.

◆ Patterns May Not Apply to All Global Markets – Marketers who base their strategies on how the PLC plays out in their home market may be surprised to see the PLC does not follow the same patterns when they enter other markets. The reason is that customer behavior may be quite different within each market. For instance, a company may find that while customers in their home market easily understand how the company's new product could save them time in performing a certain task, customers in a foreign market may not easily see the connection.

◆ Impact of External Forces – The PLC assumes customers' decisions are primarily impacted by the marketing activities of the companies selling in the market. In fact, as we will discuss in Chapter 19, there are many other factors affecting a market which are not controlled by marketers. Such factors (e.g., social changes, technological innovation) can lead to changes in market demand at rates that are much more rapid than would occur if only marketing decisions were being changed (i.e., if everything was held constant except for the company's marketing decisions).

◆ Use for Forecasting – The impact of external forces may create challenges in using the PLC as a forecasting tool. For instance, market factors not directly associated with the marketing activities of market competitors, such as economic conditions, may have a greater impact on reducing demand than customers' interest in the product. Consequently, what may be forecasted as a decline in the market, signaling a move to the Maturity stage, may be the result of declining economic conditions and not a decline in customers' interest in the product. In fact, it is likely demand for the product will recover to growth levels once economic conditions improve. If a marketer follows the strict guidance of the PLC they would conclude that strategies should shift to those of the Maturity stage. Doing so may be an over-reaction that could hurt market position and profitability.

◆ Stages Not Seamlessly Connected – Some high-tech marketers question whether one stage of the PLC naturally will follow another stage. In particular, technology consultant Geoffrey Moore suggests that for high-tech products targeted to business customers a noticeable space or **chasm** occurs between the Introduction and Growth stages that can only be overcome by significantly altering marketing strategy beyond what is suggested by the PLC. (15)

While not perfect, the PLC is a marketing tool that should be well understood by marketers since its underlying message, that markets are dynamic, supports the need for frequent marketing planning. Also, for many markets the principles presented by the PLC will, in fact, prove to be very much representative of the conditions they will face in the market. We will return to the concepts associated with the PLC in much greater detail in *Planning and Strategy with the PLC* discussion in Chapter 20.

|||||||||||||||||||||||||||||||||||||||||||||||||||||||||||||||||||||||||||||||||||||||||||||||||||||||||||||||||||||||||||||||

REFERENCES

1. *Tide* website.

2. *BIC* website.

3. *Salary.com* website.

4. *United States Department of Labor - Occupational Employment Statistics* website.

5. Reiter, C., "Mercedes Designer Goes 'Off the Charts' to Draw Younger Buyers," *BusinessWeek*, January 11, 2011.

6. *Segway* website.

7. Olson, E., "Under Armour Wants to Dress Athletic Young Women," *New York Times*, August 31, 2010.

8. Perraudin, F., "From Four Wheels to Two: Has Mini Gone Too Far?" *Time*, September 29, 2010.

9. Horovitz, B., "Savvy Marketers Let Consumers Call the Shots," *USA Today*, March 24, 2011.

10. Siriwardane, V., "How to Run a Brainstorming Session," *Inc. Magazine*, November 30, 2010.

11. Horovitz, B., "12-Inch Burger? Carl's Jr., Hardee's Test Market a Foot-Long," *USA Today*, July 16, 2010.

12. Wong, E., "Inventions That Were Accidents," *Forbes*, December 23, 2010.

13. Szoid, C., "Rent-A-Wreck Trades in Its Beat-Up Car-Rental Image," *USA Today*, July 21, 2010.

14. Rogers, E.M., <u>Diffusion of Innovation</u>, The Free Press, 1995.

15. Moore, G., <u>Crossing the Chasm, Marketing and Selling Technology Products to Mainstream Customers</u>, HarperCollins, 1991.

Full text of many of the references can be accessed via links on the support website.

Chapter 8: Distribution Decisions

Our coverage in Chapters 6 and 7 indicate product decisions may be the most important of all marketing decisions since these lead directly to the reasons (i.e., offer benefits that satisfy needs) why customers decide to make a purchase. But having a strong product does little good if customers are not able to easily and conveniently obtain it.

With this in mind, we turn to the second major marketing decision area – distribution.

In this chapter, we cover the basics of distribution, including defining what channels of distribution are, examining the key functions and parties within a distribution system, and evaluating the role distribution serves within the overall marketing strategy. Also, we look at the major types of channel arrangements and the factors affecting the creation of effective distribution channels. We conclude with a discussion of different distribution design options and look at the issues global marketers face when distributing beyond their home country.

||||||||||||||||||||||||||||||||||||||||||||||||||||||||||||||||||||||||||||||||||||||||||||||||||||||

IMPORTANCE OF DISTRIBUTION

Distribution decisions focus on establishing the path, termed **channel of distribution**, which moves the product from the marketer to the customer. For most marketers, this means making decisions on the activities that will ultimately give customers access to and permit purchase of a marketer's product.

Distribution decisions are relevant for nearly all types of products. While it is easy to see how distribution decisions impact physical goods, such as laundry detergent or truck parts, distribution is also necessary for digital goods (e.g., television programming, downloadable music) and services (e.g., income tax services). Whether a marketer is distributing products that are physical, digital, or service, the bottom line is a marketer's distribution system must be both effective (i.e., delivers a good or service to the right place, in the right amount, and in the right condition) and efficient (i.e., delivers at the right time and for the right cost). As discussed in Box 8-1, creating an effective and efficient distribution system requires the marketer carefully consider the benefits offered versus the costs for establishing and maintaining the system.

An interesting channel of distribution emerging for digital goods can be found in virtual worlds and social networks. Several marketers, including automobile manufacture Volvo and clothing retailer H&M, are selling virtual products online through interactive games and meeting places found on such sites as Second Life and Facebook. The market for distributing "pretend" goods, which has grown rapidly in Asia, South America and the Middle East, is estimated to be a multi-billion dollar market. (1)

Box 8-1

DISTRIBUTION TRADE-OFF ANALYSIS: SERVICE LEVEL VS. COST

As part of developing a successful distribution strategy, marketers strive to provide an optimal level of service to their customers. However, "optimal" does not always translate into providing the "best" distribution service options to customers. The service level marketers offer for their distribution activities is determined using trade-off analysis.

With service level trade-off analysis, the marketer compares the number and quality of distribution features (e.g., speed of delivery, ease of placing orders, order tracking, etc.) it would like to offer versus the cost of providing the features. While customers may want quick delivery, the marketer may find fast delivery an expensive proposition that significantly reduces its profit margin.

Since most distribution activities represent a cost to the marketer, the marketer's distribution system choice may not be the "best" available in terms of getting the product into customer's hands as fast as possible. Consequently, the marketer's choice for what is optimal will be determined by analyzing distribution features and costs, and evaluating how these fit within the marketer's overall objectives.

Distribution Activities

The activities involved in establishing the channel of distribution are presented in Table 8-1. While some marketers may choose to handle all distribution activities on their own, most marketers find many of these tasks are best left to others. Whether handled by the marketer or contracted to others, these activities are crucial to having a cost-effective and efficient distribution system.

Amazon is an example of a company offering services to marketers that handle nearly all distribution tasks. Through its Fulfillment by Amazon service, Amazon handles ordering, inventory management, product handing, and shipping. All the marketing company needs to do is ship its product to an Amazon storage facility and, for a fee, Amazon manages the rest. (2)

Table 8-1: Channel of Distribution Activities

Distribution Activity	Explanation
Order Processing	Includes methods for handling customer purchase requests.
Inventory Management	Includes methods to ensure the right amount of product is available to fill customer orders.
Physical Handling	Includes methods to prepare product for movement that reduces damage.
Storage	Includes facilities for holding inventory.
Shipping	Includes providing means for getting the product to customers in a timely manner.
Display	Includes having resellers place products in locations that can be seen by customers.
Promotion	Includes the need for resellers to assist in communicating products to the target market.
Selling	Includes the need for resellers to provide personal promotion to help sell product.
Information Feedback	Includes the need for methods to encourage resellers and customers to provide marketing research information to the marketer.

||||||||||||||||||||||||||||||||||||||||||||||||||||||||||||||||||||||||||||||||||||||||||||

TYPE OF CHANNEL MEMBERS

Channel activities may be carried out by the marketer or by specialist organizations that assist with certain functions. We can classify specialist organizations into two broad categories: resellers and specialty service firms.

Resellers

These organizations, also known within some industries as **intermediaries**, **distributors**, or **dealers**, generally purchase or take ownership of products from the marketing company with the intention of selling to others. If a marketer utilizes multiple resellers within its distribution channel strategy this is called a **reseller network**, which is classified into several sub-categories including:

♦ Retailers – Organizations selling products directly to final consumers.

♦ Wholesalers – Organizations purchasing products from suppliers and selling these to other resellers, such as retailers or other wholesalers.

♦ Industrial Distributors – Firms working in the business-to-business market selling products obtained from industrial suppliers.

Specialty Service Firms

These are organizations providing additional services to help with the exchange of products, though they generally do not purchase the product:

♦ <u>Agents and Brokers</u> – Organizations working to bring suppliers and buyers together in exchange for a fee.

♦ <u>Distribution Service Firms</u> – Offer services aiding in the movement of products, such as assistance with transportation, storage, and order processing.

♦ <u>Others</u> – This category includes firms providing additional services, such as insurance and transportation routing assistance.

‖‖‖

WHY DISTRIBUTION HELP IS NEEDED

As noted, distribution channels often require the assistance of others in order for the marketer to reach its target market. But why exactly does a company need others to help with the distribution of its product? Wouldn't a company that handles its own distribution functions be in a better position to exercise control over product sales and potentially earn higher profits? Also, doesn't the Internet make it much easier to distribute products, which then lessens the need for others to be involved in selling a company's product?

While, on the surface, it may seem to make sense for a company to operate its own distribution channel (i.e., handling all aspects of distribution), there are many factors preventing companies from doing so. While companies can do without the assistance of certain channel members, for many marketers some level of channel partnership is needed. For example, L.L. Bean, which sells a large percentage of its products through catalogs and over the Internet, is successful without utilizing other resellers to sell their products. However, L.L. Bean still needs assistance with certain parts of the distribution process, primarily with product shipment (e.g., FedEx, UPS and USPS). In L.L. Bean's case, creating its own transportation system makes little sense given how large such a system would need to be in order to service their customer base. Therefore, by using shipping companies, L.L. Bean is taking advantage of the benefits these services offer to the company and to its customers.

When choosing a distribution strategy a marketer must determine what value a channel member adds to the firm's products. Remember, as we discussed in Chapter 6, customers assess a product's value by looking at many factors, including those surrounding the product (i.e., augmented product). Several surrounding features can be directly influenced by channel members, such as customer service, delivery, and availability. Consequently, selecting a channel partner involves a value analysis in the same way customers make purchase decisions. That is, the marketer must assess the benefits received from utilizing a channel partner versus the cost incurred for using the services.

It should be noted, that while we talk about marketers "selecting a channel partner" it is necessary to recognize that the channel member is the one who ultimately decides which products they will distribute. In most industries, it is not possible for a channel member to handle all products sold by suppliers. Consequently, competition for gaining distribution through a specific channel member can be quite intense as many suppliers compete for a channel member's services. To gain access to a channel member often requires a supplying company have strong knowledge of the market. Additionally, it requires a well developed marketing strategy that will help in persuading a channel member to handle a product.

> *Gaining distribution can be a difficult undertaking even for companies that have a successful track record. As an example, Violight, a manufacturer of devices for sanitizing toothbrushes using ultraviolet light, sought to expand their business by developing a product for removing germs from cellphones. While the company had successfully sold their toothbrush product in drugstores and specialty retailers, Violight found gaining distributing through electronics stores to be much more challenging. The company was eventually able to convince Best Buy to distribute but only after an extensive selling effort. (3)*

Benefits Offered by Channel Members

◆ <u>Offer Cost Savings Through Specialization</u> – Members of the distribution channel are specialists in what they do and can often perform tasks better and at lower cost than companies who do not have distribution experience. Marketers attempting to handle too many aspects of distribution may end up exhausting company resources as they learn how to distribute, resulting in the company being "a jack of all trades but master of none."

◆ <u>Reduce Exchange Time</u> – Not only are channel members able to reduce distribution costs by being experienced at what they do, they often perform their job more rapidly resulting in faster product delivery. This can be seen in Box 8-2.

◆ <u>Allow Customers to Conveniently Shop for Variety</u> – Marketers have to understand what customers want in their shopping experience. Referring back to our grocery store example, consider a world without grocery stores and instead each marketer of grocery products sells through its own stores. As it is now, many customers find shopping to be a time consuming activity, but consider what

---

Box 8-2

EFFICIENCY IN DELIVERY

The evolution of channels of distribution can be tied directly to the need for efficiency in the distribution system. For instance, consider what would happen if a grocery store received direct shipment from EVERY manufacturer that sells products in the store. This delivery system would be chaotic as hundreds of trucks line up each day to make deliveries, many of which would consist of only a few boxes. On a busy day, a truck may sit for hours waiting for space so it can unload its products.

Instead, a better distribution scheme may have the grocery store purchasing its supplies from a grocery wholesaler that has its own warehouse for handling simultaneous shipments from a large number of suppliers. The wholesaler distributes to the store in the quantities the store needs, on a schedule that works for the store, and often in a single truck, all of which speeds up the time it takes to get the product on the store's shelves.

---

would happen if customers had to visit many different retailers each week to satisfy their grocery needs. Hence, resellers within the channel of distribution serve two fundamental needs: 1) they give customers the products they want by purchasing from many suppliers (termed **accumulation** and **assortment** services), and 2) they make it convenient to purchase by making products available in a single location.

♦ <u>Resellers Sell Smaller Quantities</u> – Channel members, and particularly resellers, allow purchases in quantities that work for their customers. This is an especially valuable channel function because handling orders for small quantities is not what works best for most suppliers. Suppliers like to ship products they produce in large quantities since this is more cost effective than shipping smaller amounts (see Box 10-1 in Chapter 10). The ability of intermediaries to purchase large quantities, but to resell them in smaller quantities (termed **bulk breaking**), provides customer with two key advantages. First, it makes products available to those who do not want large quantities, such as a small retail store. Second, the reseller is able to pass along to its customers a significant portion of the cost savings gained by purchasing in large volume; thus, allowing customers to purchase smaller quantities at competitive prices.

♦ <u>Create Sales</u> – Channel partners are at the front line when it comes to creating demand for the marketer's product. In some cases, resellers perform an active selling role using persuasive techniques to encourage customers to purchase a marketer's product. In other cases, they encourage sales of the product through their own advertising efforts and using other promotional means, such as special product displays.

♦ Offer Access to More Customers – For marketers, channel partners may offer access to more customers in a much shorter time frame than the marketer can accomplish on its own. This can be particularly beneficial to companies new to a market and do not have an established distribution network, or existing companies that have had difficulty gaining distribution using their own methods.

♦ Offer Financial Support – Channel partners often provide programs enabling their customers to more easily purchase products by offering financial options that ease payment requirements. These programs include allowing customers to: purchase on credit, purchase using an extended payment plan, delay the start of payments, and allowing trade-in or exchange options.

♦ Provide Information – Companies utilizing channel members for selling their products depend on these distributors to provide information that can help improve the product. High-level intermediaries, such as major retailers, may offer their suppliers real-time access to sales data, including information showing how products are selling by such characteristics as geographic location, type of customer, and product location (e.g., where located within a store, where found on a website). Even if such high-level information is not available, marketers can often count on resellers to provide feedback as to how customers are responding to products. This feedback can occur either through surveys or interviews with reseller's employees or by requesting the reseller allow the marketer to survey the reseller's customers.

Costs of Utilizing Channel Members

♦ Loss of Revenue – Channel members are not likely to offer services to a marketer unless they see financial gain in doing so. Firms obtain payment for their services as either direct payment (e.g., marketer pays specialty service firm for shipping costs) or, in the case of resellers, by charging their customers more than what they paid the marketer for acquiring the product (see *Markup Pricing* discussion in Chapter 18). For the latter, marketers have a good idea of what the final customer will pay for their product, which means the marketer must charge less when selling the product to resellers. In these situations, marketers are not reaping the full sale price by using resellers, which they may be able to do if they sold directly to the customer.

♦ Loss of Communication Control – Marketers not only give up revenue when using channel partners, they may also give up control of the message being conveyed to customers. If the reseller engages in communication activities, such as when a retailer uses salespeople to sell to customers, the marketer is no longer controlling what is being said about the product. This can lead to miscommunication problems with customers, especially if the reseller embellishes or makes misstatements

Marketing Story

Coke Pays $715 Million to Distribute Dr Pepper
USA Today

For many years, Dr. Pepper fought hard to position it-self as an alternative to cola products. So it is somewhat ironic that Dr. Pepper, owned by the Dr. Pepper Snapple Group (DPS), is working with the enemy. It has negoti-ated deals allowing its products to be distributed in the U.S. by its leading cola rivals. The company, which also markets numerous other beverage brands including 7UP, A&W, Canada Dry and Snapple, has agreed to let Coca-Cola and Pepsi distribute some of its products including the Dr. Pepper brand.

Yet, why would DPS allow these competitors to distrib-ute its products? For the most part, it comes down to customer access and product distribution. Coke and Pepsi have massive distribution networks that are supe-rior to DPS's network.

Additionally, the beverage distribution model itself appears to be changing. Previously, most beverage distribution took place within a franchise relationship where the franchisee would bottle the product by adding water and other ingredients to the syrup product it purchased from the franchisor. These independent bottlers would often distribute multiple brands, and in some cases, sell competing products.

However, this business model may be slowly fading in the beverage business. Over the last few years, consolidation has occurred within beverage distribution networks with Coca-Cola and Pepsi acquiring several independent bottlers. In effect, they have taken distribution in-house.

As noted in this story, another reason for the distribution change is the introduction of new high-end fountain dispensers. These dispensers are a powerful form of distribution for reaching certain markets, such as restaurants and sporting events.

As part of the deal, Dr Pepper and Diet Dr Pepper will be included in Coke's new "Freestyle" fountain dispenser, which can mix more than 100 drinks. Dr Pepper paid Coca-Cola between $115 million and $135 million to be the only non-Coke product on the high-tech dispenser, which is expected to be in 500 locations by the end of the summer. (4)

While access to distribution is the attraction for Dr. Pepper, what is the value Dr. Pep-per brings to Coke and Pepsi?

about the benefits the product provides. While marketers can influence what is being said by offering sales training to resellers' salespeople, they lack ultimate control of the message.

♦ Loss of Product Importance – Once a product is out of the marketer's hands, the importance of that product is left up to channel members. If there are pressing issues in the channel, such as transportation problems, or if a competitor is using promotional incentives in an effort to push its product through resellers, the marketer's product may not get the attention the marketer feels it should receive.

> *Several luxury clothing and accessory brands, who have expressed frustration with the way their products are distributed in upscale retail stores, are looking to change how their products are sold. Leading brands including Gucci, Prada and Dior, want to establish their own space within the stores. These areas, called concession, would be managed by the brands, who would design and stock the space, hire their own employees, and set their own prices. (5)*

CHANNEL ARRANGEMENTS

The distribution channel consists of many parties each seeking to meet their own business objectives. Clearly for the channel to work well, relationships between channel members must be strong. For product distribution to flow smoothly, each member must understand and trust others on whom they depend. For instance, a small sporting goods retailer trusts a wholesaler to deliver required items on time in order to meet customer demand, while the wholesaler counts on the retailer to place regular orders and to make prompt payments.

Relationships in a channel are in large part a function of the arrangement that occurs between the members. These arrangements can be divided in two main categories: independent and dependent.

Independent Channel Arrangement

Under this arrangement, a channel member negotiates deals with others that do not result in binding relationships. In other words, a channel member is free to make whatever arrangements they feel is in its best interest. This so-called **conventional distribution arrangement** often leads to significant conflict as individual members decide what is best for them and not necessarily for the entire channel (see *Channel Conflict* discussion below). On the other hand, an independent channel arrangement is less restrictive than dependent arrangements by making it easier for a channel member to move away from relationships they feel are not working to its benefit.

Dependent Channel Arrangement

With a dependent channel arrangement, a channel member feels tied to one or more members of the distribution channel. Sometimes referred to as **vertical marketing systems**, this approach makes it more difficult for an individual member to make changes to how products are distributed. However, the dependent approach provides much more stability and consistency since members are united in their goals.

The dependent channel arrangement can be broken down into three types:

Corporate

Under this arrangement, a supplier operates its own distribution system in a manner that produces an integrated channel. This occurs most frequently in the retail industry where a supplier operates a chain of retail stores. Starbucks is a company that does this. They import and process coffee and then sell it under its own brand name in thousands of its own stores. (6) It should be mentioned that Starbucks also distributes its products in other ways, such as through grocery stores and mail order (see *Multichannel or Hybrid System* discussion below).

Contractual

With this approach, a legal document obligates members to agree on how a product is distributed. Often times, the agreement specifically spells out which activities each member is permitted to perform or not perform. This type of arrangement can occur in several formats including:

- Wholesaler-sponsored – where a wholesaler brings together and manages many independent retailers, including having the retailers operate under the same name

- Retailer-sponsored – this format also brings together retailers but the retailers are responsible for managing the relationship

- Franchised Arrangement – where a central organization controls nearly all activities of other members

- Licensing Agreement – where a central organization controls some activities of its channel members, but it does not control all activities of the members

While Starbucks operates over 9,000 company stores worldwide, they also license the sale of its products to thousands of businesses. Under its Licensed Store program qualified high-traffic outlets, such as hotels, universities, and large businesses, pay a fee to sell Starbucks products. (7)

Administrative

In certain channel arrangements, a single member may dominate the decisions within the channel. These situations occur when one channel member has achieved a significant power position (see *Channel Power* discussion below). This most likely occurs if a manufacturer has brands in strong demand by its target markets (e.g., Apple) or if a retailer has significant size and market coverage (e.g., Wal-Mart). In most cases, the arrangement is understood to occur and is not bound by legal or financial arrangements.

|||||||||||||||||||||||||||||||||||||||||||||||||||||||||||||||||||||||||||||||||||||||||||||||||||||||||||||||||||

FACTORS IN CREATING DISTRIBUTION CHANNELS

Like most marketing decisions, a great deal of research and thought must go into determining how to carry out distribution activities in a way that meets a marketer's objectives. The marketer must consider many factors when establishing a distribution system. We group these into three main categories: marketing decision issues, infrastructure issues and channel relationship issues. In turn, each of these categories contains several topics of concern to marketers.

Marketing Decision Issues

Distribution strategy can be shaped by how decisions are made in other marketing areas.

PRODUCT ISSUES

The nature of the product often dictates the distribution options available, especially if the product requires special handling. For instance, companies selling delicate or fragile products, such as flowers, look for shipping arrangements that are different from those sought by companies selling extremely tough or durable products, such as steel beams.

PROMOTION ISSUES

Besides issues related to physical handling of products, distribution decisions are affected by the type of promotional activities needed to sell the product to customers. For products needing extensive salesperson-to-customer contact (e.g., automobile purchases) the distribution options are different compared to for products where customers typically require no sales assistance (e.g., bread purchases).

PRICING ISSUES

The desired price at which a marketer seeks to sell its product can impact how they choose to distribute. As previously mentioned, the inclusion of resellers in a marketer's distribution strategy may affect a product's pricing since each member of the channel seeks to make a profit for their contribution to the sale of the product. If too many channel members are involved the eventual selling price may be too high to meet sales targets, in which case the marketer may explore other distribution options.

TARGET MARKET ISSUES

A distribution system is only effective if customers can obtain the product. Consequently, a key decision in setting up a channel arrangement is for the marketer to choose the approach that reaches customers in the most effective way possible. The most important decision with regard to reaching the target market is to determine the level of distribution coverage needed to meet customers' needs.

Distribution Coverage

Distribution coverage is measured in terms of the **intensity** of product availability. For the most part, distribution coverage decisions are of most concern to consumer products companies, though there are many industrial products that also must decide how much coverage to give its products.

There are three main levels of distribution coverage - mass, selective, and exclusive.

- Mass Coverage – The mass coverage strategy (also known as **intensive distribution**) attempts to distribute products widely in nearly all locations in which that type of product is sold. This level of distribution is only feasible for relatively low priced products that appeal to extremely large target markets (e.g., consumer convenience products). A product such as Coca-Cola is a classic example since it is available in a wide variety of locations, including grocery stores, convenience stores, vending machines, hotels, and many, many more. With such a large number of locations selling the product, the cost of distribution is extremely high and must be offset with very high sales volume.

- Selective Coverage – Under selective coverage the marketer deliberately seeks to limit the locations in which its product is sold. To the non-marketer it may seem strange for a company not to want its product distributed in every possible location. However, the logic of this strategy is tied to the size and nature of the product's target market. Products with selective coverage appeal to smaller, more focused target markets (e.g., consumer shopping products) compared to the size of target markets for mass marketed products. Consequently, because the market size is smaller, the number of locations needed to support the distribution of the product is fewer.

- Exclusive Coverage – Some high-end products target narrow markets having a relatively small number of customers. These customers are often characterized as "discriminating" in their taste for products and seek to satisfy some of their needs with high-quality, though expensive products. Additionally, many buyers of high-end products require a high level of customer service from the channel member from whom they purchase. These characteristics of the target market may lead the marketer to sell its products through a highly select or exclusive group of resellers. Another type of exclusive distribution may not involve high-end products, but rather products only available in selected locations, such as company-owned stores. While these products may or may not be higher priced compared to competitive products, the fact these are only available in company outlets gives exclusivity to the distribution.

We conclude this section by noting that while the three distribution coverage options just discussed serve as a useful guide for envisioning how distribution intensity works, the advent of the electronic communication has brought into question the effectiveness of these schemes. For all intents and purposes, all products available for purchase over the Internet or through mobile technology are distributed in the same way - mass coverage. So a better way to look at the three levels is to consider these as options for distribution coverage of products that are physically purchased by a customer (i.e., walk-in to purchase).

Infrastructure Issues

The marketer's desire to establish a distribution channel is often complicated by what options are available to them within a market. While in the planning stages the marketer has an idea of how the distribution plan should be executed, she/he may find that certain parts of the distribution channel may not be what they expected. For example, a supplier of high-end, specialty snack foods may find a promising target market for their products is located in a mountain ski area in Colorado. However, the company may also discover that no suitable distributor in that area possesses the required refrigerated storage space that is necessary to store the product in the proper way specified by the marketer.

This concern is even greater when a marketer looks to expand into international markets. Marketers often find the type of distribution system they are used to employing is lacking or even nonexistent (e.g., poor transportation, few acceptable retail outlets). In fact, depending on the type of product, a marketer could be prevented from entering a foreign market because there are no suitable options for distributing the product. More likely, marketers will find options for distributing their product but these options (see *Distribution in Global Markets* discussion below) may be different, and possibly inferior, from what has made them successful in their home country. While viewed as risky, companies entering foreign markets often have little choice but to accept the distribution structure that is in place if they want to enter these markets.

Relationship Issues

An appropriate distribution strategy takes into account not only marketing decisions, but also considers how relationships within the channel of distribution can impact the marketer's product. In this section, we examine three such issues:

CHANNEL POWER

A channel can be made up of many parties each adding value to the product purchased by customers. However, some parties (see Box 8-3) within the channel may carry greater weight than others. In marketing terms, this is called channel power, which refers to the influence one party within a channel has over other channel members. When power is exerted by a channel member, they are often in the position to make demands of others. For instance, they may demand better financial terms (e.g., will buy only if prices are lowered, will sell only if suggested price is higher) or demand others members perform certain tasks (e.g., do more marketing to customers, perform more product services).

> *Because of the power wielded by leading retailers, manufacturers often find it is difficult to get more than a few of their products sold in stores. With outlets for their product limited, many manufacturers have created their own retail channel selling directly to customer over the Internet. Footwear manufacturer Crocs turned to the Internet when leading footwear and sporting goods retailers were handling only a few of their products. Besides selling a greater variety of products, Crocs also gains value feedback directly from customers. (8)*

CHANNEL CONFLICT

In an effort to increase product sales, marketers are often attracted by the notion that sales can grow if the marketer expands distribution by adding additional resellers. However, such decisions must be handled carefully so that existing dealers do not feel the new distributors are encroaching on their customers and siphoning potential business.

For marketers, channel strategy designed to expand product distribution may, in fact, do the opposite if existing members feel there is a conflict in the decisions made by the marketer. If existing members sense a conflict and feel the marketer is not sensitive to their needs, they may choose to stop handling the marketer's products.

NEED FOR LONG-TERM COMMITMENTS

Channel decisions have long-term consequences for marketers since efforts to establish new relationships can take an extensive period of time, while ending existing relationships can prove difficult. For instance, Company A, a marketer

---

Box 8-3

WHO HAS THE POWER

Channels of distribution can be dominated by certain channel members who hold something of value that is needed by other members. Examples of those holding power include:

Backend or Product Power

This occurs when a product manufacturer or service provider markets a brand that has a high level of customer demand. The marketer of the brand is often in a power position since other channel members have little choice but to carry the brand or risk losing customers. Examples include Apple and Procter & Gamble.

Middle or Wholesale Power

This occurs when an intermediary, such as a wholesaler, services a large number of smaller retailers with products obtained from a large number of manufacturers or product suppliers. In this situation, the wholesaler can exert power since small retailers, who purchase only a few items at a time, are often not in the position to purchase products cost-effectively, or in as much variety as what is offered by the wholesaler. Examples include Do It Best (hardware stores) and Independent Grocer Alliance (grocery stores).

Front or Retailer Power

As the name suggests, the power in this situation rests with the retailer who can command considerable concessions from its suppliers. This type of power is most prevalent when the retailer generates a significant percentage of sales in the market it serves and others in the channel are dependent on the sales generated by the retailer. For example, small suppliers looking to sell to Wal-Mart may be surprised to see how much information the world's largest retailer demands from its suppliers. The requirements include the submission of financial statements, evidence of product liability insurance, and samples of the product. (9)

---

of kitchen cabinets that wants to change distribution strategy, may decide to stop selling its product line through industrial supply companies, who distribute cabinets to building contractors, and instead sell through large retail home centers. If, in the future, Company A decides to once again enter the industrial supply market they may run into resistance since supply companies may have replaced Company A's product line with other products and, given what happened to the previous relationship, may be reluctant to deal with Company A. Considering these potential problems, Company A may have to give serious thought to whether breaking its long-term relationship with industrial suppliers is in the company's best interest.

Marketing Story

How a Start-Up Landed Shelf Space at Wal-Mart
Wall Street Journal

The most frustrating decision facing all consumer products marketers is the one they have the least control over – distribution. Unlike decisions related to product, pricing and promotion, meeting distribution objectives often means the marketer is at the mercy of retailers' decision to stock a marketer's product. This problem is especially challenging for marketers selling products in retail stores, where they must battle many other companies that are also trying to convince retail store buyers to sell their products.

When it comes to buyers learning about a company's products, the most common method is a "push" promotion approach, where salespeople knock on customers' doors. While getting a meeting with a retailer's buying staff is not hard for well-known companies, a selling opportunity like this is much more difficult for small companies that have yet to establish a track record. They soon discover that convincing a buyer just to schedule a meeting is as difficult as convincing them to buy the product.

For smaller firms, a better approach may be to use creative methods that capture the final consumers' attention. Labeled as "pull" promotion, these strategies are designed to target final consumers with the hope they will then ask for the product at retail stores. Once enough voices are heard, it is hoped the retailer will agree to distribute the product. (For further information on pull and push promotions see Marketing Decision Issues discussion in Chapter 11.)

Here is a story of one creative way that a small company used to build up consumer interest. After several unsuccessful attempts to obtain distribution through the use of sales calls, the company, which sells a somewhat unusual product (tongue cleaner), created a YouTube video that quickly went viral. The interest caught the attention of several retailers including Wal-Mart who agreed to place the product in 3,500 stores. While Wal-Mart claims the You-Tube videos did not influence their decision to stock the product, other retailers did point to consumers' interest in the videos as a key reason for their decision to handle the product.

Orabrush's Mr. Davis says he credits the company's social-media efforts for helping get the tongue cleaner into other retail stores. In some cases, he says store managers approached Orabrush on their own, citing requests for the product from customers who'd learned about it online. (10)

What other techniques can a small company use that may work within a "pull" promotional strategy?

||||||||||||||||||||||||||||||||||||||||||||||||||||||||||||||||||||||||||||||||||||||||||||||||||||||||||||||

OVERALL DISTRIBUTION DESIGN

Mindful of the factors affecting distribution decisions (i.e., marketing decision issues and relationship issues), the marketer may have several options to choose from when settling on a design for its distribution network. We stress that distribution options "may" to be available and are not guaranteed. This is because marketing decision factors (e.g., product, promotion, pricing, target markets) or the nature of distribution channel relationships may not permit the marketer to pursue a particular option. For example, selling through a desired retailer may not be feasible if the retailer refuses to handle a product.

For marketers, the choice of distribution design comes down to selecting between direct or indirect methods, or in some cases choosing both.

Direct Distribution System

With a direct distribution system, the marketer reaches the intended final user of its product by distributing the product directly to the customer. That is, there are no other parties involved in the distribution process that take ownership of the product. The direct system can be further divided by the method of communication taking place when a sale occurs. These methods are:

♦ Direct Marketing Systems – With this system, the customer places the order either through information gained from non-personal contact with the marketer, such as by visiting the marketer's website or ordering from the marketer's catalog, or through personal communication with a customer representative who is not a salesperson, such as through toll-free telephone ordering.

♦ Direct Retail Systems – This type of system exists when a product marketer also operates its own retail outlets under an independent channel arrangement. As previously discussed, Starbucks' own stores would fall into this category.

♦ Personal Selling Systems – The key to this direct distribution system is that a person whose main responsibility involves creating and managing sales (e.g., salesperson) is involved in the distribution process, generally by persuading the buyer to place an order. While the order itself may not be handled by the salesperson (e.g., buyer physically places the order online or by phone) the salesperson plays a role in generating the sales.

♦ Assisted Marketing Systems – Under the assisted marketing system, the marketer relies on others to help communicate the marketer's products, but handles distribution directly to the customer. The classic example of assisted marketing systems is eBay which helps bring buyers and sellers together for a fee. Other agents and brokers would also fall into this category.

Indirect Distribution System

With an indirect distribution system, the marketer reaches the intended final user with the help of others. These resellers usually take ownership of the product, though, in some cases, they may sell products on a consignment basis (i.e., only pay the supplying company if the product is sold). Under this system, intermediaries may be expected to assume many responsibilities to help sell the product. Indirect methods include:

♦ <u>Single-Party Selling System</u> – Under this system the marketer engages another party who then sells and distributes directly to the final customer. This is most likely to occur when the product is sold through large store-based retail chains or through online retailers.

♦ <u>Multiple-Party Selling System</u> – This indirect distribution system has the product passing through two or more distributors before reaching the final customer. The most likely scenario is when a wholesaler purchases from the manufacturer and sells the product to retailers.

Multichannel or Hybrid System

In cases where a marketer utilizes more than one distribution design the marketer is following a multichannel or hybrid distribution system. As we discussed, Starbucks follows this approach as its distribution design includes using a direct retail system by selling in company-owned stores, a direct marketing system by selling via direct mail, and a single-party selling system by selling through grocery stores (they also use other distribution systems). The multichannel approach expands distribution and allows the marketer to reach a wider market, however, as we discussed, the marketer must be careful with this approach due to the potential for channel conflict.

> *Retail sandwich chain Quiznos is following the lead of other food retailers, such as Subway and Taco Bell, by expanding distribution into filing stations and convenience stores. While Quiznos has over 4,000 restaurant locations, the move into fast delivery outlet represents a new distribution channel. The company estimates that conveniences store locations generate twice the sales per square foot as regular Quiznos stores. (11)*

DISTRIBUTION IN GLOBAL MARKETS

Organizations looking to distribute outside their home market may experience challenges that are significantly greater than what they face in their home market. Marketers, who are new to selling internationally, often discover the learning-curve for doing this effectively can be quite steep. In addition to potentially significant cultural differences that exist between customers in their home market and targeted customers in a new foreign market, marketers may find many other barriers to effective distribution including legal, political, and infrastructure limitations (see *Infrastructure Issues* discussion above). Consequently, upon entering a new foreign market, many companies discover that strategies they utilized successfully in their home market do not work in the new market.

Because companies often find it difficult to replicate their success when entering new markets, they may need to consider different strategies for establishing a marketing presence beyond their home country. In general, marketers have available the following options for gaining distribution in global markets:

♦ Exporting – With this distribution method, a marketer does not set up a physical presence in a foreign market. Instead, product is shipped by the company to buyers in the foreign market. In the simplest arrangement, a marketer will accept customer orders on their website then arrange for international shipment to reach the customer (e.g., FedEx shipment). In some exporting arrangements, the marketer negotiates with a marketing firm located in the foreign country to assist in generating orders, managing customers, and possibly handling some distribution activities. The main benefit of the export option is that risks and costs are relatively low. On the downside, exporting may not enable a company to realize full demand for the product since the marketer does not have a local presence and, consequently, cannot dedicate full attention to developing the market.

♦ Joint Operation – In general, this is a relationship where two or more organizations team to market products. For instance, a company may agree on a licensing arrangement where the marketer allows another company in a foreign country to market its products. This arrangement may even extend to allowing the foreign company to manufacture the product. Other forms of joint operation occur when a marketer forms a partnership with a company in the host country, often resulting in the creation of a new company. Ownership in such an arrangement may be equally split or one partner may have a greater percentage of the final company. Under this arrangement, the risk is split between the partnering organizations.

♦ Direct Investment – This represents to most involved business situation where the marketer owns nearly all key aspects of conducting business in another country. The key advantage with direct investment is the control it offers as the company can make all decisions and retain all profits. However, the risks are quite high as the marketer must often invest heavily to establish and maintain operations.

Finally, when it comes to global distribution, marketers must be aware of unauthorized distributors selling the marketer's product. Often such distributors operate in a "**gray market**" where they obtain products from legitimate distributors, who may be approved to handle a product but are not approved to sell to certain distribution outlets. These unauthorized distributors can be difficult to control and, depending on the country in which they are selling the product, their activities may prove challenging for the marketer to stop.

> *Many smaller US companies often see Canada as an attractive market to begin a move into global distribution. But they soon find the need to have a full understanding of all costs associated with exporting to Canada. For example, when a U.S. company exports to buyers in Canada they must carefully assess such issues as differences in exchange rates, shipping expense, additional packaging costs, sales tax, participation in trade shows and several others. Sometimes, when all additional costs are added, a marketer will realize that expansion to a foreign market may not be profitable. (12)*

||||||||||||||||||||||||||||||||||||||||||||||||||||||||||||||||||||||||||||||||||||||||||||||||||||

REFERENCES

1. Olson, E., "Marketing Fanciful Items in the Lands of Make Believe," *New York Times*, September 6, 2010.

2. *Amazon.com* website.

3. Barrett, A., "How to Adapt Products for Different Markets," *Inc. Magazine*, October 1, 2010.

4. "Coke Pays $715 Million to Distribute Dr Pepper," *USA Today*, June 7, 2010.

5. Dodes, R. and C. Passariello, "Luxury Brands Stake Out New Department Store Turf," *Wall Street Journal*, May 4, 2011.

6. *Starbucks* website.

7. *Starbucks* website.

8. Demery, P., "Getting Web Feet," *Internet Retailer*, March 31, 2010.

9. "Become a Supplier," *Walmart* website.

10. Needleman, S. E., "How a Start-Up Landed Shelf Space at Wal-Mart," *Wall Street Journal*, September 23, 2011.

11. Jargon, J., "Quiznos Carves Out Broader Niche," *Wall Street Journal*, March 1, 2010.

12. Klonsky, E., "How to Sell Your Product in Canada," *Inc. Magazine*, January 19, 2011.

Full text of many of the references can be accessed via links on the support website.

Chapter 9: Retailing

In an ideal business world, most marketers would prefer to handle all their distribution activities by way of the corporate channel arrangement we discussed in Chapter 8. Such an arrangement gives the marketer total control in dealing with customers, which can make it easier to build strong, long-term relationships.

Unfortunately, for many marketing organizations a corporate channel arrangement is not feasible. Whether due to high cost or lack of experience needed to run a channel efficiently, marketing organizations need third-party channel members to get their products into the hands of customers. For most companies, selling goods and services this means enlisting the assistance of resellers.

In this chapter, we begin our examination of resellers by examining the role retailers serve in reselling a marketer's products. We begin by setting out reasons why selecting resellers is an important decision that should not be taken lightly. We then turn our attention to a detailed look at retailing, which in terms of sales volume and number of employees is one of the largest sectors of most economies. We show that retailing is quite diverse, and marketers, who want to distribute through retailers, must be familiar with the differences that exist among different retail options. The chapter concludes with a look at the key concerns facing today's retailers.

‖‖‖

IMPORTANCE OF RESELLERS

As we discussed in Chapter 8, marketers must often enlist the assistance of others to get their products into the hands of customers. This is especially the case for marketers selling to the final consumer through retail stores, though business-to-business marketers also face such decisions. One main type of channel member linking marketers to their customers is the reseller, who purchases products from supplying firms and then resells these to its customers. Examples of resellers include retailers, wholesalers, and industrial distributors.

Choosing a reseller for product distribution is crucial since the characteristics of a reseller, including how they handle customers, can affect how a marketer's customers view the company and the products it offers. For instance, a reseller's reputation (e.g., high-quality vs. low-quality) and customers' experience when they visit the reseller to make a purchase (e.g., how long it takes to be serviced), may impact how customers feel about the products they purchase through the reseller. Consequently, marketers must take into consideration many issues when selecting resellers including:

♦ Is the target market served by the reseller the same as the marketer's target market?

♦ Does the reseller offer the expertise needed to address customers' questions regarding the marketer's product?

♦ Will the reseller help the marketer in promotional activities?

♦ Will the reseller share customer information with the marketer?

♦ Does the reseller carry competitor's products?

Once resellers have been identified a much bigger task lies ahead for the marketer: convincing the reseller to enter a relationship.

How to Establish Reseller Relationships

Convincing resellers to handle a product requires marketers use the same marketing skills they use to sell to their final customers. And, just as they do when selling to the final customer, marketers' first step when selling to resellers is to identify their needs, which are much different than those of the final customer. For instance, when it comes to selling to resellers, marketers should consider the following reseller needs:

♦ Products - Primarily resellers seek products of interest to their customers. For instance, a buyer for a large retailer may personally not like a particular product but, nonetheless, will purchase it as long as customers are willing to buy. Thus, selling to resellers means the marketer must show convincing evidence the customers serviced by the reseller will purchase the products.

♦ Delivery - Resellers want the product delivered on time and in good condition in order to meet customer demand and avoid inventory out-of-stocks. A product supplier must present a clearly articulated distribution plans when convincing resellers to distribute their product.

♦ Profit Margin - Resellers are in business to make money so a key factor in their decision to handle a product is how much money they will make on each product sold. They expect the difference (i.e., margin) between their cost for acquiring the product from a supplier and the price they charge to sell the product to their customers will be sufficient to meet their profit objectives.

♦ Other Incentives - Besides profit margin, resellers may want other incentives to entice them, especially if they are required to give extra effort selling the product. These incentives may be in the form of additional free products or even bonuses (e.g., money, free trips) for achieving sales goals (see *Trade Sales Promotion* discussion in Chapter 14).

♦ Packaging - Resellers want to handle products as easily as possible and want their suppliers to ship and sell products in packages that fit within their system. For example, retailers may require products be a certain size or design in order to fit on their store's shelf, or the shipping package must fit within the wholesaler's warehouse or receiving dock space. Also, many resellers are now requiring marketers to consider adding identification tags to products (e.g., RFID tags) to allow for easier inventory tracking when the product is received and when it is sold.

> *A major force in the use of RFID tags is Wal-Mart which for several years has required suppliers to include these on shipping pallets sent to its stores and has also attached these tags to individual products, including clothing. The adoption of the tags by Wal-Mart is credited with helping to sharply reduce the cost of these electronic tags. While a few years ago a single RFID tag cost more than 50 cents, the cost has now dropped to just a few cents per tag. (1)*

♦ Training - Some marketers require their resellers have strong knowledge of the products they are distributing. This is particularly pertinent in selling situations where product demonstrations are needed. To address the need for reseller knowledge, marketers must consider offering training to ensure resellers present the product accurately.

♦ Promotional Help - Resellers often seek additional help from the product supplier to promote the product to customers. Such help may come in the form of funding for advertisements, point-of-purchase product materials, or in-store demonstrations.

||||||||||||||||||||||||||||||||||||||||||||||||||||||||||||||||||||||||||||||||||||||||||||||||||||||||

WHAT IS RETAILING?

Retailing is defined as selling products to consumers for their personal use. A retailer is a reseller from which a consumer purchases products. Retailing is one of the largest sectors of most economies. In the U.S. alone, there are over 1,100,000 retail outlets that generate nearly $4 trillion in sales and employ over 15 million. (2).

In the majority of retail situations, the organization from which a consumer makes purchases is a reseller of products obtained from others and not the product manufacturer, though as we discussed in Chapter 8, some manufacturers do operate their own retail outlets in a corporate channel arrangement. While consumers are the retailer's buyers, a consumer does not always buy from retailers. For instance, when a consumer purchases from another consumer (e.g., eBay), the consumer purchase would not be classified as a retail purchase. This distinction can get confusing but, in the U.S. and other countries, the dividing line is whether the one selling to consumers is classified as a business (e.g., legal and tax purposes) or is selling as a hobby without legal business standing.

Benefits of Retailers

As a reseller, retailers offer many benefits to suppliers and customers as we discussed in Chapter 8. The major benefits for each include:

♦ Access to Customers – For suppliers, the most valuable benefits provided by retailers are the opportunities they offer for reaching the supplier's target market, building product demand through retail promotions, and providing consumer feedback. The knowledge and skills offered by retailers are key for generating sales, profits, and customer loyalty for suppliers (see *Concerns of Retailers* discussion below).

♦ Access to Product – For consumers, the most significant benefits offered by retailers relate to the ability to purchase products that may not otherwise be easily available if the consumers had to deal directly with product suppliers. In particular, retailers provide consumers with the ability to purchase small quantities of a wide assortment of products at prices that are considered reasonably affordable. Additionally, when it comes to retailers with physical locations (e.g., retail store), these are likely to be located near the retailer's target market; thereby, enabling consumers to make purchases and take home the product much more conveniently than if they had to visit a product supplier's facility or purchase via the Internet.

‖‖‖

WAYS TO CATEGORIZE RETAILERS

There are many ways retailers can be categorized depending on the characteristics being evaluated. We separate retailers based on six factors directly related to key marketing decisions:

♦ Target Markets Served

♦ Product Offerings

♦ Distribution Method

♦ Pricing Structure

♦ Promotional Emphasis

♦ Service Level

and one operational factor:

♦ Ownership

However, these groups are not meant to be mutually exclusive. In fact, in some way all retailers can be placed into each category.

Target Markets Served

The first classification looks at the type of markets a retailer intends to target. These categories are identical to the levels of distribution classification scheme discussed in Chapter 8.

♦ Mass Market – Mass market retailers appeal to the largest market possible by selling products of interest to nearly all consumers. With such a large market from which to draw customers, the competition among these retailers is often fierce.

♦ Specialty Market – Retailers categorized as servicing the specialty market are likely to target buyers looking for products having certain features that go beyond mass marketed products, such as customers who require more advanced product options or a higher level of customer service. While not as large as the mass market, the target market serviced by specialty retailers can be sizable.

♦ Exclusive Market – Appealing to this market means appealing to discriminating customers who are often willing to pay a premium for features found in very few products and for highly personalized services. Since this target market is small, the number of retailers addressing this market within a given geographic area may also be small.

Products Carried

Under this classification, retailers are divided based on the width (i.e., number of different product lines) and depth (i.e., number of different products within a product line) of the products they carry.

♦ General Merchandisers – These retailers carry a wide range of product categories (i.e., broad width), though the number of different items within a particular product line is generally limited (i.e., shallow depth). A retailer such as Target would be considered a general merchandiser.

♦ Multiple Lines Specialty Merchandisers – Retailers classified in this category stock a limited number of product lines (i.e., narrow width). However, within the product groups they handle, these retailers often offer a greater selection (i.e., extended depth) than is offered by general merchandisers. For example, a consumer electronics retailer would fall into this category.

♦ Single Line Specialty Merchandisers – Some retailers limit their offerings to just one product line (i.e., very narrow width), and sometimes only one product (i.e., very shallow depth). This can be seen online where a relatively small website may sell a single product, such as computer gaming software. Another example may be a small jewelry store that only handles watches.

Distribution Method

Retailers sell in many different formats with some requiring consumers visit a physical location while others sell to customers in a virtual space. It should be noted that many retailers are not tied to a single distribution method but operate using multiple methods.

Store-Based Sellers

By far the predominant method consumers use to obtain products is to acquire these by physically visiting retail outlets (also called **brick-and-mortar stores**). Store outlets can be further divided into several categories. One key characteristic distinguishing categories is whether retail outlets are physically connected to one or more other stores:

• Stand-Alone – These are retail outlets that do not have other retail outlets connected.

• Strip-Shopping Center – A retail arrangement with two or more outlets physically connected or that share physical resources (e.g., share parking lot).

• Shopping Area – A local center of retail operations containing many retail outlets that may or may not be physically connected but are in proximity to each other, such as a city shopping district.

• Regional Shopping Mall – Consists of a large, self-contained shopping area with many connected outlets.

Large general merchandise retailers, operating stand-alone stores, have primarily located in fast growing suburban areas, where they can acquire affordable real estate for building large stores with sizeable parking lots. But now several retailers, including Wal-Mart and Target, are placing stores in more congested downtown areas where real estate is often limited and expensive. Doing so often requires a change in store design. For instance, a Target store in downtown Chicago offers a two story design featuring a shopping cart escalator. Additionally, while a parking area is located underground, many customers travel to the store on foot, by public transportation, or by cab. (3)

Non-Store Sellers

Under this approach, retailers sell products to customers who do not physically visit a retail outlet. In fact, in many cases customers make their purchase from within their own homes.

- Online Sellers – The fastest growing retail distribution method allows consumers to purchase products via the Internet and mobile devices. In most cases, delivery is then handled by a third-party shipping service.

- Direct Marketers – Retailers principally selling via direct methods (e.g., television, catalog) may have a primary location that receives orders but does not host shopping visits. Rather, orders are received via mail or phone.

- Vending – While purchasing through vending machines does require the consumer to physically visit a location, it is considered non-store retailing as the vending operations are not located at the vending company's place of business.

Nearly all major store-based retailers are also non-store sellers since they operate their own websites. In the U.S. websites run by retailers Best Buy, Target, and Wal-Mart are often within the top 100 websites in terms of website traffic, while in the U.K. retailers Argos and Tesco also operate popular sites. (4)

Pricing Strategy

Retailers can be classified based on their general pricing strategy. Retailers must decide whether their approach is to use price as a competitive advantage or to seek competitive advantage in non-price ways.

- Discount Pricing – Discount retailers are best known for selling low priced products having a low profit margin (i.e., price minus cost). To make profits these retailers look to sell in high volume. Typically discount retailers operate with low overhead costs by vigorously controlling operational spending on such things as real estate (e.g., locate in less expensive areas), design issues (e.g., less elaborate store layout), and by offering fewer services to their customers.

◆ Competitive Pricing – The objective of some retailers, particularly those in the specialty market, is not to compete on price, though they do not want to be perceived as charging the highest price. These retailers aggressively monitor the market to ensure their pricing is competitive, but they do not desire to get into price wars with discount retailers. Thus, other elements of their marketing strategy (e.g., higher quality products, more attractive store setting) are used to create higher value for which the customer will pay more.

◆ Full Price Pricing – Retailers targeting exclusive markets find such markets are far less price sensitive than mass or specialty markets. In these cases the additional value added through increased operational spending (e.g., expensive locations, more attractive design, more services) justify higher retail prices. While these retailers are likely to sell in lower volume than discount or competitive pricing retailers, the profit margins for each product are much higher.

Promotional Emphasis

Retailers generate customer interest using a variety of promotional techniques, yet some retailers rely on certain methods more than others as their principle promotional approach.

◆ Advertising – Many retailers find traditional mass promotional methods of advertising, such as through newspapers or television, continue to be their best means for creating customer interest. Retailers selling online rely mostly on Internet and mobile advertising as their promotional method of choice.

◆ Direct Mail – A form of advertising that many retailers use for the bulk of their promotion is direct mail – advertising through postal mail. Using direct mail for promotion is the primary way catalog retailers distribute their materials. It also is utilized by smaller companies, who promote using postcards and other types of mailing methods.

◆ Personal Selling – Retailers selling expensive or high-end products find a considerable amount of their promotional effort is spent in person-to-person contact with customers. While many of these retailers use other promotional methods, especially advertising, the consumer-salesperson relationship is key to persuading consumers to make purchase decisions.

> *In addition to the promotional methods cited above, retailers also use short-term promotions, called sales promotions (discussed in Chapter 14), designed to encourage customers to undertake certain activity, such as make a purchase or visit a store. One common type of sales promotion is the issuing of **rewards cards** offering special discounts or cash back for reaching predefined purchase levels. But retailers handle these promotions in different ways and not always to the liking of its customers. For example, customers of drugstore retailer CVS are annoyed their rewards are printed on a receipt that can only be redeemed if the receipt is presented during a future purchase. Instead, customers are complaining the discounts should be stored on their rewards card, which they general carry. They believe this limits the burden of having to remember to bring the receipts. (5)*

Service Level

Retailers attract customers not only with desirable products and affordable prices, but also by offering services that enhance the purchase experience. There are at least three levels of retail service:

♦ Self-Service – This service level allows consumers to perform most or all of the services associated with retail purchasing. For some consumers self-service is considered a benefit, while others may view it as an inconvenience. Self-service can be seen with: 1) **self-selection** services, such as online purchasing and vending machine purchases, and 2) **self-checkout** services, where the consumer may get help selecting the product but they use self-checkout stations to process the purchase, including scanning and payment.

♦ Assorted-Service – The majority of retailers offer some level of service to consumers. Service includes handling the point-of-purchase transaction, assisting with product selection, arranging payment plans, offering delivery, and many more.

♦ Full-Service – The full-service retailer attempts to handle nearly all aspects of the purchase to the point where all consumers do is select the item they wish to buy. Retailers following a full-price pricing strategy often use the full-service approach as a way of adding value to a customer's purchase.

Ownership Structure

Finally, retailers can be categorized based on the ownership structure of the business.

♦ Individually Owned and Operated – Under this ownership structure, an individual or corporate entity owns and operates one or a very small number of relatively small outlets.

Marketing Story

Major Grocer Getting Rid of Self-Checkout Lanes
MSNBC

Giving customers what they want is the mantra of nearly all marketers, and for the last 50-plus years has been arguably the most fundamental concept in marketing. Marketers have been schooled to believe that success rests on giving customers what they "think" they want. Many marketers have translated this to mean customers want to be empowered in deciding what goods and services are best for them. That is, they believe most customers want to know they are in control when dealing with the marketer.

Customer empowerment can be seen across all consumer and business markets, and in many forms. But the most prominent form of empowerment is the move to offering self-service purchasing where previously the option was not available. Some examples include the growth of such customer purchase options as home improvement retail stores, at home movie purchases, and online vacation booking. For businesses, empowerment is evident with in-house publication design, online advertising, and management of product shipment.

There are several arguments to support the idea of empowering customers. First, as noted, marketers believe this is what customers want, and marketers are trained to offer goods and services that satisfy customers' needs. Second, letting customers do the work reduces marketers' costs. Essentially, this happens because labor-intensive work is shifted away from the company and to the customer. Third, with technology tied to many empowering situations, the ability to track and gather customer research far exceeds what can be obtained when the marketer performs the work. For instance, by monitoring what customers do when performing their own work marketers may learn about new needs that customers have, which can then be translated into new products and product features.

But empowering customers may have a downside as some companies are finding. As discussed in this story, by enabling customers to do work marketers often lose personal contact. Whether it is placing orders online instead of through a customer service phone call or, as discussed in this story, allowing customers to handle their own checkout of groceries, marketers may be distancing themselves from customers. The implications of loss of personal contact include: 1) the inability to up-sell customers on more expensive products; 2) less opportunity to get inside the customer's head to see what they really want; and 3) possibly the biggest concern, the reduction of customer loyalty as customers feel less connection to a particular company.

The move marks a surprising step back from a trend that began about a decade ago, when supermarkets began installing self-checkout lanes, touting them as a solution to long lines. Now some grocery chains are questioning whether they are really good for business. (6)

Has the empowerment of customers gone too far? Are there other changes retailers should consider in order to re-connect with customers?

◆ Corporate Chain – A retail chain consists of multiple retail outlets owned and operated by a single entity all performing similar retail activities. While the number of retail outlets required to be classified as a chain has never been specified, we will assume that anyone owning more than five retail locations would be considered a chain.

◆ Corporate Structure – This classification covers large retailers operating less than five locations, such as automotive dealers or furniture stores, and those operating in the non-store retail arena, such as online, catalog, and vending companies.

◆ Contractually Licensed and Individually Operated – The contractual channel arrangement discussed in Chapter 8 has led to a retail ownership structure in which operators of the retail outlet are not the out-right owners of the business. Instead, the arrangement often involves a legal agreement in which the owner of the retail concept allows the operator to run the owner's business concept in exchange for financial considerations, such as a percentage of revenue. This structure is most often seen in retail franchising (see *Franchise* discussion below).

IIIIIIIIIIIIIIIIIIIIIIIIIIIIIIIIIIIIIIIIIIIIIIIIIIIIIIIIIIIIIIIIIIIIIIIIIIIIIIIIIIIIIIIIIIIIIIIIIIIIIIIIIIIIIIIIIIIIIIIIIIIIII

RETAIL FORMATS

Now that we have presented ways in which retailers can be classified, we can use these categories to distinguish general formats or business models that best describe retail operations. These categories are designed to identify the primary format a retailer follows. In some cases, particularly with the advent of the Internet, a retailer will be involved in more than one format.

Mom-and-Pop

These represent small, individually owned and operated retail outlets. In many cases, these are family-run businesses catering to the local community often with a high level of service but relatively small product selection.

Mass Discounter

These retailers can be either general or specialty merchandisers but either way their main focus is on offering discount pricing. Compared to other store types, mass discounters offer fewer services and lower quality products.

Boutique

This retail format is best represented by a small store carrying highly specialized and often high-end merchandise. In many cases, a boutique is a full-service retailer following a full-price pricing strategy.

Specialty Store

A step above the boutique store is the specialty store, which is generally represented by mid-sized stores carrying more depth than boutique stores. The service level of specialty stores is not as focused as it is with boutiques, though customer service is a key element to their success.

> *Kitson, a retail chain located in Southern California, specializes in offering products catering to customers looking for trendy clothing, accessories and novelty goods. The retailer is frequented by Hollywood celebrities who are often photographed by paparazzi while in the store. Kitson sees promotional value in the photos taken at their store and often mentions these on their website. (7)*

Category Killer

Many major retail chains have taken what previously were narrowly focused, small specialty store concepts and have expanded them to create large specialty stores. These so-called "category killers" have been found in such specialty areas as electronics (e.g., Best Buy), office supplies (e.g., Staples), and sporting goods (e.g., Sports Authority).

Department Store

These retailers are general merchandisers offering mid-to-high quality products and a strong level of services, though in most cases these retailers would not fall into the full-service category. While department stores are classified as general merchandisers, some carry a more selective product line. For instance, while Sears carries a wide range of products from hardware to cosmetics, Nordstrom focuses on clothing and personal care products.

Warehouse Store

This is a form of mass discounter that often provides even lower prices than traditional mass discounters. In addition, they often require buyers to make minimum purchases in quantities that are greater than what can be purchased at mass discount stores. These retail outlets provide few services and product selection can be limited. Furthermore, the retail design and layout is, as the name suggests, warehouse style with consumers often selecting products off the ground from the shipping package. Some forms of warehouse stores, called warehouse clubs, require customers purchase memberships in order to gain access to the outlet.

Catalog Retailer

Many retailers, including Lands' End and L.L. Bean, have built their businesses by having customers place orders after seeing products that appear in a mailed catalog. Orders are then delivered by a third-party shipper.

Costco's Success Secrets Revealed
ABC News

Some retailing strategists believe general merchandise retailers must carry tens-of-thousands of products in order to satisfy the needs of their target market. This often means carrying the same type of product (e.g., laundry detergent) from several different suppliers.

But, in reality, there are several large retailers who are quite successful carrying extremely shallow product lines to the point where they may only carry a single brand within a product category.

A case in point is Costco, a so-called warehouse store catering to both consumers and business customers (though technically not a retailer when they sell to businesses). Their worldwide sales in 2010 exceeded $78 billion ranking them as the 2nd largest U.S.-based retailer. (8) What is remarkable is that they achieved this with an inventory of only 4.000 items compared to many other large retailers who carry well over 100,000 products.

As this video story points out, for Costco it is not about having a large number of different products, rather, it is about having the right mix of products. And the right mix requires retailers have a clear understanding of what their target market wants. Additionally, Costco's low-cost-for-bulk-purchase approach has benefited from recent economic problems, which has driven even more customers to their stores. The story also discusses Costco's store design and layout strategies.

"We keep our selection down so we can get the most of it and offer the best value, the best price." *You may not always find the same brand names from month to month because Costco buys from* *whichever company has surplus stock.* *"We really just put the best items out there. We try to keep* *it very simple."* *(9)*

In what other ways, not mentioned in this story, does Costco differ from other leading general retailers such as Wal-Mart and Target?

Convenience Store

As the name implies these general merchandise retailers cater to offering customers an easy purchase experience. Convenience is offered in many ways, including through easily accessible store locations, small store size that allows for quick shopping, and fast checkout. The product selection offered by these retailers is extremely limited and pricing can be high.

Franchise

As noted in Chapter 8, a franchise is a form of contractual channel in which one party, the franchisor, controls the business activities of another party, the franchisee. Under these arrangements, an eligible franchisee agrees to pay for the right to use the franchisor's business methods and other key business aspects, such as the franchise name. Franchises offer several advantages as discussed in Box 9-1.

> *As noted in Box 9-1, one key advantage of franchising is that business failure rates are often lower than for similar non-franchise businesses. But this does not mean that franchises rarely fail. According to information gathered from the U.S. Small Business Administration (SBA), the failure rate of several well-known franchises is exceptionally high as measured by defaults on loans obtained through the SBA. For instance, over 45% of SBA loans made to Blimpie franchises failed while the failure rate at Quiznos was 25%. (10)*

e-tailer

Possibly the most publicized retail model to evolve in the last 50 years is the retailer that principally sells via the Internet. There are thousands of online-only retail sellers of which Amazon is the most famous. These retailers offer shopping convenience including being open for business all day, every day. Electronic retailers or e-tailers also have the ability to offer a wide product selection since all they really need to attract orders is a picture and description of the product. That is, they may not need to have the product on-hand the way physical stores do. Instead, an e-tailer can wait until an order is received from a customer before placing its own order with its suppliers. This cuts down significantly on the cost of maintaining an inventory of products.

Vending

Within this category are automated methods allowing consumers to make purchases and quickly acquire products. While most consumers are well aware of vending machines for the purchase of smaller items, such as beverages and snack foods, newer devices are entering the market containing more expensive and bulkier products, such as music players, software, flowers, and cologne and have been adopted by such leading companies as Apple, Best Buy and Verizon. (11) These systems require the vending machine have either Internet or telecommunications access to permit purchase using credit cards.

> *In the U.S., the Minnesota Vikings of the National Football League are testing vending machines for distributing team merchandise. Along with its apparel partner, MainGate, the Vikings are selling shirts, trading cards and other official licensed merchandise through vending machines at the Mall of Americas. (12)*

Box 9-1

FRANCHISING BASICS

Starting a retail operation is a dream for many aspiring entrepreneurs. But the risks involved can be substantial. Whether starting a store-based or online retail outlet, the costs associated with creating a presence, such as opening a store or building a website, and acquiring inventory, can be steep. But even for retailers having the financial resources to establish a retail location, they still face the difficult hurdle of gaining customer recognition. In fact, opening a store may be easy compared to promotional efforts needed to build store traffic.

Because of the risk involved in building a retail outlet, acquiring a franchise may be an attractive option for entrepreneurs looking to move quickly from initial investment to producing revenue. In fact, the success rates for franchises tends to be higher compared with starting a business in more traditional ways. This is particularly the case when joining a well-established franchise operation. Franchise business opportunities are available in a wide variety of categories and offered by such companies as Subway, Dunkin' Donuts, 7-Eleven, and Holiday Inn. (13)

Under a franchise arrangement, a **franchisor** (i.e., franchise owner) allows others, known as **franchisees**, to employ its business model in exchange for a fee, which generally includes a portion of the generated revenue. For instance, McDonalds is a well-known franchisor that allows individuals to use the McDonalds name and methods to deliver food to consumers. Payment to acquire a franchise is usually in the form of both a one-time, upfront franchise fee and an on-going percentage of revenue.

While the cost to the franchisee may be quite high and there are often many restrictions on what the franchisee can do, this form of retailing offers several advantages. First, it allows the franchisee to open a business that may already be known to local customers; thus reducing the promotional effort required to establish awareness. Second, training provided by the franchisor may enable the franchisee to be successful much faster than if they attempted to start a business on his/her own.

For the franchisor, the key benefit of the franchise model is that it allows for faster expansion with less capital requirements since funds needed to expand the business (e.g., acquiring retail space, local advertising) are often supported by the franchisee's up-front fee. Additionally, overall revenue may grow faster in a shorter time if demand for the franchise is strong.

Retailing Format Summary

Below in Table 9-1 we summarize each retail format by using the seven categorization characteristics. The characteristics identified for each format should be viewed as the "most likely" case for that format and are not necessarily representative of all retailers that fall into this format.

Table 9-1: Retailing Format Summary

Format	Target Market	Products Carried	Pricing Strategy	Promotion Emphasis	Distribution	Service Level	Ownership Structure
Mom-and-Pop	mass specialty	general specialty	competitive	advertising direct mail	stand-alone strip center shopping area	assorted	individually owned/oper.
Mass Discounter	mass	general	discount	advertising	stand-alone strip-center	self	corp. chain
Boutique	specialty exclusive	specialty	full	selling	stand-alone strip center shopping area	full	individually owned/oper. corp. chain
Specialty	specialty	specialty	full competitive	selling advertising	shopping area shopping mall	full	corp. chain
Category Killer	mass	specialty	discount competitive	advertising	stand-alone strip center	assorted	corp. chain
Department Store	specialty	general	competitive	advertising	shopping area shopping mall	assorted	corp. chain
Warehouse Store	mass	general	discount	advertising	stand-alone	self	corp. chain
Catalog	mass specialty	general specialty	discount competitive	direct mail	direct marketer	assorted	corp. structure
Convenience	mass	general	full	advertising	stand-alone	self	individually owned/oper. corp. chain
Franchise	mass	specialty	competitive	advertising	stand-alone strip center	assorted	contractual
e-tailer	mass specialty	general specialty	discount competitive full	advertising	online seller	self	corp. structure
Vending	mass	specialty	full	none	vending	self	corp. structure

|||||||||||||||||||||||||||||||||||||||||||||||||||||||||||||||||||||||||||||||||||||||||||||||||||||||||||||||||||||||||||||||||||

CONCERNS OF RETAILERS

While much of the discussion in this chapter deals with the role of retailers in the marketing strategy for consumer products companies, it is necessary to understand that retailers face their own marketing challenges. Among the marketing issues facing retailers are:

♦ Improving Customer Satisfaction - Retailers know that satisfied customers are loyal customers. Consequently, retailers must develop strategies intended to build relationships that result in customers returning to make more purchases.

♦ Acquiring the Right Products - Customers will only be satisfied if they can purchase the right products to satisfy their needs. Since a large percentage of retailers do not manufacture their own products, they must seek suppliers who will supply products demanded by customers. Thus, an important objective for retailers is to identify the products customers will demand and negotiate with suppliers to obtain these products.

> *While determining which products are right for their customers is a key issue, retailers must also insure that the suppliers offering these products are able to deliver when needed. This appears to be a problem for small military surplus stores. For years, these stores have acquired used government products, such as clothing and military gear, and then sold these to the public. But the U.S. Government has reduced the products they make available as surplus due to concerns the products may be acquired by terrorist groups. The reduced supply has significantly affected sales in many military surplus stores, with several being forced to close their doors. (14)*

♦ Presenting Products to Generate Interest - Once obtained, products must be presented or merchandised to customers in a way that generates interest. **Retail merchandising** often requires hiring creative people who understand and can relate to the market.

♦ Building Customer Traffic - Like any marketer, retailers must use promotional methods to build customer interest. For retailers, a key measure of interest is the number of people visiting a retail location or website. Building "traffic" is accomplished with a variety of promotional techniques, including advertising, and specialized promotional activities, such as coupons.

♦ Creating an Attractive Layout - For store-based retailers, a store's physical layout is an essential component in creating a retail experience that will attract customers. The physical layout is more than just deciding in what part of the store to locate products. For many retailers designing the right shopping atmosphere (e.g., objects, light, sound) can add to the appeal of a store. Layout is also crucial in the online world where **website navigation and usability** may be deciding factors in whether a retail website is successful.

♦ <u>Keeping Pace with Technology</u> - Technology has invaded all areas of retailing, including customer knowledge (e.g., customer relationship management software), product movement (e.g., use of RFID tags for tracking), point-of-purchase (e.g., scanners, kiosks, self-serve checkout), web technologies (e.g., online shopping carts, purchase recommendations), and many more. Because adopting technology can potentially lead to having a competitive advantage, it is important retailer's by close attention to technologies impacting their market.

♦ <u>Finding Good Locations</u> - Where to physically locate a retail store may help or hinder store traffic. Well placed stores with high visibility and easy access, while possibly commanding higher land usage fees, may hold significantly more value than lower cost sites that yield less traffic. Consequently, evaluating the trade-off between store location costs and potential benefits is a necessary task when looking to expand retail operations.

> *As noted earlier, larger chain retailers, including Wal-Mart, have traditionally located their stores in suburban areas and small towns, and have stayed away from cities due to the high cost of acquiring real estate. However, Wal-Mart now realizes that, in order to continue to grow, it must expand into cities. It is doing so by downsizing their store footprint and focusing their product mix more heavily on grocery items. (15)*

REFERENCES

1. Bustillo, M., "Wal-Mart Radio Tags to Track Clothing," *Wall Street Journal*, July 23, 2010.
2. "2007 Economic Census," *United States Census Bureau*.
3. Cater, F., "Big-Box Retailers Move to Smaller Stores in Cities," *National Public Radio*, December 21, 2010.
4. Top 500 U.S. and Top 500 U.K. Websites, *Alexa.com*.
5. Lazarus, D., "Wake Up and Hear the Rewards Clamor, CVS," *Los Angeles Times*, August 12, 2011.
6. Anand, A., "Major Grocer Getting Rid of Self-Checkout Lanes," *MSNBC*, July 10, 2011.
7. Binkley, C., "How Stores Lead You to Spend," *Wall Street Journal*, November 30, 2010.
8. Schutlz, D., "Top 100 Retailers," *Stores*, July 2011.
9. "Costco's Success Secrets Revealed," *ABC News*, March 29, 2010.
10. "The Best and Worst Franchises to Own," *Inc. Magazine*, January 25, 2011.
11. For an example of advanced vending machines see *ZoomSystems* website.
12. Brunt, C., "NFL Teams Look to Vending Machines as Sales Option," *USA Today*, October 2, 2010.
13. For a list of top franchises see *Entrepreneur Magazine* website.
14. Zwahlen, C., "Military Surplus Retailers Struggle With Short Supplies," *Los Angeles Times*, May 9, 2011.
15. Bustillo, M., "Wal-Mart Sees Small Stores in Big Cities," *Wall Street Journal*, October 13, 2010.
Full text of many of the references can be accessed via links on the support website.

Chapter 10: Wholesaling and Product Movement

As we saw in Chapter 8, it is more the rule than the exception that marketers are not able to handle all distribution activities on their own. Instead, to get products into the hands of customers often requires the assistance of third-party service firms. In addition to retailers, marketers should be aware of others whose expertise in certain facets of distribution can prove quite beneficial.

In this chapter, we first examine another reselling group - wholesalers - and see how they come into play when a marketer attempts to reach the final customer. We show wholesalers exist in many formats, affect a wide range of industries, and offer different sets of features and benefits depending on the markets they serve. In the second half of the chapter, we examine the tasks that must be carried out in order to physically move products to customers. In some cases, the marketer will take on the responsibility of carrying out some functions, while other tasks may be assigned to distribution service providers. Whether handled by the marketer or contracted to others, these functions are crucial to having a cost-effective and efficient distribution system. It is worth noting that while most product movement is concerned with moving tangible products, some of the issues covered here are also applicable to intangible products, such as services, and to digital products.

||||||||||||||||||||||||||||||||||||||||||||||||||||||||||||||||||||||||||||||||||||||||||||||||||||||||||||||||||||||||||||

WHAT IS WHOLESALING?

Wholesaling is a distribution channel function where one organization buys from supply firms with the primary intention of redistributing to other organizations. A wholesaler is an organization providing the necessary means to: 1) allow suppliers to reach organizational buyers, and 2) allow certain business buyers to purchase products, which they may not be able to purchase directly from suppliers. In the U.S., there are over 430,000 wholesale operations that generate over $6.5 billion in sales and employ over 6 million. (1)

While many large retailers and even manufacturers have centralized facilities and carry out the same tasks as wholesalers, we do not classify these as wholesalers since these relationships only involve one other party, the buyer. Thus, a distinguishing characteristic of wholesalers is they offer distribution benefits for <u>both</u> a supplying party and for a purchasing party. For our discussion of wholesalers, we will primarily focus on wholesalers who sell to other resellers, such as retailers.

The website Wholesale Central provides links to over 1,400 wholesalers selling more than 50 product categories. For instance, the website lists over 40 wholesalers selling perfume products. For the most part, companies listed only sell to other businesses, such as retailers, and not to consumers. (2)

Benefits of Wholesalers

The benefits wholesalers offer to members of the channel of distribution can be significant, and involve most of channel member benefits we discussed in Chapter 8, though specific benefits vary by type of wholesaler. Yet there are two particular benefits – one for suppliers and one for retailers – that are common to most wholesale operations and are worth further discussion:

◆ <u>Provide Access to Products</u> – Wholesalers are in business to provide goods and services to buyers (e.g., retailers) that fall under one of the following conditions: 1) the buyer cannot purchase directly from suppliers because their purchase quantities are too low to meet the supplier's minimum order requirements; or 2) if a buyer purchases directly from suppliers, they will pay higher prices compared to larger purchasers, who obtain better pricing because they purchasing in greater quantities. Since wholesalers sell to a large number of buyers the size of orders they place with suppliers may match those of large retailers, which may allow them to obtain lower prices. Wholesalers can then pass these lower prices along to their buyers, which can enable smaller retailers to remain competitive with larger rivals. In this way, transacting through wholesalers is often the only way certain retailers can stay in business.

◆ <u>Provide Access to Markets</u> – Providing smaller retailers access to products they cannot acquire without wholesaler help offers a benefit for suppliers as well since it opens additional market opportunities for suppliers. That is, suppliers can have their products purchased and made available for sale across a wide number of retail outlets. More importantly, for a company offering a new product, convincing a few wholesalers to stock a new product may make it easier to gain traction in the market as the wholesaler can yield power with the smaller retailers convincing them to stock the new product. Considering a wholesaler can serve hundreds of small retail customers, the marketing efforts required to persuade a wholesaler to adopt a new product may be far more efficient compared to efforts needed to convince hundreds of individual store owners to stock the new product.

||||||||||||||||||||||||||||||||||||||||||||||||||||||||||||||||||||||||||||||||||||||||||||||||||||||||||||||||||

WAYS TO CATEGORIZE WHOLESALERS

In Chapter 9, we showed how retailers can be categorized using different characteristics. Wholesalers can likewise be grouped together, though the characteristics are slightly different.

For our purposes, we will separate wholesale operations based on four marketing decisions:

♦ products carried

♦ promotional activities

♦ distribution method

♦ service level

and one legal factor:

♦ product ownership

As we discussed with our retailer categorization, these grouping schemes are not meant to be mutually exclusive. Consequently, a wholesaler can be evaluated on each characteristic.

Products Carried

Similar to how retailers can be categorized, wholesalers can also be classified by the width and depth of the product lines they handle. The categories include:

♦ General Merchandise – Wholesalers carrying broad product lines fall into the general merchandise wholesaler category. Like general merchandise retailers, the product lines these wholesalers carry may not offer many options (i.e., shallow depth). These wholesalers tend to market to smaller general merchandise retailers, such as convenience or mom-and-pop stores.

♦ Specialty Merchandise – Wholesalers focusing on narrow product lines, but offering deep selection within the lines, fall into the specialty merchandise category. Most specialty merchandise wholesalers direct their marketing efforts to specific industries. For example, specialty wholesalers supply industries such as electronics, seafood, and pharmaceuticals.

Wholesalers are not limited to distributing only physical products. Wholesalers also exist in such industries as mortgage creation, vacation rental, and energy. Within the energy industry, one method for distributing electricity is through wholesalers. To be a wholesaler in the electricity market does not require the company be an electricity producer. So called Power Marketers purchase electricity from one supplier and then resell it to someone other than the end-use customer. (3)

Promotional Activities

Wholesalers can be separated based on the importance promotion plays in generating demand for products handled by the wholesaler. Two basic categories exist:

♦ Extensive Promotion – The main job of some wholesalers is to actively locate buyers. This occurs most often where a wholesaler is hired to find buyers for a supplier's products or where the wholesaler is aggressive in finding new customers for its business. Under these arrangements, the most common promotional activity is personal selling through a sales force, though advertising may also be used.

♦ Limited Promotion – Nearly all wholesalers engage in some promotional activities. Even in situations where a wholesaler dominates a channel, and clients have little choice but to acquire products from the wholesaler, some promotion will still occur. For instance, at times a wholesaler may need to use its salespeople to persuade buyers to purchase in larger volume than normal or to agree to stock a new product the wholesaler is handling. In other cases, especially for wholesalers selling products for business use, promotional activities may be more extensive and include advertising and other promotional methods.

Distribution Method

Wholesalers offer distribution options where customers may or may not be able to visit a physical location to acquire their purchases. For the purposes of our discussion of wholesaling, this category is separated based on whether or not a stationary location exists from which the wholesaler conducts the physical movement of products.

Stationary Location

In most common wholesaler arrangements, the wholesaler has one or more fixed facilities where product handling operations take place. However, while stationary wholesalers share the characteristic of a permanent location, they often differ on whether customers can visit these facilities:

• Customer Accessible – At certain wholesaler locations buyers can shop at the facility. In fact, retail warehouse clubs, such as Costco and Sam's Club, also function as wholesalers for qualifying businesses. In addition to selecting their orders, buyers are responsible for making their own arrangements to transport their purchases.

- Not Customer Accessible – Most operations classified as wholesalers do not permit buyers to visit their facilities in order to select items. Rather, buyers place orders via phone, over the Internet or through person-to-person contact with wholesaler's representatives. Also, in most cases, the wholesaler takes responsibility for product delivery.

Merchandise Mart Properties operates a number of stationary locations throughout the U.S. where they provide showroom space for a variety of wholesalers. For example, their LA Mart contains over 700,000 square feet of showroom space for over 100 wholesalers in the gift, accessory and furniture industries. (4)

Non-Stationary Location

Not all wholesalers carry inventory at a stationary location. In fact, some do not carry inventory at all.

- Mobile – Several specialized wholesalers transport products to the customer's location using vans or trucks. Buyers then have the ability to purchase product by either walking through the mobile facility or ordering from the wholesaler, who then selects the items from the vehicle.

- No Facilities – Some wholesalers do not have physical locations that store products. Instead, these operations rely on others, such as delivery companies, to ship products from one location (e.g., manufacturer) to the buyer's place of business.

Service Level

Wholesalers can be distinguished by the number and depth of services they provide to their customers.

- Full-Service – Wholesalers in this category mainly sell to the retail industry and, in most cases, require a strong, long-term retailer-wholesaler relationship. In addition to basic distribution services, such as providing access to an assortment of products and furnishing delivery, these wholesalers also offer customers many additional services that aid retail store operations. These services include offering assistance with: in-store merchandising, retail site location decisions (e.g., find best geographic location for a new store), store design and construction, back-end operations (e.g., payroll services), financial support, and many more.

♦ <u>Limited Service</u> – Compared to full-service wholesalers, buyers dealing with limited service firms receive far fewer services. Most offer basic services, such as product shipment and allowing credit purchasing, but few offer the number of service options found with full-service wholesalers.

♦ <u>No Service</u> – Some wholesalers follow a business model whose only service is to make products available for sale and only on a cash basis. In these instances, the buyer handles transportation of their purchases.

Product Ownership

Wholesalers can be classified based on whether they do or do not become the owners of the products they sell. By ownership we mean that **title** (i.e., legal ownership) has passed from the party from whom the wholesaler purchased the product (e.g., manufacturer) to the wholesaler. It also means the wholesaler assumes any risk that may arise with handling the product.

♦ <u>Do Take Title</u> – Wholesalers taking title own the products they purchase.

♦ <u>Do Not Take Title</u> – Wholesalers who do not take title are focused on activities that bring buyers and sellers together. Often these wholesalers never physically handle products.

||||||||||||||||||||||||||||||||||||||||||||||||||||||||||||||||||||||||||||||||||||||||||||||||||||||||||||

WHOLESALE FORMATS

Considering the criteria by which wholesalers can be categorized, it is not surprising many different wholesale formats exist. Below we discuss ten wholesale formats. While many of these wholesalers also have an online presence, we do not distinguish an "e-wholesaler" as a separate format the way we did with "e-tailers" or online retailers. The reason? While most wholesalers do operate from a brick-and-mortar facility, only a small fraction of wholesale operations permit customer shopping at their facilities. Consequently, the nature of this industry for many years has been to have customers use communication tools (e.g., phone, fax) to place orders. With the wholesale industry, the Internet simply serves as another communication option rather than a significantly different distribution channel.

General Merchandise

These wholesalers offer broad but shallow product lines that are mostly of interest to retailers carrying a wide assortment of products, such as convenience stores, and smaller general merchandise stores, such as those offering closeout or novelty products. Since these wholesalers offer such a wide range of products, their knowledge of individual products may not be strong.

Specialty Merchandise

Many wholesalers focus on specific product lines or industries and, in doing so, supply a narrow assortment of products. However, within the product lines offered there is considerable depth. Additionally, these wholesalers tend to be highly knowledgeable of the markets they serve.

Contractual

In Chapter 8, we introduced the concept of wholesaler-sponsored channel arrangements where a wholesaler brings together and manages many independent retailers. The services of these wholesalers are supplied only to the retailers involved in the contractual arrangement.

Industrial Distributors

The industrial distributor mainly directs its operations to the business customer rather than to other resellers. Depending on the distributor, they can carry either broad or narrow product lines.

Cash-and-Carry

A wholesale operation common to the food industry is the cash-and-carry where buyers visit the wholesaler's facility, select their orders pay in cash (i.e., credit purchases are often not permitted), and then handle their own deliveries (i.e., carry) to their place of business. This form of wholesaling has begun to expand outside of the food industry as large wholesale clubs, such as Costco and Sam's Club, allow qualified businesses to purchase products intended for retail sale.

Truck

As the name suggests, truck wholesaling operations are primarily run out of a truck that is stocked with products. These wholesalers often have assigned geographic territories where they regularly visit buyer's locations. In most cases, these wholesalers serve the retail food industry and industrial markets, where they offer specialty product lines.

Rack Jobber

Similar to truck wholesalers, the rack jobber also sells from a truck. However, the main difference is rack jobbers are assigned and manage space (i.e., racks) within a retailer's store. The rack jobber is then responsible for maintaining inventory and may even handle other marketing duties, such as setting product price. This form of wholesaling is most prominent with magazines, candy, bakery, and health-and-beauty products. In some trades, the name rack jobber is being replaced by the name **service merchandiser**.

Drop Shipper

Wholesalers in this category never take physical possession of products, though they do take ownership. Essentially they are shipping coordinators who receive orders from customers and then place the order with a product supplier. Shipping is then arranged so the supplier ships directly to the drop shipper's customer. Drop shipping is often most useful when large orders are placed so that transportation and product handling costs can be spread over many items (see Box 10-1).

Marketing Story

Goods to Go
Internet Retailer

Drop shipping is not only carried out at the wholesale level; it also occurs at the retail level. For instance, Internet retailers have used drop shipping arrangements with product suppliers for many years. Under this arrangement, when a customer places an order with the retailer the product is not shipped by the retailer, rather shipment is handled by the supplying company. However, the customer is often not aware of this as the packaging information (e.g., shipping label, billing receipt) makes it appear the retailer is the shipper.

Yet, why do retailers resort to using drop shippers rather than handling all shipping on their own? As this story points out, drop shipping arrangements offer two main advantages to retailers. First, it allows the retailer to expand its perceived product offerings without physically doing so. That is, a retailer can say it carries a larger assortment of products than it actually has in stock. Second, drop shipping arrangements may exist even though a retailer does actually acquire and distribute product from a supplier. The benefit for drop shipping in this case is that it protects the retailer in the event of unanticipated demand for a product. For instance, if the retailer experiences a sudden increase in customer orders, the retailer can send purchase requests to the drop shipper and not encounter delays that may occur if additional product had to be shipped first to the retailer before it is sent to customers.

One way Wine Country is responding is by relying more on suppliers to drop ship directly to consumers who place orders on WineCountryGiftBaskets.com. Since it started using drop shippers three years ago, Wine Country has been building its product line with a broader assortment of items like fresh flowers, freshly baked cookies and chocolate-covered strawberries—items it's not equipped to store in its own warehouse facilities. (5)

What are the key benefits for suppliers in a drop shipping arrangement?

Broker

A far less obvious type of wholesaler is the broker, who is responsible for bringing buyers and sellers together. However, brokers do not take ownership of products and often never handle the product. Brokers are paid based on a pre-negotiated percentage of the sale (i.e., commission) by the side that hires their services. In most cases, the relationship that develops between the broker and the buyer and seller is short-term and only lasts through the purchase. Brokers can be found in the food industry, importing/exporting, and real estate.

Agent

Similar to brokers, agents also bring buyers and sellers together, though they tend to work for clients for an extended period. As with brokers, agents generally are paid on commission. A common type of agent is the **manufacturers' representative**, who essentially assumes the role of a salesperson for a client. Manufacturers' representatives may handle several non-competing product lines at the same time and, during a single meeting with a perspective buyer, may discuss many products from several different companies.

Wholesaling Format Summary

Below in Table 10-1 we summarize each wholesale format by using the five categorization characteristics. The characteristics identified for each format should be viewed as the "most likely" case for that format and are not necessarily representative of all wholesalers that fall into this format.

||||||||||||||||||||||||||||||||||||||||||||||||||||||||||||||||||||||||||||||||||||||||||||||||||||

CONCERNS OF WHOLESALERS

The wholesale industry has served a vital role in the distribution process for well over 100 years, yet the challenges they face today are raising the stakes as many wholesalers fight to maintain their market position. Some of the issues facing today's wholesalers include:

◆ Disintermediation – The growth of the Internet as a communication and distribution channel has led many to conclude that wholesaling will lose its importance as manufacturers and final buyers learn to transact directly. This so called "disintermediation" of marketing channels is a real concern to some wholesalers, especially those that do not function as a dominate party within a distribution channel. For example, assume a retailer operating a gift card store uses a wholesaler only to purchase products from a specific manufacturer. In this situation if the manufacturer begins to offer direct purchasing to smaller customers the wholesaler may have little leverage in efforts to retain the retailer as a customer. In instances of disintermediation wholesalers face the challenge of creating greater value for their services with the intention of making the retailer's decision to switch more difficult.

Table 10-1: Wholesaling Format Summary

Format	Products Carried	Promotional Activities	Distribution Method	Service Level	Product Ownership
General Merchandise	general	limited	stationary not accessible	limited	take title
Specialty Merchandise	specialty	limited	stationary may be accessible	full or limited	take title
Contractual	general or specialty	extensive	stationary not accessible	full	take title
Industrial Distributor	general or specialty	limited	stationary may be accessible	limited	take title
Cash-and-Carry	specialty	limited	stationary accessible	no	take title
Truck	specialty	limited	non-stationary mobile	limited	take title
Rack Jobber	specialty	limited	non-stationary mobile	limited	take title
Drop Shipper	specialty	limited	non-stationary no facilities	limited	take title
Broker	specialty	extensive	non-stationary no facilities	limited	do not take title
Agent	specialty	extensive	non-stationary no facilities	limited	do not take title

♦ <u>Facility Location</u> – Wholesalers who are heavily involved in product shipment may spend considerable time evaluating sites to locate facilities. For organizations needing large facilities, the decision as to where to locate becomes more difficult and more expensive the closer the location is to major metropolitan areas. In fact, land costs in some regions of the world have risen so high that utilizing this space for wholesaling operations may not be feasible. In addition to land costs, facility location is also affected by access to adequate transportation, such as roads, seaports, airports, and rail terminals. Areas with available land often lack the infrastructure needed to support wholesale facilities unless expensive and time-consuming improvements (e.g., build highway, extend rail line, etc) are made.

♦ <u>Transportation Costs</u> – For wholesalers involved in transporting products, the worldwide rise in fuel costs has forced a close examination of how they handle product distribution. Transportation expense can represent a significant portion of overall distribution costs and these higher costs are often passed on to customers in the form of higher product prices. However, high transportation expense also presents opportunities for wholesalers. For instance, wholesalers have learned to control fuel costs by employing such methods as: using equipment and delivery vehicles that are more fuel efficient, utilizing computer routing software to determine less costly delivery routes, and offering greater incentives to customers to accept deliveries during less congested times of the day.

♦ <u>Adapting to New Technologies</u> – In addition to technologies to lower fuel costs, other distribution technologies are offering both advantages and disadvantages to wholesalers. New technologies, such as radio frequency identification tags (RFID) placed on shipped products, and real-time traffic updates allow wholesalers to maintain tighter control over their distribution activities. However, gaining the benefits associated with these new distribution technologies requires a significant commitment in terms of cost (i.e., purchasing the technologies) and time (i.e., installation and training).

♦ <u>Offering Non-Product Assistance</u> – Wholesalers are finding that offering access to products is not enough to satisfy buyers. Many customers also want wholesalers to offer additional value-added services including employee training (e.g., teach selling skills), promotional support (e.g., financial support for advertising), and assistance in managing their operations (e.g., building an online store). Keeping pace with the services demanded by customers requires constant research and communication with customers.

> *For many years, wholesalers relied heavily on their sales force to locate new customers. However, the increasing competitive environment facing wholesalers has led many to seek other methods for attracting customers. In particular, many wholesalers have followed the lead of retailers and are now using Internet marketing methods, such as search engine optimization and social networks to attract new business. As an example, Evertek, a computer and electronics wholesaler, regularly uses Twitter to promote sales, special events and other events. (6)*

MANAGING PRODUCT MOVEMENT

In addition to enlisting the assistance of retailers and wholesalers to make products available to customers, marketers also face additional concerns when trying to meet distribution objectives. In this section, we examine the tasks that must be carried out in order to physically move products to customers. These tasks include:

♦ Ordering and Inventory Management

♦ Transportation

♦ Product Storage

In some cases, the marketer will take on the responsibility of carrying out some functions, while other tasks may be assigned to distribution service providers. Whether handled by the marketer or contracted to others, these functions are crucial to having a cost-effective and efficient distribution system.

ORDERING AND INVENTORY MANAGEMENT

Having products available when customers want to make purchases may seem like a relatively straightforward process. All a seller needs to do is make sure there is product (i.e., inventory) in its possession and ready for the customer to purchase. Unfortunately, being prepared for customer purchasing is not always easy. Having the right product available when the customer is ready to buy requires a highly coordinated effort involving order entry and processing systems, forecasting techniques, customer knowledge, strong channel relationships, and skill at physically handling products.

ORDER ENTRY AND PROCESSING SYSTEMS

The marketer must have a system allowing customers to place orders. This system can be as simple as a consumer walking to the counter of a small food stand to purchase a few vegetables or as complicated as automated computer systems, where an **electronic order** is triggered from a retailer to a manufacturer each time a consumer purchases a product at the retailer's store. In either case, the order processing system must be able to meet the purchasing needs of the customer. In some circumstances, an efficient ordering system can be turned into a competitive advantage. Amazon turned its order handling system into a product feature with the patented "1-click" ordering option that streamlines online ordering by reducing the number of clicks needed to make purchases. (7)

Innovative inventory and order management systems developed by Internet retailers, such as Amazon, have changed customers' expectation when shopping at store-based retailers. This can be seen with in-store inventory. Prior to visiting a store, many customers now expect to have the option of searching for product information on a retailer's website, including seeing how much inventory is available. However, store-based retailers must consider the risk of offering updated inventory data as they may lose their ability to switch customers to related products since customers may not travel to the store if they know a product is not available. (8)

FORECASTING

Inventory management is often an exercise in predicting how customers will act in the future. By predicting purchase behavior, the marketer can respond by making sure the right amount of product is available. For most large-scale resellers, effective inventory forecasting requires the use of sophisticated statistical tools. These tools take into consideration many variables, such as past purchase history, amount of promotional effort that triggers an increase in customer ordering, and other market criteria, to determine how much of the product will be needed to meet customer demand.

CUSTOMER KNOWLEDGE

Inventory management can be fine-tuned to respond to customers' needs. As a marketer learns more about a customer, they begin to observe trends in how and when purchases are made. Combining customer knowledge with forecasting techniques allows the marketer to better estimate product demand and inventory requirements. As we discussed in Chapter 3, a key component for understanding customers is having in place a customer relationship management (CRM) system for tracking and analyzing customer activity.

CHANNEL RELATIONSHIPS

While the marketer who uses channel members to sell consumer products has access to information for their immediate customers (e.g., resellers) they often do not have access to sales and customer behavior information controlled by the party selling to the final consumer (e.g., retailer). Knowing the demand patterns at the final consumer level can give marketers good insight into how the reseller may order. Developing strong relationships with the holder of consumer information can result in the reseller sharing this information with the marketer. In fact, as we noted in Chapter 8, some retailers allow marketers direct access to real-time, store-level inventory information so the marketer can monitor how products are selling in stores. This places them in a position to respond quickly if inventory needs change.

PHYSICAL HANDLING

An often overlooked area of inventory management involves the actions and skills needed to prepare a product to move from one point to another. Some products require special attention be given to ensure the product is not damaged during shipment. Such efforts must be carefully balanced against increased costs that arise (e.g., stronger packaging) in order to provide greater protection to products. Because of this, many marketers will accept the fact that some small level of damage occurs during the distribution process.

‖‖

TRANSPORTATION

A key objective of product distribution is to get products into customers' hands in a timely manner. While delivery of digital products can be handled in a fairly smooth way by allowing customers to access their purchase over the Internet (e.g., download software, gain access to online subscription material), tangible products require a more careful analysis of delivery options in order to provide an optimal level of customer service.

Yet, as we noted earlier, "optimal" does not always translate into what a customer may consider is the best method (i.e., may not ship in the fastest way possible). This is particularly the case when companies see an opportunity to expand beyond their own country. When shipping internationally, transportation decisions can become quite complex. Not only are costs higher due to increased distance, but marketers may find transportation options are limited and unreliable. Additionally, the laws and regulations governing transportation may vary for each country. In most cases, marketers must enlist the help of third-party distribution partners who are familiar with the requirements of each foreign market the marketer seeks to enter.

> *For small companies supplying product in a limited geographic area, the transportation function may be something that they can handle on their own. While using transportation services to deliver product could offer many advantages, handling your own transportation enables small entrepreneurs to develop strong personal relationships since the seller is not only delivering product but also engaging the buyer in conversation which can lead to greater sales. (9)*

Transportation Features

In terms of delivering products to customers, there are six distinct modes of transportation: air, digital, pipeline, rail, truck, and water. However, not all modes are an option for all marketers. Each mode offers advantages and disadvantages on key transportation features. These features include:

♦ Product Options – This feature is concerned with the number of different products realistically shipped using a certain mode. Some modes, such as pipeline, are extremely limited in the type of products that can be shipped, while others, such as truck, can handle a wide-range of products.

♦ Speed of Delivery – This refers to how quickly it takes products to move from the shipper's location to the buyer's location.

> *One advantage leading online retailer Amazon has had over its competitors is its Amazon Prime program where, for a $79 yearly fee, customers obtain special benefits including unlimited 2-day shipping on most purchases. This option has been well received especially by frequent purchasers. To compete against Amazon, a large number of retailers including Dick's Sporting Goods, Toys R Us and PetSmart have joined together to offer their own program $79 yearly fee shipping service called ShopRunner. (10)*

♦ Accessibility – This transportation feature refers to whether the use of a mode can allow final delivery to occur at the buyer's desired location or whether the mode requires delivery to be off-loaded onto other modes before arriving at the buyer's destination. For example, most deliveries made via air must be loaded onto other transportation modes, often trucks, before they can be delivered to the final customer.

♦ Cost – The cost of shipment is evaluated in terms of the cost per item to cover some distance (e.g., mile, kilometer). Often for large shipments of tangible products cost is measured in terms of tons-per-mile or metric-tons-per-kilometer.

♦ <u>Capacity</u> – Refers to the amount of product shipped at one time within one transportation unit. The higher the capacity the more likely transportation cost can be spread over more individual products. This can result in lower transportation cost per-item shipped (see Box 10-1).

♦ <u>Intermodal Capable</u> – Intermodal shipping occurs when two or more modes can be combined in order to gain advantages offered by each mode. For instance, in an intermodal method called **piggybacking** truck trailers are loaded onto railroad cars without the need to unload the trailer. When the railroad car has reached a certain destination the truck trailers are off-loaded onto trucks for delivery to the customer's location.

Box 10-1

THE COST ADVANTAGE OF BULK SHIPPING

Transportation expense can represent a significant portion of the final product cost. Because of the high cost of shipping product, suppliers often find it in the best interest of the distribution channel and the final customer to ship products in bulk quantities. In general, bulk shipping reduces the per-item transportation cost.

For instance, consider what it costs to operate a delivery truck with a shipping capacity of 1,000 boxes. In terms of operational expenses for the truck (e.g., fuel, truck driver's costs, other operational costs), let's assume it costs (US) $1,000 to go from point A to point B. In most cases, with the exception of a little decrease in fuel efficiency, it does not cost that much more to drive the truck whether it is filled with 1,000 boxes of a supplier's product or if it only has 100 boxes.

Using this information it is easy to calculate the transportation-cost-per-item:

For the shipment of 100 boxes the transportation cost is:

$$\frac{\$1,000}{100} = \$10 \text{ per item}$$

For the shipment of 1,000 boxes the transportation cost is:

$$\frac{\$1,000}{1,000} = \$1 \text{ per item}$$

As this example illustrates, per-item transportation expense can be significantly reduced when marketers use bulk shipping. As we will see in Chapter 18, such advantages are a key reason suppliers offer quantity discounts to encourage large volume orders.

Modes of Transportation Comparison

Shown in Figure 10-1 are the estimated percentages of product movement (i.e., freight traffic) that occurs within the United States for the five modes of transportation that handle tangible products for 2007. Also, Table 10-2 presents a summary of the six modes compared on each of the key transportation features.

> *Transportation issues are particularly important as companies see an opportunity to expand beyond their own country. For instance, it is estimated that in 2009 worldwide transportation via ship was responsible for the shipment of nearly 8 billion tons of product between countries. (11)*

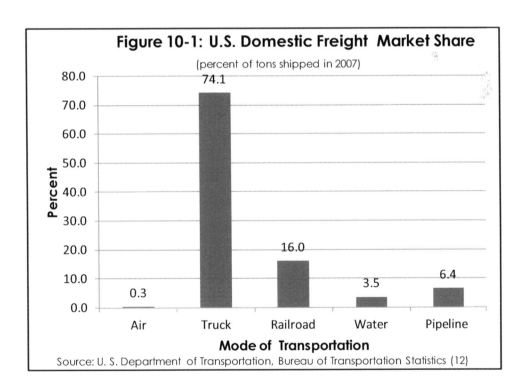

Figure 10-1: U.S. Domestic Freight Market Share

(percent of tons shipped in 2007)

Source: U. S. Department of Transportation, Bureau of Transportation Statistics (12)

Table 10-2: Modes of Transportation Summary

Mode	Product Options	Speed	Accessibility	Cost	Capacity	Intermodal Capability
Truck	Very Broad	Moderate	High	Moderate	Low	Very High
Railroad	Broad	Slow	Moderate	Low	Moderate	Very High
Air	Narrow	Fast	Low	Very High	Very Low	Moderate
Water	Broad	Very Slow	Moderate	Very Low	Very High	Very High
Pipeline	Very Narrow	Very Slow	Low	Low	Very High	Very Low
Digital	Very Narrow	Very Fast	Very High	Very Low	Moderate	Very Low

PRODUCT STORAGE

The third key element in product movement concerns storing products for future delivery. Marketers of tangible products, and even digital products, may have storage concerns. Storage facilities, such as warehouses, play a vital role in the distribution process for a number of reasons including:

♦ Hold Wide Assortment – As noted in Chapter 8, many resellers allow customers to purchase small quantities of many different products. Yet, as we saw in Box 10-1, to obtain the best prices from suppliers, resellers must purchase in large quantities. In these situations, the need exists for storage facilities that not only hold a large volume of product, but also hold a wide variety of inventory. Additionally, these facilities must be organized in a way permitting sellers to fill orders easily for its customers.

♦ Meet Unanticipated Demand – Holding products in storage offers a safeguard in cases of unexpected increases in demand for products.

♦ Needed for Large Shipping Quantities – As we noted in our discussion of transportation, manufacturers generally prefer to ship in large product quantities in order to more effectively spread transportation costs. This often means manufacturers must create storage areas in which the manufactured goods can build up in the quantities needed for such shipments to occur.

♦ Offer Faster Response – Additional storage facilities, strategically located in different geographical areas, allow a marketing organization to respond quickly to customers' needs. The ability to respond with quick delivery can be a significant value-added feature since it reduces the buyer's (e.g., retailer) need to maintain a large inventory at its own locations.

♦ Security and Backup – For digital products, additional storage facilities are not only needed to offer customers faster access to products (e.g., online content and software) but are also needed to protect against technical glitches and security threats.

Types of Warehouses

The warehouse is the most common type of storage, though other forms do exist (e.g., storage tanks, computer server farms). Some warehouses are massive structures that simultaneously support the unloading of numerous in-bound trucks and railroad cars containing suppliers' products while at the same time loading multiple trucks for shipment to customers.

Below we discuss five types of warehouses:

Private Warehouse

This type of warehouse is owned and operated by channel suppliers and resellers, and is used in their own distribution activity. For instance, a large, national retail chain may have several regional warehouses supplying its stores.

Public Warehouse

The public warehouse is essentially space that can be leased to solve short-term distribution needs. Retailers operating their own private warehouses may occasionally seek additional storage space if their facilities have reached capacity or if they are making an unusually large purchase of products. For example, retailers may order extra merchandise to prepare for in-store sales or order a large volume of a product offered at a low promotional price by a supplier.

Automated Warehouse

With advances in computer and robotics technology many warehouses now have automated capabilities. The level of automation ranges from a small conveyor belt transporting products in a small area all the way up to a fully automated facility, where only a few people are needed to handle storage activity for thousands of pounds/kilograms of product. In fact, many warehouses use machines to handle nearly all physical distribution activities, such as moving product-filled **pallets** (i.e., platforms that hold large amounts of product) around buildings that may be several stories tall and the length of two or more football fields.

Climate-Controlled Warehouse

Warehouses handle storage of many types of products including those needing special handling conditions, such as freezers for storing frozen products, humidity-controlled environments for delicate products, including produce or flowers, and dirt-free facilities for handling highly sensitive computer products.

Distribution Center

There are some warehouses where product storage is considered an extremely activity. These warehouses serve as points in the distribution system at which products are received from many suppliers and quickly shipped out to many customers. In some cases, such as with distribution centers handling perishable food (e.g., produce), most of the product enters in the early morning and is distributed by the end of the day.

> *Online grocery retailer Peapod has built a profitable service by incorporating several technological elements into their distribution system. These include a highly automated and climate controlled warehouse, where customers' orders are selected by workers and then automatically routed to the correct delivery truck. The company also uses truck-monitored GPS to identify, in real-time, where trucks are located and re-route these if needed. (13)*

Marketing Story

After 181 Years, Local Beer Stops Playing Hard to Get
Wall Street Journal

Companies, that are successful in a local or regional market, often find that to grow further they must expand beyond their core area. For many companies, this is a key point in its history. Deciding whether to move beyond its comfort zone is often a make or break decision that will impact the organization for years to come. If expansion is managed correctly, the company can expect to see continued growth, while poorly managed expansion can drain resources that may ultimately affect the health of the company.

In the age of Internet communication and low-cost package haulers (e.g., FedEx, UPS, USPS), growing distribution is a much easier task for companies selling products requiring little care in package handling. But, products needing careful handling are a different story. For these products, expanding distribution is a job the company often must handle on its own.

One company facing this situation is beer manufacturer, Yuengling. For years, the company has been primarily known as a regional brewer. As discussed in this story, Yuengling wants to grow beyond its Eastern U.S. home region. After a successful move into Southeastern states, it is now looking to expand into the Midwest. In doing so it is likely to face a number of challenges related to product movement.

Yuengling could encounter difficulty attracting drinkers as it advances westward, where many haven't heard of the brand. Competition from small-batch "craft" brewers also is likely to be stiffer in some states than it was in some of the markets in the Southeast that it entered in recent years. (14)

In terms of managing the movement of products, what are the key issues and potential risks Yuengling faces as it expands distribution?

‖‖

REFERENCES

1. "2007 Economic Census," *United States Census Bureau.*

2. *Wholesale Central* website.

3. "What Is a Wholesale Electricity Market?" *Electric Power Supply Association.*

4. *Merchandise Mart Properties* website.

5. Demery, P., "Goods to Go," *Internet Retailer*, September 1, 2010.

6. Stambor, Z., "Wholesaling 2.0," *Internet Retailer*, March 31, 2010.

7. Christ, P., "Patenting Marketing Methods: A Missing Topic in the Classroom," *Journal of Marketing Education*, 27 (1), 2005.

8. "Order Management," *Internet Retailer*, July 2010.

9. Petrecca, L., "New Sales Outlets Are a Big Deal for Small Businesses," *USA Today*, October 26, 2010.

10. Fowler, G. A., "Retailers Team Up Against Amazon," *Wall Street Journal*, October 6, 2010.

11. Review of Maritime Transport 2010, *United Nations Conference on Trade and Development*, June 2011.

12. 2007 Commodity Flow Survey, *Bureau of Transportation Statistics - U.S. Department of Transportation.*

13. Demery, P., "Peapod Keeps On Truckin," *Internet Retailer*, March 31, 2011.

14. Kesmodel, D., "After 181 Years, Local Beer Stops Playing Hard to Get," *Wall Street Journal*, October 21, 2010.

Full text of many of the references can be accessed via links on the support website.

Chapter 11: Promotion Decisions

Those unfamiliar with marketing often assume it is the same thing as advertising. Certainly our coverage so far in *Know This: Marketing Basics* has suggested this is not the case. Marketing encompasses many tasks and decisions, of which advertising may only be a small portion. Likewise, when non-marketers hear someone talk about "promotion" they frequently believe the person is talking about advertising. While advertising is the most visible and best understood method of promotion, it is only one of several approaches a marketer can choose.

In this chapter, we begin our discussion of the promotion component of the Marketer's Toolkit. We start by defining promotion, and we show how promotion is used to meet different objectives. Because communication is a key element of promotion, we take an extended look at the communication process. Next, we explore different characteristics of promotion and how different promotional methods stack up to the characteristics. Finally, we discuss factors affecting the choice of promotional methods.

||||||||||||||||||||||||||||||||||||||||||||||||||||||||||||||||||||||||||||||||||||||||||||||||||||||||||||||||||

WHAT IS PROMOTION?

Promotion is the general name given to forms of corporate communication designed to reach a targeted audience with a certain message in order to achieve specific organizational objectives. Nearly all organizations, whether for-profit or not-for-profit, in all types of industries, must engage in some form of promotion. Such efforts may range from multinational firms spending large sums securing high-profile celebrities to serve as a corporate spokesperson to the owner of a one-person enterprise passing out business cards at a local businesspersons' meeting.

Like most marketing decisions, an effective promotional strategy requires the marketer understand how promotion fits with other pieces of the marketing puzzle (e.g., product, distribution, pricing, target markets). Consequently, promotion decisions should be made with an appreciation for how it affects other areas of the company. For instance, running a major advertising campaign for a new product without first assuring there will be enough inventory to meet potential demand generated by the advertising would certainly not go over well with the company's production department (not to mention other key company executives). Thus, marketers should not work in a vacuum when making promotion decisions. Rather, the overall success of a promotional strategy requires input from other functional areas.

In addition to coordinating general promotion decisions with other business areas, individual promotions must also work together. Under the concept of **integrated marketing communication,** marketers attempt to develop a unified and highly coordinated promotional strategy in which a consistent message is presented across many different types of promotional techniques. For instance, salespeople will discuss the same benefits of a product as mentioned in television advertisements. In this way no matter how customers are exposed to a marketer's promotional efforts they all receive the same information.

> *Constellation Brands, the world's second largest wine marketer, found that integrated marketing was needed across its entire product line. At one point, Constellation was separated into four different operating units, each operating its own marketing department. In an effort to offer more consistent message, the company consolidated marketing functions, including promotion, into a single area of the company. They soon discovered that a single department enables the entire company to take advantage of newer specialized promotional options, including the use of social media. (1)*

Finally, as discussed below, promotion is not limited to the communication of product information to customers. Marketers also use promotional methods to communicate with others who are outside their target market.

Other Targets of Marketing Promotion

The audience for an organization's marketing communication efforts is not only the marketer's target market. While the bulk of a marketer's promotional budget may be directed at the target market, there are many other groups that could also serve as useful targets of a marketing message including:

◆ Target Market Influencers - There exists a large group of people and organizations with the potential to affect how a company's target market is exposed to and perceives a company's products. These influencing groups have their own communication mechanisms that reach the target market. With the right strategy, the marketer may be able to utilize these influencers to its benefit. Influencers include the news media (e.g., offer company stories), special interest groups, opinion leaders (e.g., doctors directing patients), and industry trade associations.

♦ Channel Members - Distribution channel members provide services to help the marketer gain access to final customers. Yet in many ways channel members, and particularly resellers, also represent target markets for a company's products. While their needs are different than those of the final customer, channel members must make purchase decisions when agreeing to handle a marketer's product (see Chapters 9 and 10). Aiming promotion at distribution partners (e.g., retailers, wholesalers, distributors) and other channel members is extremely important and, in some industries, represents a higher portion of a marketer's promotional budget than promotional spending directed at the final customer.

♦ Other Companies - The most likely scenario in which a company will communicate with another company occurs when the marketer is probing to see if the company would have an interest in a joint venture, such as a **co-marketing arrangement** where two firms share marketing costs. Using promotions, such as ads targeted to potential partners, could help create interest in discussing such a relationship.

♦ Other Organizational Stakeholders - Marketers may also be involved with communication activities directed at other stakeholders. This group consists of those who provide services, support, or in other ways impact the company. For example, an industry group that sets industry standards can affect company products through the issuance of recommended compliance standards for product development or other marketing activities. Communicating with this group is necessary to ensure the marketer's views of any changes in standards are known.

‖‖‖

OBJECTIVES OF MARKETING PROMOTIONS

Many view promotional activities as the most glamorous part of marketing. This may have to do with the fact that promotion is often associated with creative activity undertaken to help distinguish a company's products from competitors' offerings. While creativity is a key element in promotion decisions, many times marketers are consumed with developing a highly creative promotion (e.g., humorous advertisement featuring a top Hollywood star) only to see it fail to change a company's situation (i.e., sales do not increase).

While creativity is certainly a concern, marketers must first have a deep understanding of how marketing promotions help the organization achieve its objectives before embarking on the creative side of promotion. The most obvious objective marketers have for promotional activities is to convince customers to make a decision benefiting the marketer (of course the marketer believes the decision will also benefit the customer).

For most for-profit marketers, this means getting customers to buy an organization's product and, in most cases, to remain a loyal long-term customer. For other marketers, such as not-for-profits, it means getting customers to increase donations, utilize more services, change attitudes, or change behavior (e.g., stop smoking campaigns).

However, marketers must understand getting customers to commit to a decision, such as deciding to make a purchase, is only achievable when a customer is ready to make the decision. As we saw in Chapter 4, customers often move through several stages before a purchase decision is made. Additionally before turning into a repeat customer, purchasers analyze their initial purchase to see whether they received a good value, and then often repeat the purchase process again before deciding to make the same choice.

The type of customer the marketer is attempting to attract along with the stage of the purchase process a customer is in will affect the objectives of a particular marketing communication effort. And since a marketer often has multiple simultaneous promotional campaigns, the objective of each could be different.

> *In the U.S., there are 1.5 million nonprofit organizations leading to fierce competition for donor funds. The competition is forcing nonprofits to be creative in their promotions in order to standout. One promotional method uses printing technology to create what appears to be handwritten fundraising letters mailed to potential donors. Non-profits believe the perception of a personal letter can simulate higher contributions. (2)*

Types of Promotion Objectives

The possible objectives for marketing promotions may include the following:

◆ Build Awareness – New products and new companies are often unknown to a market, which means initial promotional efforts must focus on establishing an identity. In this situation, the marketer's promotional objectives are to: 1) ensure the message reaches customers, and 2) tell the market who they are and what they have to offer.

◆ Create Interest – Moving a customer from awareness of a product to making a purchase can present a significant challenge. As we saw in Chapter 4, customers must first recognize they have a need before they actively start to consider a purchase. The focus on creating messages convincing customers a need exists has been the hallmark of marketing for a long time with promotional appeals targeted at basic human characteristics, such as emotions, fears, sex, and humor.

♦ <u>Provide Information</u> – Some promotion is designed to assist customers in the search stage of the purchasing process. In some cases, such as when a product is so novel it creates a new category of product and has few competitors, the information is simply intended to explain what the product is and may not mention any competitors. In other situations, where the product competes in an existing market, informational promotion may be used to help with a product positioning strategy. As we discussed in Chapter 5, marketers may use promotional means, including direct comparisons with competitor's products, in an effort to get customers to distinguish the marketer's product from those of competitors (i.e., product positioning).

♦ <u>Stimulate Demand</u> – The right promotion can drive customers to make a purchase. In the case of products a customer has not previously purchased or has not purchased in a long time, the promotional efforts may be directed at getting the customer to try the product. This is often seen on the Internet where software companies allow for free demonstrations or even free downloadable trials of their products. For products with an established customer base, promotion can encourage customers to increase their purchasing by providing a reason to purchase products sooner or in greater quantities than they normally do. For example, a pre-holiday newspaper advertisement may remind customers to stock up on beverages for the holiday by purchasing more than they typically purchase during non-holiday periods.

♦ <u>Reinforce the Brand</u> – Once a purchase is made, a marketer can use promotion to help build a strong relationship that can lead to the purchaser becoming a loyal customer. For instance, many retail stores now ask for a customer's email address so follow-up emails containing additional product information or even an incentive to purchase other products from the retailer can be sent in order to strengthen the customer-marketer relationship.

Goya Foods has served the Latino food market for over 75 years. While the company has strong name recognition within Latino communities, Goya sought to expand to a larger general food market. To address their promotional objectives, that included creating awareness and stimulating demand, Goya launched a substantial promotional campaign. In addition to extensive advertising, the campaign included an experimental promotion where Goya teamed with supermarkets to recommend Goya products based on products the shopper scans through an in-store scanning system. (3)

III

THE COMMUNICATION PROCESS

Before we venture into an in-depth analysis of promotion, it is necessary to lay additional groundwork by examining how communication works. By understanding the basic concepts of communication, the marketer will have a better idea of what actions should be pursued or avoided in order to get its message out to its customers.

The act of communicating has been evaluated extensively for many, many years. One of the classic analyses of communication took place in the 1940s and 1950s when researchers, including Claude Shannon and Warren Weaver (4), Wilbur Schramm (5) and others, offered models describing how communication takes place. In general, communication is how people exchange meaningful information. Models that reflect how communication occurs often include the elements shown on Figure 11-1.

The key elements of the communication process shown in Figure 11-1 are discussed below.

COMMUNICATION PARTICIPANTS

For communication to occur, there must be at least two participants:

- Message Source – The source of communication is the party intending to convey information to another party. The message source can be an individual (e.g., salesperson) or an organization (e.g., through advertising). In order to convey a message, the source must engage in **message encoding**, which involves mental and physical processes necessary to construct a message in order to reach a desired goal (i.e., convey meaningful information). This undertaking consists of using sensory stimuli, such as imagery (e.g., words, symbols, images), sound (e.g., spoken word), and scent (e.g., fragrance) to convey a message.

- Message Receiver – The receiver of communication is the intended target of a message source's efforts. For a message to be understood, the receiver must engage in **message decoding** by undertaking mental and physical processes that give meaning to the message. Clearly, a message can only be decoded if the receiver is actually exposed to the message.

COMMUNICATION DELIVERY

Communication takes place in the form of a **message** exchanged between a source and receiver. A message can be shaped using one or a combination of sensory stimuli working together to convey meaning that meets the objectives of the sender. The sender uses a **transmission medium** to send the message. In marketing the medium may include the use of different news and information

Figure 11-1: The Communication Process

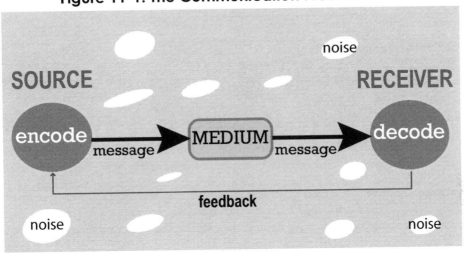

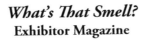

Marketing Story

What's That Smell?
Exhibitor Magazine

One area of promotion that tends to be underutilized, if not unappreciated, is scent marketing. The use of olfactory elements for marketing products has been a mainstay in certain industries (e.g., baked goods, fragrances) but has been slow to expand as a marketing tool in other areas.

At one point scent marketing seemed to have a bright future. In fact, in the late 1990s a few Internet start-up companies, including DigiScent, envisioned delivering olfactory elements (i.e., scent) over the Internet. But these ideas dead horribly during the turn-of-the-century Internet implosion and little has happened since. But this story shows scent marketing is still something that could work. While the context discussed here is its use in trade show marketing, the concepts are applicable across many industries. In particular, the discussion of the four scent strategies in this story is worth reading.

While marketers in general and trade show exhibitors in particular have typically lavished much more attention and money on sight and sound in their promotional mix, science suggests that scent marketing has far more potential: Vision and taste have three and five receptor genes, respectively, in our DNA, while smell has 350 odor-receptor genes, suggesting that nature designed us to be not only more receptive to scent but be more affected by it as well. (6)

Is this just another false start or is scent marketing really poised to take off this time?

outlets (e.g., Internet, television, radio, print), promotion-only outlets (e.g., postal mail, billboards), and person-to-person contact (e.g., salespeople).

Additionally, communication can be improved if there is a two-way flow of information in the form of a **feedback channel**. This occurs if the message receiver is able to respond, often quickly, to the message source. In this way, the original message receiver now becomes the message source and the communication process begins again.

OBSTACLES TO EFFECTIVE COMMUNICATION

While a message source may be able to deliver a message through a transmission medium, there are many potential obstacles to the message successfully reaching the receiver the way the sender intends. The potential obstacles affecting communication include:

- <u>Poor Encoding</u> – This occurs when the message source fails to create the right sensory stimuli to meet the objectives of the message. For instance, in person-to-person communication, verbally phrasing words poorly, so the intended communication is not what is actually meant, is the result of poor encoding. Poor encoding is also seen in advertisements that are difficult for the intended audience to understand, such as words or symbols lacking meaning or worse, have totally different meaning within a certain cultural groups. This often occurs when marketers use the same advertising message across many different countries. Differences due to translation or cultural understanding can result in the message receiver having a different frame of reference for how to interpret words, symbols, sounds, etc. This may lead the message receiver to decode the meaning of the message in a different way than was intended by the message sender.

*Companies seeking to sell internationally often must have their promotional material translated into the local language. For companies that do not possess the capability to handle **translations**, assistance will be needed. There are several options available ranging from low-cost software programs to high-cost language vendors. While software programs may seem an attractive option, the results are often inconsistent and could present encoding problems. One key reason for the problems is that software translations are often presented literally and not presented in the correct context used within a country. Instead, marketers are advised to hire professional, qualified translation firms who clearly understand the language requirements within local markets. (7)*

- <u>Poor Decoding</u> – This refers to a message receiver's error in processing the message so that the meaning given to the received message is not what the source intended. This differs from poor encoding when it is clear, through comparative analysis with other receivers, that a particular receiver perceived a message differently than others. Clearly, as we noted above, if the receiver's frame of reference is different (e.g., meaning of words are different) then decoding problems can occur. More likely, when it comes to marketing promotions, decoding errors occur due to personal or psychological factors, such as not paying attention to a full television advertisement, driving too quickly past a billboard, or allowing one's mind to wander while talking to a salesperson.

- <u>Communication Noise</u> – Noise in communication occurs when an outside force in someway affects delivery of the message. The most obvious example is when loud sounds block the receiver's ability to hear a message. Nearly any distraction to the sender or the receiver can lead to communication noise. In advertising, many customers are overwhelmed (i.e., distracted) by the large number of advertisements they encounter each day. Such **advertising clutter** (i.e., noise) makes it difficult for advertisers to get their message through to desired customers.

One method used to break through and be heard above the clutter created by a large number of advertisers is to find a unique approach for delivering promotional messages. Several companies, including Heinz and HSBC Bank, found such a method using food trucks. The trucks were dispatched to high traffic areas in downtown locations of major U.S. cities, where representatives talked with customers and dispensed free product. (8)

- <u>Medium Failure</u> – Sometimes communication channels break down and end up sending out weak or faltering signals. Other times the wrong medium is used to communicate the message. For instance, trying to educate doctors about a new treatment for heart disease using television commercials that quickly flash highly detailed information is not going to be as effective as presenting this information in a print ad, where doctors can take their time evaluating the information.

As discussed in Box 11-1, knowledge of the communication process can help marketers avoid these obstacles.

Box 11-1

IMPROVING COMMUNICATION

For marketers, understanding how the communication process works can improve the delivery of their message. Marketers should focus on the following to improve communication with their targeted audience:

Carefully Encode

Marketers should make sure the message they send is crafted in a way that will be interpreted by message receivers as intended. This means having a firm understanding of how their audience interprets words, symbols, sounds, and other stimuli used by marketers. This is particularly beneficial when communicating to target markets that are beyond the marketer's own experiences. For instance, marketers targeting sub-cultures that are significantly different from their own (e.g., age group difference), or marketing outside their native country may encounter cultural differences that can lead to misinterpretation. To address these issues, marketers may need to seek the help of professionals, who have a strong understanding of the culture, customs, and social behavior of the markets that will be exposed to the promotion.

Allow Feedback

Encouraging the message receiver to provide feedback can greatly improve communication and help determine if a marketer's message was decoded and interpreted properly. Feedback can be improved by providing easy-to-use options for responding, such as phone numbers and email. Additionally, the creation and management of social media sites, online forums, and corporate blogs may also enhance feedback.

Reduce Noise

In many promotional situations, the marketer has little control over interference with its message. However, there are a few instances where the marketer can proactively lower the noise level. For instance, salespeople can be trained to reduce noise by employing techniques limiting customer distractions, such as scheduling meetings during non-busy times, or by inviting potential customers to an environment offering fewer distractions, such as a conference facility. Additionally, advertising can be developed in ways that separate the marketer's ad from others, including the use of whitespace in magazine ads.

Choose Right Audience

Targeting the right message receiver will go a long way to improving a marketer's ability to promote its products. Messages are much more likely to be received and appropriately decoded by those who have an interest (see *Involvement* discussion in Chapter 4) in the content of the message.

Marketing Story

Nonprofits Look For New Ways to Get People to Give
NPR

Possibly the greatest challenge confronting most marketers is figuring out how to generate interest among potential customers. This is where promotion comes into play. Marketers use techniques including advertising, personal selling and public relations to build customer interest. Yet, on a daily basis markets are over-saturated with thousands of audio and visual promotions. This results in customers being exposed to more messages then they are able to understand and retain. In this environment, even if a marketer has excellent products, their message often gets lost among the "noise" generated by other marketers.

As discussed in Chapter 4, breaking through the clutter with a message understood and acted on by message receivers (i.e., customers) usually takes a highly creative approach. Leading consumer products firms are well aware of this and lead the way with the development of innovative advertising and other promotions.

However, compared to for-profit companies, nonprofit marketers are often not considered to be as creative with their promotional methods. This notion comes from the belief that since nonprofits lack deep pockets for promotional spending they cannot be truly innovative with their promotions. But this is not true. Many promotional methods used by nonprofits are, in fact, quite creative.

In this story, we see how nonprofit marketers are being recognized in a crowded market even with limited promotional funds. It discusses several promotional fundraising techniques intended to capture the attention of potential contributors. The techniques include the use of unique postcards, online gaming, unique gifts for donors, and several others. What is also interesting is that nonprofits are developing these promotions with the help of for-profit firms. And while not mentioned in the story, it should be pointed out that leading Internet sites, such as Google, Facebook and Twitter, are offering strong support in helping nonprofits extend their promotional efforts.

Jim O'Brien of ThinkShapes Mail in Tampa, Fla., says you can't really count on people opening letters. So his company offers postcard-like mailers in eye-catching shapes — something people might read and stick on a fridge. He holds up a paw-shaped card sent out by an animal society. (9)

What percentage of overall revenue does a leading charity spend on promotion compared to a leading consumer products company?

||||||||||||||||||||||||||||||||||||||||||||||||||||||||||||||||||||||||||||||||||||||||||||||||||||||||||||||||||

CHARACTERISTICS OF PROMOTIONS

Before we discuss the different types of promotion options available to a marketer, it is useful to gain an understanding of the features that set different options apart. In this section, we isolate eight characteristics on which each promotional option can be judged. While these characteristics are widely understood as being important in evaluating the effectiveness of each type of promotion, they are by no means the only criteria used for evaluation. In fact, as new promotional methods emerge the criteria for evaluating promotional methods will likely change.

For our discussion, we will look at the following characteristics of a promotional method:

1. Intended Audience: Mass vs. Targeted

2. Payment Model: Paid vs. Non-Paid

3. Message Flow: One-Way vs. Two-Way

4. Interaction Type: Personal vs. Non-Personal

5. Message Control: Total vs. Minimal

6. Demand Creation: Quick vs. Lagging

7. Message Credibility: High vs. Low

8. Cost Assessment: Exposure vs. Action

1. INTENDED AUDIENCE: MASS PROMOTION VS. TARGETED PROMOTION

Promotions can be categorized based on the intended coverage of a single promotional message. For instance, a single television advertisement for a major sporting event, such as the Olympics, Super Bowl or World Cup, could be seen by millions of viewers at the same time. Such mass promotion, intended to reach as many people as possible, has been a mainstay of marketers' promotional efforts for a long time.

Unfortunately, while mass promotions are delivered to a large number of people, the actual number experiencing the promotion that fall within the marketer's target market may be small. Because of this, many who use mass promotion techniques find it to be an inefficient way to reach desired customers. Instead, today's marketers are turning to newer techniques designed to focus promotional delivery to only those with a high probability of being in the marketer's target market. For example, Google, Microsoft, and other Internet search engines employ methods for delivering highly targeted ads to customers as they enter search terms. The assumption made by advertisers is that customers who enter search terms are interested in the information they have entered, especially if they are searching by entering detailed search strings (e.g., phrases rather than a single word). Following this logic, advertisers are much more likely to have their ads displayed to customers within their target market leading to a potentially higher return on their promotional investment.

The movement to highly targeted promotions has gained tremendous traction in recent years and, as new and improved targeting methods are introduced, its importance will continue to grow.

> *Several consumer products companies have shifted their advertising spending to target consumers over the age of 55. For years, this market has been ignored by leading advertisers, who generally concentrated their promotional efforts on younger customers. But given the size and spending power of the 55 and older group, several leading companies, including Kellogg, Sketchers and 5-Hour Energy, have either increased spending to this group or are targeting ads to this group for the first time. (10)*

2. PAYMENT MODEL: PAID VS. NON-PAID

Most efforts to promote products require marketers to make direct payment to the medium delivering the message. For instance, a company must pay a magazine publisher to advertise in the magazine. However, there are several forms of promotion that do not involve direct payment in order to distribute a promotional message. While not necessarily "free" since there may be indirect costs involved, the ability to have a product promoted without making direct payment to the medium can be a viable alternative to expensive promotion options.

3. MESSAGE FLOW: ONE-WAY VS. TWO-WAY COMMUNICATION

Promotions can be classified based on whether the message source enables the message receiver to respond with immediate feedback. Such feedback can then be followed with further information exchange between both parties. Most efforts at mass promotion, such as television advertising, offer only a one-way information flow that does not allow for easy response by the message receiver. However, many targeted promotions, such as using a sales force to promote products, enable message recipients to respond immediately to information from the message sender.

4. INTERACTION TYPE: PERSONAL VS. NON-PERSONAL

Promotions involving real people communicating with potential customers is considered personal promotion. While salespeople are a common and well understood type of personal promotion, another type of promotion, **controlled word-of-mouth promotion** (also called **buzz marketing**), is emerging as a form of personal promotion. This type of promotion also uses personal contact to spread information about a product. However, unlike the use of salespeople, word-of-mouth promotion is not intended to get a buyer to buy directly from the person who is doing the promoting (see *Controlled Word-of-Mouth* discussion in Chapter 16).

One key advantage personal promotions have is the ability for the message sender to adjust the message as they gain feedback from message receivers (i.e., two-way communication). So, if a customer does not understand something in the initial message (e.g., does not fully understand how the product works), the person delivering the message can adjust the promotion to address questions or concerns. Many non-personal forms of promotion, including television and radio advertisements, are inflexible, at least in the short-term, and cannot be easily adjusted to address questions raised by the audience experiencing the ad.

5. MESSAGE CONTROL: TOTAL VS. MINIMAL

Most promotions are controlled by the marketer who encodes the message and then pays to have the message delivered. However, no marketer can totally control how the news media, customers or others talk about a company or its products. Reporters for magazines, newspaper, and news websites, as well as posters on social media sites and Internet forums, may discuss a company's products in ways that can benefit or hinder a company's marketing efforts. This is particularly true with non-paid promotions where a marketer is looking to obtain a free "mention" by an influential message medium, such as a newspaper article, but has little control in getting this to occur (see *Disadvantages of PR* discussion in Chapter 15).

> *While social media holds the potential to reach a large number of potential customers, it can also lead to a distorted promotional message if not properly controlled. This can particularly be a problem for companies selling products where there are age restrictions on purchases. While most products having age restrictions operate social media sites, there are complaints that such sites should restrict those who do post and posts need to be monitored more aggressively for misleading, abusive or outrageous posts that may have been made by underage posters. (11)*

6. DEMAND CREATION: QUICK VS. LAGGING

As we discussed earlier, the success of promotional activity may not always be measured by comparing spending to an increase in product sales since marketers may use promotion to achieve other objectives. However, when a marketer is seeking to increase demand, certain promotional activities offer advantages in turning exposure to promotion into a quick increase in demand. In general, these activities are most effective when customers are offered a monetary (e.g., save money) or psychological (e.g., improves a customer's perceived group role or status level) incentive to make the purchase.

7. Message Credibility: High vs. Low

The perceived control of the message can influence the target market's perception of message credibility. For example, many customers viewing a comparative advertisement, where one product is shown to be superior to a competitor's product, may be skeptical about the claims since the company with the superior product is paying for the advertisement. Yet, if the same comparison is mentioned in a newspaper article it may be more favorably viewed since readers may perceive the author of the story (e.g., reporter) as being unbiased in their point-of-view.

8. Cost Assessment: Exposure vs. Action

The final characteristic classifies promotions based on the method by which costs are determined for running a promotion. For instance, as we will see in Chapter 12, when it comes to advertising, marketers face numerous costs ranging from promotion creation to message delivery. Costs can be assessed in two main ways: 1) based on general exposure to the promotion, and 2) based on action taken. Box 11-2 provides further insight on these options.

Box 11-2

Measures of Promotional Effectiveness

Whether a promotion is working or not is primarily determined by analyzing the cost of running a particular promotion versus the results obtained. In general, there are two main methods available for assessing promotional effectiveness: 1) measurement based on exposure, and 2) measurement based on action.

Effectiveness Based on Exposure
With the exposure method, marketers make promotional decisions based on how many people will be exposed to the promotion in relation to the cost of running the promotion. This method has been a mainstay for assessing promotion for a long time primarily because it is easy to calculate. However, the presumption of marketers using this approach is that exposure leads customers to do something, such as make a product purchase. Yet, tying exposure to a customer action is not always possible (see *Effectiveness Based on Action* discussion below); consequently, the exposure option may be all that is available.

Within the exposure method are two options:

Cost-per-Mille (CPM) - The CPM option relates to how many people are exposed to a promotion in relation to the cost of the promotion. CPM (also called **cost-per-thousand** as mille means thousand) is a commonly used promotional measurement for mass media outlets, such as print and broadcast industries, although in the online advertising industry it is also used, though it is sometimes referred to as **cost-per-impression (CPI)**. CPM calculates how much promotion costs for each 1,000 exposures. For example, if an advertisement costs (US) $10,000 in a city newspaper having a circulation of 500,000 then the CPM for that advertisement is calculated as follows:

$$CPM = \frac{\$10,000}{500,000 \, / \, 1,000} = \$20$$

A national or international television advertisement, while expensive to create and broadcast, actually produces a very low CPM given how many people are exposed to the ad.

Cost-per-Targeted Exposure (CPTE) - A low CPM can be misleading if a large percentage of the promotion's audience is not within the marketer's target market, in which case the CPTE may be a better metric for gauging promotion effectiveness. The CPTE approach looks at what percentage of an audience is within the marketer's customer group and, thus, legitimate targets for the promotion. Clearly, CPTE is higher than CPM, but it offers a better indication of how much promotion is reaching targeted customers.

Effectiveness Based on Action

An even more effective way to evaluate promotional costs is through the **cost-per-action (CPA)** metric. With CPA, the marketer evaluates how many people actually respond to a promotion. Response may be measured by examining purchase activity, number of phone inquiries, website traffic, clicks on advertisements, and other means within a short time after the promotional message is delivered.

Unfortunately, measuring CPA is not always easy and tying it directly to a specific promotion can also be difficult. For example, a customer who purchases a snack product may have first learned about the snack product several weeks before from a television advertisement. The fact that it took the customer some time to make the purchase does not mean the advertisement was not effective in generating sales, though if the CPA was measured within a day or two after the ad was broadcast this person's action would not have been counted. With the growing trend to more targeted promotions, especially those delivered through the Internet and mobile networks, combined with the development of sophisticated customer tracking techniques, the ability to compare promotion to actual customer activity is bound to one day be the dominant method for measuring promotional effectiveness.

||||||||||||||||||||||||||||||||||||||||||||||||||||||||||||||||||||||||||||||||||||||||||||||||||||||||||||||||||

THE PROMOTION MIX

Marketers have at their disposal four main methods of promotion, which taken together comprise the promotion mix. In this section, a basic definition of each method is offered while in the next section a comparison of each method based on the characteristics of promotion is presented.

ADVERTISING

This form of promotion involves non-personal paid promotions often using mass media outlets to deliver the marketer's message. While historically advertising has been a one-way form of communication with little feedback opportunity for the customer experiencing the advertisement, the advent of computer technology and, in particular the Internet, has increased the options allowing customers to provide quick feedback.

SALES PROMOTION

This promotional method covers special short-term techniques, often in the form of incentives, that encourage customers to respond to or undertake some activity. For instance, the use of retail coupons with expiration dates requires customers act while the incentive is still valid.

PUBLIC RELATIONS

Also referred to as publicity, this type of promotion attempts to encourage third-party sources, and particularly the news media, to offer a favorable mention of the marketer's company or product. This is done without offering direct payment to the third-party sources.

PERSONAL SELLING

As the name implies, this form of promotion involves personal contact between company representatives and those who have a role in purchase decisions. For instance, engaging in personal contact with members of a company's buying center (see Box 4-2 in Chapter 4). Often the contact occurs face-to-face or via telephone, though newer technologies allow this to occur online via video conferencing.

Each of these methods will be covered in much greater detail in later chapters.

> *The Girl Scouts' philosophy for promoting its Girl Scout Cookies has primarily centered on the use of person-to-person selling through in-store displays and calling on friends and neighbors. The organization had limited or outright banned other promotional options including selling online. However, the organization has now changed their view on this. They are now embracing online marketing for its potential to grow sales. The change required implementation of a safety program to help educate and protect scouts while selling online. (12)*

Promotion Mix Summary

Table 11-1 below compares each of the promotion mix options on the eight key promotional characteristics.

Table 11-1: Promotion Mix Summary

Characteristics	Advertising	Sales Promotion	Public Relations	Personal Selling
Intended Coverage	mass targeted	mass targeted	mass	targeted
Payment Model	paid limited non-paid	paid	non-paid	paid
Message Flow	one-way two-way	one-way two-way	one-way	two-way
Interaction Type	non-personal	personal non-personal	non-personal	personal
Demand Creation	lagging	quick	lagging	quick
Message Control	good	good	poor	very good
Message Credibility	low-medium	low-medium	high	medium-high
Cost Assessment	CPM – low CPTE – varies CPA - varies	CPM – medium CPTE – varies CPA - varies	CPM – one CPTE – none CPA - none	CPM – high CPTE – high CPA - high

Evolving Promotional Options

The promotion mix summary presented in Table 11-1 should be viewed only as a general guide, since promotion techniques are continually evolving, and how each technique is compared on a characteristic is subject to change. For instance, the evolution of the Internet and mobile technologies are blurring the lines between the promotional categories. This can be seen with the use of social media, such as Facebook, Twitter and YouTube.

On the surface, it would seem the use of social media for promotion should be considered advertising as it contains many of the key characteristics. However, most social media placements can be developed without direct payment to a media outlet (i.e., payment to the social media site), which is generally considered a necessary requirement for a promotion to be classified as advertising. Additionally, as we will see in the following chapters, there are several other aspects of promoting through social media that would place these promotions within other promotional categories.

For our discussion, we will continue to place social media promotions within the existing promotional categories. However, it is likely that as social media options continue to evolve, a new promotional category will eventually emerge.

Factors Affecting Promotion Choice

With four promotional methods to choose from, how does the marketer determine which ones to use? The selection can be complicated by corporate and marketing decision issues.

CORPORATE ISSUES

- Promotional Objective – As we discussed, there are several different objectives a marketer may pursue with its promotional strategy. Each type of promotion offers different advantages in terms of helping the marketer reach her/his objectives. For instance, if the objective of a subscription based genealogy website is to get customers to try their service, the use of sales promotion, such as offering a 14-day free trial, may yield better results than simply promoting through a general Internet advertisement.

- Availability of Resources – The amount of money and other resources that can be directed to promotion affect the marketer's choice of promotional methods. Marketers with large promotional budgets may be able to spread spending among all promotion options, while marketers with limited funds must be more selective with the promotion techniques they use.

- Company Philosophy – Some companies follow a philosophy dictating where most promotional spending occurs. For example, some companies follow the approach that all promotion should be done through salespeople while other companies prefer to focus marketing funds on product development and hope word-of-mouth communication by satisfied customers helps to create interest in their products.

> *With the tremendous growth experienced by social media outlets, including Facebook and Twitter, marketers have responded by including such sites in their promotional plans. Yet unlike other promotional options, where marketers can use past performance to estimate future results, making predictions in the nascent social media area is difficult. For the short term, many marketers view social media as a new promotion frontier and are willing to spend to learn more, though they also understand that corporate financial requirements may soon require they see evidence of return on investment. (13)*

MARKETING DECISION ISSUES

- Target Market – As one might expect, customer characteristics dictate how promotion is determined. Characteristics, such as size, location, and type of target markets, affect how the marketer communicates with customers. For instance, for a small marketer serving business markets with customers widely dispersed, it may be expensive to utilize a sales force versus using advertising.

- Product – Different products require different promotional approaches. For the consumer market, products falling into the convenience and shopping goods categories are likely to use mass market promotional approaches while higher-end specialty goods are likely to use personalized selling. Therefore, products that are complex and take customers extended time to make a purchase decision may require personal selling rather than advertising. This is often the case with products targeted to the business market. Additionally, as we discussed in Chapter 7, products pass through different stages in the Product Life Cycle. As a product moves through these stages, the product itself may evolve and promotional objectives may change. This leads to different promotional mix decisions from one stage to the next (see *Planning and Strategy with the PLC* discussion Chapter 20).

- Distribution – Marketing organizations selling through channel partners can reach the final customer either directly using a **pull promotion strategy** or indirectly using a **push promotional strategy**. The pull strategy is so named since it creates demand for a product by promoting directly to the final customers in the hopes their interest in the product will help "pull" more product through the distribution channel. This approach can be used when channel partners are hesitant about stocking a product unless they are assured of sufficient customer interest. The push strategy uses promotion to encourage channel partners to stock and promote the product to their customers. The idea is by offering incentives to channel members the marketer is encouraging its partners (e.g., wholesalers, retailers) to "push" the product down the channel and into customers' hands. While most large consumer products companies will simultaneously use both the pull and push strategies, due to the potential high expense of each strategy, smaller firms may find they must focus on just one approach.

- Price – Because customers generally need more time and more information when deciding to purchase higher price products, marketers of these product are more likely to engage in personalized promotion compared to lower priced products that can be marketed using mass promotion.

Marketing Story

On Campus, It's One Big Commercial
New York Times

It is probably not a huge surprise for many college students to learn that campuses are hotbeds for marketers. Aside from books and basic school supplies, each year college students spend billions of dollars on fashion, food, furnishings, and much more.

For marketers, one of the key attractions of colleges is the access these venues offer to a large number of customers within a geographically concentrated area. The potential of this market has caught the attention of a surprisingly large number of companies who see tremendous opportunity.

As discussed in this story, marketers are now flooding campuses and recruiting students to be part of their promotional army. However, companies are finding that reaching college students may require more than just advertising in the student newspaper or handing out samples in high-traffic areas. Because college students tend to be difficult to pin down to specific brands and are also often suspicious of the motives of those who are promoting, companies find that to reach this market requires creativity. For instance, American Eagle Outfitters hires "student ambassadors" to help unload and haul the belongs of newly arriving students, while Target sponsors welcome-to-school dinners.

In addition to the size of this market, another reason marketers have become so aggressive on college campuses is due to the large supply of readily available promoters. In almost all examples cited in this story, those promoting products are not full-time employees of the company but temporary hires working on commission. And, the commission may not even be in the form of cash, it may, instead, be free product. But for many of these students the real value they are receiving from their work is that it helps build up the job experience section of their resume.

This fall, an estimated 10,000 American college students will be working on hundreds of campuses — for cash, swag, job experience or all three — marketing everything from Red Bull to Hewlett-Packard PCs. For the companies hiring them, the motivation is clear: college students spent about $36 billion on things like clothing, computers and cellphones during the 2010-11 school year alone, according to projections from Re:Fuel, a media and promotions firm specializing in the youth market. (14)

What are the potential risks facing marketers who use college students as promoters of their brand?

|||||||||||||||||||||||||||||||||||||||||||||||||||||||||||||||||||||||||||||||||||||||||||||||||||||||||||||||||

REFERENCES

1. Standford, D., "Targeting Millennial Wine Drinkers Online," *BusinessWeek*, May 12, 2011.

2. Fessler, P., "Nonprofits Look for New Ways to Get People to Give," *National Public Radio*, April 6, 2011.

3. Vega, T., "Goya Aims to Expand the Neighborhood," *New York Times*, September 23, 2010.

4. Shannon, C.E. and W. Weaver, <u>The Mathematical Theory of Communication</u>, University of Illinois Press, 1949.

5. Schramm, W., <u>The Process and Effects of Mass Communication</u>, University of Illinois Press, 1960.

6. Pappas, C., "What's That Smell?" *Exhibitor Magazine*, December 2009.

7. Gillespie, K. and H.D. Hennessey, <u>Global Marketing</u>, South-Western College Publication, 2010.

8. Vega, T., "Marketers Discover Trucks Can Deliver More Than Food," *New York Times*, November 28, 2010.

9. Fessler, P., "Nonprofits Look for New Ways To Get People To Give," *NPR*, April 6, 2011.

10. Carter, B. and T. Vega, "In Shift, Ads Try to Entice Over 55-Set*,*" *New York Times*, May 13, 2011.

11. Wasserman, T., "Social Media Is Murky Area For Marketers of Alcohol," *AdWeek*, August 8, 2010.

12. Dornhelm, R., "Girl Scouts Venture Online to Market Their Cookies," *National Public Radio*, March 4, 2010.

13. Manjoo, F., "Does Social Media Have A Return On Investment?" *Fast Company*, June 22, 2011.

14. Singer, N., "On Campus, It's One Big Commercial," *New York Times*, September 10, 2011.

Full text of many of the references can be accessed via links on the support website.

Chapter 12: Advertising

Spending on advertising is huge. One estimate by marketing research firm, ZenithOptimedia, places yearly worldwide spending on advertising at over (US) $460 billion (1) while another leading research company, Nielsen, estimates this number to be more than $500 billion (2). This level of spending supports thousands of companies and millions of jobs. In fact, in many countries most media outlets, such as television, radio, and newspapers, would not be in business without revenue generated through the sale of advertising.

In this chapter, we present the first of a two-part examination of advertising with a discussion of advertising basics. We begin by covering several fundamental issues in advertising including examining what advertising is and why it is important to the marketing organization. We also look at managing the advertising effort by comparing in-house management to that offered by advertising professionals, such as advertising agencies. Finally, we identify different types of advertising and address trends facing the advertising industry.

||||||||||||||||||||||||||||||||||||||||||||||||||||||||||||||||||||||||||||||||||||||||||||||||||||||||||||||||||

WHAT IS ADVERTISING?

Advertising is a non-personal form of promotion delivered through selected media outlets that, under most circumstances, requires the marketer to pay for message placement. Advertising has long been viewed as a method of mass promotion in that a single message can reach a large number of people. But this mass promotion approach presents problems since many exposed to an advertising message may not be within the marketer's target market. Because of this, some marketers view advertising as an inefficient use of promotional funds. However, this is changing as new advertising technologies, and the emergence of new media outlets (see *Type of Media Outlets* discussion in Chapter 13), offer more options for targeted advertising.

Advertising also has a history of being considered a one-way form of marketing communication, where the message receiver (i.e., target market) is not in a position to respond right away to the message. That is, customers cannot immediately seek more information or quickly purchase a product they see advertised. However, this too is changing. For example, in the next few years technologies will be readily available to enable a television viewer to click a button to request more details on a product seen on their favorite TV program. In fact, it is expected over the next 10-20 years advertising will move away from a one-way communication model and become one that is highly interactive.

> *As we will discuss in Chapter 13, the notion that advertising in print media is a static and non-interactive is changing. This change is most often associated with the evolution of Quick Response (QR) codes, which are readable barcodes included with some print advertisements. The code is directed primarily to smartphone users. By scanning the code with their camera, users can be directed to a website, special promotion or other product information. While this form of interactive advertising may be new to customers in the United States, the QR code has been used for many years in Japan. (3)*

OBJECTIVES OF ADVERTISING

In Chapter 11, we explained five objectives that may be achieved using promotion. Advertising can address all of these, though at different levels of effectiveness.

♦ Building Product Awareness – Advertising has the potential to reach a large number of people in a short period of time. The mass communication nature of advertising makes it a particularly attractive promotional option for marketers, who are introducing new products and looking to build market awareness. Additionally, advertising can be used to help support a strategy to reposition a product (see *Product Positioning* discussion in Chapter 5) by creating awareness among a target market to benefits offered by the product that are new or that may not have been previously known.

♦ Creating Interest – Advertisements are creative productions with the power to capture customers' attention. As we will see in Chapter 13, the large number of methods for advertising presents marketers with ample ways to create appealing ads intended to excite customer interest.

♦ Providing Information – Many forms of advertising expose a targeted market to a message in a brief way and are often not suitable for providing extensive information. However, there are some forms of advertising that can convey extensive information. For instance, advertisements sent by direct mail can offer in-depth product information with the inclusion of detailed booklets, DVD videos and product samples.

◆ <u>Stimulating Demand</u> – Advertising is often used as part of a campaign to encourage a target market to make a purchase. While this certainly seems an obvious usage of advertising, in fact, by itself advertising is not the most effective promotional tool to achieve this objective. Advertisements, that on the surface appear to have the objective of stimulating demand, are generally also associated with other forms of promotion, most notably sales promotion (see Chapter 14).

◆ <u>Reinforcing the Brand</u> – Repeated use of advertising is often required to support a product. Given the number of ads a target market is exposed to on a regular basis, it almost has become a necessity for marketers to advertise consistently as they fear customers will forget about their product if competitors advertise more frequently. Companies operating in markets where competitors spend heavily on advertising must also spend in order to maintain a consistent **share-of-voice** (i.e., percentage of one marketer's spending on advertising in relation to total spending) within the market.

‖‖‖

MANAGING ADVERTISING DECISIONS

Delivering an effective marketing message through advertising requires many different decisions as the marketer develops its advertising campaign. For small campaigns involving little creative effort, one or a few people may handle the bulk of the work. In fact, the Internet has made do-it-yourself advertising an easy to manage process and has especially empowered small businesses to manage their advertising decisions.

As we will see, not only can small firms handle the creation and placement of advertisements appearing on the Internet, new services have even made it possible for a single person to create advertisements that run on local radio and television.

For larger campaigns, the skills needed to make sound advertising decisions can be quite varied and may not be easily handled by a single person. While larger companies manage some advertising activities within the company, they are more likely to rely on the assistance of advertising professionals, such as those found at advertising agencies (see Box 12-1), to help bring their advertising campaign to market.

Box 12-1

ADVERTISING AGENCY FUNCTIONS

When marketers look for advertising help they often turn to advertising agencies. The services offered by an ad agency cover both offline and online methods, and will vary depending on the size and expertise of the agency. For full-service agencies, service offerings will often include:

Account Management

Within an advertising agency, the account manager or account executive handles all key decisions related to a specific client. These responsibilities include locating and negotiating to acquire clients. Once the client has agreed to work with the agency, the account manager works closely with the client to develop an advertising strategy. For large clients, an advertising agency may assign an account manager to work full time with only one client and, possibly, with only one of the client's product lines. For smaller accounts, an account manager may manage several different, non-competing accounts.

Creative Team

Agency account managers delegate creative tasks, such as generating ideas, designing concepts, and creating the final advertisements, to the agency's creative team. An agency's creative team consists of specialists in graphic design, film and audio production, copywriting, computer programming, and much more.

Researchers

Full-service advertising agencies employ marketing researchers who assess a client's market situation, including understanding customers and competitors, and carry out tests of creative ideas. For instance, in the early stages of an advertising campaign, researchers may run focus group sessions with selected members of the client's target market in order to get their reaction to several advertising concepts. Following the completion of an advertising campaign they may use research to measure whether the campaign reached its objectives.

Media Planners

Once an advertisement is created it must be placed in appropriate advertising media outlets. Each advertising media has its own unique methods for accepting advertisements, such as different advertising cost structures (i.e., what it costs marketers to place an ad), different requirements for accepting ad designs (e.g., size of ad), different ways placements can be purchased (e.g., direct contact with media or through third-party seller), and different time schedules (i.e., when ad will run). Understanding the nuances of different media is the role of media planners, specialists who assist with the development of media strategies including looking for the best media match and negotiating promotional deals with media outlets.

‖‖‖

TYPES OF ADVERTISING

If you ask most people what is meant by "type" of advertising, invariably they will respond by defining it in terms of how it is delivered (e.g., television ad, Internet ad, etc.). But in marketing, type of advertising refers to the primary "focus" of the message being sent and falls into one of the following categories:

PRODUCT-ORIENTED ADVERTISING

Most advertising spending is directed toward the promotion of a specific good, service or idea, what we have collectively labeled as an organization's product. In most cases, the goal of product advertising is to promote a specific product to a targeted audience. Marketers can accomplish this in several ways from a low-key approach that simply provides basic information about a product (**informative advertising**) to blatant appeals that try to convince customers to purchase a product (**persuasive advertising**) including using direct comparisons between the marketer's product and its competitor's offerings (**comparative advertising**).

> *In carrying out persuasive advertising, some companies tend to go a little too far in convincing customers of the benefits of their product. Nivea, the maker of skincare and beauty products, was forced to pull a persuasive advertising campaign that some considered racist for the way it depicted black men. A similar complaint was raised for a Super Bowl ad by online couponing site Groupon which was criticized for poking fun at Tibetan culture. (4)*

However, sometimes marketers intentionally produce product advertising where the target audience cannot readily see a connection to a particular product. Marketers of new products may follow this **teaser advertising** approach in advance of a new product introduction to prepare the market for the product. For instance, one week before the launch of a new product a marketer may air a television advertisement proclaiming "*After next week the world will never be the same*" but do so without any mention of a product or even the company behind the ad. The goal is to create curiosity in the market and interest when the product is launched.

IMAGE ADVERTISING

Image advertising is undertaken primarily to enhance an organization's perceived importance to a target market. Image advertising does not focus on products as much as it presents what an organization has to offer. In these types of ads, if products are mentioned it is within the context of "what we do" rather than a message touting the benefits of a specific product. Image advertising is often used in situations where an organization needs to educate the targeted audience on some issue. For instance, image advertising may be used in situations where a merger has occurred between two companies and the newly formed company has taken on a new name. It may also be used if a problem has lead to negative publicity (e.g., oil spill) and the company wants to let the market know they are about much more than this one issue.

ADVOCACY ADVERTISING

Organizations also use advertising to send a message intended to influence a targeted audience. In most cases, there is an underlying benefit sought by an organization when they engage in advocacy advertising. For instance, an organization may take a stand on a political issue which they feel could negatively impact the organization and will target advertisements to voice its position on the issue.

PUBLIC SERVICE ADVERTISING

In some countries, not-for-profit organizations are permitted to run advertisements through certain media outlets free of charge if the message contained in the ad concerns an issue viewed as for the "greater good" of society. For instance, ads directed at social causes, such as teen-age smoking, illegal drug use, and mental illness, may run on television, radio, and other media without cost to organizations sponsoring the advertisement.

IIIIIIIIIIIIIIIIIIIIIIIIIIIIIIIIIIIIIIIIIIIIIIIIIIIIIIIIIIIIIIIIIIIIIIIIIIIIIIIIIIIIIIIIIIIIIIIIIIIIII

TRENDS IN ADVERTISING

Like most areas of marketing, advertising is changing rapidly. Some even argue that changes in the last 20 years have affected advertising more than any other marketing function. The most notable trends to have emerged include:

DIGITAL CONVERGENCE

While many different media outlets are available for communicating with customers, the ability to distinguish between outlets is becoming more difficult due to the convergence of different media types. Digital convergence, which refers to the use of information technology methods to deliver media programming, allows one media outlet to take advantage of features and benefits offered through other media outlets. This can be seen most clearly with television, which in many areas around the world is broadcast digitally using the same principles of information delivery that are used to allow someone to connect the Internet.

The convergence of television and Internet opens many potential opportunities for marketers to target customers in ways not available with traditional over-the-air television advertising. For example, technology may allow ads delivered to one household to be different from ads delivered to a neighbor's television even though both households are watching the same program.

But convergence is not limited to just television. Many media outlets are experiencing convergence as can be seen with print publications that now have a strong web presence. But even bigger potential exists for media outlets to connect with customers through digital methods. Some examples of convergence opportunities that are either currently being pursued or will be in the near future include:

- A media outlet's smartphone application that uses GPS technology to trigger a specific advertisement based on a person's physical location

- An outdoor billboard that alters its display based on a digital identifier emitted by passing vehicles

- A direct mail postcard that carries a different message based on data matchings a household's address with television viewing habits

The examples cited above represent just a few potential opportunities. The important point for marketers is to pay close attention to developments in this area as these could offer advantages for those who are early adopters.

AT&T became the first wireless company to offer location-based advertising when it began testing the delivery of ads to customers based on their smartphone's location. The program, dubbed ShopAlerts, drew interest from several leading marketers, including Hewlett-Packard, SC Johnson and Kmart, who see value in reaching customers when they are near retail locations. One downside of this service is that it can only locate subscribers within a mile of a store, rather than when the shopper is very close to a store's location. (5)

Focus on Audience Tracking

The movement to digital convergence provides marketers with the basic resources needed to monitor users' activity, namely, digital data. Any media outlet relying on computer technology to manage the flow of information does so using electronic signals that eventually form computer data. In simple form, electronic data is represented by either an "on" or "off" electronic signal. In computer language, this is further represented by two numbers "0" and "1" and, consequently, is known as **digital data**. All digital information can be stored and later evaluated. For media outlets delivering information in digital form, the potential exists for greater tracking and matching this with information about the person receiving the digital data. And tracking does not stop with what is delivered; it also works with information being sent from the customer. For instance, as we noted earlier, by clicking on their television screen viewers will soon be able to receive instantly information about products they saw while watching a television show. This activity can be tracked then used in future marketing efforts. Yet, while tracking provides marketers with potentially useful information, this research method has raised many concerns as discussed in Box 12-2.

Marketing Story

The Incidental Video Screen Is Seen by More Viewers than Prime Time
New York Times

Video screens showing television programs are popping up everywhere. Screens are now found in such venues as gas stations, elevators, doctor's offices, and public restrooms. The screens are so ubiquitous that new research suggests an enormous number of people are regularly exposed to video screens outside the home. And this does not even count computer screens. The implications for advertisers may be significant as they try to determine where to direct their promotional dollars.

This advertising channel, dubbed location-based advertising, is currently dominated by specialized networks that carry programming and handle the delivery of ads.

However, as this story mentions, these location-based programming networks have a problem. The problem is how to show advertisers how many people view these networks since an industry accepted audience measurement does not yet exist. The apparent logjam seems to rest with Nielsen, the leading auditor of television viewing data, which has only now begun to recognize the unique viewing situations faced by these networks. This issue is critical because a standardized viewing measurement is needed to enable networks and advertisers to determine advertising rates.

The networks have been pushing Nielsen to create a standard measurement so that they can better sell their ad time to agencies. "The agencies ask, 'Why are you better, why should I take some money and not run it on traditional television or somewhere else, and run it with you?' " said David Leider, chief executive of Gas Station TV. "If there's no legitimate measurement behind it, there's no point for an agency or client to look at it." (6)

This story presents both sides of the argument for having standardized measures. Which side appears to have the stronger position?

Box 12-2

AUDIENCE CONCERN WITH TRACKING

While media convergence offers marketers more options for tracking response to advertisements, as discussed in Box 1-2 in Chapter 1, such activity also raises ethical and legal concerns, particularly as these relate to customer privacy. Many consumers are not pleased to learn their activities are being monitored when they engage a media outlet. Some examples of how marketers track customers include:

Television Viewing
The advent of digitally delivered television allows cable, telephone, and satellite providers to track user activity through the set-top boxes connected to a subscriber's television. Future innovation will make the user television experience even more interactive and, consequently, open to even more tracking.

Television Recording
A **digital video recorder (DVR)** that is included with many set-top digital television boxes can track users recording habits and, based on a viewers' past activity, make suggestions for programs they may want to record. Additionally, advertising services can program the DVR to insert advertisements within a program targeted to a particular viewer.

Website Visits
Each time a visitor accesses a website they leave an information trail that includes how they got to the site, how they navigated through the site, what they clicked on, what was purchased, and loads of other information. When matched to a method for customer identification, such as website login information, the marketer has the ability to track a customer's activity over repeated visits to the site.

Internet Spyware
Downloading entertainment from the Internet, such as games, videos, and software, may contain a hidden surprise – spyware. **Spyware** is the name given to a computer program that runs in the background of a user's computer and regularly forwards information over the Internet to the spyware's owner. In some cases, spyware keeps track of websites the user has visited. The information is then used to gain an understanding of the user's interests. One form of spyware, called adware, may use the information obtained to deliver ads based on what is learned about a user's website activity.

Mobile Device Usage
A new frontier for user tracking can be found with mobile devices including smartphones and tablet "pad" computers. Tracking companies are moving aggressively into this area. For instance, The Nielsen Company, an industry leader in audience tracking, now offers data of websites visits, downloads of music, games and apps, and other activity that occur with many different types of mobile devices. (7)

ADVANCED ADVERTISING RESEARCH

In addition to the research value gained through audience tracking, there is a growing trend to incorporate other highly advanced research techniques as part of advertising decision making. One method that is increasingly gaining marketers' attention is the use of neuro-research techniques. As discussed in Chapter 2, neuro-research utilizes sophisticated brain scanning to learn how people respond to an advertisement. So called **neuromarketers** believe most processing of advertisements occurs within the unconscious part of the brain and because of this, many people cannot easily communicate what they actually like or dislike about an ad. By connecting subjects to brain-scanning equipment, neuromarketers feel they can get a much better idea of how people feel about an advertisement and, consequently, enable marketers to make better advertising decisions.

> *To measure unconscious response to advertising, California-based neuro-research firm, NeuroFocus, invites volunteers to its facility, where they are outfitted with a cap containing EEG sensors and an eye-tracking device. The research subjects are then shown various advertisements such as television commercials and website ads. The measurement devices allow NeuroFocus to match brain activity and eye-movement to specific parts of the advertisements. (8)*

AD SKIPPING AND BLOCKING

As noted in Box 12-2, television recording devices offer marketers tremendous insight into viewers' habits and behavior. Yet from the consumer side, the DVR is changing how people view television programs by allowing them to watch programming at a time that is most convenient for them. Viewer convenience is not the only advantage of the DVR. The other main reason consumers are attracted to the DVR is their ability to skip over commercials. Of course, this presents serious issues for advertisers who are paying for advertisements. As more DVR devices with ad skipping or even ad blocking features are adopted by mainstream consumers, the advertiser's concern with whether they are getting the best value for the advertising money becomes a bigger issue. Advertisers, who feel frustrated with television ad-skipping, may opt to invest their promotional funds in other media outlets, where consumers are more likely to be exposed to an advertisement.

> *The Nielsen Company suggests DVRs may not be as bad as television executives believe. Nielsen's research suggests that while viewers may not watch an advertisement at the time it is shown, if viewership is instead evaluated over a three-day period then ad viewing rises sharply, especially in the 18-to-49 year-old age group. The company suggests this is occurring primarily because these viewers are watching more television and, thus, are likely to see more ads. (9)*

CHANGING MEDIA CHOICES

There is a significant cultural shift occurring in how people use media for entertainment, news, and information. Many traditional media outlets, such as newspapers and major commercial television networks, are seeing their customer base eroded by the emergence of new media outlets. The Internet has become the principal driver of this change. In particular, a number of valuable applications tied to the Internet and mobile communication are creating new media outlets and drawing the attention of many, mostly younger, consumers. Examples include:

- Social Media – Possibly the most significant example of how media usage is changing can be seen with the rapid expansion of social media. Social networking websites, such as Facebook and Twitter, not only offer a venue for social exchange but these are also developing into locations where news and information is obtained.

> *One of the concerns expressed by marketers regarding social media is determining whether these sites truly hold potential as effective promotional outlets. One problem may be with how these outlets are viewed by customers and businesses. For instance, one study suggests consumers are more inclined to use Twitter to carry on a conversation with others (i.e., two-way communication), while businesses use it to broadcast information (i.e., one-way communication). Because of this, some experts feel marketers need to invest more time understanding how customers are using this medium. (10)*

- User Generated Video Sites – In large part due to the popularity of YouTube, what now qualifies as video media has changed. Now anyone can produce videos and post for the world to see. The result is that advertising choices for video production is no longer limited to television programs as marketers can present their ads as part of online video.

- Small Screen Video – While accessing video content over the Internet through computers linked to high-speed data networks is common, the streaming of video over wireless networks to small, handheld devices, including smartphones, is still in its infancy. Many television networks are now experimenting with making its programming available in formats suitable for small screen viewing. This includes offering marketers advertising opportunities. With the number of small screen devices continuing to grow rapidly, it is likely this format for advertising is poised for tremendous growth over a short time frame.

- Mobile Device Apps – Smartphone and tablet computer applications or "apps" are proving to offer rich new ground for advertisers. While most marketers are limiting their ads on apps to text and static image advertising, improvements in video performance and data speeds are opening the door for "in app" video ads.

- <u>RSS Feeds</u> – This is an Internet information distribution technology that is popular with news websites. With RSS feeds, new information posted on a website can be delivered instantly to anyone who has signed up for delivery. The information sent to feed subscribers can include inserted ads.

- <u>Podcasting</u> – In addition to offering RSS feeds, many news websites offer free downloadable audio and video files that can be experienced on computers, smartphones and iPod devices. While, at one time, this form of content delivery was widely used, many users are now accessing the information directly from the website rather than downloading files (e.g., watch news programming on mobile device). As this trend continues, the effectiveness of inserting ads in podcasts is likely to decline.

- <u>Online Gaming</u> – While gaming systems have been around for some time, gaming accessible over information networks is still evolving. As Internet and mobile network connections increase in speed, gamers are expected to shift away from games loaded on their local computer and, instead, access games online. This shift is opening new territory for advertisers by enabling marketers to insert special content, including product advertising, within game play.

> *Marketers see considerable opportunity for inserting ads in games played on mobile devices. While in 2010 estimated revenue for ads shown with games was less than (US) $100 million, that figure is forecasted to grow to nearly (US) $1 billion by 2015. (11)*

For marketers, these evolving technologies should be monitored closely as they become accepted alternatives to traditional media outlets. While these technologies are currently not leading outlets for advertising, they may soon offer such opportunity. As these technologies gain momentum and move into mainstream acceptance, marketers may need to consider shifting advertising spending. Marketers should also be aware that new media outlets will continue to emerge as new applications are developed. The bottom line for marketers is they must stay informed of new developments and understand how their customers are using these in ways that may offer advertising opportunities.

GLOBAL SPENDING

When it comes to the location of advertising spending, the U.S. is by far the leader with an estimated 34% of all spending occurring in that market. (12) However, the world's largest companies have recognized that to grow their business they must expand advertising beyond the U.S. market. Yet, the shift in advertising spending is likely not limited to only the top companies. Smaller firms will also need to consider expanding advertising beyond the U.S. market if they want to grow.

Trying to Move Up From a Fast-Talking, Buy-Now Approach
New York Times

Traditionally, the marketing establishment has looked down on products sold via infomercial (a.k.a., direct response marketing) as being of lower quality than competitive products sold by well established brands. Certainly the infomercial promotional method has much to do with crafting this perception of product quality. Most television viewers know too well that many infomercials are more akin to high-pressure personal selling sales pitches than what many of us have come to accept as television advertising. And this belief is fueled by the fact that few products that first entered our consciousness through infomercials have eventually transitioned to a traditional brand advertising strategy.

But that may be changing, as described in this story. Guthy-Renker, a direct response marketer with a long track record for successful marketing via infomercials, is now trying to bridge this divide by marketing one of its infomercial successes through a traditional advertising strategy.

The product being advertised is Proactiv, an acne product that can't be missed on weekend cable stations where it is heavily promoted. Guthy-Renker is advertising the product through several media outlets including spots on popular network television programs. The approach is new ground for this company and for the direct response industry.

The Proactiv campaign, which got under way last week, is being created with the help of an advertising agency, named Eleven, which is based in San Francisco. The campaign includes television commercials, magazine ads, billboards, signs and online ads, and they all resemble pitches for blue-chip brands in the skin care category. (13)

What other direct response products are suitable candidates for following a traditional advertising approach?

For marketers looking to move into foreign markets, the advertising decisions can be quite different compared to the U.S. market. Marketers may find that advertising that works in one country does not work in another. For this reason, marketers who are new to international marketing should take the time to learn how each market works and, in some cases, enlist the help of experts familiar with nuances of specific international markets.

> *The top 100 global marketers spend less than 40% of their advertising budget in the US. For instance, the world's largest advertiser, Procter & Gamble, spends two-thirds of its advertising budget outside the U.S., while P&G's principal competitor, Unilever, spent 86% of its ad budget in non-U.S. markets. (14)*

REFERENCES

1. *ZenithOptimedia*, Press Release, October 3, 2011.

2. Airlie, C., "Global Advertising Spending Rose in 2010, Nielsen Says," *Bloomberg*, April 4, 2011.

3. Rosenbloom, S., "Want More Information? Just Scan Me," *New York Times*, September 21, 2011.

4. Nir, S.M., "Nivea Pulls Ad After Online Outcry," *New York Times*, August 19, 2011.

5. Blair, N., "AT&T to Send Text Ads to Phones Based on Location," *USA Today*, February 28, 2011.

6. Clifford, S., "The Incidental Video Screen Is Seen by More Viewers Than Prime Time," *New York Times*, April 11, 2010.

7. "Mobile Measurement," *Nielsen* website.

8. Singer, N., "Making Ads That Whisper to the Brain," *New York Times*, November 13, 2010.

9. Stelter, B., "The Myth of Fast-Forwarding Past the Ads," *New York Times*, December 20, 2010.

10. Swartz, J., "Twitter and Marketing: The Real Story (or So Says a New Study)," *USA Today*, July 23, 2010.

11. "Rapid Growth Ahead for Mobile Game Ad Spending," *eMarketer*, January 10, 2011.

12. *ZenithOptimedia*, Press Release, October 3, 2011.

13. Elliott, S., "Trying to Move Up From a Fast-Talking, Buy-Now Approach," *New York Times*, May 4, 2010.

14. Johnson, B., "Top 100 Global Advertisers See World of Opportunity," *Ad Age*, December 6, 2010.

Full text of many of the references can be accessed via links on the support website.

Chapter 13: Managing the Advertising Campaign

An important objective of marketing is to communicate with its target market with the goal of creating interest in an organization's goods and services. A key method for doing this is by engaging in the consistent use of advertising. For many organizations, this entails the development of advertising campaigns, which involves a series of decisions for planning, creating, delivering, and evaluating an advertising effort.

In this chapter, we continue our discussion of advertising by taking a closer look at the decisions involved in creating an advertising campaign. Whether a marketing organization employs a professional advertising agency to handle its advertising campaign or chooses to undertake all advertising tasks on its own, a successful campaign requires a number of critical decisions including: 1) setting the advertising objective; 2) setting the advertising budget; 3) selecting media for message delivery; 4) creating a message; and 5) evaluating campaign results.

For leading consumer products companies, that spend large sums to promote their products, each of these decisions is intensely evaluated. Smaller companies with limited budgets may focus what little money they have on fewer decisions, such as message development and selecting media, and give less attention to other areas. No matter the organization's size, knowledge of all advertising campaign decisions is crucial and should be well understood by all marketers.

||||||||||||||||||||||||||||||||||||||||||||||||||||||||||||||||||||||||||||||||||||||||||||||||||||||||||||||

SETTING THE ADVERTISING OBJECTIVE

As we noted in the Chapter 12, marketing promotion, which includes advertising, can be used to address several broad objectives including: building product awareness, creating interest, providing information, stimulating demand, and reinforcing the brand. To achieve one or more of these objectives, advertising is used to send a message containing information about some element of the marketer's offerings. For example:

♦ <u>Message About Product</u> – Details about the product play a prominent role in advertising for new and existing products. In fact, a large percentage of product-oriented advertising includes some mention of features and benefits offered by the marketer's product. Advertising is also used to inform customers of changes taking place in existing products. For instance, if a beverage company has purchased the brands of another company resulting in a brand name change, an advertising message may stress *"New Name but Same Great Taste."*

> *One of the most unusual advertisements to promote a product was developed in Germany by Nestle. The company's television commercial for its Beneful brand of dog food is not only intended to capture the attention of dog owners but also capture the attention of dogs. The ad, which features a man talking to his dog, includes a high-frequency tone that dogs can hear but is imperceptible to human ears. (1)*

♦ <u>Message About Price</u> – Companies that regularly engage in price adjustments, such as running short term sales (i.e., price markdown), can use advertising to let the market know of price reductions. Alternatively, advertising can be used to encourage customers to purchase now before a scheduled price increase takes place.

♦ <u>Message About Other Promotions</u> – Advertising often works hand-in-hand with other promotional mix items. For instance, special sales promotions, such as contests, may be announced within an advertisement. Also, advertising can help salespeople gain access to new accounts if the advertising precedes the salesperson's attempt to gain an appointment with a prospective buyer. This may be especially effective for a company entering a new market, where advertising may help reduce the uncertainty a buyer may have with setting up an appointment with a salesperson from a new company.

♦ <u>Message About Distribution</u> – Within distribution channels, advertising can help expand channel options for a marketer by making distributors aware of the marketer's offerings. Also, advertising can be used to let customers know locations where a product can be purchased.

II

SETTING THE ADVERTISING BUDGET

Setting an advertising objective is easy, but achieving the objective requires a well thought out strategy. One key factor affecting the strategy used to achieve advertising objectives is how much money an organization has to spend. The funds designated for advertising make up the advertising budget and reflect the amount an organization is willing to commit to achieve its advertising objectives.

Organizations use several methods for determining advertising budgets including:

◆ Percentage of Sales – Under this approach advertising spending is set based on either a percentage of previous sales or a percentage of forecasted sales. For example, an organization may set next year's advertising budget at 10 percent of the current year's sales level. One problem with this approach is that the budget is based on what has already happened and not what is expected to occur. If the overall market grows rapidly in the following year, the budget may be well below what is necessary for the company to maintain or increase its sales. Alternatively, companies may consider allocating advertising funds based on a percentage of forecasted sales. In this way, advertising is viewed as a driver of future sales and spending on advertising is linked directly to meeting future sales forecasts. However, since future sales are not guaranteed, the actual percentage spent may be considerably higher than expected if the sales forecast is greater than what actually occurs.

◆ What is Affordable – Many smaller companies find spending of any kind to be constraining. In this situation, advertising may be just one of several tightly allocated spending areas with the level spent on advertising varying over time. For these companies, advertising may only occur when extra funds are available.

◆ Best Guess – Companies entering new markets often lack knowledge of how much advertising is needed to achieve their objectives. In cases where the market is not well understood, marketers may rely on their best judgment (i.e., executive's experience) of what the advertising budget should be.

II

SELECTING MEDIA OUTLETS

With an objective and a budget in place, the advertising campaign next focuses on developing the message. However, before effort is placed in developing a message the marketer must first determine which media outlets will be used to deliver its message. The choice of media outlets is crucial as it impacts the type of message that is created, the frequency with which the message will be delivered, the overall cost of the advertising campaign, and several other advertising decisions.

Characteristics of Media Outlets

An advertising message can be delivered via a large number of media outlets. These range from traditional established outlets, such as print publications, radio, and television, to newer evolving outlets, including the Internet and mobile devices. However, each media outlet possesses different characteristics and offers marketers different advantages and disadvantages.

The characteristics by which different media outlets can be assessed include the following seven factors:

1. Creative Options
2. Creative Cost
3. Media Market Reach
4. Message Placement Cost
5. Length of Exposure
6. Advertising Clutter
7. Response Tracking

1. CREATIVE OPTIONS

An advertisement has the potential to appeal to four senses – sight, sound, smell, and touch. (It should be noted that promotion can also appeal to the sense of taste but generally these efforts fall under the category of sales promotion, which is discussed in Chapter 14.) However, not all advertising media have the ability to deliver multi-sensory messages. Traditional radio, for example, is limited to delivering audio messages while roadside billboards offer only visual appeal. Additionally, some media may place limits on when particular sensory options can be used. For instance, some websites may only accept certain types of graphical-style ads if these conform to specified minimum size and limit smaller size advertising to text-only ads (see *Internet Advertising* discussion below).

While different media outlets offer different sensory options, these also may present the marketer with different requirements in term of what content is contained within an advertisement. For instance, popular media, such as major television networks and leading magazines, may be more restrictive on the message being conveyed in an ad, while smaller media, such as small websites and specialty magazines, may offer fewer content restrictions.

> *Toyota found that not only is advertising content affected by the media in which it appears but also by other influential forces. The automaker experienced this for an ad showing two football players' helmets colliding. While the intention of the ad was to demonstrate how Toyota's research can help improve safety across many industries, including sports, the National Football League (NFL) felt the ad was sending the wrong message. The NFL, which has become extremely concerned with the effects of concussions, insisted Toyota change their ad. The car company responded by adjusting the ad and removed the colliding helmets. (2)*

2. CREATIVE COST

The media type selected to deliver a marketer's message also impacts the cost of creating the message. For media outlets that deliver a multi-sensory experience (e.g., television and Internet for sight and sound; print publications for sight, touch, and smell), creative cost can be significantly higher than for media targeting a single sensory experience. But creative costs are also affected by the expectation of quality of the media delivering the message. In fact, media outlets may set minimal production standards for advertisements and reject ads not meeting these standards. Television networks, for example, may set high production quality levels for advertisements they deliver. Achieving these standards requires expensive equipment and high cost labor, which may not be feasible for small businesses. Conversely, a simple text-only Internet advertisement is inexpensive and easy to create.

3. MEDIA MARKET REACH

The number of customers exposed to a single promotional effort within a target market is considered the reach of a promotion. Some forms of advertising, such as television advertising, offer an extensive reach, while a single roadside billboard on a lightly traveled road offers limited reach.

Market reach can be measured along two dimensions: 1) channels served, and 2) geographic scope of a media outlet.

Channels Served

This dimension relates to whether a media outlet is effective in reaching the members within the marketer's channel of distribution. Channels can be classified as:

- Consumer Channel – Does the media outlet reach the final consumer market targeted by the marketer?

- Trade Channel – Does the media outlet reach a marketer's channel partners who help distribute its product?

- Business-to-Business Channel – Does the media outlet reach customers in the business market targeted by the marketer?

Geographic Scope

This dimension defines the geographic breadth of the channels served and includes:

- International – Does the media outlet have multi-country distribution?

- National – Does the media outlet cover an entire country?

- Regional – Does the media outlet have distribution across multiple geographic regions, such as counties, states, provinces, territories, etc.?

- Local – Does the media outlet primarily serve a limited geographic area?

- Individual – Does the media outlet offer individual customer targeting?

4. MESSAGE PLACEMENT COST

Creative development is one of two principal spending considerations for advertising. The other cost is for media placement, which includes the purchase of time, space or location from media outlets delivering the message. Advertising placement costs vary widely from extremely small amounts for certain online advertisements to highly expensive rates for advertising on major television programs (see Box 13-1). For example, in the United States the highest cost for advertising placement occurs with television ads shown during the National Football League's Super Bowl championship game where ad rates for a single 30-second advertisement are nearly (US) $3 million. (3) By contrast, ads placed through online search engines may cost less than (US) $5.

5. LENGTH OF EXPOSURE

Some products require customers be exposed to just a little bit of information in order to build customer interest. For example, the features and benefits of a new snack food can be explained in a short period of time using television or radio commercials. However, complicated products need to present more information for customers to understand the full concept. Consequently, advertisers of these products will seek media formats that allot more time to deliver the message.

Box 13-1

FACTORS IN SETTING ADVERTISING RATES

Media outlets set advertising rates using several factors, though the most important are the following:

Audience Size
The first factor refers to the number of people who experience the media outlet during a particular time period. For example, for television outlets audience size is measured in terms of the number of program viewers, for print publications audience is measured by the number of readers, and for websites audience is measured by the number of visitors. In general, the more people who are reached through a media outlet, the more the outlet can charge for ads. However, actual measurement of the popularity of media outlets is complicated by many factors to the point where media outlets are rarely trusted to give accurate figures reflecting their audience size. To help ensure the validity of **audience measurements**, nearly all leading media outlets have agreed to be audited by third-party organizations and most marketers rely on these auditors to determine whether the cost of placement is justified given the audited audience size.

Audience Type
When choosing a media outlet, selection is evaluated based on the outlet's customer profile (i.e., viewers, readers, website visitors) and whether these match the characteristics of the marketer's desired target market. The more selectively targeted the audience, the more valuable this audience is to advertisers. This is because targeted advertising funds are being spent on those with the highest potential to respond to the advertiser's message. The result is that media outlets, whose audience possess similar characteristics (e.g., age, education level, political views, etc.), are in a position to charge higher advertising rates than media outlets that do not appeal to such a targeted group.

Characteristics of the Advertisement
Media outlets also charge different rates based on creative characteristics of the message. Characteristics that create ad rate differences include:

- Run Time – such as a 15-second versus a 30-second television advertisement

- Size – such as a small box versus a full size banner Internet advertisement

- Print Style – such as a black-and-white versus a color postcard

- Location in Media – such as placement on the back cover versus on an inside page of a magazine

Media outlets vary in how much exposure they offer to their audience. Magazines and other publications provide opportunities for longer exposure times since these media types can be retained by the audience (i.e., keep old magazines), while exposure on television and radio are generally limited to the length of time the ad is broadcast.

6. Advertising Clutter

In order to increase revenue, media outlets often include a large number of ads within a certain time, space or location. For instance, television programs may contain many ads inserted during the scheduled run-time of a program. A large number of advertisements delivered through a growing number of different media outlets (e.g., smartphones, electronic billboards, etc.) create an environment of advertising clutter, which makes it difficult for those in the targeted market to recognize and remember particular advertisements.

To break through the clutter advertisers may be required to increase the frequency of their advertising efforts (i.e., run more ads). Yet greater **advertising frequency** increases advertising expense. Alternatively, advertisers may seek opportunities offering less clutter where an ad has a better chance of standing out from other promotions. This can be seen with certain news and information websites where online videos are provided. The videos may feature a five minute story but contain only a single 30-second advertisement.

> *Another contributing factor to advertising clutter is the rapid increase in the number of 15-second television commercials that are airing. Television research firm Nielsen estimates that 15-second ads now represents over 34% of all ads aired. The increase in 15-second ads means viewers are exposed to more ads. The move to 15-second ads can be attributed to reduced viewer attention span, thus requiring advertisers to show shorter ads more frequently. (4)*

7. Response Tracking

As we noted in Chapter 12, marketers are embracing new technologies making it easier to track audience response to advertisements. Newer media developed using Internet and mobile network technologies offer effective methods for tracking audience response compared to traditional media. But the newer-media is not alone in providing response tracking. Other advertising outlets, such as advertising by mail and **television infomercial** programming (i.e., long-form commercials), also provide useful measures of audience reaction.

Type of Media Outlets

While just a few years ago marketers needed to be aware of only a few advertising outlets, today's marketers must be well-versed in a wide range of media options. The reason for the growing number of media outlets lays with advances in communication technology, including the continued growth in importance of the Internet and wireless communication. This is changing how consumers and businesses are responding to advertising messages. For example, many consumers will be simultaneously exposed for several media options as they sit in front of their television. With mobile phones, computers and other devices readily present, a consumer's attention is easily taken away from television advertisements. Consequently, reaching consumers requires marketers to consider advertising through a variety of media outlets.

Below we discuss the leading media outlets used for advertising.

TELEVISION ADVERTISING

Television advertising offers the benefit of reaching large numbers in a single exposure. Yet, because it is a mass medium capable of being seen by nearly anyone, television lacks the ability to deliver an advertisement to highly targeted customers compared to other media outlets. However, television networks are attempting to improve their targeting efforts. In particular, networks operating in the pay-to-access arena, such as those with channels on cable and satellite television, are introducing more narrowly themed programming designed to appeal to selective audiences. Yet, television remains an option that is best for products targeted to a broad market.

The geographic scope of television advertising ranges from advertising within a localized geographic area using fee-based services, such as cable and fiber optic services, to national coverage using broadcast programming.

Television advertising, once viewed as the pillar of advertising media outlets, is facing numerous challenges from alternative media (e.g., Internet) and from the invasion of technology devices, such as digital video recorders (DVR) that have empowered customers to be more selective when choosing advertisements to view. To combat this, many networks and local television stations have altered the types of advertising they permit, including offering ads with shorter run-times (e.g., 15-second ads) or longer run-times (e.g., 30-minute infomercial).

Yet, for marketers, one of the key concerns with television is that it lacks effective response tracking. This has led many marketers to investigate other media offering stronger tracking options. In response, some cable and fiber optic services are experimenting with interactive advertising that enables viewers to gain more information on a product presented in an advertisement by clicking a button on their remote control. When this is done, data can be collected and customer response can be measured.

> *Marketers that rely on television advertising are exploring other options for getting DVR users to see their ads. One method is the use of contextual advertisements, which are ads designed to have a similar theme to the program being watched. For instance, during a zombie movie, the AMC network allowed Toyota to insert contextual ads featuring zombie characters. The hope was that anyone fast-forwarding would stop at the ad believing the movie was resuming. (5)*

RADIO ADVERTISING

Promotion through radio has been a viable advertising option for nearly 90 years. Radio advertising is mostly local to the broadcast range of a radio station, however, at least three options exist offering national and, potentially, international coverage. First, in many countries there are radio networks using many geographically distinct stations to broadcast simultaneously. In the United States, some networks, such as Disney (children's programming) and ESPN (sports programming), broadcast nationally either through a group of company-owned stations or through a **syndication arrangement** (i.e., business agreement) with partner stations. Second, within the last few years the emergence of radio programming delivered via satellite has become an option for national advertising. Finally, the potential for national and international advertising has become more attractive as radio stations allow their signals to be broadcast over the Internet and through smartphone applications.

In many ways radio suffers the same problems as television, namely, it's a mass medium that is not highly targeted and offers little opportunity to track responses. Yet, unlike television, radio presents the additional disadvantage of limiting advertisers to audio-only advertising. For some products, advertising without visual support is not effective. However, the restriction that radio is limited to audio-only advertising may be changing. This can primarily be seen in the form of Internet access and mobile device "apps" that not only allow radio stations to be heard but also enable audio ads to be supported by visual messages that appear on the screen of the device that is streaming the radio station.

PRINT PUBLICATION ADVERTISING

Print publications include magazines, newspapers, and special issue publications. The geographic scope of print publications varies from locally targeted community newspapers to internationally distributed magazines. Magazines, especially those targeting specific niches or specialized interest areas, are more narrowly focused compared to broadcast media. Additionally, magazines offer the option of allowing marketers to present their message using high quality imagery (e.g., full color) and can also offer touch and scent experiences (e.g., perfume).

Newspapers have also incorporated color advertisements, though their main advantage rests with their ability to target local markets. **Special issue publications** can offer highly selective targeting since these often focus on extremely narrow topics (e.g., auto buying guide, vacation guides, college and university ratings, etc.).

The downside of print publications is that readership has dropped consistently over the last few decades. Again, the emergence of the Internet is a key reason for the decline. Newspapers are particularly vulnerable and there are many who question the future viability of printed news as an important media outlet. In fact, many print publications have recognized they need to change and have slowly migrated their content to other media outlets included Internet, mobile devices, and pad computers.

INTERNET ADVERTISING

The fastest growing media outlet for advertising is the Internet. Compared to spending in other media, the rate of spending for Internet advertising is experiencing tremendous growth and in the U.S. for 2010 trails only television advertising in terms of total spending. (6) Internet advertising's influence continues to expand and each year more major marketers shift a larger portion of their promotional budget to this medium. Two key reasons for this shift rest with the Internet's ability to: 1) narrowly target an advertising message, and 2) track user response to the advertiser's message.

The Internet offers several advertising options including.

- Website Advertising – Advertising tied to a user's visit to a website accounts for the largest spending on Internet advertising. Today marketers have a large number of website advertising options available as discussed in Box 13-2.

- Email Advertising – Using email to deliver advertisement affords marketers the advantage of low distribution cost and potentially high reach. In situations where the marketer has a highly targeted list, response rates to email advertisements may be quite high. This is especially true if those on the list have agreed to receive email, a process known as **opt-in** marketing. Email advertisement can take the form of a regular email message or be presented within the context of more detailed content, such as an electronic newsletter. However, there is a significant downside to email advertising due to highly publicized issues related to abuse (i.e., spam).

- RSS Feed Advertising – As noted in Chapter 3, Really Simple Syndication (RSS) allows a marketer to send a notice that content on a website has been updated. Used widely by Internet bloggers and information websites, RSS feeds can be embedded with advertising that is automatically sent to those subscribing to the feed. The ads are then viewed when a subscriber accesses the feed through a feed reader.

- <u>In-Text Advertising</u> – This type of online advertising ties ads to text found on a webpage, such as specific words contained in articles or other content. In most cases, the text is formatted to be distinct from surrounding information (e.g., underlined words) and an ad will be triggered in the form of a pop-up box when the website visitor moves her/his cursor over the text.

> *Evidence of a shift in advertising spending from old media to new media can be seen with the promotional spending at Comcast. Between 2009 and 2010, the company dropped ad spending in newspapers by 23% while increasing spending for Internet ads by 52%. (7)*

MOBILE DEVICE ADVERTISING

Another outlet that is experiencing rapid growth as a venue for advertising is the mobile device market that includes smartphones and pad computers. The growth in mobile device advertising is being fueled by technological advances occurring with the computing power of hand-held devices as well as significant gains in speed of data delivered over wireless networks. This has spawned a new mobile advertising industry. Not only are advertisements displayed when a mobile device user opens a web browser to view Internet sites, advertisements are also embedded within specialized applications or "apps" that run on these devices. For example, advertisements may be displayed as a user is playing a gaming app.

This burgeoning method of advertising is expected to grow at tremendous rates. In particular, this market shows potential demand throughout the world with some forecasting that the largest demand may come from the Asian-Pacific region (8). The potential of the mobile advertising market has attracted a number of high-powered companies who provide technologies for serving ads to mobile devices. These include Apple, with its iAd advertising platform, and Google, with its AdMob product.

> *Apple's iAd mobile advertising platform uses information from its iTunes users to help determine what ads will be delivered. Apple uses the downloading information to determine the buying habits of customers and then serves them ads based on what is learned. With information on music, videos, apps, books, and more, Apple can determine a behavioral profile, which then can be used to assess the best type of ads to present. (9)*

DIRECT MAIL ADVERTISING

This method of advertising uses postal and other delivery services to ship advertising materials (e.g. postcards, letters, brochures, catalogs, flyers), to a physical address of targeted customers. Direct mail is most effective when it is designed in a way that makes it appear to be special to the customer. For

Box 13-2

OPTIONS FOR WEBSITE ADVERTISING

Website advertising offers a host of options for marketers to consider. Among the options are:

Creative Types
Internet advertising allows for a large variety of creative types including text-only, image-only and video. It also enables advanced interactive messages including advertising in the form of online games.

Size
In addition to a large number of creative types, Internet advertisements can be delivered in a number of different sizes (measured in screen pixels) ranging from full screen to small square ads that are only a few pixels in size. The most popular Internet ad sizes include medium rectangle (300 x 250 pixels), leaderboard (728 x 90 pixels), and wide skyscraper (160 x 600 pixels). (10)

Targeting
The leading locations for placing ads are on high traffic websites, such as search engines and other leading content sites, though advertisers can also choose to advertise on thousands of smaller, specialized websites. Ads placed on websites can be targeted by: demographics, such as ads appearing on sites more likely viewed by a certain age group; geographics, where ads only appear to visitors who access a website from a certain location; and timing, such as limiting the display of ads to certain times of day.

Placement
The delivery of an Internet advertisement can occur in many ways including: processed placement, where the ad is delivered based on user characteristics, such as in response to the entry of certain words in a search engine query; fixed placement, where an ad appears in a certain location on a website, such as at the top of the page; or on a separate webpage, where the ad appears on a different page from the main content, such as in the form of a new page or as a pop-up under, where the user may not see the ad until they leave a website or close his/her browser.

Delivery
When it comes to placing advertisements on websites marketers can, in some cases, negotiate with websites directly to place an ad on the site or marketers can place ads via a third-party advertising network, which has agreements to place ads on a large number of partner websites.

instance, a marketer using direct mail can personalize mailings by including message recipients' names on the address label or by inserting their names within the content of the advertisement.

Direct mail can be a cost-effective method of advertising, especially if mailings contain printed material. This is due to cost advantages obtained by printing in high volume. For most printing projects, the majority of printing costs are realized when a printing machine is initially setup to run a print job and not because of the quantity of material printed. Consequently, the total cost of printing 50,000 postcards is only slightly higher than printing 20,000 postcards, but when the total cost is divided by the number of cards printed the cost per-card drops dramatically as more pieces are printed. Obviously there are other costs involved in direct mail, primarily postage expense.

While direct mail offers the benefit of low cost for each distributed piece, the actual cost-per-exposure can be quite high as large numbers of customers may discard the mailing before reading. This has led many to refer to direct mail as **junk mail** and, due to the name, some marketers view the approach as ineffective. However, direct mail, when well-targeted, can be an extremely effective promotional tool.

SIGNAGE ADVERTISING

The use of signs to communicate a marketer's message places advertising in geographically identified areas in order to capture customer attention. The most obvious method of using signs is through **billboards**, which are generally located in high traffic areas. Outdoor billboards come in many sizes, though the most well-known are large structures located near transportation points intending to attract the interest of people traveling on roads or public transportation. Indoor billboards are often smaller than outdoor billboards and are designed to attract the attention of foot traffic (i.e., those moving past the sign). For example, smaller signage in airports, train terminals, and large commercial office space fit this category.

While billboards are the most obvious example, there are many other forms of signage advertising including:

- Sky writing, where airplanes use special chemicals to form words
- Plane banners, where large signs are pulled behind an airplane
- Mobile billboards, where signs are placed on vehicles, such as buses and cars, or even carried by people
- Sidewalk billboards, where signs are place on the ground

Developments in gesture and facial recognition technology have led to experimental billboards that adjust messages based on who is viewing. While such advertising devices were envisioned by Hollywood in the movie Minority Report, these technologies have evolved quickly due to its use in airport security and the gaming industry. Such technologies have also raised privacy concerns as some fear these have the capability to recognize a specific person and track their activities, such what they do while in a store. (11)

PRODUCT PLACEMENT ADVERTISING

Product placement is an advertising approach that intentionally inserts products into entertainment programs, such as movies, television programs, and video games. Placement can take several forms including:

- visual imagery in which a product is a background element of an entertainment program

- actual product use by an actor in an entertainment program

- words spoken by an actor that include the product name

Product placement is gaining acceptance among a growing number of marketers for two main reasons. First, in most cases the placement is subtle so as not to divert significant attention from the main content of the program or media outlet. This approach may lead the audience to believe the product was selected for inclusion by program producers and not by the marketer. This may heighten the credibility of the product in the minds of the audience since their perception, whether accurate or not, is that the product was selected by an unbiased third-party.

Second, as we discussed in Chapter 12, entertainment programming, such as television, is converging with other media, particularly the Internet. In the future, a viewer of a television program may easily be able to request information and purchase products that appear in a program by simply pointing to the product on the screen. As this technology emerges and as marketers explore other options (see Box 13-3), it is expected product placement opportunities will become a powerful promotional option for many marketers.

Gaining product placement in movies or on television programs can be difficult for companies to do on their own, as they often lack access to important personnel involved in making placement decisions. To overcome this, marketers often use the services of product placement agencies. These specialized businesses know the industry and are familiar with products sought by those producing entertainment programming. Additionally, these agencies maintain warehouse space close to studios so they are able to respond quickly if a product is accepted for placement. (12)

Box 13-3

OTHER SENSORY PRODUCT PLACEMENT

Product placement is not limited to movies and television. Other options are currently in use and more are being actively explored. Some additional product placement options include:

Musical Product Placement

Electronic games have become wildly popular and are often on par with television for attracting the entertainment attention of many teens and young adults, in particular, those in the important 18-25 year-old demographic. For many of today's gamers, their gaming system includes not only the gaming machine attached to a screen but also includes connections to an advanced audio system. Game developers have taken advantage of the enhanced gaming environment by populating their software with numerous songs from genres aimed at younger players. Most songs are up-tempo tunes that help create an atmosphere of excitement while players battle on the screen. After playing a game for many weeks, the gamer may be exposed to a song well over 100 times. In fact, for avid gamers, they will hear the song much more while playing video games than they will through local radio outlets. The result is that many new artists have benefited from this intense exposure, and the placement of their songs within an electronic game can be a key factor in helping to launch a successful musical career.

Scent Product Placement

The intentional inclusion of scent as a promotional aid has garnered much attention and could lead to a number of product placement opportunities. Olfactory elements have been used for several years at amusement parks to enhance customers' experience at shows and on rides. A broader consumer market will almost certainly develop with gaming most likely being the first to explore this sensory product placement option. As scent becomes a recognized sensory experience for media programming, there is little doubt scent-related product placements will follow. For instance, a bathroom scene in a movie may one day result in the smell of brand name room deodorizer wafting through the theatre.

Tactile Product Placement

Touch or feel sensations may also be a product placement opportunity. Today's gamers use feel devices to heighten the experience by way of such items as vibrating controllers and motion chairs. Sometime soon a television viewer may experience a program from several sensory angles including a tactile one. For example, a television show may not only show the visual product placement of a certain brand of automobile, the inclusion of tactile placement could suggest the smooth ride one might get from being in the real thing.

SPONSORSHIP ADVERTISING

A subtle method of advertising is an approach in which marketers pay, or offer resources and services, for the purpose of being seen as a supporter of an organization's event, program or product offering (e.g., section of a website). Sponsorships are not viewed as blatant advertisements and, in this way, may be appealing for marketers looking to establish credibility with a particular target market.

There are numerous local, regional, national, and international sponsorship opportunities ranging from a local art center to the Olympics. Exposure opportunities include signage, printed handouts, free gifts, sponsored receptions, and much more. However, many sponsorship options lack the ability to tie spending directly to customer response. Additionally, the visibility of the sponsorship may be limited to relatively small mentions especially if the marketer is sharing sponsorship with many other organizations.

OTHERS

While the advertising outlets discussed above represent the overwhelming majority of advertising methods, there are several more including:

- advertising using telephone recordings (e.g., political candidate's messages)
- advertising via fax machine (though such methods may be legally prohibited in some areas)
- advertising through inserted material in product packaging (e.g., inside credit card bill)
- advertising imprinted on retail receipts (e.g., cash machine receipt)
- advertising placed on or around another product (e.g., imprinted on plastic bags used to protect newspapers)
- advertising on equipment, tools and shopping aids (e.g., attached to grocery carts)

Some have termed the placement of ads on nonconventional media as **ad creep**. *One example is placement on public school-owned property, such as school buses and cafeterias. Yet, in a time when school districts around the US are experiencing sharp reductions in state funding, many school districts see the placement of ads as a way to generate much needed revenue. (13)*

Marketing Story

Your Brand on TV, for a Fee, in Britain
New York Times

Most product placement promotion, which is found primarily in entertainment programming including movies and television shows, is fast becoming a popular promotional method. One key reason for its attractiveness is that it offers a higher level of credibility. Program viewers may believe the product appears because the program producers selected the product and not because the marketer paid for placement.

In the early days of product placement, marketers often paid indirectly for placement. For instance, to gain visibility marketers used public relations techniques and free product to persuade producers to include their product. But what it takes to gain placement is moving away from such indirect cost methods and is now moving to requiring direct payment. As more marketers see value in product placement, the trend is for program producers to charge for placement. And marketers have responded by offering large sums to get their product included.

While paid product placement is an accepted practice in the U.S. and many other countries, this is not the case in Britain. In fact, as discussed in this story, product placement has long been banned on British television, though this has now changed. Following the lead of other European nations, Britain now allows for paid placement.

However, while over $6 billion is spent worldwide on product placement, many marketers question the potential of the British market due to limitations imposed by regulators. For instance, placements are prohibited for alcohol and junk-food products. Additionally, placements are not permitted on the BBC, the most watched network in Britain.

One of those rules is that product placements must be disclosed to viewers, something that is not required in the United States. In Britain, channels must display a small "P" in the corner of the screen at the start and end of shows containing product placements, as well as after the advertising breaks. (14)

Are the concerns expressed by British regulators still viable or is it time they rethink these?

||||||||||||||||||||||||||||||||||||||||||||||||||||||||||||||||||||||||||||||||||||||||||||||||||||||||

CREATING A MESSAGE

In our discussion of the communication process in Chapter 11, we saw that effective communication requires the message source create (encode) a message that can be interpreted (decode) by the intended message receiver. In advertising, the act of creating a message is often considered the creative aspect of carrying out an advertising campaign. And because it is a creative process, the number of different ways a message can be generated is limited only by the imagination of those responsible for developing the message.

When creating an advertising message the marketer must consider such issues as:

GENERAL MESSAGE CREATION FACTORS

When developing the message the marketer must take into consideration several factors that affect how it is created including:

- Characteristics of the Target Audience – The makeup of the target audience (e.g., age, location, attitudes, etc.) impacts what is conveyed in the message.

- Type of Media Used – The media outlet (e.g., television, print, Internet, etc.) used to deliver the message impacts the way a message will be created.

- Product Factors – Products that are highly complex require a different message than simpler products. Additionally, the target market's familiarity with a product affects what is contained in a message. For instance, a new product attempting to gain awareness in the market will have a message that is much different than a product that is well known.

- Overall Advertising Objective – As mentioned, the objective of the advertising campaign can affect the type of ad that is designed. For example, an advertisement with the objective of stimulating immediate sales for an existing product will have a different message than an advertisement seeking to build initial awareness of a new product.

KEY MESSAGE ELEMENTS

Most advertising messages share common elements within the message including:

- The Appeal – This refers to the underlying idea that captures the attention of a message receiver. Appeals can fall into such categories as emotional, fearful, humorous, and sexual.

- <u>Value Proposition</u> – The advertising message generally contains a reason for customers to be interested in the product which often means the ad will emphasize the benefits obtained from using the product.

- <u>Slogan</u> – To help position the product in a customer's mind and distinguish it from competitors' offerings, advertisements will contain a consistent phrase or group of words marketers include within their promotional message that is repeated across several different messages and different media outlets.

MESSAGE TESTING

Before choosing a message, marketers running large advertising campaigns will want to have confidence in their message by having potential members of the targeted audience provide feedback. The most popular method of testing advertising for the marketer (or its ad agency) is to conduct focus groups where several advertising messages are presented. On the Internet, advertising delivery technology allows for testing of ads by randomly exposing website visitors to different ads and then measuring their response.

EVALUATING CAMPAIGN RESULTS

The final step in an advertising campaign is to measure the results of carrying out the campaign. In most cases, the results measured relate directly to the objectives the marketer is seeking to achieve with the campaign. Consequently, whether a campaign is judged successful is not always tied to whether product sales have increased since the beginning of the campaign. In some cases, such as when the objective is to build awareness, a successful campaign may be measured in terms of how many people are now aware of the product.

In order to evaluate an advertising campaign, it is necessary for two measures to take place. First, there must be a pre-campaign or **pre-test measure** that evaluates conditions prior to campaign implementation. For instance, prior to an advertising campaign for Product X a random survey may be undertaken of customers within a target market to see what percentage are aware of Product X. Once the campaign has run, a second, post-campaign or **post-test measure** is undertaken to see if there is an increase in awareness. Such pre- and post-testing can be done no matter what the objective.

Marketing Story

Slogans in Advertising

Millward Brown

The Juice
For Everyday

ORANGE

JUICE

One technique used to position products in the minds of customers, is to develop a distinctive product slogan. By repeatedly exposing customers to a slogan, marketers hope to build product awareness and instill key product concepts. For instance, for many consumers the *"Just Do It"* slogan is instantly associated with Nike and connotes the impression of being active.

When it comes to developing a slogan strategy, marketers face several decisions. One crucial decision is determining what promotional role the slogan will serve. Some marketers view the role of a slogan in the same way they view the brand name with which it is associated. For these marketers, a slogan is for the long-term and essentially becomes embedded in the brand. This can be seen with the slogans of such brands as DeBeers (*"A Diamond Is Forever"*) and Wheaties (*"The Breakfast of Champions"*) which have seen little change for many decades. For these brands, the longevity of the slogan suggests the slogan is tied to the product in the same way the brand name is tied to the product.

Other marketers see a slogan as a marketing decision that needs to be refreshed after some period of time. An excellent example is McDonalds which has created many slogans in the last 40 years including *"You Deserve a Break Today," "It's a Good Time For the Great Taste of McDonald's," "Did Somebody Say McDonald's?"* and *"I'm Lovin' It."* Often these changes coincide with a change in the overall advertising campaign. In this way, the slogan is connected more to the advertising message and somewhat less to the brand name.

Since marketers use both long-term and short-term approaches to the role of a slogan, it begs the question: Is one approach better than the other? This issue is discussed in this story where research across many countries suggests familiar long-term slogans may have an advantage over short-term slogans. Not surprisingly this is leading many marketers to resurrect previously used slogans. Additionally, the story points to several other elements of a slogan that may improve its overall effectiveness.

Slogans are most likely to be remembered when they are included in a jingle. There is also evidence to suggest that slogans that have been used before and that are repeated within ads are better remembered. (15)

What product slogans would appear to be in need of a makeover?

||||||||||||||||||||||||||||||||||||||||||||||||||||||||||||||||||||||||||||||||||||||||||||||||||||||||||||||||||||||||

REFERENCES

1. "Nestle Ad First to Pitch to Canine Customers," *MSNBC*, September 30, 2011.

2. Schwarz, A., "Ad Change Underlines Influence of N.F.L.," *New York Times*, January 21, 2011.

3. Nakashima, R., "Super Bowl Advertisers Say the $3 million is Worth It," *MSNBC*, February 2, 2011.

4. Fredrix, E., "TV Commercials Shrink to Match Attention Spans," *USA Today*, October 30. 2010.

5. Stelter, B., "The Myth of Fast-Forwarding Past the Ads," *New York Times*, December 20, 2010.

6. IAB Internet Advertising Revenue Report, *Internet Advertising Bureau*, April 2011.

7. Database of 100 Leading National Advertisers, *AdAge*, June 2011.

8. "Gartner Says Worldwide Mobile Advertising Revenue Forecast to Reach $3.3 Billion in 2011," *Gartner,* Press Release, June 16, 2011.

9. Satariano, A., "Apple Studies User Downloads to Fine-Tune Mobile Ads," *Business Week*, July 6, 2010.

10. "Ad Unit Guidelines," *Internet Advertising Bureau*.

11. Steel, E., "The Billboard That Knows," *Wall Street Journal*, February 28, 2011.

12. Fell, J., "How to Get Your Product into a Hollywood Movie," *Entrepreneur*, February 25, 2011.

13. Rampell, C., "On School Buses, Ad Space for Rent," *New York Times*, April 15, 2011.

14. Pfanner, E., "Your Brand on TV, for a Fee, in Britain," *New York Times*, March 6, 2011.

15. "Slogans in Advertising," *Millward Brown*, May 2011.

Full text of many of the references can be accessed via links on the support website.

Chapter 14: Sales Promotion

In a time when customers are exposed daily to a nearly infinite number of promotional messages, many marketers are discovering advertising alone is not enough to move members of a target market to take action, such as convincing them to try a new product. In addition, some marketers are finding certain characteristics of their target market (e.g., small but geographically dispersed) or characteristics of their product (e.g., highly complex) make advertising a less attractive option. Still for other marketers, the high cost of advertising may drive many to seek alternative, lower cost promotional techniques to meet their promotion goals. For these marketers, better results may be obtained using other promotional approaches and may lead to directing all their promotional spending to non-advertising promotions.

In this chapter, we continue our discussion of promotion decisions by looking at a second promotional mix item: sales promotion. Sales promotions are used widely in many industries and especially by marketers selling to consumers. We show that the objectives of sales promotion are quite different than advertising, and are specifically designed to encourage customer response. Coverage includes a detailed look at promotions aimed at consumers, channel partners, and business-to-business markets. Finally, we will look at the trends shaping the sales promotion field.

||||||||||||||||||||||||||||||||||||||||||||||||||||||||||||||||||||||||||||||||||||||||||||||||||||||||||||||||||||

WHAT IS SALES PROMOTION?

Sales promotion describes promotional methods using special short-term techniques to persuade members of a target market to respond or undertake certain activity. As a reward, marketers offer something of value to those responding, generally in the form of lower cost of ownership for a purchased product (e.g., lower purchase price, money back) or the inclusion of additional value-added material (e.g., something more for the same price).

Sales promotions are used by a wide range of organizations in both the consumer and business markets, though the frequency and spending levels are much greater for consumer products marketers. In fact, by some estimates spending on sales promotion in the U.S. exceeds that of advertising. (1)

Sales Promotion vs. Advertising

Sales promotion is often confused with advertising. For instance, a television advertisement mentioning a contest awarding winners with a free trip to a Caribbean island may give the contest the appearance of advertising. While the delivery of the marketer's message through television media is certainly labeled as advertising, what is contained in the message, namely the contest, is considered a sales promotion. The factors that distinguish between the two promotional approaches are:

♦ Evidence of Time Constraint - Sales promotions involve a short-term value proposition where an advertisement does not. In general, if there is a limited time period within which action must be taken then it most likely qualifies as a sales promotion. In the contest example, a stated entry deadline would indicate a time constraint.

♦ Customer Action Required - Sales promotions require customers to perform some activity in order to be eligible to receive the value proposition. For instance, in our Caribbean trip example, customers may need to complete a form to make them eligible to be entered in the contest.

The inclusion of BOTH a timing constraint and an activity requirement is a hallmarks of sales promotion. While an advertisement may be used to communicate the elements of the sales promotion, the promotional method that rewards the customer is considered a sales promotion.

IIIIIIIIIIIIIIIIIIIIIIIIIIIIIIIIIIIIIIIIIIIIIIIIIIIIIIIIIIIIIIIIIIIIIIIIIIIIIIIIIIIIIIIIIIIIIIIIIIIIIIIIIIIIII

OBJECTIVES OF SALES PROMOTION

Sales promotion is a tool used to achieve most of the five main promotional objectives discussed in Chapter 11:

♦ Building Product Awareness – Several sales promotion techniques are highly effective in exposing customers to products for the first time and can serve as key promotional components in the early stages of new product introduction. Additionally, as part of the effort to build product awareness, several sales promotion techniques have the added advantage of capturing customer information at the time of exposure to the promotion. In this way sales promotion can act as a useful customer information gathering tool (i.e., sales lead generation), which can then be used as part of follow-up marketing efforts.

♦ Creating Interest – Marketers find sales promotions have the potential to be extremely effective in creating interest in a product. In fact, creating interest is often considered the most important use of sales promotion. In the retail industry, an appealing sales promotion can significantly increase customer traffic to retail outlets. Internet marketers can use similar approaches to bolster the number of website visitors. Another important way to create interest is to move customers to experience a product. Several sales promotion techniques offer the opportunity for customers to try products for free or at low cost.

◆ <u>Providing Information</u> – Generally, sales promotion techniques are designed to move customers to some action and are rarely simply informational in nature. However, some sales promotions do offer customers access to product information. For instance, a promotion may allow customers to try a fee-based online service for free for several days. This free access may include receiving product information via email.

◆ <u>Stimulating Demand</u> – Next to creating interest, the most prominent use of sales promotion is to build demand by convincing customers to make a purchase. Special promotions, especially those lowering the cost of ownership to the customer (e.g., price reduction), can be employed to stimulate sales.

◆ <u>Reinforcing the Brand</u> – Once customers have made a purchase, sales promotion can be used to both encourage additional purchasing and reward for purchase loyalty (see *Loyalty Programs* discussion below). Many companies, including airlines and retail stores, reward good or "preferred" customers with special promotions, such as notification of "exclusive deals" sent by email or surprise price reductions mentioned when the customer is at the in-store checkout counter.

||||||||||||||||||||||||||||||||||||||||||||||||||||||||||||||||||||||||||||||||||||||||||||||||||||||

CLASSIFICATION OF SALES PROMOTION

Sales promotion can be classified based on the primary target audience to whom the promotion is directed. These include:

◆ <u>Consumer Market Directed</u> – Possibly the most well-known methods of sales promotion are those intended to appeal to the final consumer. Consumers are exposed to sales promotions nearly every day and, as discussed later, many buyers are conditioned to look for sales promotions prior to making purchase decisions.

◆ <u>Trade Market Directed</u> – Marketers use sales promotions to target all customers including partners within their channel of distribution. Resellers, who are often referred to as trade partners, are targets for the majority of such spending. Trade promotions are initially used to entice channel members to carry a marketer's products and, once products are stocked, marketers utilize promotions to strengthen the channel relationship.

♦ <u>Business-to-Business Market Directed</u> – A smaller sub-set of sales promotions are targeted to the business-to-business market. While these promotions may not carry the glamour associated with consumer or trade promotions, B-to-B promotions are used in many industries.

In the next few sections, we discuss each classification in more detail.

CONSUMER SALES PROMOTIONS

Consumer sales promotions encompass a variety of short-term promotional techniques designed to induce customers to respond in some way. The most popular consumer sales promotions are directly associated with product purchasing. These promotions are intended to enhance the value of a product purchase by either reducing the overall cost of the product (i.e., get same product but for less money) or by adding more benefit to the regular purchase price (i.e., get more for the money).

While tying a promotion to an immediate purchase is a key use of consumer sales promotion, it is not the only one. As we noted above, promotion techniques can be used to achieve other objectives, such as building brand loyalty or creating product awareness. Consequently, marketers have available a wide assortment of consumer promotions as discussed below:

COUPONS

Most consumers are quite familiar with this form of sales promotion, which offers purchasers price savings or other incentives when the coupon is redeemed at the time of purchase. Coupons are short-term in nature since most (but not all) carry an expiration date. Also, coupons require consumer involvement in order for value to be realized. In most cases involvement consists of the consumer making an effort to obtain the coupon (e.g., print coupon from website) and then presenting it at the time of purchase. Customers are exposed to coupons in many different ways as explained in Box 14-1.

> *While consumer products companies are the primary source of coupons, retailers often augment these promotions by offering additional savings, such as doubling the value of manufacturers' coupons. The enhanced value of coupons has lead to an evolving "extreme couponer" sub-culture that invests considerable time combining both manufacturer and retailer offerings to realize significant savings. The craze, which has received a great deal of attention in large part due to the TLC network's Extreme Couponing television series, is being watched closely by manufacturers and retailers, who could cut back on coupons if more customers are drawn to extensive coupon usage. (2)*

Box 14-1

HOW COUPONS ARE OBTAINED

Coupons are used widely by marketers across many retail industries and reach consumers in a number of different delivery formats including:

Free-Standing Inserts (FSI)

The traditional approach to distributing coupons is to insert within media, such as newspapers and direct mail. This method may require the customer to remove the coupon from surrounding material (e.g., clip from newspaper) in order to use.

Printout

A delivery method common in many food stores is to present coupons at the conclusion of the purchasing process. These coupons, which are often printed on the spot, are intended to be used for a future purchase and not for the current purchase which triggered the printing.

Cross-Product

This involves the placement of coupons within or on other products. For example, a sports drink marketer may imprint a coupon for its product on the package of a high-energy snack. Also, this delivery approach is used when two marketers have struck a **cross promotion** arrangement where each agrees to undertake certain marketing activity for the other.

Product Display

Some coupons are nearly impossible for customers to miss as they are located close to the product. In some instances, coupons may be contained within a coupon dispenser fastened to the shelf holding the product, while in other cases coupons may be attached to a separate display (see *Point-of-Purchase Displays* discussion below) and customers can remove (e.g., tear off) and use at the checkout counter.

Internet

Many manufacturer and specialty websites allow customers to print coupons, or enable customers to obtain coupons via email. This form of couponing has grown rapidly in recent years due to the growth of group couponing. This form of sales promotion, made popular by such websites as Groupon and LivingSocial, provide coupons that only become valid when a minimum number of customers agree to use the coupon. The coupons generally offer significant discounts and must be acted on within a certain time frame. (3)

Electronic

The Internet is also seeing the emergence of new non-printable coupons redeemable through website purchases. These electronic coupons are redeemed when the customer enters a designated **coupon code** during the purchase process.

Mobile Device

A rapidly evolving method for coupon delivery is via messages sent to mobile devices, such as smartphones. The coupon appears along with a **Quick Response (QR)** barcode image. The customer then flashes the cellphone screen containing the image to the retailer or in front of an electronic reader that will then process the coupon. (4)

Rebates

Rebates, like coupons, offer value to purchasers typically by lowering the customer's final cost for acquiring the product. While rebates share some similarities with coupons, they differ in several keys aspects. First, rebates are often handed or offered (e.g., accessible on the Internet) to customers after a purchase is made and cannot be used to obtain immediate savings in the way coupons are used. (So called **instant rebates**, where customers receive price reductions at the time of purchase, have elements of both coupons and rebates, but we will classify these as coupons based on the timing of the reward to the customer.)

Second, rebates often request the purchaser to submit personal data in order to obtain the rebate. For instance, customer identification, including name, address, and phone or email contact information, is usually required to obtain a rebate. Also, the marketer may ask those seeking a rebate to provide additional data, including indicating the reason for making the purchase.

Third, unlike coupons that always offer value when used in a purchase (assuming it is accepted by the retailer), receiving a rebate only guarantees value if the customer takes actions. Marketers know that not all customers will respond to a rebate. Some will misplace or forget to submit the rebate while others may submit after a required deadline. Marketers factor in the **non-redemption rate** as they attempt to calculate the cost of the rebate promotion.

Finally, compared to coupons, rebates tend to be used as a value enhancement in higher priced products. For instance, rebates are a popular promotion for automobiles and computer software where large amounts of money may be returned to the customer.

> *Rebates can be offered by product manufacturers and by retailers. However, some discount retailers, such as Target and Best Buy, do not offer retailer rebates. They believe their prices are already competitive and see little need to lower price further through a rebate. Additionally, while these retailers will guide customers to manufacturer rebates by placing information on their website, they feel issuing their own rebates is not worth the inconvenience it poses to customers. (5)*

Trade-In Promotions

Trade-in promotions allow consumers to obtain lower prices by exchanging something the customer possesses, such as an older product that the new purchase will replace. While the idea of gaining price breaks for trading in another product is most frequently seen with automobile sales, these promotions are used in other industries, such golf equipment, where the customer's exchanged product can be resold by the marketer in order to extract value.

Marketing Story

Recommerce
Trendwatching

In a growing market, where many companies are introducing new products, the promotional "noise" occurring can be extremely intense. Spending on advertising is often strong as competitors are trying to stake a claim and be heard. With so much promotional activity taking place, marketers often must look beyond advertising and find other promotions that will capture customers' attention. One key way of doing this is to utilize sales promotions, such as coupons and "on-sale" promotional pricing.

Another type of sales promotion that is available, but tends to be underutilized, is the trade-in. This promotion, where customers exchange a current product they own for a price reduction on a new product, is seeing more usage across many industries. For customers, the trade-in is a nice way to feel they are getting extra value from a previous purchase and, consequently, they perceive they are giving up less to obtain a newer product. For marketers, the trade-in not only makes their customers happier, but the marketer gets the added benefit of not actually appearing to lower the product price. Instead, the marketer positions this promotion as a form of payment rather than a price reduction. Additionally, for some products the trade-in may enable the marketer to obtain certain public relations advantages. For instance, they may be able demonstrate how their trade-in promotion can be used to support environmental causes, such as explaining how they are recycling what customers trade-in or showing how they are offering a positive contribution to economically depressed regions by giving away what has been traded in.

In this story, we get a particularly good global perspective of trade-in promotions and see two market situations in which these are particularly effective. First, this type of promotion may work in markets that tend to experience relatively short life cycles, including consumer electronics and fashion. In these markets, customers are often still acutely aware of the investment they made when they first purchased the product and may be reluctant to purchase the latest offerings, unless they can obtain some value for the older model.

Trade-in promotions also work well in markets that may have an extended life cycle, where customers are likely to hold onto a product for a long time. Of course, the classic example is the automobile purchase, though there are many other industries in which the trade-in is also widely used including the purchase of business equipment.

French label A.P.C. launched the Butler Worn-Out series, where customers who brought in used jeans could trade them for a new pair at half price. The used jeans were repaired, stitched with the initials of the previous owner and resold. The range is so-called because 19th century English aristocrats would have their butlers wear their clothes first, to break them in. (6)

What type of research must the marketer engage in to ensure the trade-in promotion is worth offering?

PROMOTIONAL PRICING

One of the most powerful sales promotion techniques is the short-term price reduction or, as known in some areas, "on sale" pricing. Lowering a product's selling price can have an immediate impact on demand, though marketers must exercise caution since the frequent use of this technique can lead customers to anticipate the reduction and, consequently, withhold purchase until the price reduction occurs again.

As we will see in our discussion in Chapter 18, promotional pricing is also considered within the framework of price setting. More on of this technique will be provided in that discussion.

LOYALTY PROGRAMS

Promotions offering customers a reward, such as price discounts and free products, for frequent purchasing or other activity are called loyalty programs. These promotions have been around for many years but grew rapidly in popularity when introduced in the airline industry as part of frequent-flier programs. Loyalty programs are also found in numerous other industries, including grocery, pizza purchasing, and online book purchases, where they may also be known as **club card** programs since members often must use a verification card as evidence of enrollment in the program.

Many loyalty programs have become ingrained as part of the value offered by a marketer. That is, a retailer or marketing organization may offer loyalty programs as general business practice. Under this condition, because the loyalty program is always offered, it does not qualify as a sales promotion since it does not fit the requirement of offering a short-term value. However, even within a loyalty program that is part of a general business practice, a sales promotion can be offered, such as a special short-term offer that lowers the number of points needed to acquire a free product.

> *While many think of loyalty programs as being a new marketing promotion, these have actually been around for hundreds of years. One of the most popular predecessors to today's loyalty programs was the S&H Green Stamps program introduced in the late 19th century. With this program, customers would obtain stamps for their purchases and once they filled a book with stamps customers could trade these in for their rewards. (7)*

SAMPLES AND FREE TRIALS

Enticing members of a target market to try a product is often easy when the trial comes at little or no cost to the customer. The use of samples and free trials may be the oldest of all sales promotion techniques dating back to when society advanced from a culture of self-subsistence to a culture of trade.

Samples and free trials give customers the opportunity to experience products, often in small quantities or for a short duration, without purchasing the product. Today, these methods are used in almost all industries and are especially useful for getting customers to try a product for the first time. Sampling can take place at a person's home (e.g., included with a newspaper), in-store (e.g., through product sampling table), and out-of-home (e.g., hand outs on college campuses).

Retailer 7-Eleven uses free samples to help boost overall sales. When the convenience store retailer gave away free samples of its Slurpee product as a promotion on its unofficial birthday, July 11, they saw sales of Slurpees increase by over 38% the same day. Curiously, many customers who ended up spending to get more Slurpee may also have spent more in gasoline to get to the store than the free sample was worth. (8)

FREE PRODUCT

Some promotional methods offer free products but with the condition that a purchase be made. The free product may be in the form of additional quantities of the same purchased product (e.g., buy one, get one free) or specialty packages (e.g., value pack) that offer more quantity for the same price as regular packaging.

PREMIUMS

Another form of sales promotion involving free merchandise is premium or "give-away" items. Premiums differ from samples and free product in that these often do not consist of the actual product, though there is often some connection. For example, a cellphone manufacturer may offer access to free downloadable ringtones for those purchasing a cellphone.

CONTESTS AND SWEEPSTAKES

Consumers are often attracted to promotions where the potential value obtained is unusually high. Under these promotions, only a few lucky consumers receive the value offered in the promotion. Two types of promotions offering high value are contests and sweepstakes.

Contests are special promotions awarding value to winners based on skills they demonstrate compared to others. For instance, a baking company may offer free vacations to winners of a baking contest. Contest award winners are often determined by a panel of judges.

Sweepstakes or drawings are not skill based but rather based on luck. Winners are determined by random selection. In some situations, the chances of winning may be higher for those who make a purchase if entry into the sweepstake occurs automatically when a purchase is made. But in most cases, anyone is free to enter without the requirement to make a purchase.

A sub-set of both contests and sweepstakes are **games**, which come in a variety of formats, such as scratch-off cards and collection of game pieces. Unlike contests and sweepstakes, which may not require purchase, to participate in a game, customers may be required to make a purchase. In the United States and other countries, where eligibility is based on purchase, games may be subjected to rigid legal controls and may actually fall under the category of lotteries. In the U.S., a promotion is considered to be a **lottery** if it contains three elements: an award or prize; won by chance; and the requirement that those entering must pay for the chance. Such promotional methods are tightly controlled and may be illegal in several states.

PRODUCT DEMONSTRATIONS

Many products benefit from customers being shown how products are used through a demonstration. Whether the demonstration is experienced in-person or via video form, such as over the Internet, this promotional technique can produce highly effective results. Unfortunately, demonstrations are often expensive to arrange. Costs involved in demonstrations include paying the expense of the demonstrator, which can be high if the demonstrator is well-known (e.g., nationally known chef), setup costs, and payment for the space where the demonstration is given.

PERSONAL APPEARANCES

An in-person appearance by someone of interest to the target market, such as an author, sports figure or celebrity, is another form of sales promotion capable of generating customer traffic to a physical location. However, as with demonstrations, personal appearance promotion can be expensive since the marketer normally must pay a fee for the person to appear.

||||||||||||||||||||||||||||||||||||||||||||||||||||||||||||||||||||||||||||||||||||||||||||||||||||||

TRADE SALES PROMOTIONS

As noted in Chapter 11, certain promotions can help "push" a product through the channel by encouraging channel members to purchase and promote the product to their customers. For instance, a trade promotion aimed at retailers may encourage them to instruct their employees to promote a marketer's brand over competitors' offerings. With thousands of products competing for limited shelf space, spending on trade promotion is nearly equal that spent on consumer promotions.

Many sales promotions aimed at building relationships with channel partners follow similar designs as those directed to consumers, including promotional pricing, contests, and free product. In addition to these, several other promotional approaches are specifically designed to appeal to trade partners including:

POINT-OF-PURCHASE DISPLAYS

Point-of-purchase (POP) displays are specially designed materials intended for placement in retail stores. These displays allow products to be prominently presented, often in high traffic areas, and thereby increase the probability the product will stand out. POP displays come in many styles, though the most popular are ones allowing a product to stand alone, such as in the middle of a store aisle or sit at the end of an aisle (i.e., **end-cap promotion**) where it will be exposed to heavy customer traffic.

For channel partners, POP displays can result in significant sales increases compared to sales levels experienced at the product's normal shelf position. Also, many marketers will lower the per-unit cost of products in the POP display as an incentive for retailers to agree to include the display in their stores.

ADVERTISING SUPPORT PROGRAMS

In addition to offering promotional support in the form of physical displays, marketers can attract channel members' interest by offering financial assistance in the form of advertising money. These funds are often directed to retailers who then include the company's products in their advertising. In certain cases, the marketer will offer to pay the entire cost of advertising, but more often the marketer offers partial support known as **co-op advertising** funds.

PROMOTIONAL PRODUCTS

Among the most widely used methods of trade sales promotions is the promotional product, products labeled with the brand or company name that serve as reminders of the actual product. For instance, companies often hand out free calendars, coffee cups, and pens that contain the product logo. Table 14-1 presents a breakdown of the top 10 categories marketers use for promotional products. (9)

Table 14-1: Top 10 Promotional Products

Product	Percentage
Wearable Clothing	31.1
Writing Instruments	9.0
Calendars	8.4
Drinkware	7.0
Bags	6.5
Desk/Office/Business Accessories	5.3
Recognition Awards/Trophies/Jewelry	3.8
Textiles	3.2
Electronics	3.1
Other	2.9

SHORT TERM TRADE ALLOWANCES

This promotion offers channel partners price breaks and other incentives for agreeing to stock a product. In most cases, the allowance is not only given as encouragement to purchase the product but also as an inducement to promote the product in other ways. For instance, it may be used for: obtaining more attractive shelf space or store location; highlighting the product in company-produced advertising or website display; or agreeing to have the retailer's sales personnel "talk-up" the product to customers.

Allowances can be in the form of price reductions, also called **off-invoice promotion**, where the price is lowered based on the quantity purchased, and **buy-back guarantees**, where a manufacturer agrees to take back product that does not sell within a certain period of time.

TRADE SHOWS

One final type of trade promotion is the industry trade show. Trade shows are organized events that bring industry buyers and sellers together in one central location. Spending on trade shows is one of the highest of all sales promotions.

Marketers are attracted to trade shows since these offer the opportunity to reach a large number of potential buyers in one convenient setting. At these events, most sellers attempt to capture the attention of buyers by setting up a display area to present their product offerings and meet with potential customers. These displays can range from a single table covering a small area to erecting specially built display booths that dominate the trade show floor.

Marketing Story

Growth in Virtual Gatherings Offers Marketing Opportunities
New York Times

Every few years, a web-based business model garners attention for a unique offering that some believe will eventually be the next big thing. In the last 10 years, such web businesses as Friendster (social networking), Webvan (grocery delivery) and NetBank (online banking) were all labeled as the next big thing only to crash under the strain of poor execution, lack of funding, bad management decisions, changing technology or a host of other factors. Of course, other businesses would eventually learn from the mistakes made by these early entrants and turn these concepts into successful business models.

One recent web business to receive similar attention is Second Life, the virtual world where one can mingle with others often by masking their true identity through an avatar. While Second Life has shown some success in the gaming world, many have also touted the potential this site has for becoming an indispensable marketing tool. In particular, many feel Second Life is an ideal venue for businesses to promote products, conduct seminars, and generate sales leads. However, this has never really panned out as most companies have not embraced Second Life for businesses purposes.

But, like others that failed, the ideas developed by Second Life are now being put to work with greater success by others. The idea of virtual meeting space is alive and well on several fronts. As examined in this story, more and more companies are finding real value in participating in virtual meetings. This method is receiving particular attention from sales professionals, who are using virtual space to present products and establish sales leads. Major firms, including IBM, Cisco, and Hilton, are hosting virtual conferences. With physical trade shows continuing to struggle, many are predicting the virtual conference will someday be a legitimate alternative to the traditional trade show.

Like a physical counterpart, the virtual event allowed participants to start in a welcome area, with comfortable looking chairs (and businesslike avatars), and then hear and interact with company experts. (10)

What advantages do physical trade shows offer that cannot be matched in a virtual show?

SALES INCENTIVES OR PUSH MONEY

When the main objective of a sales promotion is to stimulate demand and increase sales, a marketer may be able to use promotion techniques that are aimed at those in a channel member's organization who also affect sales. Primarily, marketers may offer sales promotions to its resellers' sales force and customer service staff where they are used as incentives to help sell more of the marketer's product. Sometimes called push money, these promotions typically offer employees cash or prizes, such as trips, for those that meet certain sales levels.

||||||||||||||||||||||||||||||||||||||||||||||||||||||||||||||||||||||||||||||||||||||||||||||||||||

BUSINESS-TO-BUSINESS SALES PROMOTIONS

The use of sales promotion is not limited to consumer products marketing. In business markets, sales promotions are also used as a means of moving customers to action. However, the promotional choices available to the B-to-B marketer are not as extensive as those found in the consumer or trade markets. For example, most B-to-B marketers do not use coupons as a vehicle for sales promotion with the exception of companies that sell to both consumer and business customers (e.g., products sold through office supply retailers). Rather, the techniques more likely to be utilized include:

- price-reductions
- free product
- trade-in
- promotional products
- trade shows

Of the promotions listed, trade shows are by far the mostly widely used sales promotion within the business-to-business market. Trade shows, also called trade fairs, are especially critical for firms looking to expand into global markets. In many global markets, especially in Europe, trade fairs have a long history of being one of the most cost effective ways to promote products. The largest B-to-B trade fair is Hannover Messe held annually in Germany. The fair, which contains multiple industry trade shows, attracts thousands of exhibitors from over 60 countries and over 200,000 visitors. (11)

For American companies seeking to enter international markets, the U.S. Department of Commerce offers a program for locating and promoting global trade shows. Because smaller firms are often not familiar with trade fairs in other parts of the world, the Department of Commerce certifies such fairs through its Certified Trade Fair Program. (12)

||||||||||||||||||||||||||||||||||||||||||||||||||||||||||||||||||||||||||||||||||||||||||||||||||||||

TRENDS IN SALES PROMOTION

Marketers who employ sales promotion as a key component in their promotional strategy should be aware of how the climate for these types of promotions is changing. The important trends in sales promotion include:

CUSTOMERS EXPECTATIONS

The onslaught of sales promotion activity over the last several decades has eroded the value of the short-term requirement to act on sales promotions. Many customers are conditioned to expect a promotion at the time of purchase, otherwise they may withhold or even alter their purchase if a promotion is not present. For instance, food shoppers are inundated on a weekly basis with such a wide variety of sales promotions that their loyalty to certain products has been replaced by their loyalty to current value items (i.e., products with a sales promotion). For marketers, the challenge is to balance the advantages offered by short-term promotions versus the potential of eroding loyalty to the product.

COMMUNICATION AND DELIVERY

For many years consumers typically became aware of sales promotions in passive ways. That is, most customers obtained promotions not through an active search but by being a recipient of a marketer's promotion activity (e.g., received coupons in the mail). The Internet and mobile phone technology are changing how customers obtain promotions. In addition to websites offering access to coupons, there are a large number of community forum sites where members share details about how to obtain good deals, which often include information on how or where to find a sales promotion. Monitoring these sites may offer marketers insight into customers' attitudes about certain promotions and may even suggest ideas for future sales promotions.

Traditionally, sales promotions have been delivered to customers via mail, in-person or within print media. However, the Internet and mobile phone technologies, such as smartphones, present marketers with a number of new delivery options. For example, the combination of mobile devices and geographic positioning technology permits marketers to target promotions to a customer's physical location. This allows retailers and other businesses to issue sales promotions, such as sending electronic coupons to a customer's mobile device when they are near the location where the coupon can be used.

> *The leader in electronic coupon delivery is Groupon. The company, which was founded in 2008, is built on a business model that sends customers "deal-of-the-day" coupons, generally sponsored by businesses in a local area. While an attractive method for building awareness, many small companies using Groupon find revenue is low as Groupon is often paid 50% of the overall revenue that is generated. This has opened the electronic coupon market for other companies offering more attractive revenue sharing terms. (13)*

TRACKING

As we discussed in our coverage of advertising, tracking customer response to marketers' promotional activity is critical for measuring the success of an advertisement. In sales promotion, tracking is also used. For instance, grocery retailers whose customers are in possession of loyalty cards, have the ability to match customer sales data to coupon use. This information can then be sold to coupon marketers who may use the information to get a better picture of the buying patterns of those responding to the coupon, including using the information to generate instant coupons at the checkout counter.

CLUTTER AND NEED FOR CREATIVITY

In the same way an advertisement competes with other ads for customers' attention, so too do sales promotions. This is particularly an issue with inserted coupon promotions that may be included in mailing or printed media along with numerous other offerings. The challenge facing marketers is to find creative ways to separate their promotions from those offered by their competitors.

REFERENCES

1. Myers, J., <u>2010 Advertising and Marketing Investment Forecast</u>, *JackMyers.com.*
2. Bonner, J.L., "Coupon Obsessives Teach How to Get Extreme," *MSNBC*, July 7, 2011.
3. Pogue, D., "Psyched to Buy, in Groups," *New York Times*, February 9, 2011.
4. Siwiki, B., "Stores Link to the Online World," *Internet Retailer*, September 1, 2011.
5. Choi, C., "Stores Like Rebates Because Shoppers Are Lazy," *MSNBC*, November 4, 2010.
6. "Recommerce," *Trendwatching*, October 2011.
7. Starvish, M., "Customer Loyalty Programs That Work," *Harvard Working Knowledge*, July 27, 2011.
8. Horovitz, B., "Free Slurpees Come With a Twist: They May Cost You," *USA Today*, July 7, 2011.
9. "The 2010 Estimate of Promotional Products Distributor Sales," *Promotional Products Association International.*
10. Olson, E., "Growth in Virtual Gatherings Offers Marketing Opportunities," *New York Times*, December 1, 2010.
11. *Hannover Messe* website.
12. "Trade Fair Certification," *Export.gov* website.
13. Holmes, E., "Burned by Daily-Deal Craze, Small Businesses Get Savvy," *Wall Street Journal*, March 24, 2011.

Full text of many of the references can be accessed via links on the support website.

Chapter 15: Public Relations

Of the four promotional mix options available to marketers, public relations (PR) is probably the least understood and, consequently, often receives the least amount of attention. Many marketers see public relations as only handling rudimentary communication activities, such as issuing press releases and responding to questions from the news media. But in reality, in a time

when customers are inundated with thousands of promotional messages every day, public relations offers powerful methods for cutting through the clutter.

In this chapter, we investigate how public relations is growing in importance as a marketing tool and is now a critical component in helping marketers reach their objectives. We look at both the advantages and disadvantages of using PR for promotion. We see that PR uses a variety of tools to enhance the relationship between an organization and its target audience. And we show how when handled correctly, PR can allow a marketer's message to stand out compared to other promotional methods.

|||||||||||||||||||||||||||||||||||||||||||||||||||||||||||||||||||||||||||||||||||||||||||||||||||||||||||||

WHAT IS PUBLIC RELATIONS?

Public relations involves activities that are intended to cultivate positive relations with key organizations and group through the use of a variety of communications channels and tools. Traditionally, this meant a company's public relations team would work with members of the news media to publicize the organization and/or its products in an attempt to gain favorable stories in print and broadcast media. But today the role of public relations is much broader and includes:

◆ Closely monitoring numerous media channels for public comment about a company and its products.

◆ Building goodwill among an organization's target market through community, philanthropic, and special programs and events.

◆ Managing crises that threaten the image of a company or its product.

> *Following an ice storm, JetBlue Airways received significant media coverage for its decision not to cancel flights. While other airlines shutdown, JetBlue made the decision to continue flying and even kept some passengers on its planes for hours despite food supplies running low. The media quickly picked up on passenger complaints and the resulting negative publicity was fierce. However, the company's public relations team quickly mobilized and developed a plan that included placing the company's CEO out front to answer news media questions. The rapid response was credited with diffusing the issue. (1)*

In this chapter, most of our focus is on how public relations supports marketing by building product and company image (sometimes referred to as **publicity**). Yet, it should be noted that there are other stakeholders companies reach via the public relations function, such as employees and non-target market groups (see *Other Targets of Marketing Promotion* discussion in Chapter 11). Favorable media coverage about a company or product often reaches these audiences as well and may offer potential benefit to the marketer.

Finally, in most large companies, **investor relations (IR)** or **financial public relations** is a specialty area guided by specific disclosure regulations. However, coverage of this type of PR will not be provided here.

Advantages of PR

Public relations offers several advantages not found with other promotional options. First, PR is often considered a highly credible form of promotion. One of PR's key points of power rests with helping to establish credibility for a product, company or person (e.g., CEO) in the minds of targeted customer groups by capitalizing on the influence of a third-party — the media. Audiences view many media outlets as independent sources that are unbiased in their coverage, meaning the decision to include the name of the company and the views expressed about the company is not based on payment (i.e., advertisement), but on the media outlet's judgment of what is newsworthy. For example, a positive story about a new product in the business section of a local newspaper may have a greater impact on readers than a full-page advertisement for the product since readers perceive the news media as presenting an impartial perspective of the product.

Second, a well-structured PR campaign can provide the target market with more detailed information than they receive with other forms of promotion. That is, media sources often have more space (e.g., magazine story) or time (e.g., television report) to offer a fuller explanation of a product.

Third, depending on the media outlet, a story mentioning a company may be picked up by a large number of additional media resulting in a single story spreading to many other outlets. For instance, a story on a major magazine website can spread rapidly as bloggers and social media users provide links to the story.

Finally, in many cases public relations objectives can be achieved at low cost when compared to other promotional efforts. This is not to suggest public relations is not costly, it may be, especially when a marketer hires PR professionals to handle the work. Yet, when compared to the direct cost of other promotions, in particular advertising, the return on promotional expense can be quite high.

Disadvantages of PR

While public relations holds many advantages for marketers, there are also concerns when using this promotional technique. First, while public relations uses many of the same media outlets as advertising, such as newspapers, magazines, radio, TV, and Internet, it differs significantly from advertising in that marketers do not have direct control over whether a message is delivered and where it is placed for delivery. For instance, a marketer may spend many hours talking with a magazine writer who is preparing an industry story only to find that her company is never mentioned in the article.

Second, while other promotional messages are carefully crafted and appear exactly as written when these appear in predetermined a media vehicle (e.g., advertisements in newspapers), public relations generally conveys information to a member of the news media (e.g., reporter), who then "re-crafts" the information as part of a news story or feature. Consequently, the final message may not be precisely what the marketer planned.

Third, while a PR campaign has the potential to yield a high return on promotional expense, it also has the potential to produce the opposite if the news media feels there is little value in running a story **pitched** (i.e., suggested via communication with the news outlet) by the marketer.

Fourth, with PR there is always a chance a well devised PR story will get "bumped" from planned media coverage because of a more critical breaking news story, such as a significant event (e.g., earthquake), severe weather or serious crime.

Fifth, in some areas of the world the impact of traditional news outlets is fading forcing public relations professionals to scramble to find and understand new ways to reach their target markets. Unfortunately, many seasoned PR people may be slow to adapt to newer methods and, thus, may not be in a position to understand fully how these methods impact public relations. This could place them at a competitive disadvantage compared to competitors whose PR staff is well-versed in utilizing these newer methods.

Finally, marketers accustom to handling many of their own tasks may find that public relations requires a different skill set than other types of promotion. As explained in Box 15-1, for many marketers PR functions are better left to professionals.

Another potential problem with public relations occurs when it is used to spread false information. For example, in China, rumors were spread suggesting that one company's baby formula was potentially harmful to infants. It turns out these rumors were part of a PR campaign intended to boost a competitor's sales. Those responsible spread rumors through online postings that suggested the competitor's milk contained fish oil that could cause birth defects. Those responsible for the rumors were subsequently arrested. (2)

Box 15-1

THE BENEFITS OF PR PROFESSIONALS

While do-it-yourself public relations is certainly undertaken by many marketers, gaining satisfactory results can often prove difficult for those who have little experience in this promotional area. Instead, most marketers are better served by seeking the assistance of PR professionals who understand all aspects of this diverse field. Skilled PR professionals offer many advantages for marketers with the two most prominent being:

Understand the Story

An important tool for PR is the development of media relations (see *Media Relations* discussion below). Public relations professionals are trained to unearth good stories about a company and its products, which can then be presented to the media in the form of a story idea. Just like selling products, selling story ideas requires those "pitching" the story to present it in terms that will benefit the media outlet. PR professionals are skilled at presenting stories in ways that capture the interest of members of the media.

Know the Media

Knowledge of the media's market may place PR professionals in a better position to match stories to the news angles sought by specific media members. Their skill at targeting the right media may prove to be a more efficient use of promotional resources than would occur if a marketer, who has little understanding of media needs, attempted to handle this on his/her own. This skill is especially valuable for organizations looking to do PR beyond their home market. Unlike advertising, where a standardized message can often work across different countries and cultures, the message presented through PR must often be tailored for individual countries and, in some cases, sub-cultures within countries. For this reason, many companies find that undertaking PR in the global market is better left to professionals who are active within each market. (3)

III

OBJECTIVES OF PUBLIC RELATIONS

Like other aspects of marketing promotion, public relations is used to address several broad objectives including:

♦ Building Product Awareness – When introducing a new product or re-launching an existing product, marketers can use a PR element to generate customer attention and awareness through media placements and special events.

♦ Creating Interest – Whether a PR placement is an article specifically covering a product or is included within a "round up" article covering several related products, stories in the media can help entice a targeted audience to try a product. For example, around the holiday season, a festive holiday food may receive PR support with promotional releases sent to the food media, or through a free sampling event that may attract local television coverage.

♦ Providing Information – PR can be used to provide customers with more in depth information about goods and services. Through articles, collateral materials (e.g., videos, handouts), newsletters, and websites, PR delivers information to customers that can help them gain understanding of the product.

♦ Stimulating Demand – While not as effective as sales promotion for moving customers to make a purchase, PR can still be a useful technique for building demand. For example, a positive article in a newspaper, on a TV news show or mentioned on the Internet, can lead to a discernible increase in product sales.

♦ Reinforcing the Brand – In many companies, the public relations function is also involved with brand reinforcement by maintaining positive relationships with key audiences and thereby aiding in building a strong image. Today it is crucial for companies and brands to build a favorable image. A strong image helps the company grow its business and may also help protect the company in times of crises.

|||||||||||||||||||||||||||||||||||||||||||||||||||||||||||||||||||||||||||||||||||||||||||||||||||||||||||

PUBLIC RELATIONS TOOLS

Whether handling PR internally or hiring professionals (see Box 15-1), marketers should be familiar with the tools available for public relations. The key tools available for PR are discussed in detail below.

MEDIA RELATIONS

Historically the core of public relations has been media relations, which includes all efforts to publicize products or a company to members of the press (e.g., TV, radio, newspaper, magazine) and other influential voices (e.g., websites, bloggers). In garnering media coverage, PR professionals work with the media to place stories about products, companies, and company spokespeople. This is done by developing interesting and relevant story angles that are pitched to the media. It is necessary to understand that media placements only come when story ideas are of interest to the media and that no direct payment is made to the media for placements. In fact, in order to maintain the highest level of credibility, many news organizations bar reporters from accepting even the smallest gifts (e.g., free pencils with product logo) from companies.

For marketers, it is essential to know that many story ideas appearing in news outlets often start with a suggestion from a PR person. This may occur through one of the media building techniques discussed in Box 15-2 or through direct conversations with journalists. If things work out, a journalist will, at best, write a positive story with the company as a key feature or, at a minimum, include the company's name somewhere within an industry-focused article.

Another growing segment of the media market is represented by independent bloggers who are not part of an established news organization. Within some industries, bloggers have attracted a large and loyal following. Public relations campaigns targeting bloggers are rapidly gaining favor and, for many companies, represent a media outlet that carries significant influence within a target market.

The news media is frequently on the lookout for story ideas that are unique, unusual or controversial as these will often attract the attention of their customers. Athletic Propulsion Labs, a small apparel and footwear company, realized they had an attractive story idea when their basketball sneaker, which contains a spring-like mechanism, was banned by the National Basketball Association. In just a few hours of learning of the ban, Athletic Propulsion Labs sent out a press release trumpeting the ban. Their story was quickly picked up by leading news outlets including ESPN, Yahoo and the Associated Press. (4)

Box 15-2

TECHNIQUES FOR BUILDING MEDIA RELATIONS

While the objective of media relations is to obtain favorable mentions for a company or product without direct payment to a media outlet, the process of building strong media relations is by no means free. Public relations professionals "pitch" stories to reporters and news editors with the assistance of a variety of techniques that are often expensive to produce. These techniques include:

News Releases

One of the most frequently undertaken tasks of public relations professionals is the preparation of a news release (a.k.a., press release). A news release is a company prepared message that is intended to highlight one or more issues facing the company. For instance, a news release is often used to announce a new product, indicate changes occurring with existing products, and to introduce new company personnel. Today the vast majority of news releases are delivered electronically via website postings or email, though some companies are also producing audio and video news releases.

Press Kits

This is the name given to prepared materials, such as organization background, key spokesperson biographies and other supporting materials, that provide information useful to the news media. Such kits can be sent to reporters via package delivery services or accessible on a company's website. As more companies utilize press kits, the design and content have changed with many now packaged in uniquely detailed containers, such as bags, pouches, plastic cases, and cardboard tubes. (5) Additionally, press kits may include video that is intended for use within media programming. For instance, a local television news report about amusement parks may include a video that is available as part of press kits sent out by a national amusement park company.

Matte Release

Some media, especially small local newspapers, may accept articles written by companies as filler material when their publications lack sufficient content. PR professionals submit matte releases through **syndicated news services** (i.e., services that supply content to many media outlets) or directly to targeted media via email, fax or postal mail.

Industry Articles

Many industry websites and print publications allow companies to submit articles authored by company personnel, such as a CEO or Marketing Manager. Depending on the media outlet, the articles can cover specific happenings at a company or may be written with the intention of addressing a business issue. In either case, PR professionals may have significant input into the creation of the article even though they are not identified as the author.

Website Press Room

While hard copies of materials are used and preferred by some media, marketers are well served to establish an online press room catering to media needs (e.g., news releases, press kits) and providing company contact information. Many website press rooms feature RSS feeds enabling the news media to be automatically notified when new material is added.

Social Networks

In addition to company website postings, public relations professional are also making use of social networks as a method for reaching the media. While Facebook postings are widely used for PR, instant communication messaging, such as that found with Twitter, may offer more immediate impact. However, it should be understood, the effectiveness of social media will depend on whether reporters and other news media members actually follow the postings. In fact, as more companies turn to using social media for PR, the task of getting the news media to follow postings is likely to become more challenging.

SPECIAL EVENTS

These run the gamut from receptions to elegant dinners to stunts. Special events can be designed to reach a narrow audience, such as a dinner with a guest speaker targeted to individuals interested in college savings plans, or aimed at a large group, such as a strawberry festival designed to promote state tourism and targeted to a large geographic area. Stunts, such as building the world's largest ice cream sundae during National Ice Cream month, capture the attention of an audience in the immediate area, but also attract the attention of mass media, such as TV news and newspapers, which provide a broad reach. In the U.S., the Oscar Mayer Wienermobile is a classic example, providing a recognizable icon that travels the country garnering attention wherever it visits. (6) As with all PR programs, special event planners must work hard to ensure the program planned conveys the correct message and image to the target audience.

Public relations stunts have long been used to capture the attention of media outlets. Recently, companies have recognized that stunts may capture even more media attention if it is recognized by the publishers of Guinness World Records. A number of well-known companies have created PR stunts that were intended to set a Guinness record. This includes wireless provider Cricket Communications, which along with Samsung was recognized for building the world's largest working cellphone measuring 15 feet by 11 feet. The stunt generated over 38 million impressions on Cricket's website. (7)

Marketing Story

FTC: Bloggers Must Disclose Payments for Reviews
USA Today

The U.S. Government is sending a stern message to marketers and to bloggers: stop hiding your relationship. This message is contained in a document titled *"Guides Concerning the Use of Endorsements and Testimonials in Advertising"* (8) which, among other things, states bloggers who are being subsidized with money or products by a marketing company must disclose this when their blog postings offer opinions on the marketer and/or its products.

Since blogging became a lucrative activity a few years ago, marketers have sought popular bloggers and offered them incentives to review products, preferably in a positive way. In other cases, marketers have surreptitiously arranged to have blogs setup, often by employing a freelance blogger, with the sole intention of creating a positive spin for a product. According the FTC, now such activity may be viewed as "sponsored advertising" which is regulated in the United States.

Bloggers have long praised or panned products and services online. But what some consumers might not know is that many companies pay reviewers for their write-ups or give them free products such as toys or computers or trips to Disneyland. In contrast, at traditional journalism outlets, products borrowed for reviews generally have to be returned. (9)

Is it unethical for a marketer to give a product to a blogger with the understanding that the product does not have to be returned?

MEDIA TOUR

Some new products can be successfully publicized when launched with a media tour. On a media tour a company **spokesperson** travels to key cities to introduce a new product by being booked on TV and radio talk shows and conducting interviews with print and Internet reporters or influencers (e.g., bloggers). The spokesperson can be a company employee or someone hired by the company, perhaps a celebrity or "expert" who has credibility with the target audience. A media tour may include other kinds of personal appearances in conjunction with special events, such as public appearances, speaking engagements or autograph signing opportunities.

NEWSLETTERS

Marketers who have captured names and addresses of customers and potential customers can use a newsletter for regular contact with their targeted audience. Newsletters can be directed at trade customers, final consumers or business buyers and can be distributed either by regular mail, via electronic means (i.e., newsletters delivered via email, RSS feed) or through posted links on social media sites. Marketers using newsletters strive to provide content of interest to customers, as well as information on products and promotions. For instance, a bookstore may include reviews of new books, information on online book chats, and information on in-store or online promotions. A food manufacturer may include seasonal recipes, information on new products, and coupons. Online newsletters also offer the opportunity to include clickable links to retail outlets carrying the marketer's product and to videos offering additional product information.

SPEAKING ENGAGEMENTS

Speaking before industry conventions, trade association meetings, and other groups provides an opportunity for company experts to demonstrate their expertise to potential clients and customers. Typically, these opportunities are not explicitly for company or product promotion. Rather, speaking engagements are a chance to talk on a topic of interest to potential customers and serve to highlight the speaker's expertise in a field. Often the only mention of the company or its products is in the speaker biography. Nevertheless, the right speaking engagement, in front of an appropriate target audience, offers opportunities for generating customer interest.

EMPLOYEE COMMUNICATIONS

For many companies, communicating regularly with employees is essential for keeping them informed of developments, such as new products, sales incentives, personnel issues, and other changes. Companies use a variety of means to communicate with employees, including email, newsletters, and social media. In larger firms, an in-house PR department often works in conjunction with the Human Resources Department to develop employee communications.

COMMUNITY RELATIONS AND PHILANTHROPY

Organizations often realize positive results by fostering strong relations with key audiences, such as members of their regional community. Programs that are supportive of the community include: sponsoring local organizations and institutions (e.g., arts organizations, community activities, parks); conducting educational workshops (e.g., for teachers and parents); and donating product or money in support of community events. Effective community relations can help a company weather bad publicity or a crisis situation that can unexpectedly arise due to such issues as problems with a product, perceived service shortcomings, unethical behavior by management, and false rumor. Some companies also make an effort to contribute to charitable groups, especially organizations that have some relationship to the company's mission or to a key person at the company.

III

ADDITIONAL PUBLIC RELATIONS ACTIVITIES

In addition to serving as means to help achieve marketing objectives, PR professionals may undertake additional activities aimed at maintaining a positive image for an organization. These activities include:

MARKET MONITORING

Monitoring public comment about a company and its products is becoming increasingly necessary, especially with the explosion of Internet and wireless information channels. Today monitoring not only includes watching what is written and reported in traditional print and broadcast media, it requires attention be paid to discussions occurring through social media, discussion forums, blogs, and other public messaging areas (see Box 15-3). Marketers must be prepared to respond quickly to erroneous information and negative opinions about products as these can spin out of control very quickly. Failure to correct misinformation can be devastating to a product or a company's reputation.

> *There are many specialized monitoring services that can help companies keep track of news about the company and its products. These services can be used to measure the effectiveness of public relations campaigns, such as indicating how many times a company is mentioned in the news media or to see if the company is discussed in blogs and social media. For companies willing to pay large fees, monitoring firm Vocus will track mentions on over 50,000 media outlets including print and Internet. (10) For smaller firms looking to save money, the free Google Alerts service will email a listing each time a keyword, such as a company or product name, is mentioned. (11)*

CRISIS MANAGEMENT

Marketers need to be prepared to respond quickly to negative information about the company. When a problem with a product arises, whether real or substantiated only by rumor, a marketer's investment in a product can be in serious jeopardy. Today, with the prevalence of the Internet and mobile communication, negative information can spread rapidly. Using monitoring tools marketers can track the issues and respond in a timely fashion. Additionally, to manage response effectively, many companies, led by their public relations staff, have a crisis management plan in place that outline steps to take and the company spokespeople authorized to speak on behalf of the company should an event occur.

Box 15-3

MONITORING WHERE CUSTOMERS VOICE THEIR OPINIONS

Internet and mobile applications make it easy for people to offer opinions on products and organizations, and, consequently, should be monitored by those involved in public relations. The key applications to be watched closely include:

Blogs

Blogs, short for weblogs, are a phenomenon that shows just how powerful and influential the Internet has become as a communication medium. While an initial blog posting is often controlled by those responsible for managing the blog, follow-up comments may be open to nearly anyone, though some blogs will filter responses to reduce the risk of undesirable posts (e.g., spam). The topics covered by blogs are endless and literally hundreds of thousands now exist.

Discussion Forums

Discussion forums, where users can post their opinions on virtually any topic, pose both opportunities and threats for PR professionals. On one hand, maintaining a presence on an influential forum helps build credibility for an organization, as forum members recognize a company's effort to reach out to the public. On the other hand, forums can cause considerable problems for marketer as they may become breeding grounds for rumor and accusation. Because of this, public relations personnel must continually monitor forums and respond to misguided comments to help squelch rumors before these catch fire.

Social Network Sites

Social network sites combine elements of blogs and forums by allowing the creation of user content and encouraging others to post comments. However, these go a step further by encouraging the sharing of information. The most popular social networks are Facebook, Google Plus and Twitter, but there are others including photo sharing (e.g., Flickr), video sharing (e.g., YouTube), and business contact sharing (e.g., Linkedin). When possible, monitoring social networks offers the same advantages as found with blogs and forums. However, doing so may prove more difficult since access to the full contents of an individual page within most social networks requires approval by the owner of the page.

Social Bookmarking Sites

In addition to the general social networking sites listed above, several specialized websites have emerged allowing users to share links they have found to news items, blog postings, and other websites. On bookmarking sites, such as Digg, Delicious, and StumbleUpon, users can bookmark (also called **tagging**) sites and then provide the opportunity for others to see how many people are also bookmarking the same links.

News Sites

Many news publications allow readers to post comments to stories appearing on their website. Though, in some cases, comments are moderated by the news site's editorial staff, a company's public relations or marketing staff should still closely monitor to avoid the spread of rumor and to respond by offering the company's viewpoint on a specific issue.

Marketing Story

Taco Bell Using Ads to Battle Back on Beef
MSNBC

What do marketers do when their company is under attack for its marketing decisions? Some may take the approach that the best way to handle things is to diffuse the situation quickly by working hard to address the issues being raised. With this approach, the marketer will often make concessions to those who are screaming the loudest.

For instance, a marketer may remove an advertisement that a certain group feels is offensive. While the marketer may not really believe it is necessary to do so, the potential negative backlash that may arise if the ad is not removed may be viewed as too risky.

However, seeking to diffuse a potentially troublesome situation is not the only approach when a company is facing criticism. In fact, the opposite approach may be taken as some companies will respond with a public relations blitz defending their decisions. This aggressive strategy can be quite effective if the company already has significant support in the market. On the other hand, an offensive stance can draw the attention of the media and Internet bloggers, which could heighten and prolong the controversy.

A company facing such a PR issue is Taco Bell. The fast-food retailer was slapped with a class-action lawsuit claiming its tacos do not contain enough beef to be classified as a beef sandwich. In particular, the suit argues Taco Bell is engaging in false advertising by saying the product contains "seasoned ground beef" which the plaintiffs claim does not meet standards set by the U.S. Food and Drug Administration.

But Taco Bell did not take these charges lightly and responded with an all-out PR campaign including the placement of full-page ads in major U.S. newspapers explaining exactly what is in their tacos.

The print ads say, in huge letters, "Thank you for suing us. Here's the truth about our seasoned beef." They go on to outline the meat's ingredients. The chain did not say how much it is spending on the campaign, but such ads in national newspapers can cost more than $100,000. (12)

Is it possible both sides are correct?

||||||||||||||||||||||||||||||||||||||||||||||||||||||||||||||||||||||||||||||||||||||||||||||||||||||||||

TRENDS IN PUBLIC RELATIONS

Until recently most public relations activity involved person-to-person contact between PR professionals and members of the media, such as journalists and television news reporters. However, several trends are developing that alter the tasks performed by PR people. In most cases, these changes are the result of new Internet and communication technologies, which are quickly gaining widespread acceptance and becoming new media outlets. The important trends in public relations include:

UPDATING CORPORATE NEWS

Developing websites has long been a time-consuming and often overly technical undertaking for the vast majority of marketers. However, this changed with the evolution of easier to use website development applications, called **content management systems (CMS)**, which allow for quick creation and convenient updating of site information. With CMS those with access, including public relations personnel, can add information on a regular basis. In addition, posting company news to websites can be tied to RSS feeds (see Chapter 3), thereby allowing for automatic notification to those who have subscribed to the feed. Many journalists and other media members are finding RSS feeds to be a more convenient way to acquire information, particularly if they follow certain industries and can monitor specific industry information websites. By subscribing to relevant RSS feeds, members of the news media have information delivered to them, rather than spending time searching.

CORPORATE BLOGGING

Blogs may be most famous as a tool for political discussion and used as a personal journal for individuals, but these are also becoming powerful communication tools for public relations. Many companies in high-tech fields, such as eBay, Google, and Microsoft, and traditionally low-tech fields, such as General Motors, McDonalds, and Wells Fargo Bank, now produce in-house blogs that report on happenings at the company. These blogs enable company employees, including CEOs and marketers, to post messages updating company developments and, consequently, serve as a useful PR tool. As with corporate news, blog postings can also be quickly communicated to news media and others via RSS feeds.

SOCIAL MEDIA

By far the most significant trend to affect public relations in the last 25 years is the impact played by social media. In a matter of just a few years, social networks, including Facebook, Twitter, and Linkedin, have created opportunities for monitoring and communicating that are quickly raising these methods to the top of the list of PR tools. But while it offers tremendous PR advantages, social media also poses significant threats. One of the most pressing issues is that social media forces PR professionals to respond rapidly to negative or misleading information. In effect, social media is turning PR into a 24-hour job, particularly for global companies. Also, the time required to monitor and respond to the growing number of social media outlets is forcing some companies to place less emphasis on traditional public relations tasks, such as the creation of press kit materials. Since social media is still evolving as a PR tool, it is unclear if shifting workload to social media will carry the same return on investment as what is offered with traditional PR tools.

PODCASTING

The introduction of the Apple iPod and other digital audio and video players opened the door for PR professionals to distribute promotional information. The evolution of podcasting provided public relations with a quick and easy way to send out audio and video news releases, and other promotional material that was downloaded and stored on a user's digital device. However, as noted in Chapter 12, the ability for users to access information directly using wireless technology has reduced the effectiveness of podcasting. And its use in PR appears to be waning.

SEARCH ENGINE OPTIMIZATION

A key task of publicity is convincing media outlets to mention the name of a product, company, or person. For several years, Internet marketers have recognized the importance of getting their company information listed in what has become an influential media outlet - search engines. Using methods dubbed search engine optimization (SEO), marketers employ specific techniques in an effort to attain higher rankings to relevant search queries. For instance, an online clothing retailer may attempt to be one of the first websites listed when someone enters the search phrase "men's suits." If the retailer's website meets the search engine's criteria for ranking, then the website could appear at the top of the search results page, without cost to the retailer.

While, at first glance, SEO may not seem like a responsibility of public relations, it would appear to contain the main characteristics for making it so, namely getting a third-party media outlet (i.e., search engine) to mention the company (i.e., search rankings) at no direct cost the company (i.e., no payment for ranking). And, just as PR people can use methods to affect coverage within traditional media, optimizing a website can work to influence results in search engines by using techniques (e.g., **keywords**) that allow a website to fit within ever-changing search engine ranking criteria. In this way, SEO does what PR professionals do, namely obtain good placement in third-party media outlets. (13)

> *In response to the growing importance of evolving public relations methods, MDC Partners, which owns a large collection of advertising and public relations firms, decided it needed to upgrade its skills in these areas. Over a 12-month period, MDC acquired a number of smaller firms specializing in newer public relations methods including social media, blogging and search engine marketing. (14)*

‖‖

REFERENCES

1. Markowitz, E., "Recovering From a Blow to Your Brand's Reputation," *Inc. Magazine*, August 22, 2011.

2. McDonald, J., "Public Relations in China: Dirty Tricks, Scandals," *MSNBC*, October 22, 2010.

3. Rose, D., "The Four Cs of Centralized vs. Localized Message Development," *PR Conversations.com*, October 11, 2010.

4. Branch, J., "Rejection by N.B.A. Gives New Shoes Even Greater Bounce," *New York Times*, October 20, 2010.

5. Armstrong, L., "Trash Proof Press Kits," *Exhibitor Magazine*, April 2010.

6. *Oscar Mayer Wienermobile* website.

7. Vranica, S., "Fastest-Growing PR Stunt: Get Into Guinness Records," *Wall Street Journal*, October 4, 2010.

8. "Guides Concerning the Use of Endorsements and Testimonials in Advertising," *United States Federal Trade Commission*, October 2010.

9. Yao, D., "FTC: Bloggers Must Disclose Payments for Reviews," *USA Today*, October 5, 2009.

10. *Vocus* website.

11. *Google Alerts* website.

12. Schreinder, B. and S. Skidmore, "Taco Bell Using Ads to Battle Back on Beef," *MSNBC*, January 28, 2011.

13. Christ, P., "Internet Technologies and Trends Transforming Public Relations," *Journal of Website Promotion*, 1 (4), 2007.

14. Elliott, S., "Growing Appreciation for P.R. on Madison Avenue," *New York Times*, September 8, 2010.

Full text of many of the references can be accessed via links on the support website.

Chapter 16: Personal Selling

In the past few chapters, we saw how marketers can use advertising, sales promotion, and public relations to reach a large number of customers. While these methods of promotion offer many advantages, they each share one significant disadvantage: they are a non-personal form of communication. And whether a company is in retailing or manufacturing, sells goods or services, is a large multinational or a local startup,
is out to make a profit or is a non-profit, in all probability at some point they will need to rely on personal contact with customers. In other words, they will need to promote using personal selling.

In this chapter, we define personal selling, look at the advantages and disadvantages, and see how it fits within an organization's promotional strategy. We also see there is a variety of different selling roles available to the marketing organization, including some whose objectives are not tied to getting customers to buy. Finally, we examine several trends facing the personal selling field.

||||||||||||||||||||||||||||||||||||||||||||||||||||||||||||||||||||||||||||||||||||||||||||||||||||||||||||

WHAT IS PERSONAL SELLING?

Personal selling is a promotional method in which one party (e.g., salesperson) uses skills and techniques for building personal relationships with another party (e.g., those involved in a purchase decision) resulting in both parties obtaining value. In most cases, the "value" for the salesperson is realized through the financial rewards of the sale while the customer's "value" is realized from the benefits obtained from consuming the product. However, as we will discuss, getting a customer to purchase a product is not always the objective of personal selling. For instance, selling may be used for the purpose of simply delivering information.

Because selling involves personal contact, this promotional method often occurs through face-to-face meetings or via telephone conversation, though newer technologies allow contact to take place over the Internet, including using video conferencing or text messaging (e.g., online chat).

Among marketing jobs, more are employed in sales positions than any other marketing-related occupation. In the United States alone, the U.S. Department of Labor estimates that over 13 million people, or about 11% of the overall labor force, are directly involved in selling and sales-related positions. (1) Worldwide this figure may be closer to 100 million. Yet these figures vastly under-estimate the number of people who are actively engaged in some aspect of selling as part of their normal job responsibilities. While millions of people can easily be seen as holding sales jobs, the promotional techniques used in selling are also part of the day-to-day activities of many who are usually not associated with selling. For instance, top corporate executives, whose job titles are CEO or COO, are continually selling their companies to major customers, stock investors, government officials, and many other stakeholders. The techniques they employ to gain benefits for their companies are the same ones used by the front-line salesperson who is selling to a small customer. Consequently, our discussion of the promotional value of personal selling has implications beyond marketing and sales departments.

> *Creative artists often find they must convince dealers to stock their work in stores and galleries. In doing so, many feel their work alone is enough to convince someone to buy. Yet, to be successful, many artists are now finding that, by itself, the product is not enough to get a buyer to buy. These artists now realize that gaining product distribution requires they apply basic selling skills when interacting with dealers. (2)*

Advantages of Personal Selling

One key advantage personal selling has over other promotional methods is that it is a two-way form of communication. In selling situations, the message sender (e.g., salesperson) can adjust the message as they gain feedback from message receivers (e.g., customer). Consequently, if a customer does not understand the initial message (e.g., does not fully understand how the product works) the salesperson can make adjustments to address questions or concerns. Many non-personal forms of promotion, such as a radio advertisement, are inflexible, at least in the short-term, and cannot be easily adjusted to address questions that arise by the audience experiencing the ad.

The interactive nature of personal selling also makes it the most effective promotional method for building relationships with customers, particularly in the business-to-business market. This is especially the case for companies selling expensive products, as such purchases may take a considerable amount of time to complete and may involve the input of many people at the purchasing company (see Box 4-2 in Chapter 4). In these situations, sales success often requires the marketer develop and maintain strong relationships with members of the purchasing company.

> *For an 8 year period, Erica Feidner, was the top salesperson for Steinway, maker of high-end pianos. Feidner sold over $40 million worth of pianos during this period. Her success was primarily attributed to building strong relations with customers. By getting to know customers, she often learned they had unrealized musical ambitions. She would then position Steinway pianos as something that helps them achieve their unfulfilled musical goals. (3)*

Building relationships is also a critical part of the personal selling process when doing business internationally. Business cultures in such area as Asia and Latin America are often built on personal relationships between buyer and seller rather than on seeking the best business deal. While building closer business relationships may take time, salespeople, who are able to cultivate such relationships, often find greater success compared to competitors who sell on price alone.

Finally, personal selling is the most practical promotional option for reaching customers who are not easily reached through other methods. The best example lies in selling to the business market where, compared to the consumer market, advertising, public relations, and sales promotions are often not as effective.

Disadvantages of Personal Selling

Possibly the biggest disadvantage of personal selling is the degree to which this promotional method is misunderstood. Most people have had unpleasant experiences with salespeople who, in their view, were overly aggressive or even downright annoying. But as we discuss in Box 16-1, while there are certainly many salespeople that fall into this category, the truth is salespeople are most successful if they focus their efforts on satisfying customers over the long term and not focusing on their own selfish interests.

A second disadvantage of personal selling is the high cost of maintaining this type of promotional effort. Costs incurred in personal selling include:

♦ High cost-per-action (CPA) – As noted in Chapter 11, CPA can be a key measure of the success of promotion spending. Since personal selling involves person-to-person contact, the money spent to support a sales staff can be steep. For instance, in some industries it costs well over (US) $300 each time a salesperson contacts a potential customer regardless of whether a sale is made. These costs include compensation (e.g., salary, commission, bonus), providing support materials, allowances for entertainment spending, office supplies, telecommunication, and much more. With such high cost for maintaining a sales force, this is often not a practical option for selling products that do not generate a large amount of revenue.

♦ <u>Training Costs</u> – Most forms of personal selling require extensive training of the sales staff on such issues as product knowledge, industry information and selling skills. For companies that require their salespeople to attend formal training programs, the cost of training can be quite high and include such expenses as travel, hotel, meals, and training equipment, while also paying the trainees salary while they attend.

A third disadvantage is that personal promotion is not for everyone. Job turnover in sales is much higher than other marketing positions. For companies that assign salespeople to handle certain customer groups (e.g., geographic territory), turnover may leave a company without representation in a customer group for an extended period of time while the company recruits and trains a replacement.

Box 16-1

A MISUNDERSTOOD FIELD

Here is a quick question: Which of the following mental images comes closest to what you think about when you hear that someone's job involves "selling"?

1. Someone who is highly extroverted and quick with stories that keep everyone laughing.

2. Someone on a used car lot who makes every car sound like a gem.

3. Someone in a clothing store who corrals customers when they first enter and then won't leave them alone.

4. Someone calling at dinner time trying to get the "head of the household" to buy a vacation timeshare.

5. A knowledgeable, hard-working, and highly trained professional, who uses finely honed communication techniques to fully understand and satisfy the needs of his/her customers.

If you chose one of the first four options, don't feel bad, you're in tremendous company. Lots of people share the view that selling is something done by people who are manipulative, arrogant, aggressive, greedy, and only concerned about getting the sale. While there certainly are some salespeople that fit these descriptions, today the most successful salespeople are ones who work hard to understand their customers' needs with the ultimate goal of ensuring the customer is satisfied at a high level. Additionally, to understand customers, the most important characteristic of a good salesperson is not their ability to carry on a conversation, but their ability to listen to the customer.

Also, personal selling holds a key role in the promotional activities of a large number of organizations. In fact, in the business market, where one company sells products to another company, money spent to support the selling function far exceeds spending on advertising. Thus, while many people have had poor experiences with salespeople, the truth is selling is one of the most powerful methods for building customer relationships and those successful at selling are much more likely to reflect the description presented in #5. (4)

Marketing Story

10 Greatest Salespeople of All Time
Inc. Magazine

As we note in Box 16-1, sales is a highly misunderstood field. Yes, most people understand the main task of many (but not all) salespeople is to get customers to purchase products. And, because of this many have developed the perception that salespeople must be extremely aggressive and interested in only one thing – making a sale.

But, it would be shortsighted to think that making the sale is all salespeople do. In fact, they contribute to the marketing organization in many other ways. For example, the sales force is a key provider of market information since they are directly involved with customers on a daily basis. This level of contact can directly benefit those in charge of product marketing by providing valuable details on what is occurring in the market.

Companies also know having a sales force that is viewed as being only interested in making the sale may not always be good for business. Why? Because for many buyers the only contact they have with a company may be through the salesperson, consequently, a customer's perception of a salesperson is also their perception of the company. Any negative feelings they have toward a salesperson may also be the attitude they have about the company.

Yet, despite different tasks salespeople perform for a company or a company's efforts to field a customer-friendly sales force, many still equate sales success with the ability salespeople have to motivate customers to make a purchase. However, this story may offer some support for other methods that make for success in selling. While there certainly is a fair representation of dynamic sellers, such as infomercial icon Ron Popeil and Oracle's Larry Ellison, the story also includes discussion of men and women who built successful sales careers in other ways, such as through sales training, use of technology, and building strong customer relationships.

Napoleon Barragan - The founder of 1-800-Mattress was a genius at using technology to open new sales channels for his Simmons and Sealys. He was one of the first and most successful adopters of the 1-800 number, correctly predicting that consumers would be perfectly willing to have mattresses delivered to their homes sight unseen. (5)

What traits are most common among each of the sales stars profiled in this story?

||||||||||||||||||||||||||||||||||||||||||||||||||||||||||||||||||||||||||||||||||||||||||||||||||||||||||

OBJECTIVES OF PERSONAL SELLING

Personal selling is used to meet the five objectives of promotion in the following ways:

♦ Building Product Awareness – A common task of salespeople, especially when selling in the business markets, is to educate customers on new product offerings. In fact, salespeople serve a vital role at industry trade shows, where they discuss products with show attendees. But building awareness using personal selling is also important in consumer markets. For instance, the advent of controlled word-of-mouth promotion (see Box 16-2) is leading to personal selling becoming a useful mechanism for introducing consumers to new products.

♦ Creating Interest – The fact personal selling involves person-to-person communication makes it a natural method for getting customers to experience a product for the first time. In fact, creating interest goes hand-in-hand with building product awareness as sales professionals can often accomplish both objectives during the first encounter with a potential customer.

♦ Providing Information – When salespeople engage customers a large part of the conversation focuses on product information. Marketing organizations provide their sales staff with large amounts of sales support, including brochures, research reports, computer programs, and many other forms of informational material.

♦ Stimulating Demand – The most fundamental objective of personal selling is to convince customers to make a purchase. As we will see below in our discussion of selling roles, getting customers to buy is the prime function of a large segment of selling jobs.

♦ Reinforcing the Brand – Most personal selling is intended to build long-term relationships with customers. A strong relationship can only be built over time and requires regular communication with a customer. Meeting with customers on a regular basis enables salespeople to discuss their company's products and, by doing so, helps strengthen customers' knowledge of what the company has to offer.

||||||||||||||||||||||||||||||||||||||||||||||||||||||||||||||||||||||||||||||||||||||||||||||||||||||||||

CLASSIFYING SELLING ROLES

Worldwide millions of people have careers that fit in the personal selling category. However, the actual functions carried out by someone in sales may be quite different. Below we discuss the four main types of selling roles: order getters, order takers, order supporters, and sales supporters. It should be noted that these roles are not mutually exclusive and that a salesperson can perform more than one and possibly all roles.

Order Getters

The role most synonymous with selling is a position in which the salesperson is actively engaged in using his/her skills to obtain orders from customers. Such roles can be further divided into:

NEW BUSINESS DEVELOPMENT

A highly challenging yet potentially lucrative sales position is one where the main objective is to find new customers. Sales jobs in this category are often in fields that are intensely competitive, but offer high rewards for those that are successful. The key distinguishing factor of these positions is that, once a sale is made, new business salespeople pass customers on to others in their organization who handle account maintenance. These positions include:

- Business Equipment Sales – These salespeople are often found in industries where company profits are generated mainly from the sale of supplies and services that come after an initial equipment purchase. The key objective of business equipment salespeople is to get buyers to purchase the main piece of equipment for which a large number supplies and services are needed. For instance, traditionally in the photocopier industry, business equipment salespeople focus on establishing new accounts. However, once a photocopier sale is made they pass along the account to other sales personnel, who then handle sales of supplies and maintenance contracts.

- Telemarketing – This category includes product sales over the phone, whether aimed at businesses or consumers. While in the U.S. laws restrict unsolicited phone selling in the consumer market, the practice is still widely used in the business market.

- Consumer Selling – Certain companies are extremely aggressive in their use of salespeople to build new consumer business. These include: retailers selling certain high priced consumer products, including furniture, electronics, and clothing; sellers of housing products, including real estate, security services, and building replacement products (e.g., windows); and in-home product sellers, including those selling door-to-door, and products sold at "home party" events, such as cosmetics, kitchenware, and decorative products.

ACCOUNT MANAGEMENT

Most people engaged in sales are not only involved in gaining the initial order, but work to build and maintain relationships with their clients that will hopefully last a long time. Salespeople involved in account management are found across a broad range of industries. Their responsibilities involve all aspects of building customer relationships from initial sale to follow-up account servicing. These include:

- Business-to-Business – These salespeople sell products for business use with an emphasis on follow-up sales. In many cases, business-to-business salespeople have many different items available for sale (i.e., broad and/or deep product line), rather than a single product. Consequently, while the initial sale may only result in the buyer purchasing a few products, the potential exists for the buyer to purchase many other products as the buyer-seller relationship grows.

- Trade Selling – Sales professionals working for consumer products companies normally do not sell to the final user (i.e., consumer). Instead, their role is focused on first getting distributors, such wholesalers and retailers, to handle their products and once this is accomplished, helping distributors sell their product by offering ideas for product advertising, in-store display, and sales promotions.

Order Takers

Selling does not always require a salesperson use methods designed to encourage customers to make a purchase. In fact, the greatest number of people engaged in selling are not order getters, rather they are considered order takers. In this role, salespeople primarily assist customers with a purchase in ways that are much less assertive than how order getters handle their role. As might be expected, compensation for order takers is generally lower than order getters. Among those serving an order taker role are:

- Retail Clerks – While some retail salespeople are involved in new business selling, the vast majority of retail employees handle order taking tasks, which range from directing customers to products to handling customer checkout.

- Industrial Distributor Clerks – Industrial purchase situations also have clerks to handle customer purchases. For instance, distributors of building products often operate a facility where contractors shop for supplies. The person handling these transactions would likely fit the order taker role.

- Customer Service – Order taking is also handled in non face-to-face ways through customer service personnel. Usually this occurs via phone conversation, though newer technologies are allowing for these tasks to be handled through electronic means, such as online chat.

Order Supporters

Some salespeople are not engaged in direct selling activity at all. That is, they do not actively sell to the person who is the ultimate customer for their product. Examples of order support salespeople include:

- Missionary – These salespeople are used in industries where customers make purchases based on the advice or requirements of others. In this role, the sales-

Marketing Story

Sales Tips From the World's Toughest Customers
Inc. Magazine

Sales prospecting can be a tough business. Depending on the industry and products sold, turndowns by buyers can exceed 80% of sales calls made by a company's sales force. In fact, in some industries, a salesperson may be viewed as being successful if they convince less than 1% of their prospects to make a purchase. But salespeople, who are effective in finding buyers, understand that much of their success comes down to a simple concept - know your customers. Unfortunately, while this may seem relatively obvious, this concept is often lost on small business owners whose primary skills may not be in sales but must face the difficult task of getting top companies to purchase their products.

For marketers looking to establish their products within a large company, this story is worth reading. It gives insight into the purchasing activities of several large firms, such as Coca-Cola, Northrop Grumman and Dell, and offers concrete suggestions for what it takes to do business with these firms. While these suggestions may be identified as being specific to each of these companies, in reality the advice given here can be applied to a broad range of potential buyers. The suggestions can help a seller not only know about the workings of big companies, but can provide clues on how to customize a sales presentation to meet a prospect's needs.

What not to do: "The biggest no-no is not knowing our competition. People will say, 'I've got this really exciting proposal I want you to look at.' I'll say, 'Go ahead; send it to me.' Then they send it to me by FedEx. It happens every day. Just be smart. Know the company you are pitching to and know their likes and dislikes. (6)

What other "tips" or key points not mentioned by the insiders quoted in this story are essential for sellers to consider when trying to sell into large companies?

person concentrates on selling activities that target those who influence purchases made by the final customer. Two industries in which missionary selling is commonly found are pharmaceuticals, where salespeople, known as **product detailers**, discuss products with doctors (influencers) who then write prescriptions for their patients (final customer), and higher education, where salespeople discuss textbooks with college professors (influencers) who then assign these to their students (final customer).

◆ Controlled Word-of-Mouth Promotion – As discussed in Box 16-2, marketers are experimenting with another type of order supporter who specializes in
word-of-mouth promotion. This type of promotion, which also is known by
such terms as buzz marketing and **advocacy marketing**, is similar to missionary
selling in that salespeople do not actively look to make a sale. However, it differs
from missionary selling in that salespeople will talk to the eventual purchaser of
the product. While still a fairly new approach to personal selling, marketers may
one day view this as a standard personal selling option.

> *College campuses represent a hotbed for word-of-mouth promotion. By one
> estimate, over 10,000 student representatives have been hired by such companies
> as Red Bull, Hewlett-Packard and American Eagle to promote products to
> fellow students. These reps build product interest by not only handing out free
> products but also by employing social media. While technically most student
> reps are not company employees, they do receive compensation including free
> product, internship credit and, in some cases, cash. (7)*

Box 16-2

CONTROLLED WORD-OF-MOUTH PROMOTION

One of the most influential forms of promotion occurs when one person speaks highly of a
product to someone else, particularly if the message sender is considered an unbiased source
of information. Until recently, marketers have had little control over person-to-person promotion that did not involve salespeople (i.e., biased source). However, marketers are beginning to experiment with new methods of promotion that strategically take advantage of the
benefits offered by word-of-mouth promotion. Unlike salespeople who often attempt to
obtain an order from customers, controlled word-of-mouth promotion uses real people to
help spread information about a product but do not directly elicit customer orders.

With controlled word-of-mouth promotion, a marketer hires individuals to spread positive information about a product but in a way that does not make it obvious that they
are being paid to do so. This technique is especially useful when building a high level
of awareness for a new product. For example, a brewer may form a team of word-of-
mouth marketers who visit local taverns and night spots. As part of their job, these
marketers may "talk up" a new beer sold by the brewer and even purchase the product
for some customers. Yet, they may carry out their task without directly disclosing that
they are being compensated for their efforts.

While controlled word-of-mouth has received a great deal of marketer interest, this
form of promotion has also been subjected to negative publicity due to potential ethical
issues it raises. Some believe that paying people to "act" as if they are interested in a
product without any indication of their relationship with the product breaches ethical
standards. These critics feel that any type of organized promotion, where marketers
are compensated for their efforts, must come with full disclosure to those receiving the
message. It should be noted that such disclosure is a cornerstone of the ethics code of
the Word-of-Mouth Marketing Association, the leading industry group in this field. (8)

Sales Supporters

A final group involved in selling assist mostly with the selling activities of other sales professionals. These include:

♦ <u>Technical Specialists</u> – When dealing with the sale of technical products, particularly in the business market, salespeople may need to draw on the expertise of others to help with the process. This is particularly the case when the buying party consists of a buying center. In Chapter 4, we indicated that, in business selling, many people from different functional areas are involved in the purchase decision. If this buying center includes technical people, such as scientists and engineers, a salesperson may seek assistance from members of her/his own technical staff to help address specific questions.

♦ <u>Office Support</u> – Salespeople also may receive assistance from their company's office staff in the form of promotional materials, setting up sales appointments, finding sales leads, arranging meeting space or organizing trade shows exhibits.

‖‖‖

TRENDS IN PERSONAL SELLING

While the basic premise of personal selling, building relationships, has not changed much in the last 50 years, there are a number of developments impacting this method of promotion including:

CUSTOMER INFORMATION SHARING

Possibly the most dramatic change to occur in how salespeople function on a day-to-day basis involves the integration of customer relationship management (CRM) systems into the selling arena. As we discussed in Chapter 3, CRM is the name given to both the technology and the philosophy that drives companies to gain a better understanding of their customers with the goal of building stronger long-term relationships. The essential requirement for an effective CRM system is the need for all customer contact points (e.g., salespeople, customer service, websites) to gather information to share with others in the company.

But CRM has faced some rough times within the sales force for the exact reason it is important: salespeople must share their information. Salespeople historically have been highly effective at developing relationships and learning about customers, but often loath sharing this since, in effect, information is what makes them valuable. In the minds of some salespeople, letting go of the information reduces their importance to the company. For example, some salespeople feel sharing all they know about a customer will make them expendable since a company can simply insert someone new at anytime.

While the attitude toward CRM has made its implementation difficult in many companies, salespeople should understand that it is not going away. CRM and information sharing has proven to be critical in maintaining strong customer relations and salespeople must learn to adapt to it.

> *Convincing the sales force to adopt CRM may depend on how this process is presented to them. While companies are often alerted by CRM companies about potential resistance by salespeople, companies are advised not to use threats to get their sales force to embrace CRM. Instead, convincing salespeople to use CRM should be viewed just like any sales situation. Managers should present this to the sales force just as salespeople present products to customers by explaining the key benefits the sales force will obtain for accepting CRM. Companies should focus on how CRM can help increase sales force income while also improving the relationship salespeople have with their customers. (9)*

MOBILE TECHNOLOGY AND WEB-BASED COMPUTING

The move to an information sharing approach is most effective when salespeople have ready access to CRM and other information sources. Mobile technology, such as wireless (WiFi) and cellular Internet, offers such access and allows salespeople to retrieve needed information at any time. For instance, if a salesperson takes a customer to lunch, she/he can quickly log onto their company website to respond to customer questions, such as how long it may take to receive a product if an order is placed.

Additionally, there is a growing trend to make key business applications available through a browser rather than having specialized programs loaded on a salesperson's computer. For example, as mentioned many companies have moved to web-based CRM systems where simply having Internet access allows salespeople to enter and retrieve information. Additionally, office productivity applications for word processing, spreadsheets and presentations are also becoming web-accessible. The implication is that salespeople are now truly mobile as nearly all of their software applications are accessible from almost anywhere.

The sales force is also discovering that new-generation smartphones, along with handheld pad computing devices, lighten the burden of carrying laptop computers, while still providing access to much of the same information as a standard computer. While the computing power of handheld devices is still underpowered compared to conventional computers, the move to web-based computing may someday make the handheld the main instrument the sales force uses for managing information.

Finally, the sales forces' adoption of mobile and web-based technologies has made it easier for them to explore the use of social networks for building business relationships. While salespeople actively use more consumer-oriented social media (e.g., Facebook and Twitter), the most popular social network for building sales relationships is Linkedin, since it is primarily aimed at business people. Consequently, the contacts found through Linkedin tend to be of higher quality than contacts found through other social networks.

> *Many hold the perception that salespeople are not technologically savvy and overall are slow to adopt change. However, this generalization may not be accurate. Research suggests that since the mid-1800s salespeople have been early adopter of key innovations. For instance, salespeople were among the first to see the advantages of new transportation technology, such as railroad and automobile; new communication technologies, including telegraph and telephone; and new presentation technologies, including slide projection and motion pictures. (10)*

ELECTRONIC SALES PRESENTATIONS

Technology also plays a key role in how sales professionals reach prospects and existing customers. While audio/video conferencing has been available for many years by using high-end telecommunications hookups (e.g., satellite transmission), improvements in Internet access speeds, computing power, and meeting software have made electronic sales presentations a practical and cost effective alternative to in-person selling. Salespeople have several options for engaging in electronic sales presentations including:

- Online Video Conferencing – Online conferencing essentially acts in the same way as traditional telecommunications videoconferencing, with one big exception, it is delivered over the Internet. Anyone who has an Internet connection knows that delivering video over the Internet can be a trying experience as video often appears to be slow, jittery, and sometimes not even recognizable. However, these problems are quickly disappearing and real time Internet video conferencing (i.e., television quality video and audio) will soon be routinely accessible to most salespeople.

- Web/Phone Conferencing – To offset the problems associated with Internet delivery of real time audio and video, many companies deliver sales presentations using a combination of web and telecommunications. The most widely used are services that use the Internet to deliver visual material (typically a slide presentation) and telecommunications to provide voice conversation. The process has a salesperson arrange a conference time with a prospect who enters the conference by: 1) using his/her web browser to gain access to the visual presentation, and 2) using his/her telephone to call into the audio conference. Splitting the visual and audio feeds allows for smoother presentations since the conference participants' computers need only process the visual material.

- <u>Online Text Chat</u> – Online chat allows for real time communication between multiple participants using text messaging. While this form of buyer-seller communication may not be highly effective at getting customers to make a purchase, it has proven beneficial in building initial interest in products. For example, potential customers visiting a website may use the chat feature to ask a few questions about the company's products. Engaging customers this way can then lead to the customer agreeing to a phone call from a salesperson to discuss the product further.

- <u>Virtual Meetings</u> – Another electronic method that is showing considerable promise for sales is the virtual meeting. These meetings take place through special "venues" created on the Internet, which allow participants to attend while sitting in front of their computer. While marketers experimented with virtual meetings using Second Life, many companies and industry groups have now established their own virtual worlds where participants can meet and exchange information.

> *Research conducted by Market Research Media estimates the virtual events market is posed for rapid growth and will exceed $18 billion by 2015. Within this forecast, the company includes analysis of such online event tools as virtual conferences and trade shows, webinars, and 3-D virtual worlds. (11)*

ELECTRONIC SALES TRAINING

Developing the skills and techniques needed to be successful at selling requires the individual seller and the seller's company be fully committed to sales training. Sales training is the hallmark of professional selling. If there is one characteristic separating the truly successful salesperson from those who are not successful, it is the amount of training and preparation they have received.

Most organizations employing a sales force offer new salespeople an extensive formal in-person training program, often held at dedicated training facilities. The length of training programs range from a few days to many months depending on the industry. But once a salesperson has moved on to selling to customers, training does not stop. Those involved in selling must continue to stay abreast of their products, customers, markets, and competitors. While many companies continue to deliver ongoing training using the same in-person methods used when they first trained their salespeople, a large number of firms are finding that training can be just as effective using electronic options, such as delivering training over the Internet, through downloadable computer programs or via interactive DVDs.

While feedback using electronic means is not as personal as in-person training, sophisticated electronic training programs are effective in educating and testing trainees' knowledge. Also, a real trainer can be available via email, online chat, or by a phone or Internet video call if a question does arise.

Additionally, compared to paper-based materials, electronic delivery of training materials is low cost and can be made available to the entire sales force in a short time frame. Also, the use of messaging services (e.g., text message, Twitter) and email enables salespeople to be immediately notified when new material is published. This is useful when the sales force must be made aware of new information, such as a price change or new information on a competitor's product.

Despite the growing availability of methods for improving sales training, there is evidence to suggest the amount of time companies spend training their salespeople is often woefully slim. In particular, one study reports that one out of seven companies do not engage in any formal training for their sales force, while another study indicates that a large percentage of seasoned salespeople (three or more years of service) receive less than six days of training per year. (12)

Use of Customer Sales Teams

As we noted in our discussion of technical specialists, salespeople may require the assistance of others in their organization in order to deal effectively with prospects. In fact, many companies are moving away from the traditional sales force arrangement where a single salesperson handles nearly all communication with an account in favor of a team approach where multiple personnel are involved.

Teams consist of individuals from several functional areas, such as marketing, manufacturing, distribution, and customer service. In some configurations, all members share bonuses if the team meets sales goals. Clearly to be effective a team approach will require the implementation of customer relationship management systems (CRM) discussed earlier.

||||||||||||||||||||||||||||||||||||||||||||||||||||||||||||||||||||||||||||||||||||||||||||||||||||||||||

REFERENCES

1. "National Occupational Employment and Wages Estimates United States," *Bureau of Labor Statistics - U.S. Department of Labor*, May 2010.

2. Petrecca, L., "New Sales Outlets Are a Big Deal for Small Businesses," *USA Today*, October 26, 2010.

3. "10 Greatest Salespeople of All Time," *Inc. Magazine*, March 28, 2011.

4. For more information on what it takes to be successful at selling see: Anderson, R., Dubinsky, A., and Mehta, R., <u>Personal Selling: Building Customer Relationships and Partnerships</u>, Houghton-Mifflin, 2007.

5. "10 Greatest Salespeople of All Time," *Inc. Magazine*, March 28, 2011.

6. Wehrum, K., "Sales Tips From the World's Toughest Customers," *Inc. Magazine*, April 5, 2010.

7. Singer, N., "On Campus, It's One Big Commercial," *New York Times*, September 10, 2011.

8. For more details on word-of-mouth marketing see *Word of Mouth Marketing Association* website.

9. Buchholtz, C., "A Winning Sales Pitch for CRM Adoption," *CRM Buyer*, October 28, 2010.

10. Christ, P., and R. Anderson, "The Impact of Technology on Evolving Roles of Salespeople," *Journal of Historical Research in Marketing*, Spring 2011.

11. <u>Virtual Conference & Trade Show Market Forecast 2010-2015</u>, *Market Research Media*, March 2011.

12. Markowitz,E., "New Tools for Sales Training," *Inc. Magazine*, May 31, 2011.

Full text of many of the references can be accessed via links on the support website.

Chapter 17: Pricing Decisions

What do the following words have in common? Fare, dues, tuition, interest, rent, and fee. The answer is that each of these is a term used to describe what one must pay to acquire benefits from another party. More commonly, most people simply use the word price to indicate what it costs to acquire a product. For marketers, the pricing decision can be complex as many factors must be considered when arriving at the selling price for a product.

In this chapter, we begin a two-part discussion of the pricing component of the Marketer's Toolkit. We start by defining price and see how it has a different meaning for different parties to a transaction. We next look at why price is essential to marketing and to the organization. Finally, considerable attention is given to the internal and external factors that influence pricing decisions.

|||||||||||||||||||||||||||||||||||||||||||||||||||||||||||||||||||||||||||||||||||||||||||||||||

WHAT IS PRICE?

In general terms price is a component of an exchange or transaction that takes place between two parties and refers to what must be given up by one party (i.e., buyer) in order to obtain something offered by another party (i.e., seller). Yet this view of price provides a somewhat limited explanation of what price means to participants in the transaction. In fact, price means different things to buyers and sellers in an exchange:

♦ Buyers' View – For those making a purchase, such as final customers, price refers to what must be given up to obtain benefits. In most cases what is given up is financial consideration (e.g., money) in exchange for acquiring access to a good or service. But financial consideration is not always what the buyer gives up. Sometimes in a **barter** situation a buyer acquires a product by giving up his/her own product. For instance, two farmers may exchange cattle for crops. Also, as discussed in Box 17-1, buyers may also give up other things to acquire the benefits of a product that are not direct financial payments (e.g., time required to learn to use the product).

♦ Sellers' View – To the selling organization, price reflects the revenue generated for each product sold and is an essential factor in determining profit. For those responsible for marketing decisions, price serves as a marketing tool and is a key element in marketing promotions. For example, most retailers highlight product pricing in their advertising campaigns.

> *For some customers, price is the number one reason they purchase a product. Marketers targeting these customers are likely to promote their low pricing as their key marketing advantage. But some customers are so driven to buy the lowest price products that they become unprofitable to retailers. Wal-Mart found this out when they cut price on a large number of items in order to encourage more traffic to their stores. The hope was shoppers would not only purchase the lower price products but would also spend on other regular priced items. However, Wal-Mart soon found many customers were buying the bargain products and not spending on other items leading the retail giant to eliminate this pricing promotion. (1)*

Price is commonly confused with the notion of **cost** as in "*I paid a high cost for buying my new cell phone.*" Technically these are different concepts. Price is what a buyer pays to acquire products from a seller. Cost concerns the seller's investment (e.g., manufacturing expense) in the product exchanged with a buyer. For marketing organizations seeking to make a profit, the hope is a product's price will exceed its cost so the organization can see financial gain from a transaction.

Finally, while product pricing is a main topic for discussion when a company is examining its overall profitability, pricing decisions are not limited to for-profit companies. Not-for-profit organizations, such as charities, educational institutions, and industry trade groups, also set prices. For instance, charities seeking to raise money may set different "target" levels for donations that reward donors with increases in status (e.g., name in newsletter), gifts, or other benefits. While a charitable organization may not call it a "price" in their promotional material, in reality these donations are equivalent to price since donors are required to give a contribution in order to obtain something of value.

IMPORTANCE OF PRICE

When marketers talk about what they do as part of their responsibilities for marketing products, the tasks associated with setting price are often not at the top of the list. Marketers are much more likely to discuss activities related to promotion, product development, marketing research, and other tasks that are considered to be the more appealing and exciting parts of the job. One reason for the lack of attention paid to pricing is that many believe price setting is a mechanical process requiring the marketer to utilize financial tools, such as spreadsheets, to build their case for setting price levels.

Box 17-1

What Price Means to Customers

When faced with a purchase decision, most customers will evaluate the entire marketing offering and will not simply make a decision based solely on a product's monetary price. In fact, price is one of several variables customers evaluate when they mentally assess a product's overall value. As we discussed in Chapter 1, value refers to the perception of benefits received for what someone must give up. An easy way to see this is through a **value equation**:

$$\text{Perceived Value} = \frac{\underline{\text{Perceived Benefits Received}}}{\text{Perceived Price Paid}}$$

For marketers, it is necessary to recognize that the price paid in a transaction is not only financial, it can also involve other things a buyer may be giving up. For example, in addition to paying money, a customer may have to spend time learning to use a product, pay to have an old product removed, close down current operations while a product is installed or incur other expenses.

Consequently, while the monetary price is a key marketing decision, marketers must also take into consideration many other issues that can affect what customers view as the perceived price.

While pricing may not tap into a marketer's creative skills to the same degrees as other marketing tasks, pricing decisions can have significant consequences for the marketing organization and the attention given by the marketer to pricing is just as important as the attention given to more recognizable marketing activities.

Some reasons why attention to pricing is critical include:

Most Flexible Marketing Decision

For marketers, price is the most adjustable of all marketing decisions. Unlike product and distribution decisions, which can take months or years to change, or some forms of promotion, which can be time consuming to alter (e.g., creating a new television advertisement), price can be changed very rapidly. The flexibility of pricing decisions is particularly relevant in times when the marketer seeks a quick way to stimulate demand or to respond to competitor price actions. For instance, a marketer can agree to a field salesperson's request to lower price for a potential prospect during a phone conversation. Likewise, a marketer in charge of online operations can raise prices on hot selling products with the click of a few website buttons.

Marketers at Chargify, an Internet start-up company offering recurring billing service for websites, found the pricing decision is flexible in another way. Chargify had previously offered free service to certain customers hoping these customers would see the value in upgrading to a fee-based plan. The company decided to drop their "freemium" plan and announced new fee-based pricing plans, that raised the minimum starting rate from $49 to $99 per month. The company received considerable customer backlash to these decisions and quickly introduced at $39 per month plan for lower volume customers. (2)

Need for Setting the Right Price

Pricing decisions made hastily without sufficient research, analysis, and strategic evaluation can lead the marketing organization to lose revenue. Prices set too low may mean the company is missing out on additional profits that could be earned if the target market is willing to spend more to acquire the product. Additionally, attempts to raise an initially low priced product to a higher price, may be met by customer resistance if they feel the marketer is attempting to take advantage of its customers. Prices set too high can also impact revenue, as it prevents interested customers from purchasing the product. Setting the right price level takes considerable market knowledge and, especially with new products, may require the testing of different pricing options.

Trigger of Early Perception

Often times, customers' perceptions of a product are formed as soon as they learn the price, such as when a product is first seen in a store with a price tag attached. While the final decision to make a purchase may be based on the value offered by the entire marketing offering (i.e., actual and augmented product), it is possible the customer will not evaluate a marketer's product at all based on price alone. For instance, customers may form impressions of a product if they consider the price to be too high (e.g., *"that product can't be worth that price"*) or too low (e.g., *"that product must not be very good"*). It is necessary for marketers to know if customers are more likely to dismiss a product when all they know is the price. If so, pricing may become the most important of all marketing decisions if it can be shown that customers are avoiding learning more about the product because of the price.

Important Part of Sales Promotion

Many times price adjustments are part of sales promotions that lower price for a short term to stimulate interest in the product. However, as we noted in our discussion of promotional pricing in Chapter 14, marketers must guard against the temptation to adjust prices too frequently since continually increasing and decreasing price can lead customers to be conditioned to anticipate price reductions and, consequently, withhold purchase until the price reduction occurs again.

Affects Demand of Other Products

How a company prices one product can affect the overall demand for other products. This is especially the case where the demand for other products is directly tied to the demand for a main product. This is a consideration for marketers making the bulk of their profits from the sale of goods and services used to support the main product. For example, operators of gambling casinos often entice customers by offering low hotel room rates knowing they can generate higher revenue when customers visit the casino.

> *A good example of how pricing can affect the sale of other products can be seen in the smartphone "app" market. Many app providers have stirred customer interest by offering a basic version of their app for an exceptionally low price or for free. App developer Rovio, has found that free downloads of its wildly popular Angry Birds game are leading customers to not only purchase upgraded versions of the game, but they are also purchasing other products offered by Rovio, including game related toys, dolls and even a special Angry Birds iPhone case. (3)*

FACTORS AFFECTING PRICING DECISIONS

For the remainder of this chapter, we look at factors that affect how marketers set price. The final price for a product may be influenced by many factors, which can be categorized into two main groups:

♦ Internal Factors – When setting price, marketers must take into consideration several factors, which are the result of company decisions and actions. To a large extent these factors are controlled by the company and, if necessary, can be altered. However, while the organization may have control over these factors making a quick change is not always realistic. For instance, product pricing may depend heavily on the productivity of a manufacturing facility (e.g., how much can be produced within a certain period). The marketer knows increasing productivity can reduce the cost of producing each product, which potentially allows the marketer to lower the product's price. But increasing productivity may require substantial changes at the manufacturing facility that take time (and are potentially costly) and will not translate into lower price products for a considerable period of time.

♦ External Factors – There are a number of influencing factors, which are not controlled by the company but will impact pricing decisions. Understanding these factors requires the marketer conduct research to monitor what is happening in each market the company serves since the effect of these factors can vary by market.

Marketing Story

Phone-Wielding Shoppers Strike Fear Into Retailers
Wall Street Journal

As technology continues to advance us to having instant access to almost anything, retailers are facing a host of issues with repercussions that could change how retailing is done. Thanks to such technologies as search engines, product rating sites, and mobile devices, today's consumers are in a far better position to assess the value of a purchase than they have ever been. While the average consumer does not yet possess the product comparison and negotiation skills of a corporate purchasing agent, technology is helping them get closer.

The ramifications for retailers of tech-savvy consumers are tremendous, especially in terms of consumers' use of mobile devices. While store-based retailers are accustom to dealing with educated customers (i.e., shoppers who have done their research), before mobile technology these retailers at least had an advantage of providing something new once the consumer walked into the store. The retailer could offer updated product details, new promotions, new pricing and other information the consumer did not know before the store visit and, consequently, could not easily research while in the store. However, with today's mobile technologies even new information can be quickly researched by shoppers while they are still in the store.

As explained in this story, one of the key bits of information in-store consumers seek with their mobile devices is a price comparison. Shoppers can use smartphones and even pad technologies (e.g., iPad) to search other retailers to determine whether the product sitting in front of them on a display table is actually a bargain. Even easier, snapping a picture of a product's UPC code using a smartphone camera can provide the consumer with a list of places selling the same product and the prices they are charging.

But, things do not just end with a search. Possibly, the biggest slap in the face of store-based retailers comes from consumers who are willing to wait to acquire the product. These consumers may window shop at the physical store and while still in the store place the order for the product with another retailer who will ship it directly to their residence, often at no charge.

Now, marketers must contend with shoppers who can use their smartphones inside stores to check whether the specials are really so special, and if the rest of the merchandise is reasonably priced. (4)

In terms of pricing decisions, what can retailers do to take advantage of this new level of consumer shopping behavior? What about other marketing decisions?

Below we provide a detailed discussion of both internal and external factors.

Internal Factors

The pricing decision can be affected by factors that are controlled by the marketing organization, including:

Marketing Objectives and Strategy

Marketing decisions are guided by the objectives established by the leaders of the organization. While we will discuss this in more detail when we cover *Marketing Planning and Strategy* in Chapter 20, for now it is necessary to understand that all marketing decisions, including price, are impacted by the strategy formulated to meet marketing objectives. For instance, marketers whose objective is to be known as an affordable alternative to high-end products would be expected to have a marketing strategy that includes having price set at or below the price of most competitors.

It should be noted, not all companies view price as a key selling feature and, consequently, it may not play a major role in helping the marketer meet its objectives. Some firms, for example those seeking to be viewed as market leaders in product quality, de-emphasize price and concentrate on a strategy highlighting non-price benefits (e.g., quality, durability, service, etc.). Such non-price competition can help the company avoid competing against new products that sell for a lower price or protect it against potential price wars that often break out between competitive firms that follow a market share objective (discussed in Chapter 20) and use price as a key selling feature.

> *Ryanair has become one of the most popular airlines in Europe by offering no-frills, low price service. Because price is the key marketing strategy, Ryanair must make sure all other marketing decisions take this into consideration. For instance, when it comes to distribution decisions (i.e., airport location), the airline flies from many small airports that other carriers do not serve. This allows Ryanair to negotiate lower prices with the airports, which helps the company keep its overhead costs low. (5)*

Costs

For many for-profit companies, the starting point for setting a product's price is to determine first how much it will cost to get the product to their customers. Obviously, whatever price customers pay must exceed the cost of producing a good or delivering a service, otherwise the company will lose money.

When analyzing cost, the marketer will consider all costs needed to get the product to market including those associated with production, marketing, distribution, and company administration (e.g., office expense). These costs can be divided into two main categories:

Variable Costs

These costs are directly associated with the production and sale of products and may change as the level of production or sales changes. Typically variable costs are evaluated on a per-unit basis since the cost is directly associated with individual items. Most variable costs involve costs of items that are either components of the product (e.g., parts, packaging) or are directly associated with creating the product (e.g., electricity to run an assembly line). However, there are also marketing variable costs, such as certain promotional expenses (e.g., cost of redeemed coupons) that could fluctuate based on sales volume.

For marketers selling physical products, variable costs, especially for product components, tend to decline as more units are produced. This is due to the marketer's ability to receive discount pricing for large quantity purchases from component suppliers (see *Quantity Discounts* discussion in Chapter 18).

Fixed Costs

Also referred to as overhead costs, these represent costs the marketing organization incurs that are not affected by level of production or sales. For example, for a manufacturer of writing instruments that has just built a new production facility, whether they produce one pen or one million they will still need to pay the monthly mortgage for the building. From the marketing side, fixed costs may also exist in the form of such expenditures as fielding a sales force, carrying out an advertising campaign, and paying a service to host the company's website. These costs are fixed because there is a level of commitment to spending that is not affected by production or sales levels. While fixed costs are normally not associated with either level of production or sales volume, marketers still must factor these into their price, though, as discussed in Box 17-2, doing so is not always easy.

When costs increase marketers must decide whether they should pass these along to their customers in the form of higher prices. But how do you do this when the name of your company is the 99 Cent Only Store? When this Los Angeles retailer, which sells product for 99 cents or less, faced rising costs it decided to price its top end products at 99.99 cents. But that extra .99 cents did not sit well with customers, who filed class-action lawsuits saying the company was now selling products 1 cent higher than it claims. (6)

OWNERSHIP OPTIONS

An important decision faced by marketers as they are formulating their pricing strategy deals with who will have ownership of the product (i.e., holds legal title) once an exchange has taken place. There are two basic options available:

- <u>Buyer Owns Product Outright</u> – The most common ownership option is for the buyer to make payment and then obtain full ownership. Under this condition, the price is generally reflective of the full value of the product.

> **Box 17-2**
>
> ## WHAT'S THE REAL COST?
>
> Determining the cost for an individual unit can be a complicated process. While variable costs are often determined on a per-unit basis, applying fixed costs to individual products is less straightforward. For example, if a company manufactures five different products in one manufacturing plant how should it distribute the plant's fixed costs (e.g., mortgage, production workers' cost) over the five products?
>
> In general, a company assigns fixed costs to individual products if the company can clearly associate the costs with the product. For instance, it may assign the cost of operating production machines based on how much time it takes to produce each item or assign advertising expense to the specific product an advertising campaign is promoting.
>
> Alternatively, some firms may instruct the marketing department to add a certain percentage of the variable cost as a way to cover fixed costs. For example, final cost for products may be determined by adding an additional 20 percent on top of the per-unit variable cost.
>
> Finally, if it becomes too difficult to associate costs to specific products, the company may simply allocate total fixed costs by general category of product and assign it on some percentage basis. As an example, for a discount retailer's website that sells many products, the cost of operating the website may be distributed among product categories (e.g., books, hardware, women's clothing, etc.) based on user traffic, category sales as a percentage of overall sales, or some other measure. By using this approach, individual products may not see a fixed cost allocation, though the overall product category will.
>
> No matter which method is used, setting price based only on the cost of the materials and labor needed to produce a product may significantly underestimate the true costs incurred. As we will see in Chapter 18, product cost is only one of many considerations that go into determining the final price.

- <u>Buyer Has Right to Use but Does Not Have Ownership</u> – Many products, especially those labeled as services, permit customers to make payment in exchange for the right to use a product but not to own it. This is seen in the form of usage, rental, or lease payment for such goods and services as: mobile phone services, manufacturing equipment, and Internet file storage sites. In most cases, the price paid by the customer is not reflective of the full value of the product compared to what the customer would have paid for ownership of the product. It should be noted, under some lease or rental plans there may be an option for customers to buy the product outright (e.g., car lease) though this often requires a final payment.

> *Sometimes the accepted pricing model of an industry will change due to customer demand. This seems to be occurring in the college textbook market where the textbook purchase model is fading in favor of a rental model. For example, Amazon started a rental program for digital textbooks. Under this plan, students can rent books for as little as 30 days for a fraction of the regular selling price. If at the end of their rental period students still need the book, they can acquire more access time or make an outright purchase of the book. (7)*

External Market Factors

The pricing decision can be affected by factors that are not directly controlled by the marketing organization. These factors include:

ELASTICITY OF DEMAND

Marketers should never rest on their marketing decisions. They must continually use marketing research and their own judgment to determine whether marketing decisions need to be adjusted. When it comes to adjusting price, the marketer must understand what effect a change in price is likely to have on the target market's demand for a product.

Understanding how price changes impact the market requires the marketer have a firm understanding of the concept economists call elasticity of demand, which relates to how purchase quantity changes as prices change. Elasticity is evaluated under the assumption that no other changes are being made (i.e., "all things being equal") and only price is adjusted. The logic is to see how price by itself will affect overall demand. Obviously, the chance of nothing else changing in the market but the price of one product is often unrealistic. For example, competitors may react to the marketer's price change by changing the price of their product. Despite this, elasticity analysis does serve as a useful tool for estimating market reaction.

Elasticity deals with three types of demand scenarios:

- Elastic Demand – Products are considered to exist in a market that exhibits elastic demand when a certain percentage change in price results in a larger and opposite percentage change in demand. For example, if the price of a product increases (decreases) by 10 percent the demand for the product is likely to decline (rise) by greater than 10 percent.

- Inelastic Demand – Products are considered to exist in an inelastic market when a certain percentage change in price results in a smaller and opposite percentage change in demand. For example, if the price of a product increases (decreases) by 10 percent, the demand for the product is likely to decline (rise) by less than 10 percent.

- Unitary Demand – This demand occurs when a percentage change in price results in an equal and opposite percentage change in demand. For example, if the price of a product increases (decreases) by 10 percent, the demand for the product is likely to decline (rise) by 10 percent.

For marketers, the pivotal issue with elasticity of demand is to understand how it impacts company revenue. In general, the following scenarios apply to making price changes for a given type of market demand, though it should be clear these effects will only apply to relatively small changes in price:

- For Elastic Markets – Increasing price lowers total revenue, while decreasing price increases total revenue.

- For Inelastic Markets – Increasing price raises total revenue, while decreasing price lowers total revenue.

- For Unitary Markets – There is no change in revenue when price is changed.

> *In New Zealand the national rugby team, the All Blacks, has a highly loyal fan base. Because of this support Addias believed they were dealing with an inelastic market when they began selling replicas of the team's jersey to loyal fans. Addias charged customers in New Zealand nearly double the price purchasers in other parts of the world paid for the same jersey. The price difference was quickly criticized by New Zealand media, which led to an outcry among fans. Retailers handling the jerseys decided to listen to fans and lowered their price leaving them with a small profit margin, as Addias did not lower the price it charged retailers. (8)*

COMPETITOR PRICING

Marketers will undoubtedly look to competitors for indications of how price should be set. For many marketers of consumer products, researching competitive pricing is relatively easy, particularly when Internet search engines and other online tools are used. Price analysis can be somewhat more complicated for products sold in the business market. This is because final price may be affected by a number of factors including whether competitors allow customers to negotiate the final price.

Almost all marketing decisions, including pricing, will include an evaluation of competitors' offerings. The impact of this information on the actual setting of price depends on the competitive nature of the market. For instance, products that dominate markets and are viewed as market leaders may not be heavily influenced by competitor pricing, since they are in a commanding position to set prices as they see fit. On the other hand in markets where a clear leader does not exist, the pricing of competitive products will be carefully considered. Marketers must not only research competitive prices. They must also pay close attention to how these companies will respond to the marketer's pricing decisions. For instance, in highly competitive industries, such as gasoline or airline travel, companies may respond quickly to competitors' price adjustments, thereby, reducing the effect of such changes.

While gathering pricing information on products offered by competitors is research that most marketers are accustom to performing, there is other product pricing that may also affect marketers. In some cases, pricing decisions may be impacted by products that are not considered direct competitors. Here are two examples:

Related Product Pricing

Products offering new ways for solving customer needs may look to pricing of products that customers are currently using, even though these other products may not appear to be direct competitors. For example, a marketer of a new online golf instruction service that allows customers to access golf instruction via their computer may look at prices charged by local golf professionals for in-person instruction to gauge where to set its price. While, on the surface, online golf instruction may not be a direct competitor to an in golf instructor, marketers for the online service can use the cost of in-person instruction as a reference point for setting price.

Primary Product Pricing

As we discussed in Chapter 6, marketers may sell products viewed as complementary to a primary product. For instance, Bluetooth headsets are considered complementary to the primary product cellphones. The pricing of complementary products may be affected by pricing changes made to the primary product, since customers may compare the price for complementary products based on the primary product price. To illustrate, companies selling accessory products for the Apple iPad may do so at a cost that is only 10 percent of the purchase price of the iPad. However, if Apple decided to drop the price dramatically, for instance by 50 percent, the accessory at its present price would now be 20 percent of the of iPad price. This may be perceived by the market as a doubling of the accessory's price. To maintain its perceived value the accessory marketer may need to respond to the iPad price drop by also lowering the price of the accessory.

CUSTOMER AND CHANNEL PARTNER EXPECTATIONS

Possibly the most obvious external factor influencing price setting concerns what customers and channel partners expect from products they are considering for purchase. As we discussed, when it comes to making a purchase decision, customers assess the overall "value" of a product much more than they assess the price alone. When deciding on a price, marketers need to conduct customer research to determine what **price points** are acceptable. Pricing beyond these price points could discourage customers from purchasing.

Firms within the marketer's channels of distribution also must be considered when determining price. Distribution partners expect to receive financial compensation for their efforts, which usually means they will receive a percentage of the final selling price. The percentage or margin between what they pay the marketer to acquire the product and the price they charge their customers must be sufficient for the distributor to cover their costs and earn a desired profit.

> *A key issue for manufacturers seeking to maintain minimum prices is to prohibit retailers from advertising prices that are lower than the minimum. This includes the posting of prices on a retailer's website. To avoiding posting lower prices, online retailers, including Amazon, may hide the actual price until a shopper first selects the product and places it in their online shopping cart. (9)*

CURRENCY CONSIDERATIONS

Marketers selling internationally must be acutely aware of how monetary exchange rates can affect the price of its products in foreign markets. Depending on fluctuations in currency rates, a product's price in the importing country's currency can be significantly different from what the marketer has planned, which can have significant marketing implications (see Box 17-3). For instance, a company seeking to be a low-price market leader may find this strategy works when selling in its home market but when selling in an importing country with a weak currency the product's price may be at a mid-price level compared to competitive products. This could dramatically impact the perceived value of the product by customers in this market. Alternatively, if the currency of the marketer's country is weak compared to the currency in the buyer's market, a product could sell at a price that is much lower than what the marketer expects. This could lead customers in the importing country to perceive the product to be of lower quality compared to similar products selling at higher prices.

Additionally, in some situations currency issues may not even permit a buyer and a seller to negotiate an exchange. This is likely to occur when a country's currency is not widely recognized or when a currency's value is fluctuating rapidly. Under these conditions, a seller from one country may refuse to accept the currency offered by a buyer from another country. To overcome this, the two parties may agree to an exchange arrangement that does not involve currency. The primary method for carrying out this exchange is through a bartering method called **countertrade**, where a seller ships product to a buyer in exchange for receiving other product in return. As an example, a U.S. marketer of chemical products may negotiate a trade with an African mining company whose currency is not stable. The exchange may involve the U.S. company trading fertilizer in exchange for minerals mined by the African company. While the value of countertrade occurring is not easy to measure, one estimate suggests that over 20% of all world trade is undertaken in this way. (10)

Box 17-3

THE EFFECT OF EXCHANGE RATES ON PRICING

To see the impact currency has on pricing, consider what may happen to a U.S. company selling its products in Germany. For these examples assume the initial exchange rate is 1 Dollar = .8 Euros. Under the current exchange rate, if the company sells a product for $10 in the U.S. the equivalent price to customers in German will be €8. But, what might happen if the exchange rate changes?

Using a simplified example, assume a product's price in a foreign market is based on the U.S. price, and is not a set price but fluctuates based on exchange rates. Let's see what may happen as rates change under the following conditions:

Weaker Dollar – Stronger Euro
If the exchange rate moves from $1= €.8 to $1 = €.7, the rate is becoming weaker for the U.S. dollar but stronger for the Euro. This means it will now take fewer Euros to purchase the same product. In our example, where it previously required €8 to purchase the product, with a stronger Euro it now requires €7. Thus, customers in Germany perceive the product as becoming less expensive.

Stronger Dollar – Weaker Euro
If the exchange rate moves from $1= €.8 to $1 = €.9, the rate is becoming stronger for the U.S. dollar but weaker for the Euro. This means it will now take more Euros to purchase the same product. In our example, where it previously required €8 to purchase the product, with a weaker Euro it now requires €9 Euros. Thus, customers in Germany perceive the product as becoming more expensive.

It is essential to understand that with these examples the change in the exchange rate alone is affecting product pricing. Because exchange rates are not controllable by the marketer, companies selling internationally need to pay close attention to currency fluctuations to ensure the price customers pay in their local markets is consistent with the company's marketing strategy.

GOVERNMENT REGULATION

Marketers must be aware of regulations impacting how price is set in the markets in which their products are sold. These regulations are primarily government enacted meaning that there may be legal ramifications if the rules are not followed. Price regulations can come from any level of government and vary widely in their requirements. For instance, in some industries, government regulation may set **price ceilings** (how high prices may be set), while in other industries there may be **price floors** (how low prices may be set). Additional areas of potential regulation include: **deceptive pricing**, **price discrimination**, **predatory pricing**, and **price fixing**.

Marketing Story

Amazon.com to Capitulate to Macmillan Price Demand
USA Today

Setting price is one of the trickiest of all marketing decisions. Marketers have to take into consideration many factors when coming up with the right price. Some of these factors they control, such as product costs (e.g., product development, promotion, etc.), which the marketer knows must be covered. But other factors the marketer does not control and these are the ones that drive marketers crazy. For instance, what customers expect to pay and how competitors will respond are key considerations impacting pricing strategy. But for retailers there is another factor that can often override all other issues, namely what do the suppliers want you to charge for their products.

Suppliers have an important stake in the price a product is sold for at the retail level. Unfortunately, when they are dealing with large retailers (e.g., Wal-Mart), many suppliers find it is often a take-it-or-leave-it situation when it comes to what the retailer charges. That is, either the supplier accepts the price and the retail distribution that comes with it, or they reject the price and lose distribution. Of course, for most suppliers that deal with a market dominating retailer like Wal-Mart it is hard not to accept the retail price.

But Wal-Mart is not the only leading retailer that controls price. While Wal-Mart dominates the offline retail world, Amazon holds that crown in online retailing. As discussed in this story, book supplier, Macmillan, had little choice but to accept Amazon's pricing approach to ebooks when Amazon first entered this market. Amazon's approach was to sell most digital books for cheap, only $9.99. Macmillan claims they never liked this deal but felt they had little choice but to accept this pricing given that, at the time, Amazon was the only major ebook distributor. But now Apple and others have entered the ebook market and are willing to charge a higher price and give publishers a bigger cut of the revenue. This appeared to give Macmillian more bargaining power with Amazon resulting in a change in Amazon's retail pricing of Macmillan ebooks.

Amazon wants to tamp down prices as competitors such as Barnes & Noble, Sony and Apple line up to challenge its dominant position in the rapidly expanding market. But Macmillan and other publishers have criticized Amazon for charging just $9.99 for best-selling e-books on its Kindle e-reader, a price publishers say is too low and could hurt sales of higher priced hardcovers. (11)

Why would Amazon pursue a low-price pricing strategy when it launched its ebook sales when they essentially had the market to themselves and could have charged significantly higher prices?

Finally, when selling beyond their home market, marketers must recognize that local regulations may make pricing decisions different for each market. This is particularly a concern when selling to international markets where failure to abide by regulations can lead to severe penalties. For example, countries may institute tariffs on products shipped into the country. Often these tariffs are intended to protect domestic industries by raising the final selling price of product for the importing company. Consequently marketers must have a clear understanding of regulations in each market they serve.

REFERENCES

1. Gregory, S., "Has Walmart's Price Chopping Come to an End?" *Time*, October 5, 2010.

2. Del Rey, J., "How to Raise Prices," *Inc. Magazine*, January 20, 2011.

3. Mangalindan, J.P., "25 Ways of Downloading Angry Birds," *Fortune*, June 3, 2011.

4. Bustillo, M. and A. Zimmerman, "Phone-Wielding Shoppers Strike Fear Into Retailers," *Wall Street Journal*, December 15, 2010.

5. Pincott, G., "Brand Equity: What's Price Got to Do With It?" *Millward Brown*, June 2011.

6. Chang, A., "99 Cents Only Stores Sued Over Price Increase," *Los Angeles Times*, July 22, 2010.

7. Olivarez-Giles, N., "Amazon Launches College Textbook Rentals Program," *Los Angeles Times*, July 19, 2011.

8. Hutchison, J., "The Price of a Jersey Sets Rugby Fans Against Adidas," *New York Times*, August 24, 2011.

9. Stone, B., "The Fight Over Who Sets Prices at the Online Mall," *New York Times*, February 7, 2010.

10. Brady, D., <u>Essentials of International Marketing</u>, M.E. Sharpe Inc, 2011.

11. Koenig, D., "Amazon.com to Capitulate to Macmillan Price Demand," *USA Today*, February 1, 2010.

Full text of many of the references can be accessed via links on the support website.

Chapter 18: Setting Price

In Chapter 17, our coverage centered on understanding the impact pricing decisions have on marketing strategy, and how internal and external factors are likely to affect price setting. With this groundwork laid, we turn our attention to the methods marketers use to determine the price they will charge for their products.

In this chapter, our primary emphasis is to look at pricing as a five-step process. The process takes into consideration many different decisions before the marketer arrives at a final selling price. We will examine this process by first assessing how price fits into the organization's overall marketing objectives. Next, we look at several approaches for setting the initial product price. For many marketers, the initial price is not the final price and adjustments must be made. In the next step, we consider situations where marketers must make changes to their initial price and the various methods that are available for doing this. We conclude the five-step process by looking payment options marketers can choose when selling their product. We complete the discussion of pricing by looking at two additional methods, bid and auction pricing, and see how these fit within pricing strategy.

‖‖

STEPS IN THE PRICE SETTING PROCESS

For some marketers, more time is spent agonizing over price than any other marketing decision. Many times this is due to a lack of understanding of the factors that should be considered when faced with pricing decisions. To address this, we take the approach that price setting consists of a series of decisions or steps the marketer makes. The steps include:

1. Examine Objectives
2. Determine an Initial Price
3. Set Standard Price Adjustments
4. Determine Promotional Pricing
5. State Payment Options

While this process serves as a useful guide for making price decisions, not all marketers follow this step-by-step approach. Many marketers may choose to bypass Steps 3 and 4 altogether. Additionally, it is necessary to understand that finding the right price is often a trial-and-error exercise where continual testing is needed.

Like all other marketing decisions, marketing research is critical to determining the optimal selling price. Consequently, the process laid out here is intended to open the marketer's eyes to the options to consider when setting price and is in no way presented as a guide for setting the "perfect" price.

> *Some companies have turned to computerized methods for helping set the right price. So called **price optimization software** programs take into consideration many of the internal and external pricing factors discussed in Chapter 17 along with other variables, such as sales history, in order to arrive at an ideal price. The software can be particularly helpful to a field sales force by suggesting the optimal price ranges when negotiating with customers. (1)*

STEP 1: EXAMINE OBJECTIVES

As we discussed in Chapter 17, pricing decisions are driven by the objectives set by the management of the organization. These objectives come at two levels. First, the overall objectives of the company guide all decisions for all functional areas (e.g., marketing, production, human resources, finance, etc.). Guided by overall company objectives, the marketing department will set its own objectives. Marketing department objectives may include financial objectives, such as **return on investment (ROI)**, cash flow, and maximize profits, or non-financial marketing objectives, such as market share, level of product awareness, and increase in store traffic, to name a few.

Pricing decisions like all other marketing decisions are used to help the department meet its objectives. For instance, if the marketing objective is to build market share it is likely the marketer will set the product price at a level that is at or below the price of similar products offered by competitors.

Additionally, the price setting process looks to whether pricing decisions are in line with the decisions made for the other marketing areas (i.e., target market, product, distribution, promotion). Thus, if a company with a strong brand name targets high-end consumers with a high quality, full-featured product, the pricing decision would follow the marketer's desire to have the product be considered a high-end product. In this case, the price would be set high relative to competitors' products that do not offer as many features or do not have an equally strong brand name.

||||||||||||||||||||||||||||||||||||||||||||||||||||||||||||||||||||||||||||||||||||||||||||||||||||||||||||||||

STEP 2: DETERMINE AN INITIAL PRICE

With the objectives in Step 1 providing guidance for setting price, the marketer next begins the task of determining an initial price level. We say initial because, in many industries, this step involves setting a starting point from which further changes may be made before the customer pays the final price.

Sometimes called **list price** or **published price**, marketers often use this as a promotional or negotiating tool as they move through the other price setting steps. For companies selling to consumers, this price also leads to a projection of the recommended selling price at the retail level often called the **manufacturer's suggested retail price (MSRP)**. The MSRP may or may not be the final price for which products are sold. For strong brands that are highly sought by consumers, the MSRP may, in fact, be the price at which the product will be sold. But in many other cases, as we will see, the price setting process results in the price being different based on adjustments made by the marketer and others in the distribution channel (see Box 18-1).

> *In general, consumer product manufacturers not only use MSRP to suggest a price but also indicate that this is the minimum price at which a product may be sold by its retailers (also called **resale price maintenance**). But many retailers have chosen to ignore the MSRP and have tended to determine the final price in ways they see fit, which could be lower or higher than the MSRP. However, in 2007 the U.S. Supreme Court overturned a nearly 100 year-old ruling that, in most cases, allowed retailers to set the final price and instead gave manufacturers the right to set suggested prices that retailers must follow. (2) Yet, many states did not like the ruling and are now supporting retailers' in their efforts to set their own prices. (3)*

Marketers have at their disposal several approaches for setting the initial price which include:

♦ Cost Pricing

♦ Market Pricing

♦ Competitive Pricing

Box 18-1

PRICING AND THE DISTRIBUTION CHANNEL

Some marketers utilize multiple channel partners to handle product distribution. For marketers selling through resellers, the pricing decision is complicated by resellers' need to earn a profit and marketers' need to have some control over the product's price to the final customer. In these cases setting price involves more than only worrying about what the direct customer (e.g., retailer) is willing to pay. They must also be concerned with the pricing decisions resellers will make when they turn around and sell the product to their customers (e.g., final consumer).

When resellers are involved, marketers must recognize that all members of the channel will seek to profit when a sale is made. If a marketer wants to sell the product at a certain retail price (e.g., MSRP), then the price charged to the first channel member to handle the product can potentially influence the final selling price. And in some situations this may create problems causing the reseller to sell the product at a price that differs from what the marketer is expecting.

To see how problems arise, assume a marketer sets an MSRP of (US) $1.99 for a product selling through a distribution channel. This channel consists of wholesalers, who must pay the marketer $1.89 to purchase the product, and retailers who in turn buy the product from wholesalers. In this example, it is unlikely the retailer will sell the product at the MSRP since the wholesaler will add to the $1.89 purchase price to increase their profit. The retailer in turn will add to the price it pays to the wholesaler when selling to consumers. In this scenario, it is possible the retailer's price to the final consumer will be closer to $2.99 than the $1.99 MSRP.

As this example shows, marketers must take care in setting price so that all channel partners feel it is worth their effort to handle the product (see *Trade Allowances* discussion below). Clearly sales can be dramatically different from what the marketer forecasts if the selling price to the final customer differs significantly from what the marketer expects. In fact, resellers may balk at handling a marketer's product altogether if they are forced to charge a retail price that is much greater than what they believe customers are willing to pay.

The lesson here is that marketers must consider all members of the distribution channel as well as the final customer when making pricing decisions.

Cost Pricing

Under cost pricing, the marketer primarily looks at product costs (e.g., variable and fixed) as the key factor in determining the initial price. This method offers the advantage of being easy to implement as long as costs are known. But one significant disadvantage is that it does not take into consideration the target market's demand for the product. This could present considerable problems if the product is operating in a highly competitive market where competitors frequently alter their prices.

There are several types of cost pricing methods including:

♦ Markup Pricing

♦ Cost-Plus Pricing

♦ Breakeven Pricing

MARKUP PRICING

This pricing method, often utilized by resellers who acquire products from suppliers, uses a percentage increase on top of product cost to arrive at an initial price. A leading general retailer, such as Wal-Mart, may apply a set percentage for each product category (e.g., women's clothing, automotive, garden supplies, etc.) making the pricing consistent for all like-products. Alternatively, the predetermined percentage may be a number that is identified with the marketing objectives (e.g., required 20% ROI).

For resellers that purchase thousands of products (e.g., retailers), the simplicity inherent in markup pricing makes it a more attractive pricing option than more time-consuming methods. However, the advantage of ease of use is sometimes offset by the disadvantage that products may not always be optimally priced resulting in products that are priced too high or too low given the demand for the product.

As discussed in Box 18-2, markup can be done as either a percentage of cost or a percentage of selling price.

COST-PLUS PRICING

In the same way markup pricing arrives at the price by adding a certain percentage to the product's cost, cost-plus pricing also adds to the cost by using a fixed monetary amount rather than percentage. For instance, a contractor hired to renovate a homeowner's bathroom will estimate the cost of doing the job by adding his/her total labor cost to the cost of the materials used in the renovation. The homeowner's selection of ceramic tile to be used in the bathroom is likely to have little effect on the labor needed to install it whether it is a low-end, low-priced tile or a high-end, premium-priced tile. Assuming most materials in the bathroom project are standard sizes and configuration, any change in the total price for the renovation is a result of changes in material costs while labor costs are constant.

Box 18-2

DIFFERENT WAYS TO CALCULATE MARKUP

Resellers differ in how they use markup pricing with some using the Markup-on-Cost method and others using the Markup-on-Selling-Price method. We demonstrate each using an item that costs a reseller (US) $50 to purchase from a supplier and sells to customers for (US) $65.

Markup-on-Cost

Using this method, markup is reflected as a percentage by which initial price is set above product cost as shown in this formula:

$$\frac{\text{Markup Amount}}{\text{Item Cost}} = \text{Markup Percentage}$$

$$\frac{\$15}{\$50} = 30\%$$

The calculation for setting initial price using Markup-on-Cost is determined by simply multiplying the cost of each item by a predetermined percentage then adding the result to the cost:

$$\text{Item Cost} + (\text{Item Cost} \times \text{Markup Percentage}) = \text{Price}$$
$$\$50 \quad + \quad (50 \times .30 = \$15) \quad = \$65$$

Markup-on-Selling-Price

Many resellers, and in particular retailers, discuss their markup not in terms of Markup-on-Cost but as a reflection of price. That is, the markup is viewed as a percentage of the selling price and not as a percentage of cost, as it is with the Markup-on-Cost method. For example, using the same information as was used in the Markup-on-Cost, the Markup-on-Selling-Price is reflected in this formula:

$$\frac{\text{Markup Amount}}{\text{Selling Price}} = \text{Markup Percentage}$$

$$\frac{\$15}{\$65} = 23\%$$

The calculation for setting initial price using Markup-on-Selling-Price is:

$$\frac{\text{Item Cost}}{(1.00 - \text{Markup Percentage})} = \text{Price}$$

$$\frac{\$50}{(1.00 - .23)} = \$65$$

> ### Why Two Methods?
>
> So why do some resellers use Markup-on-Cost while others use Markup-on-Selling-Price? The answer to this lies more with promotion than with pricing. In particular, Markup-on-Selling-Price is believed to aid promotion, especially for resellers who market themselves as low-price leaders. This is because the amount of money a reseller makes in percentage terms is always lower when calculated using Markup-on-Selling-Price than it is with Markup-on-Cost.
>
> For example, in the Markup-on-Cost example where the markup is 30%, the gross profit is $15 ($65-$50). If the reseller using Markup-on-Selling-Price received a gross profit of $15 its markup would only be 23 percent ($50/[1.00-.23] = $65). Consequently, a retailer's advertisement may say: *"We Make Little, But Our Customers Save a Lot"* and back this up by saying they only make a small percentage on each sale. When in reality how much they make in monetary terms may be equal to another retailer who uses Markup-on-Cost and reports a higher markup percentage.

BREAKEVEN PRICING

Breakeven pricing is associated with **breakeven analysis**, which is a forecasting tool used by marketers to determine how many products must be sold before the company starts realizing a profit. Like the markup method, breakeven pricing does not directly consider market demand when determining price. However, it does indicate the minimum level of demand that is needed before a product will show a profit. From this, the marketer can then assess whether the product can realistically achieve these levels.

The formula for determining breakeven takes into consideration both variable and fixed costs (discussed in Chapter 17) as well as price, and is calculated as follows:

$$\frac{\text{Fixed Cost}}{\text{Price} - \text{Variable Cost per Unit}} = \textbf{Number of Units Needed to Breakeven}$$

For example, assume a company operates a single-product manufacturing plant that has a total fixed cost (e.g., purchase of equipment, mortgage, etc.) per year of (US) $3,000,000 and the variable cost (e.g., raw materials, labor, electricity, etc.) is $45.00 per unit. If the company sells the product directly to customers for $120, it will require the company to sell 40,000 units to breakeven.

$$\frac{\$3,000,000}{\$120 - \$45} = \textbf{40,000 units}$$

Again, it must be emphasized that marketers must determine whether the demand (i.e., number of units needed to breakeven) is realistically attainable. Simply plugging in a number for price without knowing how the market will respond is not an effective way to approach this price setting method.

Note: A common mistake when performing this analysis is to report the breakeven in a monetary value such a breakeven in dollars (e.g., results reported as $40,000 instead of 40,000 units). The calculation presented above is a measure of units that need to be sold. Clearly it is easy to turn this into a revenue breakeven analysis by multiplying the units needed by the selling price. In our example, 40,000 units x $120 = $4,800,000.

Market Pricing

A second method for setting initial price is market pricing. Under the market pricing method, cost is not the main factor driving pricing decisions. Rather, initial price is based on analysis of marketing research in which customer expectations are measured. The main goal is to learn what customers in an organization's target market are likely to perceive as an acceptable price. Of course, this price should also help the organization meet its marketing objectives.

Market pricing is one of the most common methods for setting price, and the one that seems most logical given marketing's focus on satisfying customers. So, if this is the most logical approach why don't all companies follow it? The main reason is that using the market pricing approach requires a strong marketing research effort to measure customer reaction. For many marketers, it is not feasible to spend the time and money it takes to do this right. Additionally for some products, especially new high-tech products, customers are not always knowledgeable enough about the product to know what an acceptable price level should be. Consequently, some marketers may forego market pricing in favor of other approaches.

For those marketers who use market pricing, options include:

◆ Backward Pricing

◆ Psychological Pricing

◆ Price Lining

BACKWARD PRICING

In some marketing organizations, the price the market is willing to pay for a product is an important determinant of many other marketing decisions. This is likely to occur when the market has a clear perception of what it believes is an acceptable level of pricing. For example, customers may question a product carrying a price tag that is double that of a competitor's offerings but is perceived to offer only minor improvements compared to other products. In these markets, it is essential to undertake research to learn whether customers have mentally established a price points for products in a certain product category. The marketer can learn this by surveying customers with such questions as *"How much do you think these types of products should cost you?"*

In situations where a price range is ingrained in the market, the marketer may need to use this price as the starting point for many decisions and work backwards to develop product, promotion, and distribution plans. For instance, assume a company sells products through retailers. If the market is willing to pay (US)$199 for a product but is resistant to pricing that is higher, the marketer will work backwards factoring out the profit margin retailers are likely to want (e.g., $40) as well as removing the marketer's profit (e.g., $70). From this, the product cost will remain ($199-$40-$70= $89). The marketer must then decide whether they can create a product with sufficient features and benefits to satisfy customers' needs at this cost level.

When Amazon first introduced their Kindle ebook reader, they were in a position to dictate price to book publishers, since they initial dominated this market. However, their control over pricing changed with the introduction of the Apple iPad. Apple permitted publishers to set their own price and many chose higher levels than $9.99, which Amazon had set as the maximum price. For many publishers, this higher amount has resulted in higher profit margins compared to what they make with traditional printed books. (4)

PSYCHOLOGICAL PRICING

For many years, researchers have investigated customers' response to product pricing. Some of the results point to several intriguing psychological effects price has on customers' buying behavior and their perception of individual products. We stress that certain pricing tactics "may" have a psychological effect since the results of some studies have suggested otherwise. But enough studies have shown an effect making this topic worthy of discussion.

Methods of psychological pricing include:

Odd-Even Pricing

One effect, dubbed "odd-even" pricing, relates to whole number pricing, where customers may perceive a significant difference in product price when pricing is slightly below a whole number value. For example, a product priced at (US) $299.95 may be perceived as offering more value than a product priced at $300.00. This effect can also be used to influence potential customers who receive product information from others. Many times buyers pass along the price as being lower than it actual is, either because they recall the price being lower than the even number or they want to impress others with their success in obtaining a good value. For instance, in our example a buyer who pays $299.95 may tell a friend they paid "a little more than $200" for the product when, in fact, it was much closer to $300.

Prestige Pricing

Another psychological effect, called prestige pricing, points to a strong correlation between perceived product quality and price. The higher the price, the more likely customers are to perceive it as higher quality compared to a lower priced product. (Although, there is a point at which customers will begin to question the value of the product if the price is too high.) In fact, the less a customer knows about a product the more likely she/he is to judge the product as being higher quality based on only knowing the price (see *Trigger of Early Perception* discussion in Chapter 17). Prestige pricing can also work with odd-even pricing as marketers, looking to present an image of high quality, may choose to price products at even levels (e.g., $10 rather than $9.99).

Reference Pricing

As we discuss in Chapter 4, the process involved in making purchase decisions can be quite complex. But for most customers, the purchase decision will involve a comparison of one product to another with price being a key evaluative criterion. Because of this, marketers who believe they have a price advantage will create an arrangement where customers can easily compare one product to another. As an example, a retail grocery store may price its store brand coffee slightly below a leading premium brand and then place the store brand right beside the premium brand. With effective packaging and labeling, shoppers may feel the store brand is of similar quality but sells for less. In this way, the store hopes customers use the premium brand as a reference point; thus, presenting the store's brand as being more attractive in terms of price.

Sometimes marketers want to avoid comparison to other products, especially if they sell more expensive products. One way this can be done is by making it difficult for customers to compare one product to another. This can be seen in movie theaters, where popcorn is sold in packages that make it difficult for customers to compare the price to other ways popcorn is sold. (5)

PRICE LINING

As we have discussed many times, marketers must appeal to the needs of a wide variety of customers. The difference in the "needs set" between customers often leads marketers to the realization that the overall market is really made up of a collection of smaller market segments (see Chapter 5). These segments may seek similar products but with different product features, such as different models whose product components (e.g., different quality of basketball sneakers) or service options (e.g., different hotel room options) will vary between markets.

Price lining or **product line pricing** is a method that primarily uses price to create the separation between the different models. With this approach, even if customers possess little knowledge about a set of products, they may perceive products are different based on price alone. The key is whether the prices for all products in the group are perceived as representing distinct price points (i.e., enough separation between each). For instance, a marketer may sell a base model, an upgraded model, and a deluxe model each at a different price. If the differences in features for each model are not readily apparent to customers, such as differences that are inside the product and not easily viewed (e.g., difference between laptop computers), then price lining will help the customer recognize that differences do exist as long as the prices are noticeably separated.

Price lining can also be effective as a method for increasing profitability. In many cases, the cost to the marketer for adding different features to create different models or service options does not alone justify a significant price difference. For example, an upgraded model may cost 10 percent more to produce than a base model but using the price lining method the upgraded product price may be 20 percent higher, thereby, making it more profitable than the base model. The increase in profitability offered by price lining is one reason marketers introduce multiple models. Offering more than one model allows the company to satisfy the needs of different segments. It also presents an option for a customer to "buy up" to a higher priced and more profitable model.

Competitive Pricing

The final approach for setting initial price uses competitors' pricing as a key marker. Clearly when setting price it makes sense to look at the price of competitive offerings. For some, competitor pricing serves as a central reference point from which they set their price. In some industries, particularly those in which there are a few dominant competitors and many small companies, the top companies are in the position of holding price leadership roles where they are often the first in the industry to change price. Smaller companies must then assume a price follower role and react once the top companies adjust their price.

When basing pricing decisions on how competitors are setting their price, firms may follow one of the following approaches:

♦ <u>Below Competition Pricing</u> – A marketer attempting to reach objectives that require high sales levels (e.g., market share objective) may monitor the market to ensure its price remains below competitors.

♦ <u>Above Competition Pricing</u> – Marketers using this approach are likely to be perceived as market leaders in terms of product features, brand image or other characteristics that support a price that is higher than what competitors offer.

♦ <u>Parity Pricing</u> – A simple method for setting the initial price is to price the product at the same level at which competitors price their product.

||||||||||||||||||||||||||||||||||||||||||||||||||||||||||||||||||||||||||||||||||||||||||||||||||||||||

STEP 3: SET STANDARD PRICE ADJUSTMENTS

With the first round of pricing decisions now complete, the marketer's next step is to consider whether there are benefits to making adjustments to the list or published price. For our purposes, we will consider two levels of price adjustments – standard and promotional. The first level adjustments are those we label as "standard" since these are consistently part of the marketer's pricing program and not adjustments that appear only occasionally as part of special promotions (see *Step 4: Determine Promotional Pricing* discussion below).

In most cases, standard adjustments are made to reduce the list price in an effort to: 1) stimulate interest in the product, or 2) indirectly pay channel partners for the services they offer when handling the product. In some circumstances the adjustment goes the other way and leads to price increases in order to cover additional costs incurred when selling to different markets (e.g., higher shipping costs).

It should be noted that given certain circumstances companies may not make adjustments to their list price. For instance, if the product is in high demand, the marketer may see little reason to lower the price. Also, if the marketer believes the product holds sufficient value for customers at its current list price then they may feel that reducing the price will lead buyers to question the quality of the product (e.g., *"How can they offer all those features for such a low price? Something must be wrong with it."*). In such cases holding fast to the list price allows the marketer to maintain some control over the product's perceived image.

For firms that do make standard price adjustments, options include:

♦ Quantity Discounts

♦ Trade Allowances

♦ Special Segment Discounts

♦ Geographic Pricing

♦ Early Payment Incentives

Quantity Discounts

This adjustment offers buyers an incentive of lower per-unit pricing as more products are purchased. Most quantity or volume discounts are triggered when a buyer reaches certain purchase levels. For example, a buyer may pay the list price when they purchase between 1-99 units but receive a 5 percent discount off the list price when the purchase exceeds 100 units.

Options for offering price adjustments based on quantity ordered include:

Discounts at Time of Purchase

The most common quantity discounts exist when a buyer places an order exceeding a certain minimum level. While quantity discounts are used by marketers to stimulate higher purchase levels, the rational for using these often rests in the cost of product shipment. As discussed in Box 10-1 in Chapter 10, shipping costs per unit tend to decrease as volume shipped increases. This is because the expenses (e.g., truck driver expense, fuel, road tolls, etc.) required to transport product from one point to another do not radically change as more product is shipped. Consequently, the transportation cost per item drops as more are ordered. This allows the supplier to offer lower prices for higher quantity.

Discounts on Cumulative Purchases

Under this method, the buyer receives a discount as more products are purchased over time. For instance, if a buyer regularly purchases from a supplier they may see a discount once the buyer has reached predetermined monetary or quantity levels. The key reason to use this adjustment is to create an incentive for buyers to remain loyal and purchase again.

Marketing Story
Catering to the Costco Mindset: Finding the 'Sweet Spot' in Quantity Discounts
Knowledge @ Wharton

Most for-profit marketers do not want to give products away unless they feel they will benefit by doing so. Nor do they want to lower price unless they see it as a useful way of simulating greater demand. But, marketers often find that at some point selling their products below their regular price is something they must do. Of course, marketers can simply run a "sale" where the price is lowered from its listed price. However, the problem with most sale pricing is the lower price applies to every product purchased whether a single unit or multiple units.

To encourage customers to purchase multiple units, quantity discount pricing is used, where marketers do not allow a discounted price to kick in until certain requirements are met. For instance, some marketers handle this by not lowering the price until additional products are purchased (e.g., "buy three or more and take $1 off each"). Other marketers may not want specifically to advertise a lower price, instead they choose to give away extra product if a customer purchases a certain amount (e.g., "buy three and get the fourth free"). But what level of discount should a marketer offer to encourage customers to purchase more? This is a question tackled by sellers since the dawn of commerce when street merchants and farmers' markets enticed customers with quantity discount offers (e.g., "buy two onions and get another one free"). For many marketers, determining quantity discounts is done either by using historical industry discounting methods or by undertaking their own extensive research, such as test markets.

This story looks at another approach to quantity discounting in the form of a marketing research technique called conjoint analysis. In marketing, conjoint analysis is primarily used to see how customers make product selection decisions. In simple terms, conjoint analysis looks at how customers evaluate a product when presented with different sets of features. By changing which features are presented, as well as changing the value of each feature (e.g., strong or weak), the marketer can then get an idea of the type of products customers prefer. In this story, researchers use conjoint analysis to suggest how a fictitious Internet movie distributor might best set quantity pricing if they were to compete against other online movie sites. What is interesting is this method does not involve field testing (e.g., in-store testing). Instead, customers participate through survey-type research.

So even without testing the market with trial pricing plans, the researchers were able to calculate the likely optimal price for MovieMail's DVD rental service. Iyengar and Jedidi contend that using a mathematical formula offers companies a money-saving shortcut to determining the best way to employ quantity discounts. (6)

In addition to developing product features and pricing, in what other ways can conjoint analysis help marketers?

Trade Allowances

Manufacturers relying on channel partners to distribute their products (e.g., retailers, wholesalers) offer discounts off of list price called trade allowances. These discounts function as an indirect form of payment for a channel member's work in helping to market the product (e.g., keep product stocked, talk to customers about the product, provide feedback to the manufacturer, etc.).

Essentially, the difference between the trade discounted price paid by the reseller and the price the reseller charges its customers is the reseller's profit. For example, let's assume the maker of snack products sells a product to retailers that carries a stated MSRP of (US) $2.95, but offers resellers a trade allowance price of $1.95. If the retailer indeed sells the product for the MSRP, the retailer will realize a 33% markup on selling price ($1.95/(1-.33) = $2.95). Obviously this percentage will be different if the retailer sells the product at a price that does not match the MSRP. However, the crucial point to understand is that marketers must factor in what resellers' expect to earn when they are setting trade discounts. This amount needs to be sufficient to entice the reseller to handle and possibly promote the product.

Special Segment Pricing

In some industries, distinct classes of customers within a target market are offered pricing that differs from the rest of the market. The main reasons for doing this include: building future demand by appealing to new or younger customers; improving the brand's image as being sensitive to customers' needs; and rewarding long time customers with price breaks.

For instance, many companies, including movie theaters, fitness facilities, and pharmaceutical firms, offer lower prices to senior citizens. Some marketers offer non-profit customers lower prices compared to that charged to for-profit firms. Other industries may offer lower prices to students or children.

Another example used by service firms is to offer pricing differences based on convenience and comfort enjoyed by customers when experiencing the service, such as higher prices for improved seat locations at sporting or entertainment events.

Geographic Pricing

The sale of some products may require marketers pay higher costs due to the geographic area in which a product is sold. This may lead the marketer to adjust the price to compensate for the higher expense. The most likely cause for charging a different price rests with the cost of transporting a product from the supplier's distribution location to the buyer's location. If the supplier is incurring all costs for shipping, then they may charge a higher price for products in order to cover the extra transportation expense. For instance, for a manufacturer located in Los Angeles, the transportation cost for shipping products by air to Hawaii is likely much more than it would be to ship the same amount of product to San Diego. In this situation, since the manufacturer is incurring the shipping cost, they may set a different product price for Hawaiian purchasers compared to buyers in San Diego.

Transportation expense is not the only geographic-related cost that may raise a product's price. Special taxes or **tariffs** may be imposed on certain products by local, regional or international governments, which a seller passes along in the form of higher prices.

Early Payment Incentives

For many years, marketers operating primarily in the business market offered incentives to encourage their customers to pay early. Typically, business customers are given a certain period of time, normally 30 or 60 days, before payment is due. To encourage customers to pay earlier, and enable the seller to obtain the money quicker, marketers have offered early payment discounts often referred to as **cash terms**. This discount is expressed in a form indicating how much discount is being offered and in what timeframe. For example, the cash terms 2/10 net 30 indicates that if the buyer makes payment within 10 days of the date of the bill then they can take a 2 percent discount off the invoice, otherwise the full amount is due in 30 days.

While this incentive remains widely used, its effectiveness in getting customers to pay early has diminished. Instead, many customers, especially large volume buyers, simply remove the discount from the bill's total and then pay within the required "net" timeframe (or later!). For this reason, many companies are discontinuing offering this discount.

STEP 4: DETERMINE PROMOTIONAL PRICING

The final price may be further adjusted through promotional pricing. Unlike standard adjustments, which are often permanently part of a marketer's pricing strategy and may include either a decrease or increase in price, promotional pricing is a temporary adjustment that only involves price reductions. In most cases, this means the marketer is selling at a price that significantly reduces the profit it makes per unit sold.

As one would expect, the main objective of promotional pricing is to stimulate product demand. But as we noted back in our discussion of sales promotion in Chapter 14, marketers should be careful not to overuse promotional programs that temporarily reduce the selling price. If promotional pricing is used too frequently, customers may become conditioned to anticipate the reduction. This results in buyers withholding purchases until the product is again offered at a lower price. Since promotional pricing often means the marketing organization is making very little profit off of each item sold, consistently selling at a low price could jeopardize the company's ability to meet its financial objectives.

The options for promotional pricing include:

♦ Markdowns

♦ Loss Leaders

♦ Sales Promotions

♦ Bundle Pricing

♦ Dynamic Pricing

Markdowns

The most common method for stimulating customer interest using price is the promotional markdown method, which offers the product at a price that is lower than the product's normal selling price. There are several types of markdowns including:

Temporary Markdown

Possibly the most familiar pricing method marketers use to generate sales is to offer a temporary markdown or **on-sale pricing**. These markdowns are normally for a specified period of time, the conclusion of which will result in the product being raised back to the normal selling price.

> *While it is customary for retail stores to offer a single on-sale discounted price, retailers sometimes offer different discount levels for the same product depending on the time of day a product is purchased. J.C. Penney did this with a "door-buster" sale, where customers purchasing gold jewelry between 9am and 1pm received 70% off gold jewelry, but customers purchasing after 1pm received only a 60% discount. (7)*

Permanent Markdown

Unlike the temporary markdown, where the price will eventually be raised back to a higher price, the permanent markdown is intended to move the product out of inventory. This type of markdown is used to remove old products that are: perishable and close to being out of date (e.g., day-old donuts; an older model and must be sold to make room for new models; or products that the marketer no longer wishes to sell.

Seasonal Markdown

Products that are primarily sold during a particular time of the year, such as clothing, gardening products, sporting goods, and holiday-specific items, may see price reductions at the conclusion of their prime selling season.

Not all perceived markdowns are intentional. Sometimes technology glitches show prices that are different from what the marketer intends. Customers of the online retailer 6pm.com discovered this when prices for all products, including expensive jewelry worth over $1,000, were being capped at $49.95. The technical error lasted for six hours and cost the $1.6 million. Rather than re-charging customers at the correct price, the company issued an apology and honored the price the customers paid. (8)

Loss Leaders

An important type of pricing program used primarily by retailers is the loss leader. Under this method, a product is intentionally sold at or below the cost the retailer pays to acquire the product from suppliers. The idea is that offering such a low price will entice a high level of customer traffic to visit a retailer's store or website. The expectation is that customers will easily make up for the profit lost on the loss leader item by purchasing other items that are not following loss leader pricing. For instance, as the price of gasoline has risen many gas stations are now using this as a loss leader in order to generate traffic to the inside of their business where customers will purchase regularly priced products, such as food and drinks. While loss leader pricing is a useful option for generating customer interest, marketers should be aware of potential legal issues as explained in Box 18-3.

Box 18-3

LEGAL CONCERNS WITH LOSS LEADER PRICING

Marketers should beware that some governmental agencies view loss leaders as a form of predatory pricing and, therefore, consider it illegal. Predatory pricing occurs when an organization is deliberately selling products at or below cost with the intention of driving competitors out of business. Of course, this differs from our discussion, which considers loss leader pricing as a form of promotion and not a form of anti-competitive activity.

In the U.S., several state governments have passed laws under the heading Unfair Sales Act, which prohibit the selling of certain products below cost. The main intention of these laws is to protect small firms from below-cost pricing activities of larger companies. Some states place this restriction on specific product categories (e.g., gasoline, tobacco), but Oklahoma places this restriction on most products and goes as far as requiring product pricing to be at least 6 percent above cost. (9)

Sales Promotions

As we noted in Chapter 14, marketers may offer several types of pricing promotions to simulate demand. While we have already discussed "on-sale" pricing as a technique to build customer interest, there are several other sales promotions that are designed to lower price. These include rebates, coupons, trade-in, and loyalty programs.

Bundle Pricing

Another pricing adjustment designed to increase sales is to offer discounted pricing when customers purchase several different products at the same time. Termed bundle pricing, the technique is often used to sell products that are complementary to a main product. For buyers, the overall cost of the purchase shows a savings compared to purchasing each product individually. For example, a camera retailer may offer a discounted price when customers purchase both a digital camera and a how-to photography DVD that is lower than if both items were purchased separately. In this example, the retailer may promote this as *"Buy both the digital camera and the how-to photography DVD and save 25%."*

Bundle pricing is also used by marketers as a technique that avoids making price adjustments on a main product for fear that doing so could affect the product's perceived quality level (see *Step 3: Set Standard Price Adjustments* discussion above). Rather, the marketer may choose to offer adjustments on other related or complementary products. In our example, the message changes to *"Buy the digital camera and you can get the how-to photography DVD for 50% less."* With this approach, the marketer is presenting a price adjustment without the perception of it lowering the price of the main product.

Dynamic Pricing

The concept of dynamic pricing has received a great deal of attention in recent years due to its prevalent use by Internet retailers. But the basic idea of dynamic pricing has been around since the dawn of commerce. Essentially dynamic pricing allows for point-of-sale (i.e., at the time and place of purchase) price adjustments to take place for customers meeting certain criteria established by the seller. The most common and oldest form of dynamic pricing is **haggling**, the give-and-take that takes place between buyer and seller as they settle on a price. While the word haggling may conjure up visions of transactions taking place among vendors and customers in a street market, the concept is widely used in business markets as well, where it carries the more reserved label of **negotiated pricing**.

Advances in computer hardware and software present a new dimension for the use of dynamic pricing. Unlike haggling, where the seller makes price adjustments based on a person-to-person discussion with a buyer, dynamic pricing uses sophisticated computer technology to adjust price. It achieves this by combining customer data (e.g., who they are, how they buy) with pre-programmed price offerings that are aimed at customers meeting certain criteria. For example, dynamic pricing is used in retail stores where customers' use of loyalty cards triggers the store's computer to access customer information. If customers' characteristics match requirements in the software program, they may be offered a special deal, such as 10 percent off if they also purchase another product. Dynamic pricing is also widely used in airline ticket purchasing, where the type of customer (e.g., business vs. leisure traveler) and date of purchase can affect pricing.

On the Internet, marketers may use dynamic pricing to entice first time visitors to make a purchase by offering a one-time discount. This is accomplished by comparing information stored in the marketer's computer database with identifier information gathered as the person is visiting a website. One way this is done is for a website to leave small data files, called **cookies,** on a visitor's computer when he/she first accesses the marketer's website. A cookie can reside on the visitor's computer for some time and allows the marketer to monitor the user's behavior on the site, such as how often they visit, how much time they spend on the site, what webpages they access, and much more. The marketer can then program software, often called **campaign management software**, to send visitors a special offer, such as a discount. For instance, the marketer may offer a discount if the visitor has come to the site at least five times in the last six months but has never purchased.

||||||||||||||||||||||||||||||||||||||||||||||||||||||||||||||||||||||||||||||||||||||||||||||||||||||||||

STEP 5: STATE PAYMENT OPTIONS

With the price decided, the final step for the marketer is to determine in what form and in what timeframe customers will make payment. As one would expect, payment is most often in a monetary form, though in certain situations, the payment may be part of a barter arrangement in which goods or services are exchanged.

Form of Payment

The monetary payment decision can be a complex one. First marketers must decide in what form payments will be accepted. These options include cash, check, money orders, credit card, online payment systems (e.g., PayPal) or, for international purchases, bank drafts, letters of credit, and international reply coupons, to name a few.

One of the fastest growing methods for making payment is through mobile devices. In several Asian countries, including Japan and Korea, mobile payments using smartphones have existed for several years with customers making purchases by simply tapping their phone on a payment terminal. In the U.S., this payment process is in its infancy. However, it has drawn the interest of many leading technology companies, including Google, which was one of the first to provide a smartphone application that enables phone-tapping payment. (10)

Following a devastating earthquake in Haiti, aid agencies, including the American Red Cross, quickly spread the word that donation were needed. To encourage giving, the Red Cross teamed with Network for Good, a not-for-profit payment technology company that allows charities to accept payment by mobile phone text messaging. The ease of giving resulted in a record amount of donations being received within the first few days of the disaster. (11)

Timeframe of Payment

One final pricing decision considers when payment will be made. Many marketers find promotional value in offering options to customers for the date when payment is due. Such options include:

◆ Immediate Payment in Full – Requires the customer make full payment at the time the product is acquired.

◆ Immediate Partial Payment – Requires the customer make a certain amount or percentage of payment at the time the product is acquired. This may be in the form of a down payment. Subsequent payments occur either in one lump sum or at agreed intervals (e.g., once per month) through an installment plan.

◆ Future Payment – Provides the buyer with the opportunity to acquire use of the product with payment occurring some time in the future. Future payment may require either payment in full or partial payment.

OTHER PRICING METHODS

Two pricing approaches that do not fit neatly into the price setting process we've described are bid and auction pricing. Both follow a model in which one or more participants in a purchasing transaction make offers to another party. The difference exists in terms of which party to a transaction is making the offer.

BID PRICING

Bid pricing typically requires a marketer compete against other suppliers by submitting its selling price to a potential buyer who chooses from the submissions. From the buyer's perspective, the advantage of this method is that suppliers are more likely to compete by offering lower prices than would be available if the purchase was made directly. Bid pricing occurs in several industries, though it is a standard requirement when selling to local, national, and international governments.

In a traditional bidding process, the offer is sealed or unseen by competitors. It is not until all bids are obtained and unsealed that the marketer is informed of the price listed by competitors. The fact that marketers often operate in the dark in terms of available competitor research makes this type of pricing one of the most challenging of all price setting methods.

However, a newer form of bid pricing, called **reverse auction**, is making the bidding process more transparent. Reverse auctions are typically conducted on the Internet and in most cases limited to business-to-business purchasing. With a reverse auction, a buyer informs suppliers of its product needs and then identifies a time when suppliers may bid against each other. Usually the time is limited and suppliers can often see what others are offering.

In either traditional bidding or reverse auction, the marketer's pricing strategy depends on the projected winning bid price, which is generally the lowest price. However, price alone is only the deciding factor if the bidder meets certain qualifications; thus, the low bidder is not always guaranteed to win.

AUCTION PRICING

Auction pricing is the opposite of bid pricing since it is the buyer who in large part sets the final price. This pricing method has been around for hundreds of years, but today it is most well known for its use in the auction marketplace business models, such as eBay and business-to-business marketplaces. While marketers selling through auctions do not have control over final price, it is possible to control the minimum price by establishing a price floor or **reserve price**. In this way, the product is only sold if a bid is at least equal to the floor price.

While the auction pricing business model gained wide consumer acceptance in the early years of Internet marketing, the leading online auction site, eBay, is seeing customers becoming less interested in this method for acquiring products. Instead, there seems to be more interest in fixed pricing, where customers know they can acquire the product immediately rather than waiting until the auction has ended. However, in order to place greater emphasis on fixed pricing, eBay needed to overhaul its underlying technology, which was built primarily to support auctions. The expensive upgrade was needed as fixed pricing shoppers generally seek product information in ways that are often different from those buying by auction. (12)

Marketing Story

How to Price Your Products
Inc. Magazine

Some of the most difficult decisions marketers must make are associated with pricing. As we have seen in this chapter, the process for setting price can be complex and involves a wide-range of variables. Often times, getting to the right price requires a substantial amount of research and hard work, and even then it may not result in the "best" price.

While price setting can be a cumbersome experience, it should not be taken lightly. When done poorly, pricing mistakes can prove costly. For example, if the price is set too low the marketer may lose out on potential profits and may also find it more difficult to raise prices in the future if customers become conditions to expect the lower price. Worse yet, if price set too high there may be a significant threat to overall revenue as products sit in inventory as customers turn to lower price options.

Of course, getting to the final price requires the evaluation of many variables. This story paints a very nice picture of what marketers need to consider when setting price. The story also offers sound suggestions for what it will take to get to the right price. As an added bonus, the story offers links at the end leading to even more pricing information.

"The best way to determine if the product is being priced correctly is to watch sales volumes immediately after making any change," Willett says. "This can be done by watching cash collections (if the business is cash or credit card based) or credit sales (if accounts receivables are used) for the weeks following. If a price increase is too high, customers will react pretty quickly. Also watching the competition can help - if you've made a positive change in prices; competitors are likely to follow suit." (13)

Is pricing an art or a science?

REFERENCES

1. Banham, R., "The Price is (More) Right," *CFO Magazine*, June 1, 2011.

2. Leegin Creative Leather Products vs. Psk Inc., *U.S. Supreme Court, June 28,* 2007.

3. Biskupic, J., "States Try to Counter Supreme Court's Minimum-Price Ruling," *USA Today*, December 22, 2010.

4. Rich, M., "Math of Publishing Meets the E-Book," *New York Times*, February 28, 2010.

5. Kunz, B., "How Apple Plays the Pricing Game," *MSNBC*, September 6, 2010.

6. "Catering to the Costco Mindset: Finding the 'Sweet Spot' in Quantity Discounts," *Knowledge @ Wharton*, October 27, 2010.

7. Elliott, S., "When 50 Percent Off Just Won't Do," *New York Times*, October 11, 2010.

8. Oricchio, R., "The Pricing Mistake That Cost 6PM.com $1.6M," *Inc. Magazine*, March 24, 2010.

9. Palmer, J., "Walmart Deals Carefully Exclude Oklahoma," *NewsOK*, March 2, 2011.

10. Boehret, K., "Google Mobile App Aims to Turn Phones Into Wallets," *Wall Street Journal*, September 21, 2011.

11. "Mobile Donations Make Giving Easier," *Marketplace - American Public Radio*, January 14, 2010.

12. Fowler, G.A. and S. Morrison, "EBay Attempts to Clean Up the Clutter," *Wall Street Journal*, October 31, 2010.

13. Wasserman, E., "How to Price Your Products," *Inc. Magazine*, February 1, 2010.

Full text of many of the references can be accessed via links on the support website.

Chapter 19: Managing External Forces

The bulk of material covered in the first 18 chapters is intended to give those new to marketing a basic understanding of the decisions marketers make as they work to satisfy customer needs. Our focus has largely centered on decisions marketers control, such as product design, advertising message, type of distribution, setting price, etc. Now that we have laid out the Marketer's

Toolkit, we begin a new section examining additional issues facing marketers as they manage their marketing efforts.

In this chapter, we explore factors outside of marketers' control but that play a vital role in shaping an organization's marketing strategies and tactics. As we will see, external forces present both opportunities and threats. Each force holds the potential to alter how an industry conducts its business and how individual marketing organizations make decisions. Our coverage includes in-depth evaluation of seven key external forces: demographics, economic conditions, governmental environment, influential stakeholders, cultural and societal change, innovation, and competitors.

||||||||||||||||||||||||||||||||||||||||||||||||||||||||||||||||||||||||||||||||||||||||||||||||||||||||||||

WHAT ARE EXTERNAL FORCES?

The daily routine for most marketers sees them engaging in activities related to the key marketing decisions contained within the Marketer's Toolkit we introduced in Chapter 1, namely selecting target markets, creating products, establishing distribution, developing promotions, and setting price. These decisions are considered to be controllable by the marketer who has the final say on the attributes for each.

Unfortunately, while decisions in the Marketer's Toolkit are largely controlled by the marketer, these decisions can be strongly affected by external forces that are beyond the direct control of the marketing organization. By "direct control" we mean marketers lack the power to determine the direction and intensity of a change in these forces. Instead, marketers must treat external forces as something to monitor and respond to when necessary. For example, newspaper marketers in the U.S. and Europe are experiencing a considerable shift in how consumers obtain their news in large part due to technological innovation (an external force). Some newspapers, that have recognized this key external factor, are responding by expanding their delivery of news to meet the needs of customers using these new technologies, such as delivery to handheld devices. Other newspapers, that have been slow to embrace new methods for distributing news, now face serious threats to their survival as customers by-pass them in favor of new media outlets.

> *Another industry that may soon be seeing a shift due to technological innovation is the college textbook market. Participants in this market, including publishers, college bookstores and even authors, could be impacted as more and more textbooks are presented in digital form. Additionally, the move by Amazon and other online book retailers to "rent" digital versions of textbooks could have serious marketing implications in terms of product pricing and overall book revenue. (1)*

While marketers lack direct control over external forces, in some cases they can exercise a small amount of influence over these factors. For instance, advances in mobile devices, including smartphones and pad computers, have played a pivotal role in changing how many consumers acquire information (e.g., access to online news). But while device manufacturers are credited with being the catalyst for changing a social behavior (an external force), they represent just one of several organizational groups (e.g., news media) and individuals (e.g., bloggers), whose actions were necessary for behavior to change across a large group. Thus, while one company can market goods and services with the intention of changing how a target market behaves, it is nearly impossible for one company alone to control the change.

For marketers, the key to dealing with external forces is to engage in continual marketing research. For larger companies, this may involve assigning research personnel to watch these factors as part of their day-to-day responsibilities. A research staff dedicated to monitoring external forces may offer marketers the ability to predict changes and respond well in advance of a change. For example, researchers may be able to predict how the economy (an external force) will change over the next one to two years and through this information allow the marketing organization to respond (e.g., new products, reduced price, etc.).

For small organizations that do not have the luxury of an in-house marketing research staff, monitoring change is difficult and often means they react after a change has occurred. However, new marketing research tools (see Chapter 2) are making the monitoring task much easier allowing small companies to respond quicker than they have in the past.

‖‖‖

THE EXTERNAL FORCES FACING MARKETING

For our discussion, we highlight seven fundamental external forces. Each external force is described in detail though these are not presented in order of importance. In fact, the importance of each force may vary depending on the marketing organization and the industry in which they compete. For instance, a company manufacturing technology products may feel innovative forces are more important than demographic changes. While a financial services firm may more aggressively monitor and react to economic conditions.

Demographics

Demographics involves the evaluation of characteristics of a population and how these change over time. The characteristics that are of most interest to marketers fall into two categories:

◆ Total Population – These characteristics take a broad view of the population as a whole in terms of size (e.g., number of people, number of businesses) and location (e.g., geographic region).

◆ Personal Variables – These characteristics look at how the population is changing based on individual factors such as gender, age, income, level of education, family situation (e.g., single, married, co-habitation), sexual preference, ethnicity, occupation, and social class.

We saw in Chapter 5, demographics is a key variable used to segment both consumer and business markets. In particular, demographic variables are an essential component in creating customer profiles. These profiles are based on both demographic and non-demographic (e.g., customer behavior, attitudes, lifestyles) factors and are used for grouping customers into definable market segments from which a marketer then selects its target markets. Since demographics is tied directly to identifying target markets, monitoring how demographics change is critical for making marketing decisions.

Most demographic shifts do not occur rapidly. Consequently, marketers will not see dramatic changes in a short period of time in the manner that other external forces can impact an organization (e.g., impact of a new government regulation). However, over the long term, demographics can reshape a target market requiring marketing organizations to rework their marketing strategy in an effort to appeal to a changing market.

A significant demographic change affecting nearly all companies is the shift in the geographic location of customers. Thanks in large part to the Internet, companies find their customer base has become much more internationalized. To address this shift companies have found it necessary to enhance their marketing efforts. For instance, to handle customer inquiries bicycle retailer Jenson USA uses chat software that translates up to 17 different languages. Consumers around the world can enter their questions in their own native language and the chat software will translate for the U.S.-based service staff. (2)

ADJUSTING TO DEMOGRAPHIC TRENDS

While demographic change occurs slowly, marketers can begin to see indicators of potential change by identifying small trends that may suggest a larger shift over time. By paying close attention to these trends, organizations can prepare a long-term marketing strategy to be ready when the shift becomes more apparent.

To illustrate how a marketer may respond, consider the demographic characteristic birthrate. In some countries the overall birthrate is declining, while the average age of the population is increasing (i.e., people living longer). For a company targeting the youth market with sporting products, this trend may suggest, that in coming years, it will see shrinkage in demand for its products as the youth market population declines. On the other hand, demographic data may signal to the company that another market (i.e., older consumers), which was not previously targeted, may hold potential for new products. If it is predicted that the shift will occur over several years, the sporting products company can slowly move into the new market by offering products geared toward older adults.

Economic Conditions

Since most marketers are engaged in activities designed to entice customers to spend their money, it makes sense that economic conditions represent a powerful external force. Economic analysis looks at how a defined group produces, distributes, and consumes goods and services. These groupings can range from those defined broadly (e.g., country) to those defined narrowly (e.g., small town).

Of course, the production, distribution, and consumption of products are also of high interest to marketers and, in fact, many leading scholars of marketing first studied economics before moving to marketing. In simple terms (and with apologies to both marketers and economists), the key difference between the marketer and the economist is that marketers are engaged in activity that make things happen to individual customers (e.g., create demand for products), while economists are engaged in activity showing the results marketers' decisions have on a group (e.g., study how much is being spent by certain groups).

Additionally, economists whose job it is to study a group may use hundreds of economic variables when assessing how a group is responding. Marketers tend to evaluate far fewer economic variables preferring to concentrate on those variables that affect spending behavior of consumers and businesses. For marketers, the economic variables of most interest include:

♦ <u>Income</u> – how much is being earned

♦ <u>Spending</u> – what consumers and businesses are doing with their money

♦ <u>Interest Rates</u> – the cost of borrowing money

♦ <u>Inflation</u> – how prices for goods and services are changing

♦ <u>Cost of Living</u> – the financial requirements of living in a certain geographic area

♦ <u>Employment Rates</u> – the percentage of employable people who are working

♦ <u>Exchange Rates</u> – how the value of currencies changes between countries and regions

IMPORTANCE OF ECONOMIC CONDITIONS

For many marketers, there is a relationship between level of sales and how customers are doing financially. For most products, this relationship is a direct one – as customers' financial condition improves so will selling opportunities for the marketer. A clear example of this can be seen with the sale of luxury products, where marketers are likely to see their sales grow as the target market's economic condition improves. However, other products may see improvement as economic conditions decline. For instance, during weak economic conditions marketers of career preparation services, such as those offering resume development and job search assistance, may see increased interest by workers who are unemployed or who fear their job may not be stable.

Whether an organization benefits from improving or declining economic conditions, it is necessary it monitors changes occurring in the economy in which the organization's target markets are located. In particular, marketers should watch for changing patterns in customer spending, which may indicate that a longer term change in the economy is occurring.

Changes that extend over a long term (more than six months) may be part of the **business cycle** of an economy. A business cycle is presented as a series of up (economic expansions) and down (economic contractions) measures. During expansion, an economy grows and this generally leads to more jobs, higher income, and increased customer spending. However, an economy growing too quickly can present problems of **inflation**, where product prices grow too fast. In this situation, even though customers have higher incomes they may not be purchasing more since product prices have increased. Such situations are a main reason an economy will contract or see customer spending decrease. If severe this can lead to marketers seeing a significant reduction in sales, which may indicate the presence of an economic **recession** (i.e., economic decline).

Marketing Story

The Just-in-Time Consumer
Wall Street Journal

With the U.S. economy showing only slight signs of moving out of the doldrums, many consumer products companies selling in the U.S. are still reeling and wondering when good times will return. Unfortunately, once the economy is back on track some marketers may be in for a surprise. The problem is the length of the slowed-down economy, along with continued high unemployment rates, is leading consumers to modify their buying behavior.

Over the last few years, a large number of consumers have changed how they make buying decisions. These changes include altering the types of products they purchase, focusing more effort on finding smart bargains and reducing the quantity of product they purchase at one time.

For many consumers, these changes will not be long-term. These consumers are likely to return to their pre-recession spending patterns once the economy improves. But, more and more consumers are seeing their change in purchasing habits is resulting in benefits they did not previously realize. For these consumers the new behaviors they have adopted may stay for awhile even after the economy strengthens. Many are discovering that the behavioral adjustments they were forced to accept have changed their thinking when shopping. Furthermore, they now feel their new buying behavior has turned them into better shoppers.

As this story discusses, the implications of consumers maintaining their new purchasing habits may be significant for a host of companies along the supply chain. Some companies have already accepted that consumers are changing and they are responding by adjusting their marketing strategy. Marketers are looking at all marketing decisions, particularly product design and in-store promotion, to see how they can appeal to consumers who are more conservative with their shopping dollars.

The Great Depression replaced a spendthrift culture with a generation of frugal savers. The recent recession, too, has left in its wake a deeply changed shopper: the just-in-time consumer. (3)

Are there any others ways in which the economic climate forcing consumers to change? How will these changes affect the marketing strategy of retailers and product manufacturers?

Governmental Environment

Marketing decisions must be made with an understanding of how they are impacted by international, national, regional, and local laws and regulations. For marketers, laws (i.e., acts passed by governmental ruling bodies) and regulations (i.e., requirements put in place by governmental agencies) identify rules and procedures that guide certain marketing activities. Failure to conform to requirements established by governments and their agencies may result in fines, sanctions or other legal action.

The governmental environment is a difficult external force to monitor for two key reasons. First, the number and variety of laws and regulations can be overwhelming even for the most seasoned marketer. For instance, in the U.S. alone there are potentially hundreds of laws and regulations that are either directly or indirectly targeted to marketing decisions. Table 19-1 provides a sampling of the issues covered by U.S. laws and regulations and the primary marketing decision areas these affect.

Table 19-1: Examples of Laws and Regulations in Marketing

Decision Area	Coverage
General	unfair competition, restraint of trade, environmental
Target Market	discrimination, online registration, privacy
Product	product safety, labeling, intellectual property, warranties
Promotion	deceptive and misleading claims, advertising to children, telemarketing, email spam, promotional give-aways
Distribution	tying contracts, exclusive dealerships, transportation safety
Pricing	price discrimination, predatory pricing, consumer credit purchasing, price maintenance
Other	company image, test marketing

Because the legal and regulatory environment may be different within each market targeted by a company, businesses seeking to establish a global presence may be selective as to which geographic markets they will pursue. For example, a small start-up pharmaceutical company that has developed its first product may initially look to market their product in countries that have less restrictive testing and research requirements compared to countries were approval for marketing a drug is much more involved. In this way, the company can begin to generate revenue while also gathering the needed information for entry into other, more controlled markets.

> *Until 2010, many online retailers were not required to collect sales tax for products sold to customers in states where retailers with physical locations must collect sales tax. However, due to a slowing economy which has reduced state tax revenue, many U.S. state governments have begun to demand that online retailers collect sales tax. Several leading companies, including Amazon and Overstock.com, have rejected the idea and have decided to drop thousands of marketing affiliates rather than collect the tax. The affiliates, who receive payment for directing purchasers to an online retailer's website, are located in the states where the tax issue is being raised. The retailers believe that by eliminating affiliates they will no longer be viewed as having a presence in the states and, consequently, will not need to collect sales tax. (4)*

The second reason the governmental environment proves difficult is due to the complexity inherent in understanding laws and regulations, which often makes it impossible for marketers to handle these issues on their own. Seeking legal assistance is necessary (and often costly) for most marketers no matter their size.

> *For years, television viewers have complained about how sound volume increases when television commercials appear. Advertisers, who acknowledge this happens, say they need higher sound levels in order to capture viewers' attention. However, U.S. legislators disagree and have passed the Commercial Advertisement Loudness Mitigation Act requiring broadcasters utilize technology preventing commercials from being louder than regular programming. (5)*

DEALING WITH THE GOVERNMENT

In addition to seeking legal assistance, marketing organizations may find value by engaging in either direct discussion with governmental personnel or indirect discussion through firms hired to serve as a representative for the marketing company (e.g., consultants, lobbyists). Representatives are particularly beneficial when selling internationally, where existing relationships between government personnel and a hired representative can effectively reduce bureaucratic red tape.

In situations where proposed legislation is likely to impact an entire industry, communication with the government may occur through a marketer's participation in an **industry trade group**. These groups perform many tasks on behalf of their members, including maintaining relations with governmental groups to ensure the industry's voice is heard with regard to pending legislation affecting the industry.

Finally, marketers should not view the governmental environment as always erecting obstacles. In many cases laws and regulations present marketing opportunities. For example, in response to U.S. Federal Government rules limiting the size of liquid, gel, and aerosol products that may be carried aboard an airplane, several personal care products companies (e.g., shaving cream, hair care, toothpaste, etc.) viewed this as an opportunity to market their products in new packaging that they promote as approved for airline travel.

Marketing Story

Charges Settled Over Fake Reviews on iTunes
New York Times

The U.S. Government is intending to take a more critical view of supposedly unbiased product endorsements that are actually company-sponsored promotions. In particular, the Federal Trade Commission (FTC) announced they would become more aggressive monitoring what goes on at product review websites. Their main concern is with marketers deliberately financing the posting of positive product comments, including product reviews, but failing to disclose the business relationship the poster has with the product or company they are reviewing.

The FTC made it clear they will go after marketers who do not disclose such relationships as part of their postings. According to the new guidelines, it is not illegal to pay for positive reviews as long as it is evident to anyone reading the post that the poster was compensated or has a relationship with the product or company.

This story discusses the FTC first significant action on this issue. They settled charges brought against a California public relations company who agreed to remove positive reviews they posted to iTunes. The FTC had alleged the PR company used employees and interns to post positive reviews for clients' products.

The charges were the first to be brought under a new set of guidelines for Internet endorsements that the agency introduced last year. The guidelines have often been described as rules for bloggers, but they also cover anyone writing reviews on Web sites or promoting products through Facebook or Twitter. (6)

Should this work the other way as well? Should marketers be legally required to identify whether they intentionally post a negative comment for a competitor's product?

Influential Stakeholders

Besides dealing with various governmental groups, marketers must also pay close attention to other groups that can affect marketing activity. The most important of these groups are those that have an interest or stake in the company. While such groups may not carry the same power as governmental agencies, stakeholders can still command a great deal of influence especially in terms of swaying public opinion. If their voice is strong enough, this can then lead to governmental action.

Influential stakeholders can be divided into two categories:

Connected Stakeholders

These stakeholders consist of groups that regularly interact with the marketing organization and often perform key activities that help the marketer succeed. Examples include supply and distribution partners (e.g., distributors, material suppliers), industry standards groups, and support companies (e.g., advertising agencies). To address concerns raised by these groups often requires direct communication by management with the stakeholders.

Peripheral Stakeholders

These stakeholders consist of groups that may not routinely impact the marketer unless a specific issue arises that draws their attention. Examples include religious organizations, community activists, and cause supporters. To address concerns and to communicate with these peripheral stakeholders, marketers often seek the help of public relations professionals. Depending on the circumstances, the PR strategy may involve initiating contact prior to an issue becoming public (i.e., **preemptive strategy**), or the strategy may be to take a wait-and-see approach (i.e., **responsive strategy**) before taking action.

In Venice, Italy city officials found that one way to generate revenue to help pay for the upkeep and restoration of historic buildings and monuments was to allow companies to place advertising on scaffoldings rising next to buildings under repair. While advertisers, including Coca-Cola and Bulgari, saw value in the billboards and erected ads, they quickly found a peripheral stake holder that did not like the idea. The Fondo Ambiente Italiano, a heritage protection association, publically announced their displeasure with the ads claiming these were not appropriate for the historical area in which these were placed. (7)

Cultural and Societal Change

Society is made up of many different cultural groups. As we note in Chapter 4, members of a cultural group share similar values and beliefs, which are learned and reinforced by others within the same cultural group. These shared values and beliefs lead members of a cultural group to behave in similar ways (e.g., customs, traditions, likes/dislikes, attitudes, perceptions, etc.).

Cultural groups can be viewed on several levels. At a broad level, a cultural group consists of a very large number who share basic values (e.g., ethnicity, religious affiliation). While looking at the broad level can offer some insight into how a general cultural group behaves, marketers are much more concerned with examining cultural groups at narrower levels. Such analysis of cultural groups leads to the study of sub-cultures, which consist of individuals sharing values and beliefs that revolve around specific interests. For instance, a large sub-cultural group may exist in a certain region of a country. While collectively they share basic cultural values with others in their country (e.g., sense of patriotism), they may also share special values with those in their local region that are not shared consistently throughout the country (e.g., work ethic, taste in food, etc.).

But of even more interest to marketers is the identification of smaller sub-cultures (e.g., type of shopper, music preference, online gaming enthusiast, etc.). Members of smaller sub-cultures, who share similar values, are also likely to have similar needs and, as we discussed in Chapter 5, this suggests that sub-cultures are natural for market segmentation. For marketers, it is important to recognize that a single consumer may belong to many different sub-cultures and fully understanding the structure and key values of a sub-culture can offer clues for marketing to these customers.

EVOLUTION OF CULTURAL CHANGE

Cultural values and beliefs are not stagnant, rather these evolve and change. However, the pace of change differs depending on the level examined. At the broad cultural level changes often evolve slowly. For instance, consider how people in the United States and Japan view the importance of saving money. People in the United States are more inclined to spend their earned income than they are to save resulting in a low personal savings rate for Americans. Those living in Japan are more concerned with saving and show a high personal savings rate. The difference in values toward savings has been consistent for many years and no one expects consumers from either country to alter their values in the near future.

While broad cultures tend to shift values and beliefs slowly, changes within sub-cultures can occur relatively quickly. This can be seen within the music industry which often experiences rapid shifts as a sub-culture of music enthusiasts discovers new artists and musical styles. The key for marketers targeting sub-cultures is to maintain close contact with these groups through regular marketing research. In this way, marketers can see how different sub-cultures behave. In doing so, marketers may be able to spot trends, which they can capitalize on through new marketing tactics, such as creating new products, opening new sales channels or offering more value to their customers.

An excellent source for learning about changes occurring within sub-cultures is the website Trendwatching.com. This website offers monthly briefings on trends that marketers should closely watch. For instance, a trend the website labels as Mass Mingling suggests young adults world-wide are not being isolated in their homes by technology, as some have predicted. Instead, social media and other innovations are being used as an aid in creating face-to-face gatherings. By understanding this trend, marketers can use technologies to encourage customers to gather at specific locations, where the marketer will then have product promotion and customer relationship opportunities. (8)

Innovation

Arguably the external forces with the greatest potential for changing how marketers and industries compete are those associated with innovation. When most people think of innovation, they immediately assume it has to do with computers and other high-tech equipment. While today the majority of innovative new products rely in some way on computer technology, it is not a requirement for something to be regarded as innovative. Instead, an innovation is viewed as anything new that solves needs by offering a significant advantage (e.g., more features, more convenient, easier to use, lower cost, etc.) over existing methods.

For example, a designer of automobiles may develop a new layout for a car's dashboard using existing products (no new technologies). This new design reduces the amount of time a driver must take his eyes off the road in order to select a radio station. If this new layout is viewed positively by customers, governmental groups, and the media it may gain widespread acceptance by other vehicle manufacturers who will make similar designs available in their products.

As noted in the above example, for an innovation to be truly influential it must be widely adopted within a targeted group (e.g., within an industry, by a target market). Once adopted an innovation becomes significant if it leads to behavioral changes including changing how consumers and businesses satisfy their needs. These changes present both opportunities and threats to marketers.

Because of the potential innovation has in affecting products and industries, it is no surprise that many marketing organizations direct significant funds to researching this external force. In fact, in many industries, such as pharmaceuticals and computers, spending on technological research and development represents a significant portion of a company's overall budget.

INNOVATION IN MARKETING

Marketers in many industries know that innovation through new product development is vital to remain competitive. But product decisions are not the only areas affected by new developments. As we've discussed throughout this book, innovation can affect almost all marketing areas as outlined in Table 19-2.

Many of the benefits shown in Table 19-2 are driven by the evolution of communication technologies including the Internet and mobile devices. These communication technologies are transforming how all functional areas of an organization perform work. However, it can be argued that no functional area has been more affected than marketing (see *Marketing to the Connected Customer* discussion in the Appendix). Over the next decade, it is expected that the effect of communication technologies on marketing will continue to grow and marketers are well served to embrace it.

Table 19-2: Innovation in Marketing

Marketing Area	Effect of Innovation
Marketing Research	Creates new ways to conduct research, including more sophisticated methods for monitoring and tracking customer behavior and analyzing data.
Targeting Markets	Allows for extreme target marketing where micro marketing is replacing mass marketing. For customer service, technology makes it easier to manage relationships and allows for rapid response to customers' needs.
Product	Creates new digital goods/services. Incorporation of innovation into existing good/service enhances value by offering improved quality, features, and reliability at a lower price.
Promotion	New techniques allow better matching of promotion to customer activity and individualized promotion. Makes it easier for sellers to offer product suggestions and promotional tie-ins.
Distribution	Creates new channels for product distribution and customer transaction (e.g., mobile device purchasing). Allows more control over inventory management and closer monitoring of product shipments.
Pricing	Enables the use of dynamic pricing methods.

Procter & Gamble has long been an innovator in using the latest technologies to aid their marketing efforts. As an example, since 1997 the company has employed virtual reality tools and today they have 19 virtual solution centers where research is conducted. These centers allow P&G to conduct virtual shopping research, that includes using 3D technology for presenting consumers with new product designs and to show how these products appear on store shelves. (9)

Competitors

For many marketers, the final external force is the one most relevant to immediate day-to-day decision making. While the other external forces we've discussed tend to be examined periodically (or in some cases rarely), monitoring competitor activity is often a daily undertaking.

Monitoring competitors can serve several goals:

Competitors as Threats

The most obvious reason to monitor the competition is to see how they are responding in the same markets in which the marketer operates. Many larger companies, recognizing the importance of keeping tabs on their competition, have created specific positions, and even departments, focusing on gathering and analyzing competitor data. These **competitive intelligence** programs mainly employ high-tech methods, principally the Internet, to locate information about competitors, such as news reports, government filings (e.g., patents, stock reports), and changes to competitors' websites. Even small sized marketers can track competitors' actions. For instance, there are several news and information services that will alert a marketer (usually via email) when a competitor is mentioned in the news.

One inexpensive method used to learn about a competitor is to monitor the job posting section of their website or on Internet job sites. New postings may indicate what type of new business the competitor is pursuing, especially if the postings are detailed. (10) Additionally, competitive intelligence can be undertaken by tracking blog postings made by company executives, Twitter postings, and company email blasts. (11)

Competitors as Partners

While many may consider competitors as the enemy, there are situations where competitors can present opportunities. This happens often to large companies that offer a broad product line serving many target markets. In some markets, a company may compete aggressively with another firm, but in other markets it may make more sense for both to work together. This can be seen in the computer industry where Apple, which once would not consider building computers with Intel processors since these were used by competitors that run the Microsoft operating system, has now adopted these processors for much of its computer line.

Competitors of Tomorrow

In many industries and, in particular technology-focused industries, the most dangerous competitors are the ones that have yet to emerge. Because technology-dependent industries, such as computers, consumer electronics, and pharmaceuticals, rely heavily on innovative new products, serious competitors can appear quickly from what seems to be out of nowhere.

For instance, news organizations have been quickly and dramatically impacted by online video sharing services. The most influential innovator to affect these industries is YouTube, which in only 18 months moved from a small three-person startup working out of a garage to dominating the online video industry leading to its acquisition by Google for $1.6 billion. (12) The ease by which videos can be posted and made available for mass viewing essentially allows nearly anyone to become a broadcaster and, consequently, a threat to traditional news outlets.

Today, most news organizations recognize the impact of YouTube and have responded by altering their methods for delivering information, such as offering their own online videos. However, many other media companies, that were slow to adapt to the changes occurring in their market, are struggling to survive. The effect of the emergence of new competitors on news outlets remains to be seen, though for many their long-term survival is in doubt.

||||||||||||||||||||||||||||||||||||||||||||||||||||||||||||||||||||||||||||||||||||||||||||||||||||||||||||||||||||||||||||||||||||||

REFERENCES

1. Olivarez-Giles, N., "Amazon Launches College Textbook Rentals Program," *Los Angeles Times*, July 19, 2011.

2. Stambor, Z., "Smarter Service," *Internet Retailer*, March 1, 2011.

3. Byron, E., "The Just-in-Time Consumer," *Wall Street Journal*, November 23, 2010.

4. Lifsher, M., "Amazon Won't Collect Sales Tax; Cuts Off California Affiliates," *Los Angeles Times*, June 30, 2011.

5. Gregory, S., "Congress Tells Commercials to Quiet Down," *Time*, December 15, 2010.

6. Helft, M., "Charges Settled Over Fake Reviews on iTunes," *New York Times*, August, 26 2010.

7. Povoledo, E., "Behind Venice's Ads, the Restoration of Its Heritage," *New York Times*, September 18, 2010.

8. "Mass Mingling," *Trendwatching.com*, June-July 2010.

9. Ackerman, A., "P&G Shapes the Store," *Consumer Goods Technology*, September 16, 2011.

10. Steiner, C., "Six Ways to Spy On the Competition," *Forbes*, May 24, 2010.

11. Helm, B., "How to Use Competitive Intelligence to Gain an Advantage," *Inc. Magazine*, April 2011.

12. Lidsky, D., "The Brief but Impactful History of YouTube," *Fast Company*, February 1, 2010.

Full text of many of the references can be accessed via links on the book's companion website.

Chapter 20: Marketing Planning and Strategy

As we have seen through the first 19 chapters, marketing is a complex field. To achieve long-term success marketers must not only consider decisions for each of the components contained in the Marketer's Toolkit, they must also understand how these elements work together to achieve the goal of creating value for customers and the organization.

In our final chapter, we see that the key for ensuring the marketing components work together is to have a full understanding of the marketing planning process. We begin with a discussion of the importance of planning and show why the development of a Marketing Plan is a necessary undertaking for nearly all marketers. As part of this discussion, we distinguish between strategies and tactics and examine the role these play in the planning process. Next, to aid in our understanding of planning, we see how the Product Life Cycle (PLC) offers valuable guidance for marketing decisions. We cover in detail the circumstances marketers face as their products move through the PLC and why marketing decisions must be continually fine-tuned to adjust to these changes. Throughout this discussion, we see how the PLC can offer insight into what challenges marketers may face as the market for their product continues to evolve.

||||||||||||||||||||||||||||||||||||||||||||||||||||||||||||||||||||||||||||||||||||||||||||||||||||||||||||||||||

IMPORTANCE OF PLANNING

As we have seen throughout this book, marketers consider many factors when making decisions. Of course, the main factors are those directly associated with how customers respond to an organization's marketing efforts, such as how they react to changes in a product, new advertisements, special pricing promotions, etc.

But when making decisions marketers face other concerns that are not directly customer related. For instance, we have discussed how marketing decisions (e.g., lowering price) may place pressure on other areas of the organization (e.g., production, shipping). Other examples include:

◆ Marketers must be aware of how their decisions fit with the overall objectives of the company. For example, a company whose goal is to be the low-price leader may have concerns if the company's marketing department wants to market a high-end product since this would go against the reputation and core strengths of the company.

♦ In Chapter 19, we showed that marketers' decisions may affect peripheral stake-holders, who are not directly connected to the marketing organization but have the potential to impact the organization if issues arise that draw their attention.

♦ Marketing decisions also directly affect an organization's financial condition. Marketers' efforts generate the funds (i.e., sales) needed for the company to survive but do so while using company resources. Controls must be put in place to ensure the results of what the organization spends through marketing meet expectations (e.g., meets return on investment goals).

Because marketing decisions have both internal and external impact, marketers are wise to make their decisions only after engaging in a careful, disciplined planning process. **Planning** is a deliberate process in which the marketer looks to gain a full understanding of current circumstances and then use this knowledge to prepare for future events. For marketers, planning is an essential task that must be continually undertaken. As we will see, shifting market conditions, including changing customer needs and competitive threats, almost always means that what worked in the past will not work in the future. This requires organizations to respond with revisions in how a product is marketed.

Marketing planning is also necessary since it is often a prerequisite for obtaining funding. Whether one is a marketer in a large corporation seeking additional money for his or her department, or is part of a small startup company looking for initial funding, requests for money almost always requires the presentation of a supporting plan.

Finally, it is risky for marketers to make hasty, off-the-cuff decisions without regard to the potential implications. Instead, marketing decisions should be made with consideration of how these affect others both inside and outside the organization.

> *The Smart "fortwo" Minicar is a unique small car that initially targeted European city dwellers looking for an inexpensive vehicle for getting around town. When first introduced in the U.S. in the early 2000s, interest in the car was high and sales were encouraging. But within a few years sales dropped and Smart decided they needed a new plan for marketing the car. The planning process included extensive customer research which indicated that many people thought the car was too small. This led Smart to update its strategy, including targeting the car to environmentally-friendly consumers and expanding promotion through product placements in movies and on television. (1)*

‖‖

THE MARKETING PLAN

The central point in planning for marketing decisions is the development of a Marketing Plan. We define the Marketing Plan as a well-researched marketing analysis that attempts to explain what has happened in the past and outlines steps that will be taken in the future. The scope of the Marketing Plan depends on the company and industry. For instance, a small technology company may have a less elaborate plan that is highly flexible and can be quickly adapted to meet the needs of a rapidly changing market. A more established marketing organization, such a large consumer products firm, may create a highly structured plan that clearly identifies all activities taking place over a 12-month period.

For companies operating separate units in different international markets, a different Marketing Plan is often needed for each market even though the same product is sold in each location. This is often necessary since the market conditions for one market may be significantly different than another market and, because of this, require a different marketing approach.

> *International markets are particularly susceptible to requiring different plans. Many U.S.-based companies discovered this as they have struggled with their efforts to establish their products in Asian countries. After several false starts, companies have learned that a marketing plan that works in the U.S. may not work in Asia. For instance, General Mills needed to alter its Bugles chips to appeal to local tastes. This included producing the snack out of rice and potato, in addition to the corn product that is popular in the U.S. market. (2)*

Whether the marketer is creating a short plan intended to cover just a few months or a full-blown document that guides it for a year or more, nearly all plans require the undertaking of significant marketing research to gain stronger insight on the market. With knowledge of the market, the marketer can then begin to build the plan which will include the following six key concepts (3):

1. SITUATION ANALYSIS

The situation analysis is designed to take a snapshot of where things stand at the time the plan is developed. This part of the Marketing Plan is extremely important and quite time consuming as it looks at the current situation in terms of: 1) the components of the Marketer's Toolkit (target markets, product, distribution, promotion, and pricing); 2) the competition; 3) the financial conditions facing the organization; and 4) external forces.

2. MARKETING OBJECTIVES

The ultimate purpose of a Marketing Plan is to lead to actions that will help the organization meet a goal. The goal is reflected in one or more objectives the organization expects to achieve with its marketing efforts. The objectives flow from the top of the organization down to the marketing department. Objectives can be in the form of financial goals, such as profits, sales volume or return on investment, or marketing goals, such as achieving a certain level of **market share** (i.e. percentage of market held by organization) or a certain number of visitors to a store (i.e., store traffic).

> When it comes to coffee brands, Starbucks is one of the world's most widely recognized names. However, the company also produces another coffee brand, Seattle's Best. Starbucks, which positions this product as a lower-price alternative to its better known sibling, has set $1 billion in sales as the brand's key marketing objective. While still several years away from achieving its target, the marketing planning to reach this goal emphasizes expanding distribution to at least 100,000 outlets. Seattle's Best is now available on cruise ships and vending machines, and the company is even testing cafes inside several Canadian Wal-Mart stores. (4)

3. MARKETING STRATEGY

Achieving objectives requires the marketer engage in marketing decision making which indicates where resources (e.g., marketing funds) are directed. However, before spending begins on individual marketing decisions (e.g., where to advertise) the marketer needs to establish a general plan of action summarizing what will be done to reach the stated objectives. The information produced at this stage of the planning process helps guide the development of specific tactical programs (see *Strategy and Tactical Programs* discussion below).

4. TACTICAL MARKETING PROGRAMS

Marketing strategy sets the stage for specific actions that take place. **Marketing tactics** are the day-to-day activities marketers undertake and involve the major marketing decision areas. As would be expected, this is the key area of the Marketing Plan since it explains exactly what will be done to reach the marketing objectives. Of course, the majority of what is covered in this book deals with these decisions.

5. FORECASTS AND MARKETING BUDGET

Carrying out marketing tactics almost always means that money must be spent. The marketing budget lays out the spending requirements needed to carry out marketing tactics. While the marketing department may request a certain level of funding they feel is required, in the end, it is upper management that will

How LEGO Revived Its Brand
BusinessWeek

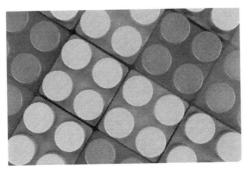

One of the trickiest planning decisions facing marketers is deciding when to move beyond what has made them successful and tackle something new. This is because at some point, nearly all companies find growing their business requires they branch out into new areas that are often unfamiliar.

For instance, companies will begin marketing new products that are significantly different compared to the products that made them successful. Or maybe they continue to produce the same products but target markets they previously did not target.

Whatever the change, there is always risk involved when making marketing decisions in unfamiliar ground. What makes things worse is when the decisions require the company possess skills that are beyond their general core competencies.

For example, just because a furniture company's product design team is skilled at creating office furniture does not mean the company can use the same team to branch out successfully to other furniture markets, such as marketing outdoor furniture. The skills of the designers may be quite different. Unfortunately, most companies that fail when expanding to new markets often do not realize what their real core competencies are until it is too late.

This story looks at one such case involving the Lego toy brand and how this company lost its way when they ventured into new areas. The story shows how Lego tried to expand into several areas only to find sales suffer for the entire company. Yet this story is not only about the problems Lego faced it also provides guidance on what it took for this company to recover.

The company's problems began in the late 1990s, when it stopped focusing on design. Back then, company executives wanted to extend the brand, venturing off on wild forays into new product development. The prototypical example: Galidor, a legendary bomb inside the walls of LEGO. (5)

What are the key marketing concepts that Lego seemed to ignore?

have the final say on how much financial support is offered. In most cases, such requests must be justified by showing what is expected to happen if the money is spent. For this, marketers must develop forecasts that may include estimates of sales volume, number of customer visits, level of product awareness, coupon usage rates, and many others.

6. IMPLEMENTATION AND ANALYSIS

This part of the Marketing Plan identifies how and by whom the tactical programs are carried out. In many cases, a timeline is presented showing when tasks will occur and who will be responsible. Additionally, the Marketing Plan shows how and when success will be measured. For instance, a retailer planning a new department within its national chain may undertake analysis of department sales once per week to see whether the marketing programs are meeting expectations.

> In some situations, the principle objective of a Marketing Plan is to prepare a product line for sale to another company. Over the last few years, Procter & Gamble has been doing this for nearly all its food product brands. The consumer-products giant has moved out of the food business by selling off such leading brands as Pringles, Folgers, Jiff, Crisco and several others. (6) By dropping out of the food product category, P&G will now focus its products in two main categories, beauty and grooming, and household care. (7)

STRATEGY AND TACTICAL PROGRAMS

As noted above, one of the most crucial concepts of the marketing planning process is the need to develop a cohesive marketing strategy that guides tactical programs for the marketing decision areas. In marketing, there are two levels to strategy formulation: General Marketing Strategies and Decision Area Strategies.

GENERAL MARKETING STRATEGIES

These set the direction for all marketing efforts by describing, in general terms, how marketing will achieve its objectives. There are many different General Marketing Strategies, though most can be viewed as falling into one of the following categories:

Market Expansion

This strategy looks to grow overall sales in one of two ways:

- <u>Grow Sales with Existing Products</u> – With this approach, the marketer seeks to increase the overall sales of products the company currently markets. This can be accomplished by: 1) getting existing customers in current markets to buy more, 2) getting potential customers in current markets to buy (i.e., those who have yet to buy), or 3) selling existing products in new markets.

- <u>Grow Sales with New Products</u> – With this approach, the marketer seeks to achieve objectives through the introduction of new products. This can be accomplished by: 1) introducing updated versions or refinements to existing products, 2) introducing new products that are extensions of existing products, or 3) introducing new products not previously marketed.

Market Share Growth

This strategy looks to increase the marketer's overall percentage or share of the market. In many cases, this can only be accomplished by taking sales away from competitors. Consequently, this strategy often relies on aggressive marketing tactics.

Niche Market

This strategy looks to obtain a commanding position within a certain segment of the overall market. Usually the niche market is much smaller in terms of total customers and sales volume than the overall market. Ideally this strategy looks to have the product viewed as being different from that of companies targeting the larger market (i.e., product positioning).

> *Large online news websites, including AOL and Yahoo, have seen considerable decline in their audience in large part due to the evolution of niche websites. Consumers appear to be more attracted to getting information from specialized websites focusing on such topics as sports, politics and gossip. AOL, which was had difficulty building its own niche offerings, has been forced to respond to this trend by acquiring specialized sites, such as Huffington Post (politics) and TechCrunch (technology). (8)*

Status Quo

This strategy looks to maintain the marketer's current position in the market, such as maintaining the same level of market share.

Market Exit

This strategy looks to remove the product from the organization's product mix. This can be accomplished by: 1) selling the product to another organization, or 2) eliminating the product.

DECISION AREA STRATEGIES

These are used to achieve the General Marketing Strategies by guiding the decisions within key marketing areas (target marketing, product, distribution, promotion, pricing). For example, a General Marketing Strategy that centers on entering a new market with new products may be supported by Decision Area Strategies that include:

- <u>Target Market Strategy</u> – employ segmenting techniques

- <u>Product Strategy</u> – develop new product line

- <u>Distribution Strategy</u> – use methods to gain access to distribution partners that service the target market

- <u>Promotion Strategy</u> – create a plan that can quickly build awareness of the product

- <u>Pricing Strategy</u> – create price programs that offer lower pricing versus competitors

Achieving the Decision Area Strategies is accomplished through the development of detailed Tactical Programs for each area. For instance, to meet the Pricing Strategy that lowers price below competitors' products, the marketer may employ such tactics as: quantity discounts, trade-in allowances or sales volume incentives to distributors.

||||||||||||||||||||||||||||||||||||||||||||||||||||||||||||||||||||||||||||||||||||||||||||||||||||||||||

PLANNING AND STRATEGY WITH THE PLC

As we have seen, there are many components to consider within the marketing planning process. In fact, for many marketers creating the Marketing Plan represents one of the most challenging and burdensome tasks they face. Fortunately, over the years marketing academics and professionals have put forth theories, models, and other tools to aid planning. Possibly the most widely used planning tool within marketing is the Product Life Cycle (PLC) concept, which we introduced in Chapter 7. The PLC suggests a product goes through several stages of "life" (Development, Introduction, Growth, Maturity, and Decline) with each stage presenting the marketer with different circumstances to which they must react.

As we will see, the PLC helps the marketer understand that marketing planning must change as a product moves from one stage to another. For example, marketers will find what works when appealing to customers in the Introduction stage is different than marketing methods used to attract customers during the Growth stage.

For the rest of this chapter, we offer a detailed discussion of how the PLC can aid marketing planning. The discussion is presented using the following assumptions and techniques:

- ◆ The chief scope of analysis is at the product form level where many companies offer products with similar benefits. In Chapter 7, we suggested that hybrid cars would be an example of a product form (see *Levels of Analysis in the PLC* discussion in Chapter 7). In most cases, a product form is a market with certain characteristics that change over time.

♦ We break down each stage and discuss market characteristics in terms of the following key internal and external factors:

- Level of Competition
- Nuances of the Target Market
- Available Product Options
- Price Level
- Promotional Focus
- Distribution Strategy
- Total Industry Profits

♦ While, at the general level, the PLC is divided into five main stages, we view most stages as consisting of sub-stages that result from noticeable changes in market characteristics.

♦ While market characteristics are evaluated for the product form, we offer strategy guidance for individual brands that compete within these specific markets.

♦ The PLC is tightly linked to the Diffusion of Innovation discussed in Chapter 7. It is necessary to keep in mind the five adopter categories: Innovators, Early Adopters, Early Majority, Late Majority, and Laggards.

Development Stage

The Product Life Cycle begins long before a product is brought to market. While technically sales do not start until the next stage, marketers must address many of the same issues they will face once the product is launched. Much of what happens in the Development stage follows our discussion of New Product Development in Chapter 7, where marketing research is the key element in planning. Most of what occurs in this stage is experienced only by companies who are on the forefront of innovation of a new product form.

In our discussion, the Development stage is divided into two distinct sub-stages: Early Development, with characteristics outlined in Table 20-1, and Late Development, with characteristics outlined in Table 20-2.

EARLY DEVELOPMENT STAGE

For firms developing a new product form, this stage (see Table 20-1) is primarily concerned with marketing research. This stage is equivalent to the *Concept Development and Testing* step for new product development. Customers and distribution partners are only involved to aid in information gathering, often through focus group research.

Because the product form is still in early development, the marketer has yet to determine whether the company will move forward with a full product launch.

Table 20-1: Early Development Stage

Key Factors	Market Characteristics
Competition	No real competition exists since the product is in early development, much of which is in-house and not readily viewable to competitors. However, from a research perspective, competitors are now being identified.
Target Market	The target market exists only in marketing research terms. Possibly a small number of target customers are used to assist with research.
Products	The product exists only in the form of ideas and prototypes. Inventory is not yet available.
Prices	Pricing is non-existent unless a company charges its research customers a fee to be part of early product testing.
Promotion	Promotion has yet to occur as companies continue to refine their products and build their marketing plans.
Distribution	Mostly limited to internal analysis of possible distribution alternatives, though there may be some communication with a limited number of distribution partners in order to gauge interest.
Industry Profits	At this stage, there are costs only.

LATE DEVELOPMENT STAGE

Products that have moved to the late stage of development (see Table 20-2) have done so because marketing research suggests there is strong potential for success. By this point, a marketer has a real product (not just ideas) and is in the position to test it in the market. Consequently, this stage matches the *Market Testing* step for new product development. Firms electing to test their product in real "test markets" will do so using all their marketing tools.

Table 20-2: Late Development Stage

Key Factors	Market Characteristics
Competition	While a marketer may not face competition in terms of sales, they may face competitive pressure from companies developing similar products, such as competition to acquire materials or technologies for product development, competition to line up product evaluators, and competition to get the early word out about the product to the news media. Additionally, competition may exist in the form of other types of products that potential customers currently use to satisfy needs targeted by this new product form. If these competitors are aware that a new product form is being developed, they may increase efforts to sell their products with the intention of reducing the market's need for the new product.
Target Market	Companies may test market the product among a small group of customers or within a selected geographic market.
Products	Companies researching the product form begin to produce small quantities of the product, primarily for testing or to build initial awareness (e.g., for display at trade shows).
Prices	Initial market price is discussed and if there are active test markets the company may be testing different price levels.
Promotion	Promotion often begins prior to product launch as marketers prepare the market for the product's arrival. Emphasis may be on public relations in an attempt to encourage the media to discuss the product prior to launch. If a real test market is used, companies may be testing several promotional options including advertising and sales promotion.
Distribution	For a product sold through distributors, the ground work is being laid to build the distribution network. In some cases, distributor education and training will start prior to product launch.
Industry Profits	A small amount of revenue may be generated if real test markets are used, but overall marketers continue to experience substantial costs.

Introduction Stage

This stage represents the launch of the new product form by one or more companies. It is done only after the marketer has created a detailed Marketing Plan. In many cases, tactical marketing decisions (target marketing, product, distribution, promotion, pricing) have been adjusted as the product has gone through the Development stage.

The Introduction stage is divided into two distinct sub-stages: Early Introduction, with characteristics outlined in Table 20-3, and Late Introduction, with characteristics outlined in Table 20-4.

EARLY INTRODUCTION STAGE

For the early entrants in the market, a crucial goal is to create awareness for the product form. If customers can see that the product form holds similar characteristics to existing products then the marketers' task is easier since their job becomes one of convincing customers that this new product form is better than what they are currently using (e.g., *"this new style running shoe offers performance and comfort features not found with traditional running shoes"*).

However, if the product form is significantly different from existing products then the marketers' job may be far more difficult. Under these conditions (see Table 20-3), marketers must not only make customers aware of the new product, but they must also educate customers as to what the product is, how it works, and what benefits are derived from its use. For some products, such as technology products, conveying this message can prove difficult as customers may not fully understand how the product works and, consequently, not see a need for the product. Whether customers understand the product or not, this stage requires promotional spending directed to addressing the need for customer education and building awareness. Also, education and awareness alone are not enough; customers must often be enticed to try a product through special promotional efforts (e.g., free trials).

In the technology industry, it is common to see companies selling competing products offering similar benefits, yet do so by employing different, often incompatible methods. Such products often confuse consumers. They fear that one product may ultimately win the battle and leave the purchasers of the other product with something that may not be supported in the future. A classic example of this occurred in the early days of video players where VHS players ultimately defeated Beta players. A current example appears to be playing out in the tablet computer market that includes eBook readers (e.g., Amazon Kindle) and pad computers (e.g., Apple iPad). The market has attracted many competitors and analysts are suggesting this crowded market is likely to see the emergence of only one or two top products, with all others eventually being displaced. (9)

Table 20-3: Early Introduction Stage

Key Factors	Market Characteristics
Competition	In many cases, when two or more companies are working to be first to market with a new product form, one company will be out ahead and for a period of time have the market to it-self. However, this does not mean there is no competition. The company launching the product still faces competition from ex-isting products that customers previously purchased in order to satisfy their needs.
Target Market	To establish interest in the market for a new product form, marketers will initially target Innovators and, to a larger extent, Early Adopters.
Products	From the target market's perspective, product options are limited, since only one or a very small number of companies are selling products. Because of the uncertainty of whether the product will be accepted by a larger market and because of the expense in-volved in producing products in small volume (primarily due to low demand,) there are few product options available.
Prices	In most cases, marketers follow a pricing strategy called **price skimming** in which price is set at a level that is much higher than can be sustained once competitors enter the market. Price skimming allows the company to recover development and ini-tial marketing costs before the onslaught of competitors eventu-ally force prices lower.
Promotion	For products considered to be a leap ahead of existing products, early marketers may have some difficulty explaining how the product satisfies customers' needs. This is particularly an issue with high-tech products. In this situation, the marketer must engage in a promotional campaign designed to educate the mar-ket on the general product form and not necessarily focus only on promoting a specific brand. Additional sales promotion may be used to encourage product trial. Also, the sales force may begin a strong push to acquire distributors.
Distribution	Upon product launch marketers continue efforts to build their distribution network. As we saw in the Development stage, the focus of marketers is to find distributors committed to handling the product.
Industry Profits	Marketers often experience low profits or, most likely, a loss as the cost of acquiring customers (i.e., promotion) is high. Additionally, marketers may need to pay back development expense to the corporation or to other investors.

LATE INTRODUCTION STAGE

Early entrants continue to create awareness and educate customers, but their promotional orientation may shift to a "buy-our-brand" approach if more companies enter the market. Thus, at this stage (see Table 20-4), marketers begin to position their products with the intention of separating themselves from the competition.

In many ways, this stage is where the real competition begins and aggressive marketing tactics are likely to be the norm in the very near future. However, those selling in this market must understand, that because the mass market (i.e., Early Majority) has yet to purchase in large numbers, there is still a high level of uncertainty as to whether the product form will be successful. This is especially the situation with high-tech products. As noted in the *Criticisms of the PLC* discussion Chapter 7, for technology products a chasm may appear that clearly separates buyers in this stage from potential buyers in the Growth stage. Overcoming this may require a significant change in the marketing effort that may include redesigning the product to make it much easier to use.

Table 20-4: Late Introduction Stage

Key Factors	Market Characteristics
Competition	By this stage, any company that was alone in launching the new product form is alone no longer, as it is highly likely at least one competitor has entered the market.
Target Market	Marketers are now engaged heavily in getting a high percentage of Early Adopters to accept the product.
Products	With competitors entering the market, choices available to customers expand, though the differences between competitors' offerings are often not significant.
Prices	Product pricing remains high, though any competitors entering at this stage may attempt to compete with the early entrants by offering a lower relative price.
Promotion	The promotional message is still one designed to educate the market on the benefits of this new product form, yet with more competition, there is a noticeable increase in the use of advertising that highlights a company's brand. Also, personal selling and sales promotion have increased especially targeting the channel of distribution as entrants attempt to secure distributors.
Distribution	The number of distributors continues to increase with many now offering products from several market entrants (which at this point may still be only a few).
Industry Profits	Losses continue to mount due to high marketing costs and the need to recover development expense. Losses may be even higher than anticipated if the target market adopts slower than forecast or if more companies enter than expected.

Growth Stage

The Growth stage is characterized by product sales increasing, often at an extremely rapid rate. This is seen by large percentage sales increases over previous periods (e.g., 50 percent increase in sales from one quarter to the next). This is an indication the product has advanced beyond Early Adopters and is now being purchased by the mass market (i.e., Early Majority). It is also the stage when early entrants begin to realize profits, though the fact the market is now profitable invariably leads to increased competition. It is also the time when competitors use aggressive techniques to position their brand in a way that will separate it from the onslaught of new entrants.

For many products, the Growth stage is represented by three distinct sub-stages: Early Growth, with characteristics outlined in Table 20-5, Middle Growth, with characteristics outlined in Table 20-6, and Late Growth, with characteristics outlined in Table 20-7.

EARLY GROWTH STAGE

In the early part of the Growth stage (see Table 20-5), marketers are seeking to expand the market beyond the Early Adopters and into the mass market. They do this by using Market Expansion strategies (see *Strategy and Tactical Programs* discussion above) including: 1) Grow Sales with Existing Products, by getting new market segments to buy, and 2) Grow Sales with New Products, by introducing new models containing different sets of features. The latter strategy is used not only to appeal to new customers but also to encourage repeat purchasing by existing customers.

Additionally, greater emphasis is placed on using promotion to continue building awareness and driving interest in the product form. This is due to: 1) the need to reach a broader market, and 2) to maintain an effective **share of voice** (i.e., percentage of all promotions in the market), so the marketer's message is not lost among competitors' increased promotional spending.

One market seeing early growth is rooftop gardening. This market consists of products used to grow flowers, vegetables and fruits atop buildings, primarily in large cities. Several companies have tapped into the rising interest by introducing a number of products including heating and watering systems and plant growing bins. One company, Sky Vegetable, is even planning to construct a collection of hydroponic rooftop farms to provide produce to major cities including New York and San Francisco. (10)

Table 20-5: Early Growth Stage

Key Factors	Market Characteristics
Competition	Only a few competitors are in the market as others wait to see whether the mass market will adopt the product. However, competitors, who sell products customers previously purchased to satisfy needs now addressed by the new product form, may be getting very aggressive in their marketing tactics as they sense the new product form to be a threat.
Target Market	Continued focus is on Early Adopters, but marketers begin to identify new market segments containing the Early Majority.
Products	A basic product sold to the Early Adopters remains, but plans are underway to introduce products with different configurations, such as more options (e.g., advanced model) and fewer options (i.e., stripped-down model). This is needed in order to satisfy many different potential segments of the mass market.
Prices	The average selling price may remain high, especially in cases where market demand is strong but only a few competitors exist.
Promotion	Promotions are broadened with more emphasis on mass advertising and sales promotions that encourage product trial. Also, personal selling and sales promotions to distributors continue as marketers attempt to make inroads into distributors that target the mass market.
Distribution	Marketers look for new channels that enable the product to begin to reach the mass market. For instance, consumer products may look to gain distribution in large discount retailers.
Industry Profits	The early market entrants may begin to experience profits as early development costs have been covered and overall demand is gaining steam.

MIDDLE GROWTH STAGE

In the middle part of the Growth stage (see Table 20-6), the objective is to continue a Market Expansion strategy. The most likely strategy is to seek out new market segments that have not been targeted. Sometimes this can be done using the same products previously introduced, though in most cases entering a new market will require revisions to existing products.

This stage is also a time to focus on product positioning. The idea is to use marketing decisions to affect customers' perceptions of a brand by trying to either: 1) separate a brand from other products (i.e., differentiate), or 2) bring a brand closer to competitors' offerings (i.e., equivalency). For the **product differentiation approach**, marketers use promotional methods showing why their brand is different, while the **product equivalency approach** suggests how the brand is equal to other brands but offers notable advantages, such as lower price.

Marketing Story

Crowded Coupon Industry Competes for Users
MSNBC

The early Growth Stage of the Product Life Cycle is certainly an interesting place for companies and customers. For many companies, this is an exciting time as climbing sales leads to company expansion. For early adopting customers, it is a time to experiment with different products and communicate their experiences to others. Thanks to an influx of competitors and customers, the market can change quickly forcing companies to adjust their marketing plan on a continuing basis.

An example of an industry in the early Growth Stage is the burgeoning online coupon market populated by such names as Groupon and LivingSocial. While coupons as a sales promotion technique are far from being new, what makes this a unique product form is the process by which a promotion becomes active. While original coupon websites were primarily static sites containing images of printable coupons, the newer coupon sites often require group participation in order to take advantage of a promotion. Consequently, we can view these as social promotion websites.

While there has been extensive media coverage of sites offering social promotion, as discussed in this story, the long-term prospects for this market are uncertain. The problem is a classic one for new products. While Innovators and Early Adopters have already tried social promotions, they make up a relatively small percentage of total online consumers. Success in social promotion will only come when the much larger Early Majority market also purchases these promotions. If these customers do buy, then expect several social promotion companies to become highly successful brands. If the Early Majority does not buy, then most social promotion companies will face the same fate as many other once high-flying companies whose market was not sustained.

One problem facing these companies is that few consumers have actually tried daily deal-type coupons, so it is unclear just how big the market can get. A poll released last month by Harris Interactive, conducted on behalf of the American Institute of Certified Public Accountants, found that only 10 percent of those surveyed had purchased a group coupon in the past year. (11)

What other Internet companies, that were early entrants in a market, did not make it out of the early Growth stage?

Late-to-market competitors may use a **penetration pricing** approach to establish a position in the market. Penetration pricing intentionally sets a price that is below long-term pricing in order to capture a large share of the market. In many cases, the firm will raise price once the product is established.

Finally, some marketers also determine that it is time to focus on specific segments of the market via a Niche strategy approach. In this way, they may be shielded from competition that exists in the larger generally market, especially if the niche market is much smaller than the general market and is not likely to attract the interest of larger brands.

Table 20-6: Middle Growth Stage

Key Factors	Market Characteristics
Competition	More competitors are attracted to the market as they see the potential for high profits. Competitors selling products customers previously purchased to satisfy needs may be extremely aggressive (may be entering the Maturity stage of their product form's PLC) resulting in substantial price reductions.
Target Market	The Early Majority sector of the mass market begins to purchase in higher volume and, depending on the product, existing customers (i.e., Early Adopters) may be purchasing again. Those in the Late Majority are becoming customers.
Products	Companies increase the number of product offerings in order to differentiate themselves from competitors. In most cases, new product offerings improve on the performance or benefits offered by earlier products. However, the target market may begin to feel burdened by too many choices.
Prices	As more competitors enter with more product options, prices may begin to fall, though the effect may not be felt as strongly if demand remains high. Pricing may be somewhat more competitive if large companies, with strong financial backing, are now entering. It may also be competitive in smaller segments, where multiple companies are trying to establish a niche.
Promotion	Emphasis has shifted away from building awareness of the general product form to heavy advertising and sales promotions centered on promoting individual brands. Heavy selling and sales promotion continues with distributors.
Distribution	Distribution reaches saturated levels as all possible channels are now handling the product.
Industry Profits	Marketers, who were early entrants, may begin to see high profits as demand is increasing while the pricing levels remain fairly strong. Depending on the product, unit cost of production may be dropping as manufacturing levels increase.

LATE GROWTH STAGE

Many marketers find this to be the most difficult part of the PLC. The late Growth stage (see Table 20-7) is a turbulent time with firms fighting to survive as market growth slows. This is not to say that overall sales are declining but that the percentage of growth from one period to the next is declining. For instance, sales over a three-year period may show an overall increase, but it is occurring at a decreasing rate compared to the previous years (e.g., 20%, 15%, 10%).

The key objective for a marketer is to remain competitive by maintaining a power position (e.g., leading brand name) or by achieving an insulated position within a niche. Brands may use promotional tactics that keep existing customers happy (e.g., coupons, improved customer service) and entice new customers to try the product (e.g., rebates, extended payment, try-before-you-buy). Distribution partners are encouraged to remain loyal through such actions as attractive pricing, promotional assistance, and customized packaging.

Table 20-7: Late Growth Stage

Key Factors	Market Characteristics
Competition	The market begins to see slower growth and companies find themselves in a highly competitive market. Fierce battles may occur on some fronts, such as within segments where demand is falling faster than in other segments.
Target Market	The overall market is still growing in terms of sales volume, especially as the product spreads to the Late Majority. But there is some evidence that, while sales are increasing, overall growth is occurring at a decreasing rate compared to previous time periods.
Products	With many competitors offering numerous product options, customers may be overwhelmed and confused by the choices available. Where customers do not fully understand the product (e.g., technology product) they may be more comfortable buying top brands or products sold at leading distributors (e.g., top retailers).
Prices	The average price is falling rapidly as market growth begins to slow and competitors struggle to maintain their market share. Price wars may break out.
Promotion	There is heavy spending on advertising and especially on sales promotions offering purchase and re-purchase incentives.
Distribution	With demand beginning to slow, some distributors cut back on the number of products they stock. They may even threaten to stop carrying products if leading product marketers do not offer additional incentives.
Industry Profits	Marketers begin to see a leveling off of profits as overall revenue flattens due to slowing demand and falling prices. However, marketing costs still remain high.

Maturity Stage

At some point in time, sales slow down for the product form. Instead of double-digit growth from one period to the next, the industry limps along with low, single digit sales increases or worse. There are two key reasons why this occurs. First, the market has become saturated and a large majority of potential customers has already purchased the product. In the case of products that have a long **buy-cycle** (i.e., time between repeat purchases), the infrequency of repurchase results in slow sales for some time. Second, customers have moved on to purchase other products that are seen as replacements for this product form. In this situation, the growth of the product form may have been interrupted with the introduction of a new product form (e.g., external backup hard drive replaced by "cloud" storage).

The slowing of market growth is a signal the product form may have reached the Maturity stage of the PLC (see Box 20-1). In our discussion, the Maturity stage is divided into two distinct sub-stages: Early Maturity, with characteristics outlined in Table 20-8, and Late Maturity, with characteristics outlined in Table 20-9.

Box 20-1

WHEN MARKET GROWTH SLOWS

Reaching the Maturity stage in the PLC means that marketers can no longer count on the growth in the overall market as the trigger for increased company sales. This can be best explained with an example.

- Period 1 – Market Size 100,000 units Market Share 10% Total Company Sales 10,000 units

- Period 2 – Market Size 200,000 units Market Share 10% Total Company Sales 20,000 units

- Period 3 – Market Size 200,000 units Market Share 10% Total Company Sales 20,000 units

As shown, during the growth stage (Period 1 to Period 2) a marketer may see product sales increase without the need for an increase in market share. Under this market condition, the marketer can still do well without having to grow its percentage of the market. In fact, if its market share dropped to 6 percent in Period 2 they would still realize an overall sales increase compared to the previous year (200,000 x 6% = 120,000 units). But in Period 3 overall market sales have leveled off and maintaining the same level of market share no longer leads to increased growth. This situation makes for a very competitive market as companies fight to increase sales by increasing their market position.

EARLY MATURITY STAGE

In the early part of the Maturity stage (see Table 20-8), the key objective is to enact strategies that enable a product to survive in the face of strong competition driven by decreasing demand. In fact, marketers may be happy following a Status Quo strategy intended just to maintain their market position. Unfortunately, this may prove difficult as this stage (called the **shakeout stage**) leads to many products failing or being absorbed by competitors (i.e., companies merge, products are sold).

In order to survive marketers may need to resort to tactics designed to "steal customers" from others, which often involves significant price promotions (e.g., heavy discounting) or strong promotions intended to improve image or solidify a niche. Marketers, who have avoided competing on price, may be in a better position to weather the storm if they have convinced the market their product contains unique features that few others offer. This can be the case if they have successfully established a strong position in a niche market.

A more likely scenario for companies at this stage is to investigate new ways to grow the market in an effort to extend the Growth stage of the PLC. The use of **resurgence tactics** includes such measures as:

- Changing how customers use the product including: encourage more frequent use or more consumption per usage (e.g., consume 2 units instead of 1 unit); suggest new benefits that can be obtained from using the product (e.g., has added health benefits not previously promoted); or suggest new uses for the product with messages whose tone says: *"Did you know our product can also do this?"*

- Finding new markets not previously targeted, such as moving beyond the consumer market into business markets, or expanding to global markets.

- Developing new product options (i.e., product line extensions) that offer more or better features (e.g., easier to use, safer, more attractive) that may get existing customers to re-purchase more quickly than they would normally.

- Heightening interest by changing image through heavy promotion and package redesign.

- Competing with lower priced brands by offering an alternative low-price product through private branding arrangement with distribution partners (see *Private Label or Store Branding* discussion in Chapter 6).

One method marketers use to discover new uses for products is simply to ask customers. Many companies have discovered their customers are using products for purposes for which the marketer was not aware. For instance, laundry stain remover Zout was originally targeted to hospitals as bloodstain remover. However, once on the market, it was discovered that medical personnel were using the product to remove other types of stains. Zout was then re-positioned as a consumer cleaning product. (12)

Table 20-8: Early Maturity Stage

Key Factors	Market Characteristics
Competition	By far the fiercest competition takes place at this stage as marketers move to grab customers from weakened competitors. At this stage, many competitors fail or merge with others.
Target Market	Little or no growth is occurring as the market is saturated or the target market looks to other products to satisfy its needs. Laggards may start buying but only if they can no longer purchase products they previously purchased to satisfy their needs.
Products	Many products are still marketed though some level of **product standardization** has occurred. Any new models introduced do not lead to significant improvement in product performance. At best, the new models offer minor, incremental improvements.
Prices	The average price continues to fall possibly below cost as competitors attempt to remain in the market. Price wars occur in many segments.
Promotion	Heavy competitive advertising and extensive promotions take place with the objective of getting existing customers to switch (for their repeat purchases). The same occurs in the distribution channel as marketers try to encourage distributors not to drop the product from their inventory.
Distribution	Distributors continue to reduce their inventory and promotional expense for the product form. They also become extremely selective on the products they will carry.
Industry Profits	Industry profits fall rapidly and many firms lose money as they increase spending in hopes of remaining in the market.

LATE MATURITY STAGE

If companies have failed to extend the PLC in the early part of the maturity stage, it is highly likely the product form may never again experience growth. Instead, companies will continue to market the product, albeit with little effort other than making it available to customers who have been purchasing it for some time.

By the late part of the maturity stage (see Table 20-9), the companies that are still selling may no longer consider the product to be important for the future of their company. However, this does not mean the product no longer holds value. In fact, the product may be extremely valuable for the profit it continues to generate (a.k.a. **cash cow**), which is then used to fund new products. Consequently, some attention is still paid to the product but only to ensure that it is still available for those who want to purchase.

Marketing Story

Mocked as Uncool, the Minivan Rises Again
New York Times

Product Life Cycle theory teaches that when a product reaches the Maturity stage marketers face a tough decision. At this stage, the market is seeing slow growth, yet many competitors still remain. Even with a slowing market, internally these companies are looking to grow sales, as that is what is almost always expected. But, realistically in a flat market if one competitor is increasing sales, it must mean others are losing.

Needless to say, the Maturity stage is a tough place to be. Faced with a highly competitive and potentially money losing market, marketers must decide whether to continue to sell their product or abandon it (e.g., sell to another company, retire it from the market). For marketers who are not willing to let go, they must look to strategies intended to grow product sales once again.

As we saw in the Early Maturity Stage discussion, there are several approaches to re-growing sales that collectively fall under the resurgence tactics approach. These tactics include changing target market aspects of the product's marketing strategy, such as convincing customers to use the product more frequently and targeting the product to new markets.

While target market strategies can be highly effective, a more common approach to extending the life cycle is to pursue strategies designed to alter the product itself, such as introducing new models with new features and changing packaging.

This story offers insight into how automobile manufacturers are extending the product life cycle of the minivan. The story describes changes auto makers have made to grow minivan sales following a period of very slow growth. These include key product design changes intended to give the minivan a more car-like look and feel. The new features are highlighted in advertisements that are worlds away from the family-friendly ads that have long been the theme of minivan promotion.

Having spent recent years making minivans more child-friendly through amenities like dual-screen entertainment systems and reconfigurable seating, the automakers are now focused on making them more appealing to adults, especially men, who have shied away from the vehicles and their connotations. (13)

What other class of consumer motor vehicles is also in the Maturity stage? What can be done to extend the life cycle of this product?

Table 20-9: Late Maturity Stage

Key Factors	Market Characteristics
Competition	The competitive landscape has stabilized. The only survivors remaining consist of a few market giants and several small niche firms.
Target Market	The market has very few first-time buyers and almost all companies now focus on getting existing customers to remain loyal.
Products	There is a significant reduction in the introduction of new models. Any new models focus mostly on just a few minor performance enhancements and stylistic improvements.
Prices	Overall prices stabilize and may rise due to limited competition.
Promotion	Large competitors begin to cut back on expensive promotions designed to attract new customers and focus on reminder promotions to loyal customers.
Distribution	Overall distribution has stabilized with few new distributors agreeing to handle the product. For products sold in retail stores, there is a noticeable reduction in shelf space devoted to the product.
Industry Profits	Companies see profits recover as demand stabilizes, pricing rises, and overall marketing costs drop.

Decline Stage

A product form has reached this stage when it becomes clear the market is no longer able to sustain itself. Like the Maturity stage, the Decline stage (see Table 20-10) may last a long time especially for products that have been adopted by a large percentage of the market, who are not inclined to change how they satisfy their needs (i.e., Laggards).

Since the end of the product form is seen as inevitable, there are no sub-stages here. In fact, marketers are faced with Market Exit strategies when they reach the Decline stage. There are two ways marketers can address this. First, companies may consider a **milking** strategy that involves getting the most out of the product in terms of sales without spending any additional funds to support the product. This strategy works best if a sizable market remains that is loyal to the product and not particularly price sensitive. A customer base with these characteristics allows a marketer to ride through the decline stage for some time while earning sizeable profits.

Second, companies may look to sell off or divest the product. In some situations, this can be done by first investing in the product in order to make the product more attractive to potential buyers.

However, discontinuing a product does not mean a company no longer earns revenue from the product form. Many discontinued products, especially those used in business and industrial settings, will continue to earn money through support services, such as selling supplies and service/repair contracts.

Table 20-10: Decline Stage

Key Factors	Market Characteristics
Competition	As time goes on firms drop out until no one is producing the product.
Target Market	Mostly consists of Laggards, who have been loyal to this type of product for a long time and have not moved on to newer products.
Products	No new improvements are introduced and some models are discontinued.
Prices	Prices may be rising as competitors drop out and companies still in the market have little incentive to engage in price competition. Also, there may be a large, loyal market that may not be sensitive to price increases. However, some companies looking to get out of the market but that have existing inventory may drastically markdown product to encourage rapid sales.
Promotion	Companies limit promotions to occasional reminders to loyal customers though overall little is spent.
Distribution	With declining demand distributors are removing products. The marketer may even make the decision to remove the product from unprofitable distributors. Sales may shift to online distribution or via non-traditional channels.
Industry Profits	For companies remaining, profits may be stable and possibly significant if this stage takes a long time to play out.

III

REFERENCES

1. Carney, D., "Sales Stalling, Smart Takes to the Street," *MSNBC*, August 14, 2010.

2. Chu, K., "Fast-Food Chains in Asia Cater Menus to Customers," *USA Today*, September 7, 2010.

3. For a detailed tutorial on creating a Marketing Plan see *KnowThis.com's* **How to Write a Marketing Plan Tutorial**.

4. Patton, L., "Starbucks Targets Folks Who Shun Starbucks," *BusinessWeek*, April 21, 2011.

5. Greene, J., "How LEGO Revived Its Brand," *BusinessWeek*, July 23, 2010.

6. "P&G's Pringles Chips Headed to Diamond Foods," *USA Today*, April 5, 2011.

7. *Procter & Gamble* website.

8. Carr, D., "News Trends Tilt Toward Niche Sites," *New York Times*, September 11, 2011.

9. Hsu, T., "Tablet Computer Market at Rising Risk of a Bubble Burst," *Los Angeles Times*, March 10, 2011.

10. Runk, D., "Companies Cater to Rooftop Gardeners," *MSNBC*, June 18, 2010.

11. Linn, A., "Crowded Coupon Industry Competes for Users," *MSNBC*, May 10, 2011.

12. Wong, E., "Inventions That Were Accidents," *Forbes*, December 23, 2010.

13. Bunkley, N., "Mocked as Uncool, the Minivan Rises Again," *New York Times*, January 3, 2011.

Full text of many of the references can be accessed via links on the support website.

Appendix: Marketing to the Connected Customer

Throughout this book, we have seen how the Internet and mobile technology are dramatically impacting the field of marketing. In particular, the use of mobile technologies, such as data applications ("apps") installed on smartphones and tablet computers, has expanded dramatically (1). There now exists hundreds of thousands of applications for mobile devices (2)  and customers are quickly finding that such products are often more convenient for accessing information compared to using a web browser.

For marketers, the combination of Internet access and mobile device applications has lead to a society of Connected Customers who, for much of their day, have the means to seek information, shop for products, and converse with others from almost anywhere. These Connected Customers present significant opportunities for marketers.

Yet, surprisingly many companies have not developed a rational strategy to cover these economic drivers. Considering the Internet has been used effectively by marketers since 1994 and mobile devices have evolved to become an indispensable communication tool, any organization without a strategy to utilize these for marketing is likely missing significant opportunities, while also opening the organization to potential threats (see *Innovation* discussion in Chapter 19).

Below we examine 10 reasons why marketers must make the Connected Customer a vital part of their overall marketing strategy. Much of this has been covered elsewhere in the book, but these issues holds such importance for marketing that it should not be underestimated and, consequently, warrants additional emphasis.

1. THE GO-TO PLACE FOR INFORMATION

Possibly the most important reason why companies need to include the Internet and mobile technology in marketing strategy is because of the transformation that has occurred in how customers seek information. While customers still visit stores, talk to sales representatives, look through magazines, and discuss product information with friends, an ever-increasing number of customers turn to the Internet and mobile applications as their primary knowledge source. In particular, they use search engines as their principle portal of knowledge as search sites have become the leading destination for anyone seeking information. Additionally, the growth of social media has led to these sites becoming powerful venues for product information and recommendations. Finally, customers are increasingly accessing information via mobile devices, such as smartphones, which also provide additional information retrieval options through specialized data applications. Marketers must recognize that the Internet and mobile technology are where customers are heading first for information and, if the marketer wants to stay visible and viable, they must follow.

2. What Customers Expect

The Internet and mobile applications are not only becoming the resource of choice for finding information, these are also the expected location where customers can learn about products and make purchases. This is especially the case for customers below the age of 30. In many countries, nearly all children and young adults have been raised knowing how to use the Internet and mobile technology. Once members of this group dominate home and business purchases they will clearly expect companies to have a strong Internet and mobile presence.

3. Captures a Wide Range of Customer Information

As a data collection tool, the Internet and mobile technology are unmatched when it comes to providing information on customer activity (see Box 1-2 in Chapter 1). For instance, each time a visitor accesses a website they leave an information trail that includes how they got to the site, how they navigated through the site, what they clicked on, what was purchased, and loads of other information. When matched with methods for customer identification, such as login information, the marketer has the ability to track a customer's activity over repeated visits to the site. Knowing a customer's behavior and preferences opens up tremendous opportunities to cater to a customer's needs and, if done correctly, the customer will respond with long-lasting loyalty.

4. Allows for Extreme Target Marketing

The most efficient way for marketers to spend money is to direct spending to those who are most likely to be interested in what the marketer is offering. Unfortunately, efforts to target only customers who have the highest probably of buying has not been easy. For example, consider how much money is wasted on television advertisements to people who probably will not buy. Yet, the unrivaled ability of websites and mobile devices to identify and track customers has greatly improved marketers' skills in targeting customers who exhibit the highest potential for purchasing products. Because of today's targeting technologies, marketing techniques for reaching the Connect Customer offer most marketers a more effective and efficient use of marketing funds compared to traditional targeting methods.

5. STIMULATES IMPULSE PURCHASES

Whether customers like it or not, the Internet and mobile technology are proving to be the ultimate venue for inducing impulse purchases. Much of this can be attributed to marketers taking advantage of improvements in: 1) technologies that offer product suggestions based on a customer's behavior when using browsing the Internet or using a mobile device; and 2) technologies that streamline the purchasing process. But online and mobile impulse purchasing also takes advantage of the "purchase now, pay later" attitude common in an overspending credit card society. How this plays out over time, as many customers become overwhelmed with debt, will need to be watched and could impact marketers' activities.

6. PERMITS CUSTOMIZED PRODUCT OFFERINGS

Companies know they can develop loyal customers when goods and services are designed to satisfy individual needs. This has led many marketers to implement a micro marketing strategy (see *Customized or Micro Marketing Strategy* discussion in Chapter 5) offering Connected Customers options for configuring their goods or services. The interactive nature of the Internet and mobile technologies makes "build-your-own" a relatively easy to implement purchasing option. An empowered customer base, that feels a company will deliver exactly what they want, is primed to remain loyal for long period of time.

7. TAKES PROSPECTS RIGHT TO THE SALE

No other form of communication comes close to turning exposure to promotion into immediate customer action in the way the Internet and mobile technologies do. These technologies enable Connected Customers to make purchases immediately after experiencing a promotion. Prior to today's technologies, the most productive call-to-action was through television infomercials that encourage viewers to call toll-free phone numbers. However, moving customers from a non-active state (i.e., watching television) to an active state (i.e., picking up the phone to call the number) is not nearly as effective as getting people to click on an ad while they are actively using the Internet or their mobile device. Today's marketers must understand that technology leads customers to making quicker decisions. While encouraging quick decisions may not be ideal for all product purchases, for many marketers this evolution in customer purchasing must be accepted and made available.

8. CONVEYS PERCEPTION OF BEING A FULL-SERVICE PROVIDER

For distributors and retailers, the Internet and mobile technologies make it easy to be a comprehensive supplier. Unlike brick-and-mortar suppliers, who are often judged by the inventory that is actually on hand or services provided at a store, Internet websites and mobile commerce companies can give the illusion of having depth and breadth of inventory and service offerings. This can be accomplished by placing goods and services information on the company's website or within an app so these are viewable customers. However, behind the scenes certain orders are fulfilled by outside suppliers via shipping and service agreements. With such arrangements, customers may feel they are dealing with providers offering full-service, when in reality a certain percentage of the goods and service are obtained from other sources.

9. LOWERS COSTS AND PROVIDES BETTER SERVICE

Internet and mobile technologies are replacing more expensive methods for delivering goods and services, and for handling customer information needs. Cost savings can certainly be seen with products deliverable in digital form (e.g., music, publications, graphic design, etc.), where production and shipping expenses are essentially removed from the cost equation. Cost savings may also be seen in other marketing areas including customer service where the volume of customer phone calls may be reduced as companies provide online access to product information (see *Customer Service Technologies* discussion in Chapter 3). Field salespeople may also see benefits by encouraging prospects to obtain product information online prior to a face-to-face meeting. This may help reduce the time devoted to explaining basic company and product information, and leave more time for understanding and offering solutions to customers' problems. As these examples suggest, the Internet and mobile technologies may lower administrative and operational costs while offering greater value to customers.

10. CREATES A WORLDWIDE PRESENCE

The Internet and mobile networks are communication and distribution channels offering global accessibility to a company's goods and services. Through a website or wireless application, a local marketer can quickly become a global marketer and, by doing so, expand its potential target market to many times its current size. Unlike the days before electronic commerce, when marketing internationally was a time-consuming and expensive undertaking, the uploading of files to establish a website is all that is needed to create a worldwide presence. While developing mobile apps takes somewhat more effort than creating a website, and establishing a website or app does not guarantee international sales (there is a lot more marketing work needed for the site to be viable internationally), the Internet and mobile networks provide a gigantic leap into global business compared to pre-Internet and wireless devices days.

Marketing Story

The Dirty Little Secrets of Search
New York Times

Most companies looking to build a successful online presence must rely heavily on search engines to drive customer traffic. In a perfect world, though, this is not what most marketers would want since they do not have complete control over an important method for acquiring customers. But as things currently stand, performing well on search engine queries is vital and marketers have little choice but to deal with it by developing a search engine marketing strategy. And what does it mean to have a successful search engine marketing strategy? The best measure of success is high visibility on the list of links returned to someone's keyword search (called organic search results). Yet, what many marketers, especially those in small firms, do not realize is that gaining high rankings is not easy. It takes work and it takes understanding how search engines operate.

While a few years ago understanding the basic workings of search engines was not all that difficult, things have become much more complicated. This has led to the evolution of a new industry, dubbed search engine optimization (SEO), that is populated by businesses claiming to know the techniques needed to improve a website's search engine rankings. The services to improve search engine rankings fall into two camps: white hats and black hats. The white hats essentially optimize a website by following rules laid out by search engines. Unfortunately, while these may improve the rankings, the time frame for improvement could be long term and may not necessarily result in the website getting into the first 10 listings, which is often a key goal. Black hats, on the other hand, look for methods that will propel a website's rankings more quickly. However, some of these methods go against the requirements laid out by search engines. If the methods used by black hats are identified as being inappropriate, a search engine may penalize the website by dropping it in the rankings or removing its listing all together.

As discussed in this story, retailer JCPenney's website was flagged by Google as not playing by the rules. Google claims black-hat techniques were used to fool Google into thinking the JCPenney website was relevant for a large number of search terms. During a four-month period that included the holiday selling season, these techniques helped JCPenney leap to the top of Google rankings for a large number of search terms. Google responded by penalizing JCPenney including wiping them off the first page of search results for most terms.

Search experts, however, say Penney likely reaped substantial rewards from the paid links. If you think of Google as the entrance to the planet's largest shopping center, the links helped Penney appear as though it was the first and most inviting spot in the mall, to millions and millions of online shoppers. (3)

Is it possible unethical competitors can undertake activity to scam search engines in ways that are intended to negatively impact another company's website?

REFERENCES

1. Newark-French, C., "Mobile Apps Put the Web in Their Rear-view Mirror," *Flurry. com*, June 20, 2011.

2. "App Store Metrics," *148Apps.biz*.

3. Segal, D., "The Dirty Little Secrets of Search," *New York Times*, February 12, 2011.

Full text of many of the references can be accessed via links on the support website.

Index

44607307R00237

Made in the USA
Charleston, SC
29 July 2015